IRELAND'S ENGLISH QUESTION

IRELAND'S ENGLISH QUESTION

Anglo-Irish Relations 1534-1970

PATRICK O'FARRELL

SCHOCKEN BOOKS • NEW YORK

Contents

Preface

The introduction to this book implies why it was written – because I became convinced that there was a way other than that usually followed, a way strangely neglected, of writing the history of Anglo-Irish relations. This conviction developed from a detailed investigation of the period 1887–1923, a study which still proceeds and which will, I hope, issue one day in something which will dig much deeper than I can here. What I have tried to do here is to pursue a theme – generally a religious theme – over a longish historical course, hounding it very closely when my case seemed to demand this, at other times letting my discussion have fairly loose rein to move along a general path.

That I came to be in a position to begin this subject, I owe generally to His Excellency, Dr Eoin MacWhite, formerly Irish Ambassador in Australia, now Ambassador of Ireland in the Hague, and an authority on Russian writing on Irish history: in a particular respect I am indebted to Professor T. Desmond Williams of University College, Dublin. The assistance of University College, Dublin and the University of New South Wales made possible my research work in Ireland and Rome, and support from the Australian Research Grants Committee made it possible to microfilm, for use in Australia, such material as the Redmond Papers.

For access to ecclesiastic archives I am particularly in the debt of His Eminence Cardinal Gilroy, and the Archivist of St Mary's Cathedral, Sydney, Very Reverend Monsignor C. J. Duffy; His Eminence Cardinal Conway, Archbishop of Armagh; Very Reverend Monsignor D. Conway, formerly Rector of the Irish College in Rome; Very Reverend Father T. Fagan and Father K. Condon of All Hallows College, Dublin; Most Reverend H. Murphy and Father P. J. O'Callaghan of Limerick, and Very Reverend Professor Patrick J. Corish of St Patrick's College, Maynooth. Of course, none of the churchmen from whom I have received help – and the number has been very numerous – are necessarily in agreement with the views presented in this history: the responsibility for these is my own. But I would like to express my warm gratitude not only for their generous help, but for friendly hospitality which I will always remember.

I wish also to record my thanks to the Directors, Librarians and staffs of the National Library of Ireland, the Library of University College,

Dublin, Trinity College Library, Dublin, the University of New South Wales Library, the National Library of Australia, and to Reverend Dr C. Tierney of St Patrick's College Manly, N.S.W. I am most grateful to Mrs E. E. Dryer of Singleton, N.S.W. for the use of her late husband's very extensive library of Irish material, and also to the Irish National Association of Sydney. Reverend Professor F. X. Martin (O.S.A.) and Reverend Father Cyril Halley lent me typescripts on which I have drawn. Mr A. E. Cahill of the University of Sydney made helpful comments on the earlier sections of the book. The year I spent on the staff of University College, Dublin was one in which the staff of the History Department all contributed, in that most general and pleasant way of formation and information, to the making of this book. In a similar way, I acknowledge the help of my colleagues here. A more precise debt I owe to those Fourth Year Honours students with whom I have conducted seminars on Anglo-Irish relations since 1967: their intellectual stimulus and criticism have been very valuable.

Clichés and sentiment are part of life and history. I would like to think that my father and mother who came from Borrisikane, Co. Tipperary to New Zealand in the early years of this century might have enjoyed this book. And had it not been for my wife's help, it would not exist.

Patrick O'Farrell
School of History
University of New South Wales
May 1970

IRELAND'S ENGLISH QUESTION

INTRODUCTION

Defining the Question

'The Irish Question', as shorthand for denoting historically the problems of relationship between England and Ireland, is a term which obscures, constricts and distorts: it is a political term, comparable in categorising utility with, say, 'The Eastern Question'. Its popular origin and setting are in the peculiar politics of Victorian England; and as a descriptive label it is indubitably British. A study of 'The Irish Question' construed in this sense throws light, no doubt, on British nineteenth-century politics – a considerable historical literature testifies to this. But its view of the Irish in the Question is superficial and confined to the few – the few superficially constructed in the image and likeness of nineteenth-century political Britain. But is it in this sense, and on this level, that the nature and destiny of the Question may be best understood? Or to confront the central problem – what, basically divided Ireland from England? Were the two essentially irreconcilable?

Not surprisingly, the usual, and even the most illuminating, answers to these central questions have fallen into the standard historical categories of political, social and economic, with an overwhelming emphasis on the political. Given the relationship between the two countries, an Irish Question seemed to require a British answer, and the dominant notions and terminology of modern Britain were those of politics, society and economics, the sentience of the secular: the Irish themselves came to adopt these very natural and readily intelligible forms of protest and explanation. Thus (above all other propositions) a passionate Irish nationalism contended with a determined British imperialism; and a desire for social and economic justice and self-determination rebelled against social degradation and economic exploitation.

This is true – as far as it goes. On the surface, the situation has a familiar modern simplicity. The Irish wanted freedom and prosperity. The problem lay in Britain's unwillingness or inability to confer these things.

'The Irish Question', as traditionally understood, dates from the Legislative Union of 1800 by which Irish politics were absorbed directly into British political life. This merging, and the whole development of human affairs in the post-French Revolution era, produced an outlook and understanding in which the Irish impingement on the British mind took very largely a political form. The outcome (reflected and perpetuated in the absorption of historians with the nineteenth-century complexion of Anglo-Irish affairs) was a pronounced and sometimes exclusive emphasis on the political and nationalist elements in the relationship.

A concentration on politics and nationalist agitation neglects a vital fact, which stands as contradiction: Ireland and the Irish were not politically modern. Whatever they developed of a modern political outlook was not Irish, but British, derived from their rulers, or European. The Ireland subdued by England in the sixteenth and seventeenth centuries had few political forms, and those were rudimentary, without effective unity or organisation. English rule forced the Irish to adopt English political forms, both because it imposed these forms by sheer force, and because the Irish, finding no adequate counterparts in their own cultural tradition, had no alternative but to accept the efficient political structures the English gave them. The same may be said for political ideologies, notably nationalism. The European nationalism of the sixteenth century amounted essentially to the consolidation and centralisation of certain geographic areas into single and distinct political units, or nation states: it was a process of power and politics. Ireland was a victim of the operation of this process in England: no signs of the process had emerged in Ireland.

Confronted with Irish resistance and hatred, the English developed a set of responses which were contradictory, or at least disparate. They refused to accept – and the refusal goes down to the nineteenth century – that the task of blending Ireland with England would be any less successfully completed than the absorption of Scotland, Wales or Cornwall. At the same time they tended to explain Irish recalcitrance in terms akin to those in which they conceived of themselves – nationalist terms. They tended to lump their opponents in Ireland under a nationalist term, 'The Irish'. It was easy to explain Irish hatred in nationalist terms: the Irish hated the English because they were English, a racial term which had a largely nationalist connotation for the English. Perhaps it would be an exaggeration to suggest that the English unconsciously invented Irish nationalism to explain the bitter resistance to the rule of their own nationalism, and that the Irish swiftly adopted and adapted this invention as a congenial and potent weapon. Nevertheless, it is certain that the English were responsible for the introduction into Ireland of modern political consolidation and centralisation, the nationalism of power and politics. And in so doing the English laid the essential foundations for nineteenth-century nationalism. That nineteenth-century nationalism amounted to a rebellion against the earlier phase of nationalism, the rebellion of principle, emotion, ideology and myth-cult against the rule of power and politics.

Politics and nationalism – the English imposed their form and terms on Irish-English relationships. More (and herein lay their enduring conquest), they structured the Irish political mind – but they did not, and could not, provide its content.

That is to say, the Irish did not contrive their own political framework and ideologies; they accepted what the British (and Europeans) had contrived for them. Their quarrels with Britain took place mainly within that framework and in the language of those ideologies. But this does not mean that these were the fundamental matters at issue. The political quarrels of the Irish were largely among themselves. Ireland's dispute with Britain, however much it was within the realm of politics, was not about politics. The quarrel with Britain was not about what they had in common, but what was held in difference – a total world view. This world view was composed of several closely integrated elements – race, culture, temperament perhaps, historical experience and development, and religion; with religion both pivot and linch-pin. These are the essential foundations, upon which the political activity and ideologies of the nineteenth and twentieth centuries are so much mask and overlay.

Race? Gael and Saxon. Culture? That of a rural peasantry remote from a world of commerce and industry. Historical experience? Ireland and England were divided by much more than long experience of defeat and disaster on one hand, triumph and prosperity on the other, the living legacies of failure and success. They were divided by their tenancy of time. England was always modern, up to any moment; Ireland remained in contrasting relationship, a constant anachronism. Tudor England, the emergent nation state, sought to rule an Ireland of family clans and semi-feudal chiefs. Victorian England, giant of the industrial and commercial world, ruled an Ireland in which the seventeenth and earlier centuries breathed strongly still. Nor was this rift of years merely one of social and economic development, though that alone would have been hard enough for government and politics to bridge. England and Ireland were divided spiritually, by faith – by hope and charity too. The Counter Reformation began in Ireland in 1534, with the revolt of Lord Offaly, Silken Thomas. When did it end? In England it died, if it had lived that long, with James II, with the seventeenth century. In Ireland the

Counter Reformation lived vigorously on. Until the disestablishment of the Church of Ireland in 1869? Until the Free State? Does it still live, residually, in Ian Paisley's Ulster?

The religious factor is usually accepted as important in determining the course of relations between Ireland and England. Accepted – but very seldom understood, and almost invariably undervalued or misconstrued. Those indifferent to religion, or who hold it in contempt, usually do more than minimise or distort religious influence; they fail to appreciate its character. In an age of faith, all politics are religion: conversely, in an age of politics, all religion is politics. The common English view reduced Irish religion to the intelligible terms of power politics: it failed to see religion in the crucial terms of belief. The secular-political view of Ireland and its history still neglects or obscures the role of religion – or, becoming obsessed with its ubiquity, interprets it as a political structure similar to, but much worse than that of any party. The historical dynamism of religion is thus assessed in terms of its direct political expressions. Yet, if religious men, clerical and lay, were divided over political questions, as they consistently were, they were united in central belief: their unity is of more historical significance than their divisions. For the Irish, insofar as they were religious, could neither comprehend nor accept the indifferent secularism or enlightened humanitarianism of modern England. For them, its level of intelligibility was that of a standing affront and persecution. Failing to understand the secular as such, they converted it into the terms of religion. National education became a giant impious conspiracy to destroy the faith; democracy appeared as a devilish device to undermine the hierarchies established to administer God's will and order. While the English mind secularised the spiritual and sacred, the Irish mind saw all in terms of Heaven and Hell. To the Irish there was no world of the neutral affairs of men. Eternity cast its light – or glare – into the ante-room of daily life, colouring all that was there.

To say that English and Irish were ignorant of each other, misunderstood each other, is to say not nearly enough, though these things are true. Ireland and England were divided by differing views of reality, understandings so divergent that what was precious and meaningful to the one, was worthless and incomprehensible to the other. ' In the lives of their saints there is a wild if fantastic splendour; but they have no secular history.' So wrote J. A. Froude of the Irish, adding, ' for as a nation they have done nothing which posterity will not be anxious to forget ': a people without a secular history deserves oblivion. The contempt was mutual. Ireland's was mirrored in the disgust of Frederick

Engels in 1869: 'Ireland still remains the Holy Isle whose aspirations must on no account be mixed with the profane class-struggles of the rest of the sinful world.'

No secular history. How many of the basic problems of Anglo-Irish relations are compressed into that scathing indictment? And what if it be found a true bill? Is there a case for trying the long historical conflict between Ireland and England as a confrontation between the sacred and the profane; the battle of faith and other-worldliness against reason, sound commerce and the worldly-wise; a nation of saints contending with a nation of shop-keepers; is this another form of that English attempt to make the spiritual subservient to the secular, so brilliantly demonstrated in 1964 in Felix Raab's *The English Face of Machiavelli*?

As the British understood it, ' The Irish Question ' was a question of politics, or more broadly, a secular question. To construe it so was natural, for all that they ever succeeded in fully imposing on the Irish was their politics and forms of government. Divided by race, culture, history and religion, politics was the sole common ground on which English and Irish could meet intelligibly, could effectively communicate.

The constriction of the problems of the relationship to the political, substantially worsened the situation. It gave these problems a false appearance of simplicity which intensified their powers of bafflement and frustration. It rendered Irish attitudes apparently the more totally irrational and unintelligible, exacerbating tension and friction. The narrowly political construction the British put on their dealings with Ireland had the automatic effect of placing the Irish in the wrong. The purpose of all government, all politics, is to govern effectively, and given the axiomatic purity of British political intentions, the inescapable fact that Ireland was ill-governed could be attributed only to the Irish and their deliberate frustration of British good intentions. Thus the clichés – wild, ungovernable, unstable. The Irish, it seemed to the British, in being not amenable to government, were *per se* uncivilised. Moreover, to see the problem as political meant to interpret Irish resistance as treason; that is, resistance was *ipso facto* justification for depriving the Irish of the rights of subjects, land and goods if not liberty or life. The dominant British view ran thus: the Irish hated British government; but British government was the best form of government, enshrining law and order so as to permit liberty, prosperity and civilisation. By their rejection of it, the Irish stood self-convicted as lawless, improvident, lazy, stupid and uncivilised – by nature. The British sought to govern Ireland well. The Irish made this impossible. Therefore, they were to blame for their own misfortunes. From this standpoint, stressing government and politics, the

Irish reaction to Britain as the hated oppressor seemed incredibly perverse and irresponsible, indeed a crime against England.

The British paid less attention to the fact that insofar as the problems generated by Ireland were seen as political, these problems became the tool of, or at best dependent on, political factions and parties in England. The cynical use made of the Irish situation in the 1780s by Fox and the Whig Opposition in their attempt to destroy Pitt is one of many variations on this theme which may be extended down to the Liberals' behaviour after 1906. Usually, this entanglement with English politics worked to the detriment of Irish affairs. Where it did not, as in some social legislation, the benefits were largely marginal or accidental. What the English regarded as constructive Irish legislation, the Irish regarded as extorted and partial remedies of enduring injustices.

The English rendered everything Irish down to the realm of politics – at best. For it might be more accurate to argue that for substantial decisive periods, in the sixteenth and seventeenth centuries particularly, but as late as 1916-21, the British saw their Irish problems as basically military. Peace reigned never long enough, nor was the threat of English force ever so remote, for the English to ever rid themselves of the reputation of harbingers of violence and war. The hatreds that developed were a natural consequence of a situation of belligerence which merely waxed and waned, never disappearing. And the habit of belligerence worked to vitiate all attempts at political solution. With relations between Ireland and England so often those of force, be it that of war, riot or coercion, these relations showed a constant and quasi-natural tendency to revert to these violent conditions, in the absence of settlement of the problems at issue. It could be contended that the early establishment of a habit of violence in the attempted settlement of Irish affairs rendered a peaceful solution a very remote possibility.

A great deal may be – and has been – said within the historical framework of Anglo-Irish relations conceived as a governmental problem, whether military or political. But was government the real matter at issue, or merely the only commonly intelligible symptom or expression of it? The history of English appraisals of the Irish problem is, at bottom, a history of bewilderment, punctuated by brief periods of temporary satisfaction when it seemed that the mystery had been dispelled, that the problem might be solved in some neat, practical and invariably political way – union, religious concessions, land reform, Home Rule – only to founder again.

The bewilderment was excusable. How could the English know the Irish, or what they wanted if the Irish did not know this themselves – or persisted in caricaturing themselves? How much of the Irish character was play-acting for English benefit? Was the 'Paddy', the stage-Irishman, the ape of *Punch*, a real person; or was he a deliberate dramatisation and exaggeration of those characteristics which the English came to believe the Irish possessed – lazy, fey, drunken, amusing, riotous? Were the Irish acting up to an English image, filling out the lines of some convenient English cartoon? Often they were, sometimes to please the English, more often – or at the same time – they took out a quiet vengeance: such a caricature insulted the English more than the Irish who filled the role, because it was a disguising and withholding of the real self, and essentially an act of contempt for fools. The Irish, or some of them, were haughty indeed; more so, in their subjugation, than their masters. True, the act sometimes became reality, or part of the chameleon that was the Irishman – but confronted with that chameleon the English often remained colour-blind: they saw only a violent green.

The good political intentions of the British need no explaining away; they need an Irish, not an English context. It is in the Irish context and in Irish terms that an explanation must be sought for the belief that Britain was more than an oppressor, rather a kind of anti-Christ, the origin and source of all evils. It seldom occurred to the British to ask themselves that most fundamental of Irish questions – why did the Irish hate them? Why were the Irish unruly? Why did the Irish do this or that? – these were much debated questions. But seldom, why do the Irish feel as they do, why do they harbour, and for so long, hatred? Seeing no cause in themselves, the emotion baffled them.

More basic than any question regarding the political devices to which the British were put in order to govern Ireland, is the simple question – why did these devices fail? Traditionally, the answer has been sought within the framework of the devices themselves – they were too late, defective as instruments, not properly implemented, and so on. Too little attention has been given to the possibility that political solutions were insufficient because the problem was not essentially political.

It was historical and religious, and a problem of identity. To the Irish, British government both represented and continued to perpetrate a crime against their selves, their history and their religion. British government, whatever form it took, represented destruction, not of political forms (the Irish had few) but of their life, their very selves; not so much of their external governances as of their interior selves. The Irish reaction was to fashion out of their past a history of extraordinary living dynamism. The Gaelic revival at the end of the nineteenth century took intellectual

Ireland back to the pre-British past. But popular Ireland had long fed
ravenously on the more immediate British past, in oral tradition, and
particularly in the second half of the nineteenth century in a multitude
of printed sources, newspapers, penny magazines, John Mitchel's histories,
the aggressive pieties of *Persecutions of Irish Catholics* and *The Battle
of the ᶠaith in Ireland*. A tiny group of intellectuals led by Yeats or A. E.
wandered with Oisin in a far past from which they conjured up a mystical
future. The people dwelt in less distant realms. Nineteenth-century
Ireland experienced a curious, perhaps unique telescoping of time, a
compression of the popular experience of four centuries into one. Famine,
Mountjoy, Land League, Penal Laws, Cromwell, Grattan's Parliament
all merged together to take their place as a living yesterday. Time,
sequence, size, perspective all vanished until present reality encompassed
the simultaneous experience of all that had passed. History, as past, had
ceased to be.

This historical telescoping, unintelligible to the English or ridiculed
by them, both derived from the experience of English rule and was its
deepest enemy. Irish identity, self-consciousness, came to be integrally
dependent on an anti-English understanding of history. When the actualities failed, or could not be distorted or mythologised to make an Irish
point, religion was pressed to fill the gap, provide the authority:
' Ireland's title to independence does not rest upon any Act or Treaty –
it comes from God' (*Sinn Féin* 5 May 1906).

Fundamentally, English rule fossilised Ireland. It prevented the
Irish from developing their own institutions, and it gravely hindered their
development as a people. This hindrance took two major forms. The relationship with England in the form imposed in Tudor times prevented
the free growth and change of Irish identity. Failing to destroy that
identity, it provoked a reaction in which the Irish clung stubbornly to
the only identity they knew, while the years, and centuries, passed. Thus,
eventually, Counter Reformation Ireland, a historical and religious relic,
out of time but very much in place, confronted modern, secular, industrial
Britain. Much that was of spiritual and human value had been retained.
Nevertheless, for Ireland whatever was British had become suspect,
tainted, not least that modern, social and economic progress characteristic
of the oppressor nation. But not only did English rule arrest the internal
development of Irish self-awareness, preserving it in a pre-modern condition, it also gave that self-awareness a savage directional twist – towards
England, erecting the Irish-English relationship into an Irish obsession.
To Britain, ' The Irish Question ' was one of many questions, and usually
not the most important. To Ireland, the English question was, or came

to be, the only question: all the questions Ireland might have asked of herself, in some quest for modern self-realisation, were asked of Britain, and asked in the language of the seventeenth century, the only language the Irish really knew. It may be argued that the Irish continually avoided their own, self-induced problems by blaming them on the English, but it is hard to take to task those under siege as guilty of making for themselves a prison of their citadel.

This situation had deeply destructive effects on nineteenth- and twentieth-century attempts to solve the problems of the Anglo-Irish relationship. Any English attempt to remedy these problems after 1800 was always partly irrelevant. Set in the present, these attempts could not remedy the past. Gladstone's consciousness of the need to atone for cruel and inveterate injustice on Britain's part raises inescapably the question – was it possible to atone for a whole history? Moreover, the English were divided as to whether or not there was anything to atone for. Would the English disown their history because the Irish disliked it, branded it tyranny? Even if they did, nothing could obliterate what had actually happened.

And the Irish and English differed very sharply about what had happened and what it signified. From the same facts, the Irish concluded that the English were invading tyrants, thieves, destroyers and heretics, while the English saw themselves compelled by necessity to govern firmly a part of their realm which was barbarous and insubordinate. Added to this was a contrasting popular reception of history. The English common people (save for the old resentment of ' the Norman yoke ') hardly gave their history a serious thought: the present was their glory, be it Trafalgar, Balaclava or Mafeking. To the Irish, overwhelmed by an inglorious, annihilating present, the past offered a dramatic escape and a heroic refuge. Yet a bitter refuge, for far down the corridors of time there was no escape from the English. Present discontents drew on those that had passed, reinforcing, hardening, deepening, and above all complicating and extending those discontents as past and present coalesced. Any attempt to remedy *present* discontents and grievances was always inadequate because the present was so fused with a past which no one could undo. Those English who attended at all to Irish history paid too much attention to what was Gaelic, or dismissed the Irish view as myth-making. There was indeed a good deal of myth in Irish history, but its factual dynamic – as a weapon against England – was real enough, and situate in modern British times. Even if it had been all myth, the problem remained for the English that the Irish believed in it: it was a continual source and dynamic for hatred. All of this, and much else, the

English preferred to avoid. As A. P. Thornton has pointed out, the
English have preferred not to investigate their political failures, have
ignored them: ' Ireland, the other island, still receives cavalier treatment
in the textbooks of British history.'

History and religion linked at one obvious point – the particular history
of Ireland as Ireland, apart from England's governmental contrivances,
had been, was, religious: religion and religious division was its focal point,
its identity and coherence. There was much more to the linkage than
that. The substance of Irish history was religious; so too were its concepts,
its grasp of the past.

It was characteristic of post-Reformation Irish religion, an inevitable
consequence of its situation, that its strength lay in faith, leadership and
loyalty. So dominant was the role of faith that it took on, in Irish understanding, almost an equivalence with religion – ' The Faith '. Contem-
plation, and the intellectual aspects of religion had no place in a belief
proscribed and under siege. Irish religion was bereft of all the ' ologies '
save one, and that scarcely a science – martyrology. One salient feature
of the history of Ireland derives directly from this religious disposition –
the concept of martyrdom applied to a whole people, and later a nation.
As martyred saints had suffered from the sixteenth to the eighteenth
century for their faith, to retain what they treasured as their real meaning
and true human identity, so Ireland suffered for being herself. The Irish
people, in their own self-image, stood as living martyrs, in communion
with dead martyrs through the offices and prayers of their church.
Martyrdom – sanctity through suffering, purification through deprivation
– was a living vital continuum in Irish history, Irish affairs.

And particularly in the relationship with England. The question,
' what agent of Satan had inflicted martyrdom on the holy Irish?', was
readily asked and readily answered. England, the English. So the English
unwittingly wrought the canonisation of the Irish – in actuality for some
few of them, ' The Irish Martyrs ' so called – in spirit for the people as
a whole. Thus the English raised up against themselves a people who
were as convinced of their superiority in the spiritual realm as the
English were of theirs in the temporal; who might even pity the English,
as saints might sorrow for the wickedness of their executioners, or, more
likely for those of less pure clay, hate their persecutors for their blindness, their arrogance, and their thoughtless cruelty. Preposterous though
it might seem to the English, they were detested in Ireland because they
were alien, and in nothing were they more alien than in their heresy and
secularism. Persecution warps all involved in it, yet those who wield it

die more fundamentally. Ultimately, the victims have the surer basis for justification.

If religion be the opium of the people, the Irish were addicts. Their addiction – no drug, but strength and sustenance – was, in large part, English-induced. And that not merely as a retreat to, and promise of, a world unspoiled, Irish, unravaged by the English. For the very strength of the English – in government – confirmed Irish dispositions in a religious mould.

In this way. English government in Ireland was a continuing failure. It maintained English possession and ultimate power, but it did not maintain law, order and stability, nor gain an effective Irish acceptance. From beginning to end it retained a coercive edge, remained foreign. Indeed its spirit of violence was foreign to the tenor and principles of government in England itself. If – at least in the English view – the basic problem of Irish government was that of ridding Ireland of its inherent anarchy and violence, English government was more than a continuing failure: in fact it added to and compounded anarchy and violence in Ireland. It was a common English view that anarchy in Ireland derived from the Irish, but some Englishmen saw that much of it derived from English policy. Critics like Froude saw a basic fault in England's failure effectively to pursue and enforce particularly those policies and laws which might have Anglicised Ireland – English settlement and Protestant proselytising. England's inability to do this, in terms of its limited resources and other preoccupations, do not fully explain this neglect. Reluctance, unwillingness, are also factors: to embark on that policy of protracted violence, terror even, necessary to achieve Anglicisation, affronted the English conscience. Recognisable too is a lack of self-confidence, an uncertainty of conviction. In religious terms – and these are central to an explanation of England's failure in Ireland – that failure was the failure of the Church of England to conquer Catholicism – if failure be the appropriate word, for Anglicanism can scarcely be credited with the attempt.

So it was that the net result of English policy in Ireland, achieved in those sixteenth and seventeenth centuries when English assertive energy was great and self-doubts few, was to effect a work of destruction. What was destroyed was the loose social and political forms of the old Gaelic Ireland. In their place the English attempted to erect the centralised political forms of modern England. The substitute had no roots in the soil: it had to be propped up by the English until the Irish could learn to accept and use it. In the meantime, old Ireland lived on, not politically (for that area was England's strength and place of jealousy) but historically, culturally and religiously. Religion had a quasi-political organisation, national in scope, hierarchical in structure, determined on autonomy. The English saw this. Hence their early efforts to destroy the Irish Catholic episcopacy: they recognised an authority structure which might, indeed would, conflict with their own. This potential rival and the dangers of conflict worried the English. However, the real menace of religion to English rule lay less in what it might do, than in what it was – a structure of faith and authority. In Catholicism the Irish could find the form, means and organisation to preserve and develop their ancient separate identity, their meaning and ultimate integrity.

As the family chiefs and leaders were destroyed, the leadership of bishops and priests rose to take their place. From the beginning there was a confusion of roles. The Catholic Confederacy of 1642-9 witnessed bishops and priests taking the initiative towards a provisional government, constitution making, leading troops into battle. In the hidden Ireland of the eighteenth century, bishops and priests quietly, and by default, took the place of the ancient chiefs. What England had crushed and swept aside came to exist in another form, reappearing energetically in the nineteenth century, sometimes actually in the form of episcopal clansmen – Doyle, MacHale, Cullen, Walsh, O'Dwyer, Logue, each with his party and privileged dependants – more often in the form of lay bishops – O'Connell, even Parnell, De Valera, a whole host of others. This new clan structure was ridden with the same personal factionalism as had marked its ancient family form. Now, however, more was at stake than family or personal honour and property, pride or profit. Religion, the contest for men's souls, was the ground of battle. And religion embraced more than itself, for, led by bishops and priests, it had become the depository for Irishry. The weapons were different, less bloody: the impulses were the same. No leader could easily tolerate another above him. Faction was their life. Bishops rose up against each other, MacHale against Cullen, O'Dwyer against Walsh – or was it Cullen against MacHale, Walsh against O'Dwyer? Bishops united temporarily, precariously, to overthrow those factions that challenged their sway, or offered competing definitions of Irishry or of the rules of religion: they fought Young Irelanders, Fenians, Land Leaguers, Parnellites, revolutionaries, republicans. Sometimes they won. Sometimes they compromised, avoided or accepted, or rendered innocuous. They were never defeated.

The Irish church came to represent Irish identity in such a profound way as to render all those who challenged it somehow foreign, less than Irish, and this to their extreme disadvantage. If the church did not accept them, or they it, they withered and died. The church would not accept English rule. Rule from England perhaps, but not a Protestant or a secular establishment in Ireland, not English rule as historically established. The nineteenth-century secularisation of the English mentality made it more, not less repugnant. Many of the old Protestant modes and attitudes remained, or were carried over in secular forms. An attitude of mind which came to see religion as reactionary superstition, with Catholicism its most noxious form, met absolute rejection from an Irish church which was coming to see itself as a strong and holy bastion against an evil world determined to make war on God Himself. That church, with its own deep-rooted establishment and traditions, its own authority structure, could make effective its refusal to accept English rule. It was of minor consequence if that refusal was made partially, politely, even with subservience – refusal it was. Moreover, the church added to this negative role of rejection, a positive substitute: it offered – or imposed – a spiritual self-government for Ireland. As Sean O'Casey said bitterly, referring to Maynooth: 'this College is the brain, the body, the nerve and the tissue of the land, controlling two-thirds of the country, influencing it all.' No one could claim anything like such a role for Dublin Castle, centre of British power. Indeed, the church could provide the Irish not only with a form of common government and mode of common identity and expression, but also with its own form of imperialism, ecclesiastical or spiritual. If the sun never set on the British Empire, neither did it set on the Irish empire – in that it was Roman, Catholic, American, Australian, Argentinian, universal, an empire of race and religion.

In short, the term 'The Irish Question' obscures the obvious – that this was a question created by the English. It was they who were the invaders, the conquerors, the owners and the rulers. Seen simply, in English terms, it was their problem, for which the faults of the Irish were to blame. And the basic Irish fault is simply expressed – the Irish were not English: the enduring error of the English in Ireland was their perennial and unshakeable assumption that the Irish were really English, and their determination to insist that, even if the Irish were not English, they must become so. The question, why were the Irish not English and why they refused to become so, is probably the only historically impartial 'Irish Question'.

Implicit in this question is another – who were the Irish, and what did they want? The essence of the Irish role in the Anglo-Irish relationship is often seen too simply as objection to English rule. It is the

English who have had to wrestle with the complexities of devising solutions to the problems of relationship – violence, coercion, concilia- tion, plantations, union, Home Rule, partition, Free State, and so on. Certainly the relationship with Ireland posed the British with political questions in which they were fertile in devising unsatisfactory political answers. However, the problems of the relationship were much wider and deeper than politics, and cut both ways, and with equal complexity. ' The Irish Question ' forced the British to engage in self-questioning, to look at themselves, their principles and values. Their habit of seeing Ireland as politics narrowed their introspection to one superficial facet of what was at stake, and even there, as the history of Britain's im- perial decay testifies, they learnt little, save how to make the same errors in other places. The questions the relationship with England forced on the Irish were more profound, more agonising: who were they, and what did they want? Their devising of answers to these crucial questions of identity and aims were just as impermanent and unsatisfactory as were the British attempts to satisfy them. In fact, the two searchings, the British for an answer, the Irish for a meaning to their question, interacted on each other to their mutual frustration. No proposed external solution could ever satisfy the Irish, calm their troubles, for they as a people knew neither who they were, nor what they wanted – these were problems they would have to solve for themselves, themselves alone.

PART ONE

The Range of Answers
1534-1800

Given that England became determined that Ireland must be a subject province, and that Ireland would not welcome this spontaneously, the courses of action open to England were necessarily limited. The alternatives, pursued in parallel or sequence, amount to an old imperial syndrome – military conquest and occupation; settlement of colonies and the erection of a colonial ruling class; legal embodiment and establishment of the colonist's modes, values and supremacy, together with repression of native culture; tuition of the natives in the way of life of the colonists, and eventually some degree of, or participation in self-government. This last stage presupposed a voluntary continuance of subject status, and a substantial acceptance by both colonists and natives of the imperial will.

Such was, more or less, the theory. Practice, as witnessed since the American Revolution, raised the possibility of a further stage in which colonial rejection of the imperial connection takes place. But Ireland is no exemplar of this pattern or process. Irish rejection of the English connection does not come at the end of the development of an imperial process; every element of that process is rejected, and at every stage. Those interpretations which see Ireland as England's first colony are blind to all other than economic facts. For, even at the most basic preliminary level of force, military conquest and occupation, on which any real colonisation was dependent, Ireland constantly rejected English imperialism. England found it frequently necessary to reconquer Ireland – up to 1921 – and even in those quieter periods between military excursions, the level of open and covert defiance of English authority remained high, and garrison activities strenuous. It has been common to regard the relationship of Ireland and England as marked unfortunately and abnormally by the eruption of periodic violence and disaffection; it might be more realistic, particularly on taking a longer view, to see it as a history of continuing hostilities in which the periods of relative peace are those of exhaustion. Or simply, the normal mode of Anglo-Irish relations was war, hot or cold, not peace.

What is under study then, is not essentially a colonial relationship, but a protracted and unique condition of actual and incipient war. The fact that, from the English side of the Irish Sea, the relationship seemed colonial, or even closer, is relevant only as testimony to English misunderstanding. The Irish reaction, not English intentions or hopes, determined the realities of the relationship.

All Britain's imperial devices were repelled, some constantly, others fitfully. Before considering the history of these devices, an initial question – why did England determine to subject Ireland? For politico-religious reasons; more political than religious in English understanding, more religious than political in Irish. The purpose of this chapter is to review the construction of the politico-religious prison in which Anglo-Irish relations were kept thereafter: this is the period in which the essentials of that structure were fabricated.

Prior to Henry VIII's Reformation, the English monarchy had, by and large, left Ireland to its own devices. The English hold was slight, not extending far from Dublin. Certainly, since Henry II had begun a Norman invasion in 1171, that monarchy had claimed, and contrived policies and legislation to support, the title to 'lordship of Ireland'. This largely nominal and feudal form of dominion had been claimed more for negative than positive reasons – an attempt to prevent the growth of any independent power in Ireland which might rival that of Norman England. But if, in terms of the actualities of monarchic power, Celtic Ireland remained almost untouched, in terms of the feudal territorial ambitions of Anglo-Norman barons the conquest was real and violent enough, though partial and haphazard: at its height at the beginning of the fourteenth century, Norman control extended over half the island. The three centuries that followed the Norman invasion saw the growth of basic and salient features in the relationship between England and Ireland.

The first of these features was that the relationship was less one of conquest than of unsuccessful conquest. The crucial characteristic of the Norman 'conquest' of Ireland is that it failed, issuing in a historical pattern of almost continuous conflict with the native Irish. Together with such stimuli as the Scottish invasion of 1315, the Norman invasion produced an Ireland in which war and disorder became a way of life, three centuries of mutual tutelage in violence, a heritage not lightly lost.

The second feature is an outcome of the first. Failing to conquer Ireland, the Anglo-Normans established not so much a colony as a garrisoned foreign province, the Pale, whose foreignness was proclaimed in law and asserted by violence. The Statutes of Kilkenny in 1366 formally attempted to segregate the two races, making marriage or concubinage high treason, proscribing Irish dress or language among the English, encouraging the duty of war on the hostile Irish. An enactment of 1475 gave this segregation a clear physical form: a deep ditch was to be constructed so as to enclose the lands of the English Pale, by then shrunken to a coastal strip fifty miles long and twenty wide. A tiny English ghetto looked out upon a despised and hostile world, seeing itself as an oasis of civilisation in a desert of savagery. The history of Irish partition began with the Pale. True, its inhabitants were to take on much that was Irish, become ' Anglo-Irish '. Yet ' Old English ' is the better term to make the point – that they were foreign, and conquerors. The Pale, as a device for segregating and Anglicising, failed. In English appraisals, its failure has been deemed more significant than continuing attempts to make it succeed. But the Pale concept, as inclination and attitude of mind, remained a constant force in Irish affairs. One Pale failing, the English built a multitude, not with ditches, but with those high stone walls, those plantations of masking trees, which ringed estates and stand there still, their purpose not inclusive of what lies within but exclusive – of that Irish world without. As with the land itself, so with the country of the mind and heart: there too the English built enduring Pales.

The obverse of this constitutes a third characteristic. Foreign to the Irish, the Anglo-Normans also became foreign to the English, as they developed their own interest in their own lands and, often, took up the language and customs of the Irish. Hence there grew an intermediate group, neither Irish nor English. (The negative catches this situation better than the positive form – both Irish and English.) This group was not of a normal colonial type. Its American equivalents had strong popular support, its Indian equivalents had close ties to the mother country. The Old English, or Anglo-Irish, were alien to both populace and mother country, and were distrusted by both. Lacking secure roots in either its old country or its new, this group tended towards restlessness and irresponsibility. Its local rule was exploitative and often corrupt; its face towards England was resentful of royal authority, assertive towards self-government, and at the same time insistent on maternal protection.

A fourth salient feature of the Anglo-Irish relationship is neglect. This became a habit of English government, in the form of lack of consistent thought or action, of exertion alternating with inaction, of temporising and vacillation. Scotch, Welsh or Continental politics, or its own domestic problems constantly absorbed the English monarchy, to its neglect of Irish affairs. Later, the claims of empire took precedence. The result was a flock of evils – inefficient, ineffective government obviously, the protraction of dissensions and quarrels, the growth of absenteeism, and the reduction of policy to mere stop-gaps to maintain Ireland as a source for what the English wanted – money and men-at-arms. Conquest, pacification and government meant a level of expenditure which the English monarchy was unable or unwilling to incur. The outcome was simply this – that Ireland was neither conquered, pacified nor governed.

I

Conquest

The Tudor conquest of Ireland, beginning with Henry VIII's destruction of the Geraldine league, and ending with Elizabeth's defeat of Hugh O'Neill in 1603 exhibits both the strengths and weaknesses of Tudor power. This conquest, unlike that of the Normans, broke the public authority systems of Gaelic Ireland, and substituted those of England acting through a Dublin executive. If the public establishment of an English executive, legislative and judicial system be conquest, conquest this was. Yet outside of governmental forms, what had been achieved? Little save destruction. Certainly not peace, nor law nor order.

The Tudor period saw sown the seeds of perennial attitudes. The English need to conquer Ireland was real and urgent. Ireland was Yorkist, anti-Tudor, in political sympathy, providing a base for pretenders such as Lambert Simnel in 1487. By the time of Henry VIII's accession, English laws and customs prevailed only in a tiny area around Dublin, so far had Ireland degenerated into anarchy and lawlessness. This situation offered a vulnerable prospect to a foreign enemy, and Henry was in the process of accumulating enemies, notably the Holy Roman Emperor. The consequent argument is as old as the English connection: it was necessary to English defence to establish a firm English government in Ireland, so that Ireland would not become a base for England's enemies. Against this was the other argument that England should permit, if not encourage, dissension in Ireland on the assumption that if the Irish were fighting among themselves they would not attack the English. Both these arguments influenced English policy in Tudor times and thereafter, to issue in a variant of the classic divide and rule. The major element of variance consists in this – the fostering of division was a major factor in making effective rule impossible.

Both of these English arguments sprang from fear – fear of what might happen to England if Ireland was left to itself: either a foreign enemy would occupy Ireland as a base to attack England, or the Irish would unite to attack England, or, worst of all both these things would happen at once. Fear is not a perceptive or magnanimous emotion: it is blind and harsh. The fact that it was fear which impelled English policy towards Ireland does much to explain the nature of the relationship. From the English viewpoint, the conquest of Ireland was not aggression, but the prevention of potential aggression against themselves; that is, essentially, self-defence, a strategic necessity. This gave it a logical and immediate justification in English eyes. What complicated this imperative was that aggression against the Irish was necessary to forestall their potential aggression and establish the necessary defensive position, and further, that Tudor power, all of a piece in England, presented a contradiction in Ireland in that there its assertion represented two realms of power – temporal and spiritual. It signified not only physical conquest, as had Norman power, but also religious. The English failed to appreciate this crucial dualism. To them, their religion was a mark of their national independence, an instrument of state, and essentially a subordinate matter: it had not been a point of really serious contention in England – why should it be in Ireland?

Conquest is possible only by the assertion of superior force. England's failure to conquer Ireland is readily understandable if the division between temporal and spiritual be taken as real, and the spiritual given primacy, as it was in Ireland. England had superior temporal force, military and governmental. But English spiritual forces were notably inferior. The decisive nature of this inferiority on the field of spiritual battle can be exhibited in political terms.. The traditional Irish modes, overwhelmed in the temporal order by the English, found ready refuge and expression in the spiritual where, indeed, an alternative, very strong, and national structure of government already existed. To destroy this refuge, the Tudors used weapons of the temporal, not the spiritual order; weapons that were so totally inappropriate to the enemy as to foster what they sought to destroy.

From a hostile Irish viewpoint, Henry VIII's standpoint was totally contradictory and untenable. The English monarchy's lordship of Ireland was based formally on a Papal grant, given in 1155 by Adrian IV, with the approval of the leaders of the Irish Church. From the 1530s, Henry was seeking to build his lordship into a kingdom, while at the same time challenging the very Papal authority from which his title derived. If Henry's predecessors had received the governance of Ireland from the Pope, as feudal vassals, Henry had forfeited it by his apostasy, to say nothing of his adultery. So ran the Irish clerical argument, bolstered eventually by the Counter-Reformation papacy itself; the Bull *Rex Hiberniae* in 1555 gave Ireland to the Catholic monarchs Philip and Mary. The revolutionary essence of Henry's Reformation was much more obvious to the Irish than the English. Sir Thomas More's perceptions were almost unique in England, where most saw nothing revolutionary at all, no real break in their continuum: thus, some English commentators were to regard Irish adherence to Catholicism as wholly a product of a perverse tendency in all England's quarrels to take the opposite side. But for the Irish, who reasoned from religious premises, there was no escaping the conclusion that Henry was a religious revolutionary, and that his rebellion transformed the Irish political situation. In that he had defied the Pope he was a heretic, an evil enemy of Christ's true Church: moreover, his breach with Rome was clearly an act of treason against the Pope whereby he had lost his right, his God-given authority, to govern. Henceforth, whatever force the English Reformation monarchy might muster, its Irish critics saw spiritual and moral right as clearly against it. Henceforth the Reformation monarchy could rely on might alone. The King's Bishop of Meath reported in the late 1530s: ' In the Irishry, the common voice runneth that the supremacy of our sovereign lord is maintained only by power, and not reasoned by learning.' In this view, English government was tyrannical by definition: it was not according to law. From this point on, the relationship of England and Ireland was set firmly in the form of might against right.

This became apparent early in Henry's reign notably in the rebellion of Silken Thomas. By the late 1530s English observers were reporting that priests were preaching ' that every man ought for the salvation of his soul fight and make war against our sovereign lord the King's Majesty and his true subjects ': death in such a cause would ensure heaven. Henry hoped to civilise – that is, Anglicise – the Irish without compulsion. His policy of bribery – with titles and honours, with confiscated monastic lands, or with English confirmation in the title to lands traditionally claimed – had some, largely temporary, success with the chiefs. But it did not reach the people: indeed it was at their expense, in terms of land holding and monastic services. The destruction of the monastic system was unpopular, breeding enemies not friends. It deprived the Irish of social services and an education system: those who wanted education were forced to seek it abroad, acquiring habits of thought very different from the English. The deprived friars were thrown into a wandering crusade against their despoiler: real sovereignty, they preached, rested with the Pope. Traditionally in Ireland the clergy had to look to the Pope, not the King, in matters of Church government, reform and preferment, and for temporal support they had looked to Irish rulers not English. So the Reformation, accepted so quietly in England, made no progress in Ireland. And before the Parliament which declared Henry VIII King of Ireland, in 1541, had dissolved, Jesuit agents of the Counter-Reformation had landed in Ireland to reinforce a clergy already actively committed to denying Henry's claims.

The future of Anglo-Irish relations was determined by the failure of the Reformation in Ireland. This proposition is not to be understood as referring merely to the obvious consolidation of antagonistic religious persuasions, but, in a related sense, as pointing to the total and irredeemable failure of English moral authority in Ireland. From the 1540s the English began a rapid moral abdication in their Irish policies – abdication, for it was not so much that the Reformation failed in Ireland as that it was never seriously attempted on a religious level. The Papacy won by default. No serious attempt was made to win a willing Irish allegiance to the reformed religion, or even to promulgate its teachings – or to place its claims, and those of its king, on an ethical basis. And what the Papacy had won by default was vital to the political aims of the English – moral authority on which political authority was so dependent. England's failure to contest the religious future in Ireland on ethical grounds, or indeed any other ground than that of coercion, amounted to an abdication of any moral claim to governing authority. Simply, to the Irish, the English had forsaken any right to govern, and force remained the only determinant of their relationship. The centuries that followed the Reformation were a protracted variation on that central theme.

Any explanation of why the Reformation failed in Ireland, however it may stress positive factors which favoured Catholicism, cannot escape the simple negative fact that little effort was made to bring the King's religion to the people, let alone make it attractive or even acceptable to them. The great mass of the population did not even hear the new faith: there was virtually no one to preach it, and those few who did were unintelligible – they did not speak Irish. The Gaelic linguistic bond was not only a cement which held together the Irish, but a barrier which kept out the English. The Catholic clergy had the Irish to themselves: they were, on the whole, dedicated, familiar, Irish speaking, bonded to the people by a common suffering and totally committed to Pope against King. On this situation the official religion made virtually no impingement. It was the religion of an alien power and establishment, subject to and exploited by the State, which remained within the Pale and mirrored the Pale's state of mind. In the Irish view it stood self-condemned (for it attempted no answer) as heretical, a political device designed to bolster and exalt English power. The motivation for this ' heresy and new error in England ', as the Irish annalists saw it was ' pride, vain-glory, avarice and lust '. This image of English religion had implicit in it an image of the English, an image which was to endure. Protestantism meant liberty for England; in Ireland it was synonymous with conquest and confiscation. Much more than this, it was wrong and evil, the product of vicious impulse, an impious Satanic war on God and His Church. This was the picture projected by the priest: the Irishry had no other. The English response to this is represented by Francis Bacon – the idea that the Irish were too savage to accept the reformed religion which reflected a superior level of civilisation – and by Sir George Carew, who saw witchery, the devil, in Irish resistance. By the 1590s these two responses were mingling in a conviction of holy superiority, foreshadowing the mind of Cromwell, patent in the warning of Lord Deputy Burgh to Tyrone that God would destroy the counsels of the wicked against his anointed. The Irish saw direct links between England and Satan. The Anglican ritual was dubbed ' the devil's service '. They crossed themselves when Protestants passed, to protect themselves from the devils who possessed those souls. When Sir John Norris, Lord General of Ireland, died in 1597, an Irish historian recorded the circumstances as these: Norris had been playing cards, when Satan, to whom Norris had sold his soul, appeared (black, and dressed in black), reminded him of his contract, and seized his soul on the spot. The lesson drawn was that combat with Norris was combat with the devil also, incarnate in his instrument on earth.

Such was one, the popular, level of consciousness which translated Irish affairs into a war between God and Satan. There were other levels, other modes for understanding these affairs, other terminology in which they might be expressed, though the religious viewpoints remained the constant determinants. From a Catholic standpoint, Elizabeth's succession as Queen in 1558 made the political situation even clearer: her legitimacy was voided not only by heresy but by birth – born out of wedlock she had no title to the throne. From this conclusion it was natural that the Catholic Irish should seek another King, of the true faith – Philip II of Spain. Natural, but not traditional, indeed an innovation.

Irish leaders, notably Hugh O'Neill, were eventually to grasp that survival in freedom depended on the adoption of such new political forms as the dynamic English threat made necessary. Localism and petty dynasticism were not enough when confronted by strong central power.

But however much the language and forms were political or economic, the Irish point of departure remained religious. The rebellion of James Fitzmaurice in 1569 pivoted on the Catholic question: his enthusiasm gave it the character of crusade against English heresy. It has been argued that religion alone would not have produced a rebellion, that Irish fear of losing lands to English colonisation is what prompted it. Whatever the truth of this, the rebellion makes very clear the central importance of religion as medium, justification and context for taking up arms against the English. Medium in the sense that Catholicism was the common Irish (and Old English) inheritance and experience and one which mobilised the only organisation as extensive as Ireland itself, the priesthood. Justification in that it provided a moral setting for idealism and ample righteous overlay for those prompted by material self-interest. Context in that it gave Irish affairs a wide and deep crucial significance in relation to the Papacy's total European policy of Counter Reformation: the Bull *Regnans in excelsis*, excommunicating Elizabeth and releasing her subjects from obedience was issued in 1570. True, the Fitzmaurice rebellion got relatively little help from Spain, the champion of the Counter Reformation, despite the Irish resolve to accept the Spanish King: Philip did not see Ireland – poor, barbarous, dangerous – as much of an asset. And true again, the Papacy was much more concerned with the larger and more powerful England than Ireland, and its policy was to win England back by the avoidance of actions which might antagonise her rulers. It would be a mistake to over-emphasise the Romanism of Ireland's stand, or at least to misunderstand its nature. Romanism was a flag, a battle cry, a non-English habit of mind, rather than a headquarters. But the effect on the English of the coalition of the Queen's excommunication with Irish rebellion and the threat of Spain was to breed a very real fear, centred on an intense hatred of the Papacy and all its allies.

This fear (a fundamental constant in the ensuing history of English attitudes towards Ireland), if not justified by facts, had a firm basis in Irish intentions. Irish rebels saw their crusade as involving more than the fate of Ireland. As the English Jesuit Nicholas Sanders wrote from Spain in 1577, ' the state of Christendom dependeth upon the stout assailing of England '. When Fitzmaurice landed from Spain at Dingle in July 1579 he was preceded to the shore by friars and a bishop, complete with crozier and mitre: Fitzmaurice declared that he would deliver Ireland from both heresy and tyranny. Here, as throughout Irish history, to make a distinction between religious and political aims is to falsify reality. In the evolution of the English mind, there was a strong tendency both to subordinate religion to politics, and to separate them altogether. Not only did such tendencies fail to allow for the thinking of a people who accepted no such subordination or separation, it also contrived, drawing on its own cynicism and political obsessions, to depict religious declarations as a sham. If the English had divorced religion from politics, in Ireland they remained truly married: Fitzmaurice's proclamations make their union clear as well as the essentially theological and legal basis for his actions.

> The cause of this war is God's glory, for it is our care to restore the outward rite of sacrifice and the visible honour of the holy altar which the heretics have impiously taken away. . . . Natural law empowers us to defend ourselves against the very manifest tyranny of heretics. . . . Pius V had deprived Elizabeth, the patroness of those heresies, of all royal power and dominion. . . . Thus we are not warring against the legitimate sceptre and honourable throne of England, but against a she-tyrant who has deservedly lost her royal power by refusing to listen to Christ in the person of his vicar. . . . we are fighting for our faith, and for the Church of God; and next . . . we are defending our country, and extirpating heretics, barbarians, and unjust and lawless men. . . . We are on the side of the truth and they on the side of falsehood; we are Catholic Christians, and they are heretics; justice is with us, and injustice with them. . . .

The 'we' and the 'they' in this division are not racial but religious terms: so it was that Nicholas Sanders, Jesuit but Englishman, spent three years in Ireland organising rebellion which brought the Irish bloodshed, famine and confiscation—but was never betrayed.

The Spanish Armada was part of this crusade: there were Irish priests on board with the Spanish and Portuguese. The crusade appeared on Irish soil again with the rebellion of Hugh O'Neill in 1595 in ' God's just cause ', fighting for ' the Catholic religion, and liberties of our country '. That this cause was also that of Irish lands and an Irish way of life does not diminish its sacred character, it merely renders it more human. The medieval crusade was no less a crusade for its greed for land and gold and power, and in Ireland the priesthood had succeeded in imparting to the temporal aspects of the old Irish system—landholding for instance—

something of the sacred nature of the old religion. Nothing was secular to the Irish: what was *temporal* had its sacred place in God's plan. Given this integration, an attack on any part of the old Irish system was an attack on all of it, and those who attacked it were no mere plunderers, they were enemies of God.

The English utterly failed to comprehend the religious basis of Irish resistance. Their explanations were cultural and racial. Since the Norman invasion, the normal relationship between Celtic Irish and English had been that of conflict. The Tudor period saw this confrontation become both intimate and desperate in a way not so before. Seeking to subdue the Irish, the English developed, in an atmosphere of fear and as justification for aggression, a set of cultural and racial judgements which formed the enduring basis of the English view of Ireland. In part, these judgements took a religious form which received its extreme development in the seventeenth century – Puritanism. More basic were impressions of an anthropological kind, characteristic of an emergent Renaissance imperialism.

By the end of the sixteenth century, the English image of the Irishman was that of a savage. As Margaret Hodgen has pointed out,

> While sovereigns of the realm were struggling to pacify the tribal Celts and the Puritan colonists in North America were wrestling with the Red Indian for his soul and his lands, all frontier antagonists looked more or less alike. . . . they were enemies, they were ignorant, and they were animal-like. . . . the epithets used to describe the folk on Britain's Celtic border were interchangeable with those applied to the Negroes in Africa or to the Indians across the Atlantic.

Such images supplied a moral basis for a righteous subjugation or extermination of Negroes and Indians: the Spanish were in advance of other Europeans in that they questioned what others assumed – that these ' savages ' were not men, not moral beings, not capable of Christian virtue – then the basic test of civilisation. And to the English the Irish were savages.

Any ethic of conquest (and civilisation demands ethics if not morals) postulates the inferiority of those subjugated; ethical inferiority, not merely inferiority in strength. Yet inferiority in strength is very important. It seemed to the English natural that the backward, savage Irish should be easily conquered. That they failed to subdue the Irish increased not English respect, but English hatred and the rationalisation of Irish success as the product of the very depths of their savagery, bereft of morality or principle. English administrators continually blamed their failure on the despicable nature of the people. Sir William Fitzwilliam saw himself as a man banished ' among unkind people, a people most accursed, who lusted after every sin. Murder and incest were everyday matters, and a lying spirit brooded over all the land.' Or Sir Henry Sidney in 1567: ' matrimony among them is no more regarded in effect than conjunction between unreasonable beasts. Perjury, robbery and murder counted allowable. Finally, I cannot find that they make any conscience of sin. . . .' In the same year George Wyse of Waterford saw ' a " menye " of brute beasts ' who knew neither God nor their prince. Tremayne saw a people without conscience or morality. What was normal or sport to the Irish – wandering, cattle raiding, violence – the English saw as crime, irresponsibility, evil. Here was a realm in which ' the wicked, better acquainted with darkness than light, have chosen to wallow in their own filth and puddle of tyranny, oppression, rape, ravine and spoil '. Succinctly, and to some British the case was still so in 1919, the Irish problem was that they could not govern themselves nor would they allow others to govern them.

And naturally, the depravity of the people was reflected in the depravity of their usages. To the English, savagery had more than political connotations, it had virtually a political and economic equivalence – the absence of a strong central government and of a stable system of landholding and agriculture. Irish political and economic organisation had not progressed much past the tribal stage, with some feudal overlays. Its concepts of wealth, land tenure, political power and justice were appropriate to that stage. The Irish admitted composition – a money-fine recompense – for murder, and liability extended from an offender to his relatives and descendants. Their capital consisted of cattle. They cultivated no land. They were nomadic. They had no money system. Their relationship one to another was highly personalised. They had no towns. They slept in the open, or in wretched huts. They talked in Gaelic. Their appearance, half-naked, long hair, clad in animal skins, always armed, was wild. They were superstitious, idolatrous perhaps. William Camden wrote in 1586, ' I cannot tell whether the wilder sort of Irishry yield divine honour unto the moone '; Camden, like other Englishmen, did not see those religious usages which were familiar to him, but those which were not – the pagan heritage; the Spanish, such as those wrecked in the Armada, saw both. So the Irish appeared strange, alien, crude and primitive. Their polity was based on predatory war, which had become a way of life, partly even a sport.

All this was an abomination to the English. This was ' beastliness ', nauseating, contemptible and inexplicable, partly because it was primitive and unfamiliar, partly because of its seeming instability, its appearance of gross and anarchic disorder.

The English conceived their major problem in Ireland as the eradication of disorder: this was an almost total misconception of the real problem they faced. They sought to impose order on Ireland, which in their minds meant the destruction of the existing system and the substitution of their own. But the existing system was in fact no system: it had its rationale in what the English took to be anarchy but what the Irish understood as their individual liberty. The destruction of this disorder did not automatically mean the creation of order. On the contrary, it meant the further extension and entrenchment of disorder. England's governmental problem in Ireland was conceived to be the establishment of English authority. It ought to have been conceived as the creation of order – as the English understood it – where none existed. For while in England authority and order were essentially synonymous, one and indivisible, in Ireland they were separate. In Ireland the English opted for the wrong alternative, for no secure authority can be based on a social order discordant with it.

Given English assumptions (that Ireland should be like England), the continued Irish rejection of English authority seemed also a rejection of civilisation. The very fact that the Irish rejected English authority proved that they were inferior, for their behaviour in this showed them to be incapable of assuming equality. Irish pride and pretensions, instanced in the behaviour of Irish leaders (Shane O'Neill at Elizabeth's court in 1562 is an example), seemed to English observers ludicrous and totally unjustified, indeed perverse.

So, schemes for civilising Ireland always rested on the initial assertion of English power and authority. Acceptance of this power and authority would denote a first step away from barbarism. In Essex's 1573 view, once the Irish had been compelled to obedience ' they would be easily brought to be of good religion '. The reverse was in fact true: it was religion which determined obedience, which demanded the rejection of the English authority structure. The old Irish religious order, and it was an order, remained untouched, unchallenged at its own level and on its own ground. Thus, those interpretations (Froude's for instance) which explain the Irish problem's continuance as fundamentally due to insufficient or inconsistent application of English power misconstrue that problem. Its solution lay, if anywhere, not on the level of authority or power, but on the level of order or social system – and the old order, reduced to a religious form, remained intact. That order, of its nature aristocratic and hierarchical, yet individualist, regional, local, and very personal in its structure and internal relationships, was inaccessible to the assertion of power alone. Alien power, far from destroying it, confirmed it by driving it in on itself and by cutting off the winds of change. Hence, the Anglo-Irish problem became static and stagnant for centuries. English power preserved the old order in Ireland by way of simple reaction.

When the English paused to consider why their victory in Ireland was assured, their answer depended on what they saw as a characteristic of the Irish – disunity: ' Thus it ever was in Ireland: the natives fought among themselves, and so lost all.' In keeping with their own political habits, they equated both power and identity with national unity. Certainly it was fatal for old Irish political independence that it failed to evolve a centralised government at the time when England was rapidly developing into a strong nation state. However, this failure did not destroy, as the English assumed it would, Irish power and identity, for that lay not in political unity, but in a peculiar oneness as a religious people: therein lay Irish strength. And therein lay the stalemate of Anglo-Irish relations – their power systems were not the same. The English could impose their political structure. They could do much to banish the superficial forms of old Irish life. They could not conform the Irish mind, whose salient characteristic was religious faith. Driven from their old politics and their old modes, the Irish took refuge in that faith. So secure was that refuge, so determined its defence, that the English were forced eventually to restrict their attempts to politics. To attempt to extend their dominion to faith was to place what was most desired, political control, in greater hazard and defy that realists' maxim that politics is the art of the possible. Moreover, for England, faith was to become, of itself, little valued. Politics was to become not merely predominant but almost sufficient unto the life of man.

But, from the Tudor viewpoint, what else could be done? Irish affairs could be approached only on the field of power. To suggest that a patient civilising programme, within the existing framework of Irish life, may have worked a congenial transformation neglects the fact that the Irish chiefdom, with its jurists and minstrels, its ancient customs and fierce localism, was committed to preserving an old order to which centralised power, any great single aggregation of governing power, was anathema. It was naturally resistant to monarchic claims even if these were not foreign. Moreover, as the Tudors were to find by experiment, the Irish politico-economic system was totally unsuited to be a vehicle for the expanding power they wished to assert. So, the system was not only resistant to take over, it was useless to the English monarchy's ambitions. Its destruction was logical, but impossible – imposible because it was more than a political system, it was a way of life. All that could be done was to crush those parts of it which obtruded into the political air. The rest remained in the soil. The cost of destroying the old order at the top was to confirm it at the bottom.

The Tudor conquest of Ireland was a bitter process which set the basic tone of Anglo-Irish relations thereafter. Ireland's seeming disorder and anarchy were first seen as a challenge by the centralising Tudors; then, as they failed to impress their will, as an affront, all the more galling for the English contempt for the Irish as savages. Failure to pacify Ireland produced an English reaction in which frustration bred harshness – and a basic irresponsibility. This irresponsibility sprang from the fact that Ireland became the grave for both English reputations and English good intentions. This fostered a very general English wish to get out of a country in which life was nasty and hazardous and failure virtually assured: Sir Anthony St Leger regarded Ireland as hell, Sir Henry Sidney merely as purgatory. All other policies failing, sheer force alone remained. And in regard to that, small doses failing, the only course was to increase the dose. As Elizabethan rule tightened on Ireland, the history of conquest became the history of atrocity, as the establishment of English authority was pursued through the spreading of fear: ' fear, and not dandling, must bring them to the basis of obedience,' Grey, the Viceroy, told the Queen in 1581. Insecurity and anarchy reigned, not English power. An unpaid soldiery lived off the land, killing, burning and looting. English rule, or attempted rule, became synonymous with violence and inefficiency. The Pale itself was insecure, a nest of corruption. The symbols of the 1570s were starvation, pestilence, wolves in the desolated areas, and impaled Irish heads. In 1580 Elizabeth felt compelled to deny that it was her intention to extirpate the inhabitants of Ireland. But that was the tendency of her policy: much of the country was deliberately laid waste in order to starve the Irish into submission. English rule became equated with destruction – of lives, agriculture and prosperity, of civilisation itself, whether Irish or English. To the English or at least Elizabeth, this was the reduction of rebellious subjects to obedience, the putting down of treason. ' The very name of Conquest in this case seemeth absurd to us,' wrote the Queen in 1599; for the intention was merely ' to reduce a number of unnatural and barbarous rebels and to root out the capital heads of the most notorious traitors.' To the Irish, conquest was famine and massacre. By early Elizabethan times, the English had taken on the image in Ireland of heretics and murderers, possessed by a Satanic pride which drove them to ceaseless conquest, and courting the imminent destruction by God of their sole possession – power. As the conquest proceeded Irish thought and emotion were rendered down to hatred and the desire for vengeance.

> May we never taste of death nor quit this vale of tears
> Until we see the Englishry go begging down the years,
> Packs on their backs to earn a penny pay
> In little leaking boots, as we went in our day.

By 1603 superior force under Mountjoy – who saw the Irish as ' swine ', ' a generation of vipers ' – had decided the political situation: an autonomous Gaelic society was at an end; law, landholding, officialdom, the entire politico-economic authority structure, were English. The Irish lords of Ulster had fled, and James I established a colony there. By 1603 Mountjoy's success could be seen in the multitudes that lay dead and unburied, torn by famished dogs, dead with mouths stained green by eating nettles, docks, grass. In their famine, the product of English conquest, the Irish had eaten their own dead, fed on shamrock. Dead too was Elizabeth's Irish dream expressed in her instructions to Sir John Perrot in 1583 – increase the revenue without oppressing the subject, reduce the army without impairing its efficiency, punish rebels without driving them to desperation, reward loyal people without cost to the Crown. These instructions mirror the thoughtless unreality of English good intentions: the facts of English policy towards Ireland were force, famine, hatred and death.

English attempts to conquer Ireland sprang from political considerations: they raised up a religious crusade. That determination to preserve the old forms of Irish life provided part of the motivation for this crusade makes it no less a crusade. The old religion, with its universalist claims and traditions, was hostile to the new nationalism, the independent pretensions of the new nation states: the old Irish forms fitted readily and subserviently into the old religious context. To embark, as did Irish leaders, clerical and lay, on a policy of restoring the Catholic faith to its liberty in Ireland, expressed a totality in which religious faith, individual liberty, property and sense of belonging, life pattern and place, all knitted into one meaningful dynamic. Seen politically, this was centrifugal determination contending with centralising power, feudal separateness fighting national unity, localism against centralism. Seen religiously it was the reverse – universalism and concepts of totality pitted against nationalism and compartmentalism, part of the great European struggle between

Catholicism and Protestantism in which Ireland was cast as a bright hope of the Counter Reformation. Even those writers who see this religious framework tend to see it as vestigial, what the Irish fell back on as every other remnant of their old civilisation was stripped from them. This is to diminish religion to the dimensions of any other social factor, a last social resort to which in weakness the Irish were reduced. It is more true to see it as a faith, that is, a core of assured conviction, of self-meaning and spiritual identity, in on which the Irish were driven. And a real faith embraces and makes centrally meaningful *all* things – men and money, land and love, poetry and poteen.

So deep and habitual has become, among Irish as well as English, the obsession with the superficialities of political forms, that it has become customary to describe the seventeenth century alignment between Catholic religion and resistance to English rule as ' the growth of Catholic nationalism ', and to see in this century the development of the idea of Irish nationality through the instrumentality of a church which provided a common consciousness. The political terminology is misleading. A national Catholicity can be seen, Catholic nationalism, no. Catholicism had universal not national ambitions: its whole mode and frame of mind were hostile to nationalism. What was occurring in the seventeenth century was not that a common Catholicism was giving rise to an Irish nationalism, but that a total Irish identity (nationalism is too political, too narrow a term) was finding, under coercive pressure, its strongest, most coherent expression in Catholicism. The Gaelic word *sasanach*, the name given to the Saxon, the Englishman, came also to mean Protestant.

The living coherence of Ireland from the Tudors to the French Revolution, rested not on the growth of nationalism, but on the continued life and growth of Catholicism. When nationalism as a new democratic principle of communal coherence was born in the late eighteenth and early nineteenth centuries it presented a tremendous problem to Ireland, for it conflicted very violently with the old hierarchical principle, Catholicism. Both principles promised liberty, and both, in a sense, liberty from the English. But the political implications of Catholicism in Ireland were always misunderstood by the English. Whereas the Irish saw Catholicism as expressing their identity and as enshrining their aspirations towards individual liberty, the English could never construe Catholicism as anything other than the enemy of liberty. They could never conceive of it as a creative force, inducing popular change. Progress in Ireland they identified entirely with their own efforts and policies. Nor could they understand the attraction of Catholicism's promise of ultimate liberty, liberty from the imprisonment of this world. The English under-stood well enough the new political secular nationalism when it appeared. They failed to appreciate its Irish context. It was its emphasis on liberty as a sacred principle that gave secular nationalism its great appeal in nineteenth century Ireland. Fraternity the Irish already had, equality also, in religious life (and with their tradition of hierarchy and authority they cared little for equality in other forms), but fullness of liberty they did not have – and Catholicism for three centuries gave them vigorous tutelage in the pursuit of that principle. Nor did the English discern that, so far as it concerned their rule, the inner history of nineteenth century Ireland consisted of the war between religious and secular structures of communal identity. Where the English saw one Ireland, there were two. Where they saw Catholicism as reactionary, nationalism as revolutionary, these creeds were in Ireland two hostile and competing answers to the same Irish question, that of identity apart from England.

Nothing could exhibit more clearly the religious interpretation the Irish placed on their liberties than their loyal reaction to the Stuart monarchy, which was widely believed to be Catholic in sympathy. It has been common to denigrate this parade of loyalty as a pretence, but the Irish support for the Stuart monarchy is evidence not of duplicity, but of mis-taken judgement. On the accession of James I, the clergy, driven under-ground by the Tudor conquest, reappeared throughout Ireland, a natural development if the Stuart accession was taken to signify the end of religious oppression. In English eyes, however, the clergy appeared very differently: ' Priests and Jesuits swarmed everywhere ', agents of the Papacy dedicated to the destruction of English power. Catholic confidence in the Stuarts was misplaced. They had no intention of tolerating Catho-licism, looked on Ireland with distaste, and saw it as a source of revenue in their financial difficulties. The Stuart impingement on Ireland com-bined, as did the Tudor, religious intolerance, political imperium and worldly greed.

But it was a change in the religious component of this amalgam that sparked off the decisive 1641 rebellion – Irish fear of the anti-Catholic designs of a Puritan Parliament. It is a remarkable feature of that much disputed historical event that those English commentators of the time who explicitly denied that religion was the cause of the rebellion used explanations which point to its centrality: ' they have had too much liberty and freedom of conscience in Ireland and that hath made them rebel.' Nor can there be any doubt about the religious complexion of the Irish Catholic Confederacy which took the field in 1642. This grew from a synod of bishops at Kells in March 1642 which determined on the establishment of a Council with authority to rule and govern, initiative which found response among the nobility and led to the appointment of a provisional government and the drawing up of a constitution. The objective was a Catholic Ireland, loyal to the Stuart Crown. The war that followed was a crusade, faithful versus heretics. Yet, at the same time, this was a land war, the Irish contending for repossession of Ulster, the English determined to meet the cost of subduing the Irish by further forfeitures. Its two aspects, religion and land, divided the Irish mind and forces. Those of Papal crusading mind had as ultimate goal an Ireland whose victorious soldiers would not rest until they had crushed heresy in all the British Isles: theirs was the imperialism of the Counter Reformation. Others, narrowly Irish, looked no further than the resurrection of old Ireland, and their old Irish lands. The Confederacy was riven by internal divisions, personal jealousies and contrasting motives, but it was, nonetheless, Catholic. The Irish bishops called the tune in negotiations with a hard pressed Charles I who in August 1645 agreed to re-establishment of the Catholic religion in return for Irish military support against Parliament's Army.

This religious dominance may be seen in the activities of Rinuccini, Papal Nuncio in Ireland from 1645 to 1649, whose object was to secure the restoration of the public exercise of the Catholic religion. This cause had the support of nearly all the clergy and people even to the extent of acceptance of Rinuccini's proposition that ecclesiastical authority was superior to the temporal ' and that ignorance of the true source of power had ruined the neighbouring kingdom.' But the crusading pattern was complete, down to its flaws, its worldliness and contradictions. The lawyers and the nobility – save for Owen Roe O'Neill – could not stomach Rinuccini's dictation. Some of the Confederacy wanted land, others vengeance. And its armies, for all their avowed Catholicity, remained barbarous and cruel, to Rinuccini's sorrow. In all of this there was nothing of Irish nationalism. There were those whose allegiance was simply Papal, Ireland envisaged as a Papal fief. There were those, like O'Neill, whose patriotism was Catholic and monarchist, with no plans for Ireland as a separate nation. And there were those whose loyalties were personal, local and self-interested. England's own contrivances, the destruction of divine right monarchy, did much to cast Ireland's political mind adrift and wandering. The Stuart monarchy offered at least some possibility of the Irish reconciling their political and religious loyalties. This possibility died with the Stuarts. The monarchs that followed them were totally foreign.

In August 1649 Cromwell came to Ireland to begin a work of reconquest, an enterprise designed both to break the power of the Stuarts in
Ireland and to colonise. Colonisation was impelled not merely by ideas of
gain, but by conviction that the godly should rule whatever earth they
might wrest from the ungodly. Furthermore, Cromwell was determined to
destroy Catholicism. At the end of 1649 the prelates of Ireland voiced
their conviction that Cromwell so intended, and pointed out that this
necessarily involved the extermination, banishment or transportation of
the Irish people, the confiscation of their land and property, and the
colonising of Ireland from England. Cromwell's reply, in March 1650,
confirmed this and revealed his convictions: they reflected the mind of
Puritan England. Catholicism was ungodly, anti-Christian, a work of the
devil, tyrannous and false. He would not tolerate the saying of the mass,
nor papists themselves. As to the Irish, they had without provocation
treacherously rebelled against their legitimate English rulers and had
seized the rightful lands and property of English settlers whom they had
barbarously massacred. The Irish were totally to blame for the ruin of
the country and for England's need to incur the vast expense of a just
war against them. For this they must pay by confiscation of their lands.
To Cromwell it seemed that English rule in Ireland had ' the blessing of
God in prosecuting just and righteous causes ' and was rightfully maintaining ' the lustre and glory of English liberty.' And, should the Irish renounce their evil ways, they too could participate equally in all the benefits
of English rule.

Puritan policy in Ireland revived that of Mountjoy – destruction of
the means of life, with all that entailed – famine, plague, wolves, canni-
balism, death everywhere. The aim, if not the achievement, is apparent
in the formula for lasting peace devised by the parliamentarian Colonel
Jones: ' removing all heads of septs and priests and men of knowledge
in arms, or otherwise in repute, out of this land, and breaking all kinds
of interest among them, and by laying waste all fast countries in Ireland,
and suffer no mankind to live there but within garrisons.'

It might be argued that the pursuit of such a policy doomed Anglo-
Irish relations to a history of hatred. But had the crusade of the Catholic
Confederacy encountered a secular reverse, the consequences of the
Counter Reformation may have been less enduring. As it was, this crusade
was met full tilt by a counter crusade, that of Puritanism. One religious
fanaticism, that of England, engaged and overthrew the forces of another,
that of Ireland. The English were to rid themselves quickly of what was
to seem a brief crusading abberation: its legacy was not primarily
religious, but in civil liberties. But Cromwell the Puritan had defeated

the Irish Catholics, thus burning the cause of the Counter Reformation, the impress of religious division, deep into Irish soil. So it was that the war attracted vast rumours, myths and exaggerations – that a million English Protestants had been murdered by blood-thirsty Papists, that Cromwell's massacre at Drogheda was an enormity virtually without human parallel. And so hatreds and responses were cast firmly in a religious mould: Irishman and Englishman each had branded on his mind a blackened religious image of the other. Ways and means aside, the Tudors lacked the conviction, the will, to impose their religious policy on Ireland. Conviction and will Cromwell had in abundance. He came too late, only to confirm a die already cast.

A last crusade was to come. It perished at Aughrim in July 1691 when the Irish, commanded by the Frenchman St Ruth, who saw his army as engaged in mortal conflict with heresy and hell, were defeated by William I's polygot Protestants. Crusades had failed against conquest, but the religion that impelled them remained.

2
Colonisation

Conquest and colonisation were closely related. Nevertheless, in their Tudor phase particularly, the histories of these two movements illustrate that continuing duality in English involvement in Ireland which remained a crucial factor in frustrating reform – the conflicting demands of public, governmental policy, and of private personal interests. Colonisation was not an official Tudor policy. Henry VIII opposed it. Elizabeth reluctantly tolerated it. To the monarchy, those who urged Irish colonisation – like Sir Humphrey Gilbert – argued that if Englishmen were offered the prospect of carving out estates in Ireland, the problem of the imposition of English authority and civilisation would soon be solved. Or simply – it was a stock argument – colonists were a means of pacifying Ireland, that is, a way of serving royal policy. Elizabeth, however, saw the defects of this argument, that colonisation might complicate rather than solve the problem. She saw that the dispossession of the Irish and the introduction of English settlers in their stead would scarcely forward that policy of conciliation constantly stressed in her instructions to her Irish officials. As a policy, conciliation had more to recommend it than its humanity. It was also cheap: conquest was an expensive business. The risk was that English colonists, instead of making the Crown's task easier, would make it harder and more expensive by arousing Irish resistance and committing the Crown's armed forces to their personal ambitions, interests and defence. And so it was to happen: a pattern was established whereby English government policy became inextricably involved with, and often subservient to, the affairs of a small group of English settlers.

The argument that colonisation would aid pacification bore little relation to the real reason it was advocated, a reason consistently economic. Tudor adventurers soon began to distinguish between the Irish people – savage, depraved, lazy – and Ireland itself, green and fertile. Some Englishmen, those in the Renaissance tradition of the Spanish conquistadores, began to dream of fame and profit in Ireland. In that golden age nothing seemed impossible to bravery and will and imagination. Ireland seized the imagination of England's conquistadores, Raleigh, Essex, Sir Richard Grenville; here was a career for adventurers, an outlet for imperial ambitions such as those of Essex who, in his own eyes, cut a Roman imperial figure; here too was rich land. From the 1570s, plans for colonising Ireland became fashionable, complete with programmes for eradicating any Irish competitors to an English colonial aristocracy and for building up an Irish labour force. Such plans differed little from those directed towards the Americas at the same time: no rights were conceded to existing inhabitants, any resistance would be crushed. So it was that the colonies of Virginia and Ulster were born under the same aegis and regarded in England as similar enterprises – with Indians and Irishmen occupying equivalent roles.

Initially then, while the basis of the monarchy's Irish policy was strategic, the basis of colonisation plans was imperial and economic. Irish colonisation, as envisaged by Tudor adventurers, was a manifestation of the rapid growth of English economic imperialism in its first, visionary stage. However, plans were one thing, implementation another. Ireland proved no Eldorado. It was tenaciously hostile to settlers, destroying them or driving them home. The basic fault was that the English were too few, and rulers only. The Irish tenantry remained.

It was when government policy sanctioned and supported private interest that colonisation came to have an enduring impact on the Irish situation. Both Stuart and Puritan governments encouraged colonisation, or as the Irish saw it, confiscation, and both for the same reasons – economic. The flight of the Irish earls in 1607 left Ulster open to the English. Holding these lands to be forfeit, the English had no misgivings about seizing them and driving off nomads and all others than the tenants they needed. The utter dominance of the profit motive is apparent in the vicious contradictions of plantation policy. On the one hand there were established those enduring characteristics of English landowning in Ireland, absenteeism and neglect of tenants. On the other, the landowners discouraged British settlers so as to get higher rents from Irish tenants. The English deliberately constructed a system in which some Irish were relegated to tenants on what they regarded as their own land while others were driven off. Further, these plantations introduced a new racial and religious complication; Scots Presbyterians, a community hostile both to Catholicism and the English religious establishment. Thus there was imported into Ireland an English issue – Anglicanism versus Dissent – which further paralysed Protestantism and absorbed energies which might have been applied to Irish affairs. Although Protestantism in Ireland was now divided, the Protestant-Catholic division not only remained, but was now, in addition to its previous racial connotation (English-Irish), given an equivalence in the very soil on which men lived: landowner and landless, landlord and tenant.

The effect of the English plantation policy is illustrated by Bishop Rothe's comment on the Wexford plantation of 1613, which

> drove from their well established and ancient possessions harmless poor natives encumbered with many children and no powerful friends . . . driving the desperate to revenge and even the more moderate to think of taking arms. They have been deprived of weapons but are in a temper to fight with nails and heels and to tear their oppressors with their teeth . . . excluded from all hopes of restitution or compensation . . . so constituted that they would rather starve upon husks at home than fare sumptuously elsewhere, they will fight for their altars and hearths, and rather seek a bloody death near the sepulchres of their fathers than be buried as exiles in unknown earth or inhospitable sand.

Conquest meant the establishment of English authority. Colonisation meant that the Irish would be deprived of both altar and hearth, twin centres of their lives; it bred desperation and rebellion.

The crucial wave of colonisation was that which followed the Cromwellian Act of Settlement in 1652. This Act, essentially, gave all Ireland save the province of Connaught, to English and Scots Protestant landowners. The Irish were ordered to remove themselves to Connaught, or renounce Popery and profess Protestantism. The conjunction between landholding and religion was thus made direct: the alternative, to Hell or Connaught, meant to the Irish what it said – choose between your religion and your land. The contrivance by the English government of such an alternative had two obvious effects – to inextricably link religion and economics, soul and soil, and to render the choice intolerable. No Irishman could choose between altar and hearth without hatred of the power that had forced him to abandon one or the other. Some, especially among the nobility, avoided the choice by voluntary exile, a further depriving of Ireland of its natural lay leaders, a further consolidation by default of the influence and power of the priests who remained. And that power and influence among the Irish were further increased by that bond between soul and soil the English had cemented further.

True, as before in other Irish colonisations, the transplantation was not carried out in any way fully. It was physically impossible to arrange such a vast movement of population as the 1652 Act required. The immigration of English labour failing, it was impossible to cultivate the land without the help of the natives – that is, in Puritan eyes, ' those whose principles in all ages carry them forth to such brutish and inhuman practices, which consent not with human society.' Nevertheless, transplantation on a large scale did occur, not only to Connaught but to the West Indies. But, again as before, colonisation in the sense of widespread or intensive English settlement did not take place: Cromwell's success (if it be such) lay almost entirely in transferring property from Irish to English owners. Thereafter, the Irish occupants lived in a land they no longer owned, and the English owners, by and large, owned a land in which they did not live.

Ownership of land acquired in this way bred a complex to justify it, a developing sense not only of superiority in civilisation, but of moral superiority, righteousness. The legacy of Puritanism was to be this, the conviction that the English were conferring a great benefit on the Irish by managing their affairs, seeking to redeem them from savagery and Romish superstition. At first this took a religious form, patent in Cromwell, who saw his massacre at Drogheda as ' a righteous judgement of God upon these barbarous wretches.' Of his Irish campaigns he asked: ' Is it an arm of flesh that doth these things? Is it the wisdom and counsel, or strength of men? It is the Lord only.' This vivid belief in the active generalship of God in the English cause did not long outlast Cromwell: the assumptions and attitudes it generated endured. Henry Cromwell may be quoted to illustrate these, shorn of religious verbiage. Commenting in 1655 on a scheme for deporting Irish girls to Jamaica, to remedy a scarcity of women in the young English settlement there, he wrote: ' Concerning the young women, though we must use force in taking them up, yet it being so much for their own good, and likely to be of so great advantage to the public, it is not in the least doubted.' W.

Steuart Trench, reminiscing of the 1845 famine, could not understand Irish denunciation of Lord Lansdowne's emigration scheme: emigrants would be better off and so would those left behind. The English were convinced of their superior knowledge of what was good for the Irish.

Nowhere is this clearer than in regard to that central Puritan virtue, work. Before the Puritan period there had been a fairly general English belief that the Irish were lazy, but that characteristic had been seen as one among many, equally odious. However, from the middle of the seventeenth century there grew, to be firm and strident by the nineteenth the English conviction that the great vice of Ireland was idleness. At first this vice was seen in terms of the Protestant ethic: the Godly man was industrious and thrifty. And of course the reason why the Irish were idle was that they were ungodly, priestridden. Clarendon, in Ireland in 1686, wrote to Rochester: ' It is scarce possible for any that have not been here to believe the profound ignorant bigotry the nation here are bred in by the priests, who, to all appearance, seem to be as ignorant as themselves. The generality of them do believe that this kingdom is the Pope's; that the King has no right further than the Pope gives him authority; and that it is lawful for them to call in any foreign power to help them against those who oppose the jurisdiction of the Church.' What Clarendon viewed with incredulous astonishment, as some absurd delusion, was a conviction reached a hundred years before by application of traditional legal principles as Irish Catholics understood them. A century had not altered the Irish position: Clarendon noted that those Irish who rejected this view of Papal authority in Ireland were ignored and of little consequence, but nevertheless would not take side against those with whom they disagreed. However, for the English, a century had transformed what had once been at least understood into something preposterous. As religion ceased to be the centre of English life, the idea that Romanism was spiritually poisonous was giving way to the assumption that it was intellectually degrading, a mark of ignorance. The same process occurred in regard to the virtue of work: the religious connotations disappeared, but not the moral. The outcome was a formula which was common down to the nineteenth century: repress Romanism and encourage industry: get rid of the priests and make the people work and all would be well with Ireland. This formula was to be given further refinement, but its basic assumption was that of a crude economic determinism. The argument went thus: it was obvious that Ireland and England were divided by religion. Catholicism was a religion of idleness and ignorance. Protestantism was a religion of prosperity. If Ireland could be made prosperous, Catholicism would die there, and the great source of difference between Ireland and

England happily removed. Given that the Irish were patently unable to do this themselves, the English would have to do this for them. That is, English governments, administrators, colonists, settlers, landlords, managers, had a clear moral duty to conduct Ireland's affairs to produce prosperity, the cure of all ills and divisions.

Like all other English solutions to the problem of Ireland, this formula was very imperfectly applied. A first reason was the unsecuring of the Cromwellian settlement by the Stuart Restoration which though not revolutionising Irish land ownership did occasion another big land re-distribution, and re-imposed the authority of the Anglican Church. The Anglican-Presbyterian battle flared again in Ireland to the detriment of English rule. The Restoration atmosphere was that of the divine right of freeholders: where English religion and English profit had once proceeded together, profit alone was left to rule – the new gentry of post-Puritan Ireland were nominally Anglican, actually indifferent. As for the English at home, so for the English abroad; by the time of the Navigation Acts of the 1660s, the sacred had given way to the profane in which trade and profit were dominant English interests. Perhaps Ireland might have been seduced from its hatreds by prosperity, perhaps prosperity and Protestantism went together, as many Englishmen thought. The experiment was never tried. At the end of the seventeenth century, after the battles of the Boyne and Aughrim and the Treaty of Limerick, Ireland was militarily annihilated. Force, it seemed, had solved the Irish question. Thereafter Ireland could be treated as a colony of exploitation, as colonisation on the basis of absentee ownership, and the Navigation Acts had foreshadowed. Ireland was fitted into the mercantilist stereotype: it must not be allowed to compete commercially with England.

The major effect of colonisation, as it occurred throughout the seventeenth century, was to further confirm Irish-English relations in a religious form. Religious discrimination, initially made for religious reasons, was, as the eighteenth century progressed, less and less spiritually meaningful for the English: they believed in it less and less for religious reasons. But they clung to it tenaciously as an effective device for distinguishing and ensuring their own supremacy. For the English, religion was moving from the realm of spiritual conviction into that of social characteristic. Religion remained the means whereby the English marked off their socio-economic Pale and their political autocracy: the English defined their secular world in anti-Catholic religious terms. They thus helped to maintain the age of the Counter Reformation in Ireland, the sacerdotal age, which belonged to priest and priesthood.

This they did not only by insisting that religion be the touchstone for everything in Ireland, but also by preserving colonisation in its seventeenth century form, by thereafter excluding further English immigrants who might, perhaps, have brought less narrow minds. The historical petrifaction of Ireland was a joint Anglo-Irish achievement. After the Williamite confiscation (1690-1703), colonisation in Ireland virtually came to an end. Protestantism had erected an ascendancy and intended to preserve it. An Irish labour force suited the Protestant gentry very well. The aristocratic satisfaction of governing the inferior and ignorant Irish apart, to import English labour would cost money and undermine the basis of the ascendancy: English Protestant settlers would be troublesome, insist on English rights, demand equality. Seventeenth century colonisation from England had produced a landowning gentry whose dominance of Irish political life and influence in England enabled them to impose their will on Ireland, which was to maintain their own ascendancy and keep down taxation.

Colonisation had the contradictory effects of rendering the Irish situation both stagnant and potentially explosive. The stagnancy was apparent in the internal situation, the potential for change in the relationship between colonists and mother country.

3
Legal Discrimination

The Tudor period proved that allegiance to the Crown in religious affairs could not be secured by the promulgation of laws. Such legislation as the 1560 Act of Uniformity, which compelled attendance at the state church on Sundays, had no positive value. Little attempt was made to enforce it: it could not be enforced outside the Pale because of lack of machinery to do so, and to try to enforce it inside the Pale ran the risk of provoking disaffection. This religious legislation operated mainly as a simple political test, less to make Catholics conform or to destroy Catholicism, than merely to achieve a ready-made division in Ireland into Catholics and Protestants. (It was also, in a sense, bribery: failure to conform might not incur punishment, but conformity secured rewards and privileges.) Little attempt was made to secure Ireland's allegiance to the Crown's religion. Efforts were almost immediately rendered down into ensuring that non-allegiance must be debarred from all areas of Irish life judged important by the English. This negative intention is the rationale of penal laws from sixteenth to eighteenth centuries: they were a self-confessed testimony to a basic failure to spread English law and order. It is true that these penal laws tended to bring English government into contempt in that their ineffective or casual positive implementation demonstrated that government was weak and inefficient. But the penal laws served their purpose in protecting that area in which English – and Anglo-Irish – strength lay, that of politics.

The only effective implementation of penal laws occurred when they related directly to the central political structures. The fact that these laws had their real bite in politics, and were contrived through politics, though the basis of their construction was religion, determined the battleground and terminology of Irish-English conflicts from the eighteenth century to the twentieth. They concentrated the attention of the Irish on this political field. That is, all Irish grievances came to be translated into political terms, or at least to seem soluble only (and entirely) by political activity and measures. This political obsession at the panacea level developed first among those who were in a position to take some political action, that is, the Anglo-Irish Protestants.

And its initial development among them was natural too in that the Anglo-Irish were much closer to the English, the earliest European victims of politics as a pathological condition. So far was Tudor government confined in its prison of the political that it could not conceive of its religious policies in Ireland as religious: they were policies, expedient courses of action. From the English viewpoint what they were pursuing in Ireland was not religious conversion or religious persecution, but a campaign against disloyalty.

The English reaction to the Irish religious situation was a logical consequence of their own complete subjection of church to state and of the relative ease with which they had disposed of Catholicism in England. Their official view of religion had taken on such a political complexion as to deprive them of any real understanding of it, as religion, as faith. The Tudor view was that Irish Catholicism was a conspiracy against the state, a political enemy. In fact Irish Catholicism was a religious enemy, its repudiation of the English monarchy being based wholly on that monarchy's heresy – which had, within an outlook in which religious principles governed the whole of life, direct political implications. What the Irish took to be fundamentally a matter of religion, the English took to be clearly a matter of politics. So what was to the English prosecution of treason was to the Irish persecution of religion. The Attorney General of Ireland, Sir John Davies, complained in 1608: ' The priests excommunicate the jurors who condemn a traitor. The Irish will never condemn a principal traitor.' Confusion was complete: religious loyalty to the Irish meant political treason to the English: to profess loyalty to the English entailed apostasy and heresy to the Irish, and it was these spiritual offences which incurred the spiritual punishment of excommunication. This became increasingly incomprehensible to the English who never failed to be indignantly astonished, as was Wentworth in 1634, that 'priests and Jesuits' sought to influence elections by promising excommunication to those who voted for Protestants.

The English were blind to the spiritual facts. The Counter Reformation was not essentially a political movement, but a religious and spiritual one, designed to reform and strengthen the church's spiritual life as well as regain ground lost to error. Certainly some of the agencies used to pursue that end were political: the English confused the agencies with the essence. The first Jesuits found Ireland religiously neglected, ignorant, and often far from that state of holiness and morality which a healthy spirituality would produce. But they found Ireland faithful, and to build on that was their mission. Indeed, the major mission of priests to Ireland was self-evident – it was to minister to the spiritual condition of the people. The English failed to see this because the religious crusades which formed in Ireland were directed against English power and were thus, whatever their motivation, rebellions – and because, on the whole, (Puritanism aside) in the higher policy-making levels of English government and church, there was little interest in the people's spiritual condition, only in their political condition. What they cared for so little themselves, they could not conceive of others valuing deeply. Montesquieu's observation of the 1730s underlines this point – ' There is no religion in England. If anyone mentions religion people begin to laugh.' Such people came to see allegiance to the Pope of Rome as an allegiance of the same order as allegiance to a foreign prince. Political loyalty was the only loyalty they understood.

So, the totality, the real meaning of Irish resistance escaped them. English officials would concede to the Irish no principles, no impulses, other than those of treachery and rebelliousness: claims for religious freedom and individual liberty were a mere pretence. These were a sham: as Sir George Carew warned in 1611, the Irish would rebel ' under the veil of religion and liberty '.

Yet, if the English were blind to the reality of the Irish religious position, the Irish certainly undervalued the political implication of their stand: they saw everything in religious terms. This was a traditional habit of mind, but it was also a product of the strong religious element in their social leadership. As English conquest progressed and Ireland's natural lay leaders died or fled, clerical leadership became stronger by default, and by missionary influx. These spiritual leaders were often not Irish by race, or if they were, usually continental by training. Their cast of mind, all their reactions, were firmly religious. As the English fitted Irish resistance into political categories, so Irish leaders fitted English activities into religious categories. A group headed by the Archbishop of Cashel, reporting to Spain in 1612 referred to ' an old artifice of persecutors to get up charges of treason and conspiracy against the Christians to cover their own malice and wickedness and their hatred of the Church. . . . The object of the English in all these injuries is no other but to destroy the spirit and energy of the Irish, and compel them to become fugitives and leave their lands, or remaining, to make them crouch in subjection like slaves, and thus root out the Catholic faith.' If the English saw the Irish as traitorous savages, the Irish saw the English as evil men engaged in rebellion against God. That monstrous and dis- ordered evil expressed itself in a multitude of ways – greed for land and wealth, lust for conquest and killing, the urge to destroy true re- ligion. To the Irish, all these things, attacks on their lives and property as well as their religion, were manifestations of the same evil. It was the duty of those who sought the good to resist this evil in every form, temporal or spiritual. The cult of the good, the extraordinary and rapid development of veneration for saints and martyrs is the reverse of this deep apprehension of the evil the English appeared to embody. The cult took extreme forms: when Bishop O'Devany was hanged, drawn and quartered in 1612, Catholics cut off his fingers and toes, even his flesh, as sacred relics.

That Irish Catholics should believe that they possessed the true religion and that the English were moved, not by simple error, but by irreligious evil, is readily explicable. If the English valued their own religion, why did they not promote it? The Crown's proselytising began and remained almost entirely at the level of legal discrimination against those who did not conform. The other obvious means of proselytising, that of spreading the new religious ideas by ministering and preaching up and down the country, was almost entirely neglected. The natural conclusion was that the English were not interested in their religion as such, only its political implications. The Tudors had seen that the dissemination of English religion and culture through church and school was essential if these were to gain acceptance. Much legislation related to the provision of free education in parish schools. But the responsibility for financing and implementing these plans was left with the Established Church – which did nothing. Or almost nothing. The Charter Schools of 1733 were a failure as a mode of instructing the children of 'the popish and other poor natives . . . in the English tongue and in the principles of true religion and loyalty.' (The objectives of these schools reveal much of the English attitude towards the Irish: they aimed to promote Protestantism, loyalty, and, through an apprenticeship system, labour and industry as a cure to the habitual laziness and idleness of the Irish.) The particular failure of these schools lay in the fact that few Catholic parents could be induced to send their children. The general difficulties which lay in the way of a positive Anglican proselytising policy are obvious. The largest was probably the language barrier: Catholic priests training for the Irish mission learnt Irish and brought from Europe devotional books written in Irish. And there was the Anglican obsession with the Protestant dissenting groups, which Anglicans detested and endeavoured to persecute. Nevertheless, basic reasons why the Established Church never really attempted the conversion of the Irish lie within its own nature. It was weakened by its subjection to parliament, by its domination by the English appointees and their low religious quality, by its constant involvement in political affairs, by plurality and non-residence, above all by worldliness and indifference. The situation was something more than the simple neglect of that aspect of imperialism which consists in the tuition of the natives in the way of life of the colonising power: as a religious and cultural example, that life had nothing to commend it to the Irish. All this being said, the governing factor in the neglect of a positive policy of conversion relates squarely to the nature of the colonial situation. The colonists had established division and exclusion as the fundamental principle of government. The dividing line between colonists and natives was religion, a religious test determined the basis of ascendancy and privilege. The whole of the political, social and economic structure rested on the existing religious division: a tiny privileged Protestant group ruled a large excluded Catholic population. If Protestantism were spread the ascendancy would first suffer a dilution, and then the whole structure of privilege would collapse.

Naturally, those who had a vested interest in this structure sought to protect it, and naturally they did so by the continued assertion of the principle on which it rested, religious division. And law was the natural embodiment for this, once military force had destroyed concerted violent opposition. The physical facts of garrison colonisation made penal laws imperative – to define clearly the privileged garrison class, to protect them against challenge or dilution, and ultimately to act as deterrents and sanctions, as a substitute for mass force of arms, in a world traditionally hostile. That these laws related exclusively to religion, not to race or social position, was natural in that the English construed religious profession as determining the division between loyalty and disloyalty. However, by the eighteenth century, the religious division of society had also become convenient in that its effect was to preserve a privileged regime. Where other privileged groups in other times and places had rested their existence on divisions of race or colour or wealth, the Anglo-Irish ascendancy had, ready-made, a religious barrier to use for their purposes. Religious discrimination, enshrined in a set of penal laws, became the device whereby the Anglo-Irish established and maintained their ascendancy in every field, political, social and economic – except the religious. Whereas they monopolised politics, dominated economics and determined the social situation, they had, in effect, abandoned religion to the Irish. The outcome was curious. The principle for the exclusion of the Irish from control of Irish life was established not in those areas in which they were weak or inefficient, but in that area in which they were strong indeed. The English discriminated against the Irish not on the basis of Ireland's weaknesses but on the basis of its strength. Inevitably the consequence was to confirm that religious strength, giving it meaning and coherence as the great cause in which the totality of Irish grievances might be subsumed. The history of English conquest had shown that the Irish could be defeated in the fields of military power and political organisation. The history of English religion had shown that they could not be defeated in that sphere. Yet the penal laws, the policy of conquest adapted to the era of colonisation, applied to the religious field. Of the nature of the situation they could be neither effectively repressive nor remedial, merely exclusive. After the military conquest, the concept of the Irish as enemies and the Irish situation as one of hostilities remained basic to the English. The penal laws made no creative impingement on this problem, indeed they worsened it in leaving the Irish to their own religion-oriented world.

By the eighteenth century, Ireland had become subject to two political determinants, the Ascendancy and the English government. If in the broadest sense, the aims of these two interests were identical – the preservation of English control of Ireland – their ideas on how this might best be achieved were often in conflict. This conflict, which was to remain a vital factor governing the situation down to Irish independence, was often to result in the mutual frustration of both Ascendancy and government, to the paralysis of any Irish policy. Fundamentally its elements were the Ascendancy's enduring determination to preserve its ascendancy pitted against the government's wish as circumstances dictated to make conciliatory or expedient political gestures towards the mass of the Irish. This abrasion is first evident in the matter of post-1691 penal laws. These were an Ascendancy contrivance and did not reflect the inclinations of the English government. William of Orange's own leanings towards toleration and that promised by the treaty of Limerick were bound to be casualties to the Ascendancy's appraisal of its own threatened position, and the need of the English government to support that Ascendancy as a garrison. Nevertheless the English government, with its lack of interest and conviction, could and did, do much to weaken the penal law policy.

But, to reiterate, the purpose of the penal laws passed after 1691 was exclusive and segregatory, designed to give a sense of security and power to the Protestant minority, and provide a weapon to which a fearful Ascendancy might resort if placed under serious threat. As they were not intended to be salutary or reformative, the matter of consistent positive enforcement was of no importance: it was enough for these laws to exist. Indeed irresponsible enforcement would defeat their purpose, if thereby more Protestants were created. The series of statutes prohibiting Catholicism would have extirpated Catholicism in Ireland very quickly had they been enforced, but they were not. Even if the wish and will to enforce them had been present, the machinery to do so was absent. The only consistent enforcement was in matters of property and politics, matters which touched Protestant preserves, and there the laws were efficient enough, ensuring conformity and destroying the remnants of the Catholic landed class. As for the mass of the population, lacking property or any basis for political power, they were not normally prosecuted.

While the penal laws were dominantly a device to preserve the interests of the Ascendancy, until 1766 they had formal political justification, a fact which many Irish commentators overlook. That, from the receiving end, the penal laws looked like and indeed amounted to religious persecution does not alter the fact that, in the main, despite their religious form, they were devised as political expedients to exclude disloyalty and ensure English power and control: the means was religious but the end was political. Until 1766 the Pope continued to recognise the Stuart claimant to the English throne. Irish Catholics, and particularly clergy, were thus naturally regarded as disloyal – or worse still, actively loyal to the Pretender and consequently potential rebels. Real fear for the security of the Hanoverian monarchy was felt strongly in England up to the accession of George III in 1760: the fact was that, Papal policy aside, many Irish were supporters of the Stuart Pretender or sympathetic to England's political enemies, as was evidenced by the Irish Brigade in the French Army. That their loyalty was regarded with deep suspicion was understandable enough. That this was a political rather than a religious fear is obvious in the fact that it was felt most deeply by those whose position was most directly threatened by any change in the Irish situation – the Protestant Ascendancy. In contrast, England, while determined on political control of Ireland, failed to see that religious persecution was essential to this. The Hanoverian kings tolerated Catholic worship in Hanover, and – again, political expediency is obvious – were unwilling to offend Continental allies, notably the Emperor, and later France, by any crusade against Catholicism.

Certainly a massive crusade impelled by enthusiasm and conviction would have been necessary: the practical difficulties of imposing the penal laws were very great. The wholesale refusal of the clergy to take the oath of abjuration of the Pope required of them in 1709 practically voided that Act. The scheme for registration of priests, introduced in 1703 and designed to ensure that Catholicism would eventually die for want of priests, was evaded. Party strife within Protestant Ireland and tension between Irish Parliament and English government militated against enforcement. However harsh and sweeping the anti-Catholic laws passed by the Irish Parliament, it had to rely on the Dublin Castle executive to administer them. That executive reflected the policy of the English government which was, except in times of disturbance, to leave the Catholics alone: as the Lord Lieutenant put it in 1739, referring to priests, ' it has been the maxim here, while they give no disturbance to the Government, to let them alone '. Even if enforcement was decided, communications made this very difficult. The West was so remote as to be semi-independent. Local officials (where they were not, in fact, Catholics) were so overburdened with duties, so corrupt, and so outnumbered by Catholics, that little was attempted. Where it was, local warning systems, guile and resistance, usually allowed evasion.

This situation enraged some few Protestants, but, in keeping with the real nature of the penal laws, it was acceptable to the Ascendancy generally: they got what they wanted – the exclusion of Catholics from land ownership and politics – and they did not want to endanger this, or peace generally, by needless provocation of a people whose reaction they might not be able to control. Cases of large groups of Catholics successfully defying the law and its enforcement officers by rescuing captured priests were numerous enough to make magistrates unwilling to expose the law to mass challenge. And the fact was that, on the whole, the Catholic clergy avoided provocation on their part. They pursued their business quietly, a business not political, but spiritual, the consolidation of the position of their church. So peaceable became their ways that in the second half of the century the Dublin executive was asking the Catholic bishops – still proscribed by law – to use their influence to prevent riots. Which they did. Priests preached civil obedience, and, for example in Dublin in 1748, threatened rioters with denial of the sacraments: frequent excommunications of Whiteboys and members of other secret societies indicate they meant this seriously.

Scholars of an older Irish generation who saw the penal laws as a bitter relentless persecution, vicious in its perfection and rigorously imposed, impelled by demoniac hatred of the Catholic people, tend to attribute the survival of Catholicism to a stubborn heroic reaction, or divine sustenance on the principle that the blood of martyrs was the seed of Christians. Given that the facts point towards political motivation, religious indifference, and very occasional enforcement, other, at least supplementary, explanations seem required. Excluded by law from the authority structures which went with politics and property, Irish Catholics were driven back on the laws of their own religion and the authority structure of their own church: to use an intelligible political cliché, the penal laws confirmed Irish Catholicism as a state within a state. It is true that the laws provoked bitter Irish resentment and hatred. They also attracted contempt, in that the English government was demonstrably either unable or unwilling to enforce them. It was natural that this should foster an Irish disrespect for law and for English authority behind that law, and also breed a sense of pride and power among a people who found they could flout or easily evade the law.

It seems true to say that Catholicism survived in penal Ireland because no determined or effective attempt was made to destroy it – to imprison it, yes, but even within its prison it had enough freedom to grow. Indeed its circumstances had one immense redeeming feature: untrammeled by that state interference so characteristic not only of religion in England, but also on the continent, the church in Ireland remained free to be itself, and within clear limits of prudence, to manage its own affairs. Naturally its growth was coloured by its prison environment. The Irish church acquired in the eighteenth century certain enduring character-istics of wide historical significance. One of these was the pursuit of quietude. The price of comparative freedom of ministry in a penal law situation was the exercising of care not to antagonise either the govern-ment or local Protestants. Practical toleration depended on Catholics making no trouble. The grass-roots strength of Irish religion is certainly related to the energies of priests and people being necessarily restricted to the internal fundamentals of prayer and the sacraments. The threat, if not the actuality of persecution, fostered a religious life of great simplicity and intensity. The penal laws had placed the Irish in a religious ghetto in which they might live more or less as they pleased, except that attempting to break out was prohibited. This fostered a community of spirit which tended to overlay the sharp regional and family differences of old Ireland and became a source of latent social strength and cohesion.

The penal laws also enforced a change in the nature of the Irish priesthood. One result of the deprivation of Ireland of educational facilities was that many of the priests were continental trained, distiguished by a strong ultramontanism, which put them and the people to whom they ministered even more at odds with the nationalist-political outlook of the English. Another consequence of the educational void was that many priests were inadequately trained, or little better than ignorant. Whatever the consequences of such ignorance for the character of the Irish church, its social implications are clear: such priests were closer to the people than a learned priesthood would have been. This closeness to the people was evident in every sphere. Priests and people shared a common proscription and persecution, a common humiliation and poverty. Priests wore no distinguishing dress. Poverty made it difficult or even impossible for the people to support clergy, so some priests took to farming and cattle raising for their support: this practice involved priests directly and personally in land grievances, and other such secular affairs. Merged with their people in this intimate way, many of the clergy, in exercising their natural community leadership, did not distinguish between spiritual and temporal grievances. This worked to the advantage of Ascendancy and government when the priests' influence was used to dampen the outward expression of discontent, but the close links between religious influence and secular affairs were potentially a source of great danger to the *status quo*, as was evidenced at the time of Daniel O'Connell. By the early nineteenth century, the priesthood could mobilise Ireland. The weight of their eighteenth century influence was conservative, but this was not always so, as is apparent in the case of Father Nicholas Sheehy, executed in 1766. From an English viewpoint his priesthood was largely irrelevant, but his championing of the grievances of his flock in rents and tithes was a crime. To the Irish, to whom priests were both spiritual and temporal leaders, such activity was natural to the priesthood and his execution was therefore construed as an attack on the priesthood. The English government deliberately encouraged the church to use its influence to maintain order in civil affairs, thus blurring further any Irish distinction between religion and politics and emphasising

the greatest cohesive force and source of grievance in Irish life.
Imprisoned, the Irish church fell back naturally for sustenance on the
past. This had more than religious significance, for the past was full
of wrongs and hatreds and grievances of all kinds. The fact that mass
continued to be said in the places where churches and monasteries had
once existed, and that the old parish boundaries were carefully preserved
witnessed to more than mere sentimentalism. The eighteenth century
church lived and prayed among the ruins of the seventeenth, maintaining as did no other body in Ireland a direct and open linkage with old
Ireland and its glories, real or supposed. The mass said in the ruins of
some old church had threefold significance: it was the spiritual witness
of an existing community, its setting was both the ancient glory and
freedom that once had been, and a continuing reminder of the visitation
of an evil destruction in more recent times. No one forgets, in a land
of ruins, if the ruins be monuments to their own defeat and subjection.

Latent in the close cohesion between priests and people that developed in eighteenth century Ireland were sources of potential tension
and conflict. One such was that, obviously, the laity who had lost one set
of natural leaders – family chiefs or landowners – gradually began to
evolve another set. The penal laws debarred Catholics from the landowning class. The more energetic and enterprising Catholics turned to
trade. By mid-century an ambitious and wealthy Catholic commercial
class was growing. In its attitude towards the Ascendancy and the
English connection this class was, like the clergy, conservative. But its
conservatism was far more basic. The clergy's conservatism was expedient, to protect religion from persecution; that of the commercial
class was inherent, deriving from the fact that their wealth was built in
and on the existing politico-economic relationships. This class bridged, to
their profit, Irish and English interests, and any dislocation of the liaison
threatened them. The conservative significance, for Irish history, of the
growth of a class of natural leaders who had a vested interest in the
continuance of Anglo-Irish relations at least in the form of close economic
ties, has been little appreciated. The history of Guinness's brewery from
1759 illustrates the more paternal aspects of this development; William
Martin Murphy, villain of the 1913 Dublin strike, is one of a historical
multitude of owners and employers who testify to its exploitative conservatism. This new class, emergent in the eighteenth century, had
economic dynamism, but seldom of a national kind. By the end of the
eighteenth century Catholic Ireland had evolved two sets of leaders,
religious and commercial, neither with much nationalist potential, but
with the religious leadership possessing far more inclination towards

securing fundamental change in Ireland. Little conflict occurred between these sets of leaders, for each acknowledged, implicitly, the strength of the other in its own sphere. The commercial classes accepted and supported the clergy: there was little of the anti-clericalism characteristic of the European bourgeoisie. On the other hand the clergy offered no intrusion into the economic life of trade and industry: the land, English-owned, was another matter. So there grew in Irish life, otherwise so deeply imbued with religious values, a divorce between religion and economics which still endures. Its effect was to constrict gravely the revolutionary potential of religious cohesion and to inhibit and distort the development of Irish identity.

The interests of religion and commerce were antagonistic but the antagonism seldom surfaced, mainly because the commercial classes never had cause to challenge the social pre-eminence of the clergy. That pre-eminence was based on leadership, and the commercial classes, as such, never wished to assert claims to popular leadership: their main desire was to be left alone, which the clergy respected. (Later when the commercial classes aspired to political leadership of Ireland the situation was different and frontal conflict with the church did occur.) The more immediate point of tension within Catholic Ireland as it developed in the eighteenth century was over the question of appropriate tactics. Priests and people were at one in their rejection of English and Ascendancy oppression. And they were generally at one in seeing this oppression as both religious and secular in expression. The point of potential division was not ends, but means, not aims and objectives but tactics. Bishops and clergy favoured a quiet and conciliatory policy so as to avoid a recurrence of active persecution. The laity, whose way was in the world, were more concerned with, and more victims of, the world's ways. Following their faith in full defiance of the law, strong in sense of community and of harsh deprivation, hating, the laity were far less prone to accept the authority behind ineffective law. The Act of Union in 1800 made the nineteenth a political, not a religious, century for Ireland, and tactics is the essence of politics. Some, and increasingly more and more, of the laity came to believe that the church's relatively passive tactics were useless or worse.

Catholic Ireland entered that political century under grave liability. Again, this was a consequence of the penal laws. Catholics had been debarred from political life for over two centuries. Deprivation of the reality of political experience encouraged political unreality in its two most obvious forms – incompetence through inexperience, and the utopian, visionary political mind which, given the area where alone effective Irish freedom had continued to exist, was bound to take a religious, semi-mystical form.

4
Self-Government

In the second half of the eighteenth century there developed in Ireland a constitutional movement which set the tone and limits of the overwhelming weight of Irish demands down to 1916. This movement, aiming at some degree of self-government, sprang from the English and Scots Protestant colonial Ascendancy: a natural corrollary of the colonisation process was that the colonists would eventually wish to have a greater say in determining their own affairs. In one sense, the situation so produced became a major determinant in shaping future Anglo-Irish affairs: in another, it was a prodigious source of delusion.

In the sixteenth and seventeenth centuries relations between England and Ireland were direct and total, in that all the Irish were involved. In the eighteenth century these relations had been constricted artifically so as to reduce the effective Irish element down to a tiny group of Anglo-Irish Protestants centred on Dublin and its Parliament. The demands of this group, and their general objectives, may be described as orthodox colonial (indeed they were largely derivative from those of the 13 American colonies) and, putting aside the unique garrison situation, unexceptional. These demands were constitutional, political and economic, language readily intelligible to eighteenth century England, even if the points made were not welcome. It seemed to those engaged in the consequent controversies, that Ireland and England had come at last to talk the same language even if they were engaged in argument: the political and economic terms in which the English government had always viewed Ireland were substantially confirmed and reinforced by the fact that the Irish, apparently, were at last responding in the same terms. Given this common language, and the fact that the only existing political actualities were English government and Irish Parliament, English understanding of Irish affairs naturally remained constricted to their political aspect. The concept of Ireland as an imperial problem, as a constitutional and political problem, born in the eighteenth century and living very strongly until the 1921 Treaty and after, was a very narrow one, in that it accepted, as a definition of the problem of Ireland, that which had been contrived and imposed by a small Protestant Ascendancy living in Ireland. This imperial definition represents a very great part, and sometimes the entirety of the English appreciation of the difficulties of the relationship with Ireland.

That this was a delusory definition is evident enough. It was a definition made by Englishmen: its initial Irish proponents were Protestants of English descent living in Ireland in a garrison situation. Its terminology and concepts were English, reflecting the constitutional and legal traditions of England, particularly the principles on which political and civil rights had been asserted in the seventeenth century. William Molyneaux's influential and typical pamphlet, *The case of Ireland's being bound by acts of parliament in England stated*, published in 1698, argued, against England's claim to legislate for Ireland, referring to John Locke's theories and stressing the natural rights of Englishmen to their own governance, wherever they might reside. And of course, the proponents of this conception of Ireland's problems as constitutional were a small, isolated colonial elite whose very existence was a major component of all Irish problems and whose grievances were more generally colonial than they were distinctively Irish.

To interpret the Irish question in terms of constitutional relationships and political pressures is, then, a very narrow, partial, and essentially English view. It has been observed that the historical study of the eighteenth century has shown a very strong imbalance towards the late years of the century: is this because these years, crammed as they are with politics, are so much more intelligible to the English and their Irish imitators? A good deal has been made, and rightly, of the relationship of Irish affairs to imperial development, and indeed to the twentieth century disintegration of empire. The reasons for this relationship need not be political, even though its effects may be. Men, even Englishmen, cannot live by politics alone, but they can die from them readily enough. The same may be said for political structures: if the empire may be said to have died of political causes, perhaps this is in the sense that a diet of politics was insufficient to sustain its life. So far as Ireland was concerned, England's political understanding of the matters at issue was a delusion of paramount importance. Its consequences were to confuse the Ascendancy's grievances with Ireland's grievances, to greatly inflate the Ascendancy's role as a determinant in Irish affairs, and to render nugatory so much of England's attempt to improve its Irish relationship in the nineteenth and twentieth centuries. Anchored firmly to the political ground marked out by the late eighteenth century Ascendancy, this attempt was irrelevant to the great mass of the people, who did not see themselves as an imperial problem, and irrelevant to the basic matters which agitated them. This is to put aside the question of whether British attempts to solve Irish problems after 1800 had much to do with Irish problems at all, but a great deal to do with English conscience, moral self-comfort and political necessity.

At first view, the statement that political – that is, constitutional or imperial – solutions to Ireland's problems were fundamentally unhelpful and irrelevant, might seem extreme, even absurd: the whole complexion, so blatantly political, of Anglo-Irish relations in the nineteenth and twentieth centuries appears to give it the lie. Yet the fact remains that the ultimate determinant lay, not in politics, but in violence in 1916, and the ultimate relationship lay not within some political framework embracing both England and Ireland, but in independence. The political complexion of Anglo-Irish relations is deceptive, for it masks the fact that this was the face put on those relations by the English and by the Ascendancy: it draws attention away from the reasons why Catholic Ireland turned to politics – not from preference, or habit of mind, but from necessity.

There was a strong English tendency to think of all those who lived in Ireland, colonists and celts, as one turbulent people. The effect of this, as has been noted often, was to press colonists and celts together in common hostility to England: each recognised in the other a potential ally, at least up to the point where their interests diverged. Related to this was the English impression that the colonists' grievances and Ireland's grievances were identical, and the almost exclusively political or economic construction by the English of the matters at issue. Faced with this, and by the fact that the colonists had begun to call an anti-imperial government tune (and that in a political key) the celts, simply in order to communicate at all, to exhibit a face recognisable to the English, took up political causes and language familiar to their masters. A neat example is the Catholic Petition of 1778, based on an appeal ' to the spirit of British laws against oppression or persecution on account of religious belief.' This kind of Irish approach has been construed usually, by implication – for the explicit point seems to have escaped notice – as quite natural political tactics, as in the activity of the Catholic Committee in the 1780s and 1790s. Tactics it was, the adoption of the modes of politics because this was the only avenue of human affairs which their opponents understood, and which was potentially available to the Irish as a means of alleviating their grievances. Natural to them it was not, in the sense of being traditional, or springing from any Irish source: historically, until the eighteenth century, Irish claims against British oppression had been based on Irish laws or customs, or canon law and religious principle.

By the end of the eighteenth century they were attempting to work through the laws and principles professed by their rulers. The importance of the constitutional and imperial concept of Irish problems is that it imposed British modes and limits on Irish agitation. Catholic Ireland accepted this as the only available path towards its aims, and soon became habituated to it: the only means to its ends was to play politics better than the English could, beat them at their own game. The danger was, of course, that the ends would be obscured or forgotten and the means cultivated as ultimate ends. Out of this frame of mind eventually grew the Home Rule movement, to find a logical home under the wing of a British political party. From the many and excellent explanations which have been given for the failure of the Home Rule movement, one simple reason obtrudes. Neither its simplicity nor its congeniality to the taste of Irish revolutionaries ought to diminish its force: all imperial, constitutional, or political solutions to the Irish question failed because they were British – circumstances wrecked Home Rule before it had come to be, but whatever its influence or sway, its destruction was implanted in its nature: it was a British solution to an Irish problem. It postulated that what the Irish wanted was self-government within a British political structure. But what the Irish wanted was what they had claimed in the sixteenth and seventeenth centuries when they had been able to state this in their own language, not in the foreign language of the eighteenth century Ascendancy – they wanted complete self-determination, independence from Britain. And Home Rule, like all British solutions, postulated a fundamental Irish constitutionalism akin to that of England, automatic respect for the processes of law and the structures of order. But force, and reliance on violence as a solvent, was ingrained in the Irish tradition. The Irish had always rejected British solutions, rejected them outright, or claimed that they were not enough. Why should Home Rule be any exception? Only if, as a solution, its Irishness demonstrably outweighed is Englishness – and this simply was not so.

The basic principles of Home Rule – that is, self-government within an imperial framework – were first asserted in modern Ireland by the Protestant Ascendancy. Its view of Ireland's problems was bound to differ from that of the English government if only because of context. The Ascendancy's life was set in the Irish situation: the English government saw Ireland from a distance and as one of many problems. The Ascendancy's standpoint was traditional to Ireland in that colonists' resentment of interference from the mother country was as old as the Normans. The English response was traditional also in its resistance to any efforts to subtract from its degree of control. The Ascendancy's position was traditional to Ireland, but it was not traditionally Irish: it was traditionally colonial, and the English reaction traditionally that of the mother country. What occurs at the end of the eighteenth century is a typical colony-mother-country dispute, very close to the American model, but of no direct relevance to the totality of the Irish situation. Its indirect relevance, however, was of crucial importance. It determined the mode and terms for conflict in the future, in that it drew Catholic Ireland into political life on the basis it had established. It gravely retarded the achievement of any solution to the basic problems of the Irish-English relationship in that it discredited (through the Ascendancy's irresponsibility and incompetence) the whole idea of Irish self-government in the eyes of the English, while at the same time mythologising the idea of an Irish Parliament in the minds of the Irish. To the English the short career of the Irish Parliament after 1782 demonstrated that the Anglo-Irish could not control Ireland to England's satisfaction; how much worse would the Irish be themselves? To the Irish, England's poisoning and ultimate termination of the parliamentary experiment consecrated the idea of an Irish Parliament pure, but on the English model, as a bright and shining ideal. The idea that the solution to all Ireland's problems lay in securing an Irish Parliament is the dominant political idea in Ireland from Grattan to 1916. Two vital points: this was an English concept, initially championed by the Protestant Ascendancy; and, in that it took on the character of a panacea, and became an endpoint for Irish objectives, it was a continual source of unreality, delusion and self-deception – a gigantic irrelevancy.

In so far as the assertion of parliamentary rights in Ireland was an affair of the Protestant Ascendancy, it was a movement neither patriotic nor rooted in reality. The outlook and position of the Protestant Ascendancy made patriotism impossible for them, even for those with a genuine belief that their interests were Ireland's interests. The Irish Parliament represented an oligarchic self-interest, riddled by both domestic corruption and that induced by the English government's policy of buying off opposition. It might claim to speak for Ireland, but it spoke merely for itself, demanding constitutional and economic concessions whose value was almost entirely restricted to the Ascendancy it represented. However, its superficially anti-English appearance from time to time lent some countenance to its claim to represent the cause of Ireland, particularly when, from the 1770s, the Dublin administration attempted to secure pro-English government management of the Parliament by corrupt insertion of its own nominees and the ejection of critics. That this was superficial is amply evidenced, as in 1773 when a tax on absentee land revenues was rejected by the Irish Parliament. The simple fact was that political Ireland, the Ascendancy, could not afford patriotism: it depended for its existence on England. What the Ascendancy found objectionable was British oppression defined as neglect and discrimination, not the English connection. And, of course, as Henry Maxwell saw in 1704, complete union with England, with the colonists represented in the British Parliament, was, theoretically at least, just as satisfactory a solution as an extension of self-government, to the problem of English ignorance and neglect of Irish affairs, disregard of the views of the Ascendancy's leaders and discrimination against their trade, commerce and industry. What was totally unsatisfactory to the Ascendancy was the position of the eighteenth century Irish Parliament, a political situation neither of effective integration in the British system nor of effective autonomy within it – under Poyning's laws of 1494 the Parliament was subject in the matters it might discuss to the authority of King and Council in England and it had no control whatever over the Dublin executive which implemented the policy of the English, not the Irish, government. This situation had become most irksome in that the policies of the English government often ran contrary to the Ascendancy's tastes and interests. British legislation adversely affecting Irish trade was an obvious sore point, but there were others. Given that English governmental policy was much more receptive to Catholic claims and grievances than the Ascendancy thought it should be, the Ascendancy took English policy to foreshadow betrayal of them into Catholic hands, or at best a playing of colonists off against Catholics and bringing each group into dependence on England for protection against the other. To the colonists the constitutional and political situation seemed one in which England would not govern Ireland properly itself, nor would it allow Irish Protestants to do this for her.

There were two alternative escapes for the Ascendancy from this intolerable position – union with England, or a greater degree of self-government. The fact that it was the self-governing alternative the Ascendancy pursued in the second half of the eighteenth century was largely determined by American example. Certainly self-government held more dignity, appealed more to pride, but what was mainly at stake for the Ascendancy in Ireland was not pride, but position and interest. Their situation was very different from that of the American colonists from whom they borrowed arguments and propaganda. The difference was simply that, whatever they might demand, the colonial Ascendancy in Ireland was imprisoned by its ultimate dependence on English power for its continued existence. The realities of the Irish situation were obscured by the dominance of American colonial problems from mid-century, not only through the effect of reducing the English government's concern with Irish affairs, but also by dictating the terms in which both English and Irish were to debate the issues. So it was that the Irish Parliament seemed patriotic: it was using American language. The English government was itself deluded. By 1769, Viscount Townsend, reacting from his American experience, had apparently become convinced that the Irish Parliament sought to take over the government of Ireland, diminish English authority, and indeed move on to independence. The Duke of Rutland echoed this in 1784. This was absurd, as in calmer moments, the government itself was aware. If the Anglican Ascendancy in Ireland could delude itself occasionally, as is evident in Swift, that Catholic Ireland was of no account and destined for disappearance, the English cabinet was more hard-headed. It rejected an Irish Habeas Corpus Bill in 1774 on two grounds – that it was ' a solecism in politics to make the constitution of a colony the same as that of the mother country ', and that ' The Catholics must either be admitted to the protection of it or excluded. If they were admitted, the peace of the country could not be secured. If they were excluded four-fifths of the people would be deprived of their constitutional rights '. This recognised the realities of the situation: Ireland was a colony in which the existence of a Catholic majority was a prevailing determinant. Political Ireland was Protestant, and Protestantism was the badge and test of the Ascendancy. Whatever patriotic noises political Ireland might make, its necessity, whatever Grattan's views on toleration, was to defend Protestantism and the English connection – and the greater of these was the English connection. Political Ireland was a garrison and it was doomed to extinction if it repudiated its headquarters. It was irresponsible enough to move some distance in this direction, but as the absentee land-tax fiasco showed, it retained sufficient caution to stop short of suicide. Yet, if it would not stand by any fundamentally divisive Irish issues, nor would it accept its role as a garrison. Protestant Ireland fell between two stools: it pretended to a role it did not possess, nor would itself fully accept, that of leading a colonial freedom movement. Rejecting complete alliance with Catholic Ireland, which must eventually have swamped them, the Protestant Ascendancy was both obsessed by and forgetful of its garrison role. Its forgetting is easy to explain: by the end of the eighteenth century the Ascendancy had been in existence long enough to regard its position as the natural order of things. Its unique amalgam of elegance and crudity, leisure and roistering, violence and political argument, were accepted thoughtlessly by those who enjoyed its warm intimacy – witness the memoirs of Sir Jonah Barrington. This society wanted independence: it assumed a continuance of its overlordship of the native Irish; it wanted a qualified independence from England, an independence of such a kind as to be enough to give them control over their own affairs, but with sufficient links to rely on the availability of English power for protection. In asserting what they believed to be their rights they forgot what were their duties, as conceived by England – to act as an Irish garrison. As Ireland degenerated into disorder and then rebellion in the 1790s their incompetence in this role stood revealed. They were irresponsible, incompetent, and, fundamentally, they did not possess sufficient power to govern the four-fifths of Ireland which was alien or hostile to them. Their rule had no roots in popular support nor sufficient resources of coercive power. The bid of Protestant Ireland to control Irish destinies was ended by England, which by the Act of Union, put an end to the separate ambitions of the Protestant Ascendancy to govern Ireland itself. But these ambitions were absurd, unrealistic and destructive of their own position.

Clear testimony to this is the history of the Volunteer movement, which had grown, from the late 1770s, as a defence corps of Protestants pledged to defend Ireland and to ensure internal security in a situation where British troops had been withdrawn and sent to America. Using this very considerable military force as a threat to a hard-pressed England, the Irish Parliament secured apparent independence in 1782. While not inventing the dictum that England's difficulty – in this case the American war – was Ireland's opportunity, the Irish Protestant Ascendancy certainly acted on it and gave further proof of its validity. When Edmund Burke remarked in the House of Commons that the Irish had learnt at last that they could obtain justice from England only at the sword's point, the observation was valid enough, but ' the Irish ' to whom he referred were not in any real position to rest their own power on assertion of that principle against England. Force, particularly successful force, breeds force. The 1798 rebellion is too seldom seen in the direct context of the threat of force which brought about the 1782 ' constitution ' – the 1782 revolution. Hussey Burgh had told the Irish House of Commons in 1779, ' Ireland is not at peace; it is smothered war. England has sown her laws as dragon's teeth, and they have sprung up as armed men.' This was the voice of Protestant colonialism, but the words could equally well have been those of Catholic Ireland. Having used the threat of force to attain its ends, the Irish Parliament refused to entertain the demands of its own Volunteer Army – many of whom came from the ' disfranchised Presbyterian and Catholic groups – for parliamentary reform. The Volunteer movement fell to pieces, but it paved the way for the United Irishmen who were to lead the 1798 rebellion.

As an instrument for stable and enduring self-government, the Irish Parliament had nothing to recommend it or suggest its likely continuance. Its liberties, as conceded by Britain in 1782, rested on the threat of force in a situation where the tides of force, through temporary American circumstances, were flowing in its favour: when those tides should turn, as they naturally would, to favour the greater power, then the future of Irish self-government would rest on its working in a manner acceptable to Britain. The areas of British sensitivity and concern were obvious – what foreign, defence and trade policies would a self-governing Ireland pursue, and would the Irish government be able to maintain British law, order and control in Ireland? The strategic question was what caused the British government most anxiety, private British interests were worried most by economic questions. The Irish aspiration to commercial autonomy, or preference on English markets aroused the jealous fear (and pressure group activity) of English merchants and manufacturers who demanded the rigorous application of those mercantilist doctrines so disadvantageous to Ireland. On neither the strategic nor the economic grounds was the prospect of Irish self-government anything better than an irritant and an uncertainty to the English. And then there was the fact that in asserting their claims, Irish parliamentarians had entangled themselves deeply in British politics, particularly with the causes of the British opposition, and spectacularly during the Regency crisis of 1788-9. In this crisis they had, prior to any British decision on the Regency, invited the Prince of Wales to so act in regard to Ireland, an aggressive assertion of the principle of Irish parliamentary independence which perished painfully in the face of George III's regaining of his sanity. The fortunes of the champions of Irish self-government were thus linked ominously with those of the British opposition, a fatal liability when that opposition became identified with the cause of revolutionary France.

The response of the leaders of the Irish Parliament to British anxiety, suspicion, and hostility towards the post-1782 relationship between the two countries was vague and unreal. Henry Grattan and his friends expressed confidence that the relationship would work on the basis of goodwill and understanding. As Lord Charlemont put it to the Marquis of Rockingham in 1782, 'Bind us to you by the only chain that can connect us – the only chain we will ever consent to wear – the dear ties of mutual love and mutual freedom.' Wishful, narrow thinking. Perhaps it was possible for Protestants, Irish and English, to love one another, but their Irish context was not conducive to the reign of love. Mutual freedom was impossible, because the Protestant Irish were in the last resort dependent for their mode of existence on Britain. In any case, was it possible to give political form to these 'dear ties'? Fox stated the problem to the British House of Commons in 1785 – to find some system which would protect and further 'the general interests of the empire' at the same time as preserving 'the full emancipation and independence' of Ireland. Such a system was not found: its absence was alarming to a British ministry confronted with the emergence of an independent Ireland legally free to pursue a policy hostile to British interests – which is what British commercial interests claimed it would do. But the absence of this system would be intolerable if the Irish situation became a strategic menace. And so it happened. The Irish Parliament itself took no actions detrimental to British security, but it failed to prevent the development of a situation which was. Then, fear, that enduring element in British attitudes towards Ireland, became the operative determinant in British policy once more.

The fall of the 1782 constitution is partly circumstantial. Fear of revolutionary France and its radical contagions dominated British political affairs and became the context in which an inefficient and unrealistic Irish Parliament became intolerably dangerous. The breakdown of self-government in Ireland 1782-1800 is readily explicable within the confines of politics. Politics are of their nature pragmatic and circumstantial, inevitably local and limited in their applicability. Only principles have any potential for constancy or universality. Put simply, politics dictated one course of action and attitude in Ireland, another in England. Politics in Protestant Ireland dictated insistence on a high degree of constitutional and financial independence (at least in theory if not in practice), trade freedom or preference, and the maintenance of an unreformed franchise as the basis of the existing political power structure. British politics necessitated insistence on a low degree of Irish constitutional independence, Irish contributions towards imperial defence, the maintenance of mercantilism as discrimination against Irish commercial interests, and sufficient parliamentary reform as to ensure stability in Ireland by the mitigation of Dissenters' and Catholics' grievances. Britain had the political means, through corruption and patronage, to disintegrate and confuse Irish politics. The political confrontation existed: the Irish Parliament would not accept Pitt's minimum requirements. And the French Revolution, accompanied by the degeneration of Ireland into internal anarchy capped by the 1798 Rebellion, made a solution to the political deadlock and confusion urgent and inescapable.

The political determinant, then, was British security, expressed in the constitutional question of what political forms, structures and relationships might best guarantee it. Had Ireland remained secure and stable under the 1782 constitution, Britain would have had neither reason nor cause to intervene to change it. The view of Pitt and his government was that Catholics were the major potential source of trouble in Ireland and that they ought to be conciliated, won over to the government, and involved in the totality of Irish life, by political concessions. Such was the conviction which forced upon a reluctant Irish Parliament a Catholic Relief Act giving them votes in 1793. The contrary conviction – that Catholics must be excluded from political power – was expressed in the rejection, in 1795, of Grattan's Catholic Relief Bill which would have admitted them to parliament.

Writing in the 1890s, W. E. H. Lecky summed up the significance of this situation. 'If the Catholic question had been settled in 1793, the whole subsequent history of Ireland would probably have been changed. The rebellion of 1798 would almost certainly either never have taken place, or have been confined to an insignificant disturbance in the North and the social and political convulsions which were produced by the agitations of the present century might have been wholly or in a great measure averted.' Lecky's regrets were British, Protestant and aristocratic, an analysis made with hindsight which he shows Grattan to have made with foresight: an 'ignorant and excitable Catholic population . . . detached from the influence of property and respectability . . . prey to designing agitators and demagogues ' – and priests. ' By giving full political power to the Catholic democracy, and at the same time withholding political power and influence from the Catholic gentry [who were few, and effusively loyal] the legislation of 1793 materially hastened this calamity, and it was in the long popular agitation for Catholic emancipation that the foundation was laid for the political anarchy of our own day.'

The flaw in Lecky's argument that the admission of Catholic gentry to Parliament would have settled the Catholic question is apparent in his remark that ' The presence of ten or twenty members of this class in Parliament would have had a conciliatory effect out of all proportion to its real importance.' He does not speculate on what would have occurred when its ' real importance ' became apparent. Lecky makes the error, typically English in its politicality and its nineteenth century assumptions, that the significance of religion in the Irish situation was that it marked the class barrier between democracy (or rather rabble) and gentry. Seeing class conflict as central to Irish agitation he assumed that if some Catholics were admitted to the ranks of privilege and governance that agitation would lose its leadership and direction, be channelled from destructive to creative purposes. Identify Catholics of substance and intelligence with the *status quo* and they would help to protect it. Protect it against what? A deluge of forty shilling Catholic freeholders. Protestant Ascendancy had issued in a situation in which the removal of religious disabilities meant opening Ireland to a democratic flood. Sir Lawrence Parsons speaking in 1793 against a forty shilling Catholic franchise declared,

> If they had all been Protestants for fifty generations back, I would not consent to the overwhelming of the Constitution by such a torrent . . . a copious adulteration of rabble. . . . I do not now desire you to consider them as differing from you in religion, but merely their poverty, their numbers, their ignorance, their barbarous ignorance, many of them not being able even to speak our language, and then think whether giving them the franchise will not be a most pernicious vitiation of the Constitution. . . . By granting franchise to the inferior Catholics, you give it to a body of men in great poverty, in great ignorance, bigoted to their sect and their altars, repelled by ancient prejudices from you, and at least four times as numerous as you are.

Religious emancipation had now become firmly identified with the danger of a loosening of the bonds of aristocratic society.

Despite themselves, the English and the Protestant Ascendancy had converted the religious question into a dynamic political one. The big political question, at the end of the eighteenth century was – were Catholics, any Catholics, to be given any political rights. The point at issue was political – the stability of Ireland. Some, dominantly the Ascendancy, argued that this was best secured by complete exclusion of Catholics; others, the English governments, that it was to be achieved by partial admission. The resultant compromise destroyed the old political system but did not create a new.

In all of this, the Protestant Ascendancy emerged discredited. To obtain the constitution of 1782 they had revived force as a means for securing political change and they could be by no means certain that they could confine its use to themselves. Indeed they had courted its use against them: having secured the position they wanted, they had repudiated and repulsed important elements in the movement that had placed them there. They had shown conspicuous unreality in their attitude towards the British connection and an inadequate appreciation of their position within Ireland itself. Tragically, this unreality, confusion, vagueness and wishful thinking was most marked among those, like Henry

Grattan, who most valued the ideals of generosity, tolerance and good-will. Grattan's message to the Irish Parliament was that distinctions of religion and race were no longer valid or necessary. He asked, ' Are we to be a Protestant settlement or an Irish nation?' It was a false alterna-tive: it assumed that the removal of religious distinctions would confirm the existing politico-economic system, not destroy it. Grattan rejoiced ' in the relaxation of the penal laws against our Roman Catholic fellow-subjects ' and conceived ' these measures to be fraught with the happiest consequences to the union and prosperity of the inhabitants of Ireland.' An idyllic picture conceived in the isolation of Ascendancy Ireland. Henry Flood saw the facts: the penal laws were not laws of religious persecution, they were a political necessity: ' What will be the consequences if you give Catholics equal powers with Protestants? Can a Protestant Constitu-tion survive? The majority will attempt to alter the Constitution, and I believe they will be repelled by the minority.' The inescapable situation was, given that religious division was the basis of the Ascendancy, that any attempt to reduce religious division was to undermine the Ascendancy.

And to arouse Catholic Ireland as an ally in a fight for political liberties was dangerous indeed. To offer Catholic Ireland a political outlet for its energies and grievances was to conjure up a vast unpredict-able force that the Irish Parliament might not be able to control. Parlia-ment's champions of Ireland's constitutional liberties were not interested in Catholic deprivations as such: they wanted Catholic support for patriotic objectives, and they were concerned by the political principles transgressed by Catholic deprivations. This concern, in such men as Grattan, did much to transform Catholic grievances stemming from religious disabilities into political grievances uttered in terms of infringe-ment of freedom and equality. And this was to invite another Catholic crusade, this time in that political field so clearly marked out by the philosophers of the Enlightenment and their English precursors, and by revolutionaries in America and France.

But according to the reasoning of patriotic Parliamentarians, Catho-lics would support the agitation for Irish self-government, and that being achieved, they would take their allotted place in the happy and harmonious structure which the Ascendancy envisaged, and which, of course, they would control. Flood sketched the future: ' We will give you all tolera-tion to your religion; we will not give you political power.' Even that was to promise too much. Given the fate of Grattan's attempts to secure Catholic emancipation through the Irish Parliament, it was apparent that whatever self-government meant to Protestant Ireland, it meant continued exclusion from power for Catholics. Thus self-government became identified in Catholic eyes with anti-Catholic policies: their prison was all the more odious for its declared Irish patriotism. On the other hand, the movement among these Irish patriots towards political recognition of Catholics gravely weakened their own political support, for under that threat many Protestant landowners swung away from reform towards support of the *status quo*.

So it was that the situation of Catholics continued to contravene the political principles at the heart of the Irish patriotic movement – such as that enunciated at the Dungannon Volunteers' convention in September 1783: 'Those only are free who are governed by no laws but those to which they assent either in person or by their representatives freely chosen.' As in France a few years later, the party of reform had promulgated general principles on which it had acted and from which, when it had achieved its objectives, it had excluded all save itself. As in other revolutionary situations, the movement for change once begun could not be arrested until its central principles had worked themselves out. The principles of the revolution of 1782 were political: they did not find their absolute expression until after 1916, and then, of course, only in politics. The ferment at the end of the eighteenth century opened a way for Catholicism to channel its grievances into politics: in one sense this was a liberation, in another it was an enslavement, the acceptance of a strait-jacket.

PART TWO

The Elements of the Question
1800-1870

I

The Nature of the Union

The Act of Union, which merged Ireland with Great Britain in the United Kingdom, came into force on 1 January 1801. The fact that this Union endured for 120 years suggests that it was a success: so it was, if the retention of British power in Ireland be the test. Stripped of the apologies of that time – Pitt's peroration on the advantages to Ireland in January 1799 – and the vast accretions of vindication since, the Union amounted simply to a strategic device, a last resort to maintain British power in Ireland. Of course, supporters of the Union never, in their arguments, disguised the strategic necessity, but their constant tendency was to make a virtue of it and thus to convert a last political resort into a grand constructive principle. This overlaid and obscured the realities of the Union relationship, but it was from the iron realities, not from pro-Unionist gilding, that the fundamental legacies of the Union derived.

The Union testified to the failure of the Irish Protestant Ascendancy to govern Ireland. Having won constitutional independence in 1782, the Irish Parliament demonstrated its inability to please England, to pacify Ireland, or prevent its degeneration into rebellion in 1798. In 1794 Grenville had distilled the essence of English policy: ' Ireland must be governed in the English interest '. So Pitt proposed Union as the only way in which Ireland, and consequently Britain, might be secured against a situation which would allow a French invasion: Union was conceived as the only effective means available of gaining a firm military control of a weak point in Britain's defences against revolutionary France. Crudely, the Union was an urgent and naked assertion of British power in what seemed an emergency situation. As G. C. Bolton has pointed out, there is no evidence that Union was any long-considered and well-planned attempt to solve Irish problems (in which Pitt was notoriously uninterested); rather is there ample indication that the embarrassing and dangerous failure of the existing Irish government – and the absence of any viable alternative administration within Ireland – compelled Pitt to reluctant intervention. Union sprang not from assertive imperialism, but from the conviction that the only secure solution to the problems of Irish government was English government. Still less did Union stem from any belief that it was a way of solving Ireland's problems as such: it was conceived as a device to protect England from the consequences of Ireland's problems.

Rendered down to its essentials, the Union appears, in the context of its implementation, a political device for evading the basic problems of the Anglo-Irish relationship, and a falling back on the last resort of government, reliance on force. Neither the Irish nationalist thesis that the Union was an English plot, nor the Unionist contention that it represented a solution to the problems of the relationship, recognise the accidental necessity which is at the heart of the Union. Being a necessity, a settlement of Anglo-Irish relationships at a level which avoided the basic problems, and a last resort, the Union was peculiarly unresponsive to pressures for change: indeed its nature as a political structure was such that any proposed change threatened its destruction. At the same time, its finality – in the sense of its representing the exhaustion of the alternative methods by which England sought to dominate Ireland – bred in those committed to it the conviction that the Union was utterly sacrosanct: on the Union they must stand, or fall.

In terms of its rigidity and finality, the Union was a structure which not so much re-organised Anglo-Irish relations as imprisoned them: either the Irish prisoners would be reformed, or they would attack their gaolers and, perhaps eventually, break out. What were the prospects of reform and conciliation?

Pitt's government at the time of Union was clearly aware of the urgent need for reform in Ireland. Had the deficiencies of the Irish Parliament been merely in the realm of military or police power, Britain could have supplemented this without removing that parliament. But its deficiencies, Pitt believed, also lay in matters of attitude and policy: it had failed to concede necessary reforms and was therefore partly responsible for discontent and rebellion. The verdict of Cornwallis, Viceroy in 1798, on the Irish Parliament was, that 'blinded by their passion and prejudice they talk of nothing but strong measures, and arrogate to themselves the exclusive knowledge of a country, of which, from their mode of governing it, they have in my opinion, proved themselves totally ignorant'.

Pitt's plan for the peaceful government of Ireland linked Union with Catholic emancipation: union plus emancipation would solve the Irish question: union was necessary not only for strategic reasons, but for long-term pacification, by enabling that emancipation of Catholics which an Irish Protestant Parliament would not accept, while at the same time rendering emancipation innocuous by absorbing it into the Protestant majority of a United Kingdom. Pitt's appraisal was accurate in that he saw the religious issue as the crucial one within Ireland, and Union as the only context in which it might be solved to England's strategic satisfaction. The King's obdurate refusal to countenance any concessions to Catholics scotched Pitt's plan to combine emancipation with Union, and this, it has been suggested, from the beginning gravely prejudiced the Union as a potential solution to the problems of Anglo-Irish government. However, it is difficult to see either how any effective emancipation would have been possible in 1801, or if it had been effected then, that it would not, in the nature of things, have led to conflict eventually.

Very few Englishmen saw Union as an opportunity for reform in Ireland: for most, Union, in itself, was reform enough. Pitt's priorities are clear. Had he been an Irish reformer he would have seen Union as a means towards the end of securing that crucial reform, emancipation: as an English statesman he saw Union as a means to rule Ireland, a means by which he could also bolster that rule by conciliating Catholics. But Union was the first and dominant necessity. Anything else was subordinate. Nor was Pitt's wish to emancipate Catholics impelled by principle or abstract theory; it was a tactical device to strengthen the basic political device of Union. Perhaps it was this prevalent acceptance of Union as a device, nothing more than a means of solving a strategic problem, that explains the indifference and neglect so characteristic of the attitudes of English statesmen towards Ireland. The Union from this viewpoint, represents the ultimate degeneration of British policy: having consistently defied attempts at government, Ireland under the Union would merely be held, an operation for which England would always possess ample force. Given that the Union had thrown Anglo-Irish relations back to the ultimate determinant of force, the indifference, neglect and extraordinary ignorance of Ireland and Irish conditions displayed by English politicians is readily explicable – Ireland was more a military problem than a political one. Against this, of course, is the fact that the Union, by intimately involving Irish problems and energies in British politics, had profound and radical effects on British affairs, a theme pursued in E. Strauss's *Irish Nationalism and British Democracy*.

But so far as British policy towards Ireland was concerned, the Union remained, until 1921, the ultimate and immutable point of reference, and ultimately the Union itself rested on force.

It is impossible to define the extent to which the existence of a final back-stop of force debilitated or corrupted British policy-making for Ireland, but it is evident that if there could be no departure from Union, objections to Union, or to policies pursued under it, were unlikely to get serious attention unless they were supported by agitation sufficiently violent to threaten the Union itself. That is to say, their committal to the Union as unchangeable tended to close English minds to pro-Irish protests based either on argument or assertion of abstract rights, and to prevent Englishmen themselves giving much serious attention to the basic causes of Irish unrest, unless and until that unrest took some practical form, usually that of violence. Even then, it was the effects, not the causes of unrest which claimed English attention: given that the Union was final, it was pointless to investigate complaints against it, and natural to assume that any fault must lie not in the Union but in those who criticised it. The presumption that the Union was immutable does much to explain why there is so little and such slow development in English attitudes to Irish problems, and why the English reaction to demands for change in Ireland tended towards religious and racial denigration of the Irish as a people rather than serious investigation of their complaints. As a framework for a political relationship, the Union structure so imperiously presumed harmony, and a static harmony moreover, that any discordance led naturally to resort to violence. On the English side, force was not only a final determinant, it was also a standing threat and deterrent, and an occasional short-cut. On the Irish side, appeals and arguments, principles and theories unavailing, violence was the only way of drawing serious attention from Britain.

Thus the Union reduced Anglo-Irish relations to the realities of power at the same time as depriving the Irish situation of whatever possibilities it possessed of a natural internal development and redress. The Union represents the final stage in the historical fossilisation of Ireland. But not only did Union frustrate the emergence of indigenous solutions to Irish problems, it forced on Ireland an inappropriate English political mould. Most Englishmen recognised that Ireland was different from England, many saw that it was distinct; yet they would make little or no political recognition of these differences and distinctions. Inappropriate legislation was imposed or maintained, appropriate legislation denied. The basic fault of the Union was not in any offence it gave to Irish national aspirations, but simply in that it made no allowance whatever for the differences between Ireland and Britain, or for the particular fundamental problems of Ireland.

Yet the very fact of Union implies that England had accepted the task of governing Ireland. In opposing the Union, C. J. Fox claimed ' we ought not to presume to legislate for a nation with whose feelings and affections, wants and interests, opinions and prejudices we have no sympathy '. The point was lost in a Parliament which saw Union as a strategic necessity and little else, and paid no real attention to the implications Fox referred to: the Union passed both Houses of English Parliament with scarcely a ripple of interest. What was self-evidently the only course to be taken hardly merited a debate on principles, morality, and consequent problems and obligations. Certainly, the Union implied that now England presumed to govern Ireland, but very few Englishmen realised what that meant or consciously accepted the responsibility. Governing Ireland meant securing it against invasion or rebellion and this concept of government, from which the Union had sprung, continued, for many English politicians, to demark the extent of their interest in Irish affairs. Speaking in April 1845, Lord John Russell asked the House of Commons, ' Are we not bound to say to the people of Ireland: " We engaged at the time of the Union to govern Ireland in a spirit of equality with England – we engaged to consider Irishmen as we consider Englishmen: to allow the same rights and privileges to the Irish as we claim for ourselves, and to consider the questions with regard to Ireland as we would consider them with regard to ourselves "?' The simple practical answer to Russell's question was, no. Whatever he might argue were the implications of Union, most English politicians did not regard the Union as any engagement to respect the equal rights and privileges of the Irish, but as a necessary device to keep order in Ireland, a very different thing.

Given this very narrow, indeed quasi-military concept of the government of Ireland, prevalent among English politicians, the Union had little immediate impact on the internal realities of Irish government: it effected no governmental revolution. As before, the Protestant Ascendancy ruled. The Union amounted to a declaration of British no-confidence in the Protestant Ascendancy, yet it confirmed their rule. It deprived them of independent constitutional power and thus of their means of defending their ascendany by the exclusion of Catholics. The Ascendancy responded by attempting to convert Union into the vehicle for what Union had theoretically ended – their effective rule. They fell back into complete reliance on the Union as support for their position. Pitt had intended Union as the context for such necessary reforms as the Ascendancy had refused to make, but it could equally well be used as a context for denying reforms: George III told Parliament: ' my inclination to an Union with Ireland was principally founded on a trust that the uniting of the Established Churches of the two kingdoms would for ever shut the door to any further measures with respect to the Roman Catholics '. The King's inclinations were immediately decisive in the matter of emancipation, and so weak was the English urge towards Irish reform generally, that the Ascendancy's convulsive embrace of Union was amply sufficient to strangle what little potential for reform it held. The continuing success of the Ascendancy in determining the nature of the Union (such that the Unionist Party in British politics eventually became a decisive vehicle for the enduring interests of the Irish Protestant Ascendancy) is readily explicable. Apathy, indifference and pro-Ascendancy prejudice in English political life was a big factor. So was the nature of the Union as a strategic device. The Union altered the formal structure of Irish government: it did not alter the Ascendancy. The Ascendancy remained in an advantageous position to frustrate any British policy unpalatable to it. If its obstruction or general behaviour led to internal disturbance, or foreign invasion, the nature of the Union compelled Britain to support the Ascendancy however fool-hardy or provocative the Ascendancy had been. Consequently the effect of the Union was to foster irresponsibility among an Ascendancy which could rely ultimately on British protection and support. The Union did not end the Ascendancy's government of Ireland; it did weaken if not destroy whatever positive potential for responsible government the Ascendancy possessed, and reduced its political function to a negative, defensive reaction. It is in this sense that the Union made it vastly more difficult for Britain to contrive any kind of good government in Ireland, because the Union encumbered Britain with the burden of Ascendancy policies, their odium and sterility. Prior to Union it was possible, to some degree, for Britain to choose between the interests of the Ascendancy and those of Catholic Ireland in order to pursue a policy of her own. Union, by identifying Ascendancy and British government, gravely limited the scope of British policy: it strengthened the tendency to do nothing, as any change might undermine the position of the Ascendancy on which British government relied: it tended to constrict British intervention to police action merely, or to limited reluctant conciliation. Indeed, given British inclination and the existence of the Ascendancy, the Union by which Britain claimed the government of Ireland saw the Irish – Protestant and Catholic – largely left to their own internal affairs until these became intolerable to Britain.

Pitt had linked Union with relief to Catholics – tithe reform and emancipation. The proof of the Union pudding was to be in its religious eating: the history of Anglo-Irish relations was influenced decisively by its immediate consequences for religion. Bolton remarks that if Pitt had had his way, ' the Catholic question might have been adequately settled, instead of being left to identify itself with the nationalist cause at the time of O'Connell's agitation '. This perhaps over-values the potential of Pitt's measures as solvents and under-values the strength of the Catholic question, but it remains true that the Union and its circumstances confirmed the matter of religious division as the central one in the new political structure.

On giving the Royal Assent to the Act of Union in August 1800, Cornwallis reported, ' there was not a murmur heard in the street, nor I believe an expression of ill-humour throughout the whole city of Dublin.' Why? Putting aside the fact that turbulent Ireland remained crushed and cowed after the ruthless repression of the 1798 rebellion, the explanation is this: anti-Unionists could not agree on any viable alternative to Union, and, in any case, many of them had been bought off by the British government; and because Catholic Ireland was not opposed to Union, or tended to support it. In 1801, Castlereagh, then Chief Secretary for Ireland, reminded Pitt that the British government had courted clerical and generally Catholic support for Union by allowing Catholics to believe that it would be followed by relief measures. Indeed, wrote Castlereagh, the Union ' could not be carried if the Catholics were embarked in an active opposition to it, and . . . their resistance would be unanimous and zealous if they had reason to suppose that the sentiments of ministers would remain unchanged in respect to their inclusion '. Pitt needed no reminding of this, but the King's opposition, and prevailing apathy or hostility (' I care no more for a Catholic than I care for a Chinese,' one Member of Parliament remarked) rendered him powerless to fill the expectations of Catholic relief his government had deliberately aroused.

The Irish Catholic hierarchy generally had supported Union. This was logical in view of the intransigent Protestantism of the Irish Parliament, from which Catholics could expect very little, and in view of the cultivated anticipation that Union would bring emancipation and other measures of Catholic relief. It was in this context that, in 1799, the Irish bishops accepted the insistence of the British Government that, in view of the feelings of Protestant extremists, it retain a veto over Irish episcopal appointments. Seen in the light of related and imminent Catholic relief measures, this concession seemed tolerable.

But from a Catholic viewpoint, the Union turned out to be a cheat: no relief was forthcoming. Worse still, the Union, shorn of its supposed reform trimmings, now emerged as a bastion of Protestant Ascendancy even stronger than the old Irish Parliament. From the outset of Union, Irish Protestants claimed an integral and indissoluble relationship between Protestantism and the constitution of the United Kingdom. In 1805, John Foster, once speaker of the Irish Parliament, told the House of Commons:

> Remember that you have settled us in Ireland under the faith of your protection: that on that faith we claim as our inheritance all the blessings of that glorious constitution which our ancestors and yours have fought and bled for – the Hanoverian succession, the illustrious House of Brunswick on the throne, a Protestant king, with Protestant councillors, Protestant lords and Protestant commons. That is what I call Protestant Ascendancy in the true sense of the phrase, and while I can utter my voice in this house I will ever demand it for my country.

This contention that the Union was a Protestant constitutional structure was a major factor in ensuring that the extension to Irish Catholics of ' the blessings of that glorious constitution ' would be met with bitter resistance, down to Ulster's threat of civil war against Home Rule. In urging Catholic emancipation, Henry Grattan argued, ' The question is not whether we shall show mercy to the Roman Catholics, but whether we shall mould the inhabitants of Ireland into a *people*: for as long as we exclude Catholics from natural liberty, and the common rights of man, we are not a *people*.' Very few Irish Protestants cared. Before the Union they had emphasised their claim to distinctive Irishness so that they could rule Ireland in some independence of Britain. After the Union had tied them to Britain, they emphasised what they had in common with Britain, their Protestantism, again so that they could rule Ireland. Given that the Union was established without inclusion of Catholic emancipation or any Irish reform, and that it claimed to be perpetual and unchanging, it lent itself very readily to an ultra-conservative if not static Protestant interpretation of its essential nature, which once established was extremely difficult to alter.

Yet at the same time, the very fact of Union implied that England had accepted the task of governing Irish Catholics: the Union directly imported religious energies, division and contention into English politics. As a political structure, the Union presumed a basic commonality and harmony between England and Ireland, yet it embraced a profound and bitter religious division and animus. Was it possible that the Union could contain such a division and the challenge it presented, while surviving unchanged? It had long been claimed in England that Protestants and Catholics had conflicting loyalties. Within Protestant England, given that the Crown was head of the Church, all the loyalty structures were internal. But the Catholics of Ireland professed spiritual allegiance to a religion of which the Roman Pontiff was earthly head, and they saw the English monarchy as leader of a heresy. Could the Union unite such conflicting allegiances, indeed could it contain them at all, short of the exertion of constant force? Not if the Union was Protestant, and substantially Protestant it was.

Once the matter of the Union and its administration had been cast into a Protestant-Catholic confrontation it never lost the essence of that complexion: it became a system which divided instead of united the elements it contained.

Moreover, the Union provided a ready-made political issue to which the fundamentally religious divisions could relate themselves. Coming at the beginning of the nineteenth century, the abolition of the Irish Parliament went against the emerging trend towards self-government in English colonies and the development of nationalism in Europe. Seen in this relationship, the Union, in terms of contemporary constitutionalism and politics, was not a step forward, but a retreat into the past: it represented a substantial loss of ground to Ireland. As such it offered an obvious cause to be championed – regaining that ground. And as most Protestants had abandoned that cause, indeed opposed it, its championing fell naturally to the Catholics. Thus, the whole period of the Union is dominated in the political sphere by an Irish Catholic agitation to destroy or modify the Union and its related policies. This agitation, though it appeared to be forward-looking, was in fact reactionary: in seeking change it sought, at times even explicitly – as in O'Connell and the Home Rule movement – to get back to some equivalent of the constitutional situation of 1782-1800. Seen from this angle, the Union served England's interests very well (and this may account in part for its longevity) for it masked the real problems of the relationship between England and Ireland: it diverted majority attention away from a questioning of the basic nature of that relationship into a questioning of a particular political form which had been imposed on that relationship by England. The point of attention became the operation of the Union; the point of Irish constitutional reference became the immediate pre-Union structure. In the Union, England had allocated to the Irish a portion of a common political abode. Finding themselves in the servants' quarters, the Irish pressed for better accommodation, and became so totally absorbed in that demand that very few entertained the idea that the abode might be a prison from which they might seek to escape.

It was the Protestant character of the Union that ensured that Catholic Ireland would oppose it, and the policies associated with it. This point, or at least its extraordinary force, seems to have escaped the English whose minds tended towards pragmatic and material interpretations: the agitation against the Union system was never completely intelligible to the English. Having found Union necessary to England, they tended to see it as a silk purse where the Irish Catholics saw a Protestant sow's ear. They argued that, given England's prosperity and progress, Ireland must benefit from the Union. On the expectation that human actions are dominated by material motives, the Irish Catholic unwillingness to acquiesce in the Union, to settle down under English rule, seemed incredibly perverse and irresponsible, revealing (or confirming) grave defects in the Irish Catholics as a people, a conclusion which avoided entertaining doubts about the virtues of the Union. In the light of such preconceptions, Irish Catholic claims to rights and principles seemed petty and absurd. The English tendency – derived not only from the conviction that the Union was appropriate, theoretically perfect and certainly immutable, but also generally from a pragmatic political philosophy hostile to abstract theorising about the rights of man – was not so much to argue against Irish assertions of rights, as to ignore them, dismiss them without consideration. This failure to consider or engage Irish arguments does much to explain both the violence endemic to the relationship and why claims to abstract rights and assertions of principle became a feature, to the degree of obsession, of Irish discontent and agitation. Given the religious nature of Irish society, this obsession which came to flourish in nationalist forms, had firm roots in popular religious dispositions which went back to the Reformation. The Union gave these dispositions a political focus: it had raised and then dashed Catholic expectations; it had taken on a Protestant character which drove Catholics into a deep hostility to it: and it left vacant the championship of the cause of Irish freedom, a position into which Catholic Ireland readily moved.

2

The Question of Religion

What had been a tolerable arrangement in the pre-Union atmosphere of expectation of emancipation, appeared very different when this expectation proved false. When Grattan proposed in 1808 that Catholic emancipation be enacted with the proviso that Britain retain a veto over

Irish episcopal appointments, the issue erupted into a fierce controversy in which the Irish hierarchy repudiated the veto, even in the face of a Vatican rescript approving it. The anti-veto movement was inspired and led by Daniel O'Connell. That the Union had taken on an anti-Catholic complexion provided him with the opportunity to link the Catholic religious impulse with his own brand of liberal democratic nationalism. The veto issue, testifying as it did to the vital importance attached by the British government to the influence exercised by the clergy over Irish affairs, was an ideal means of identifying the rights of the church with the rights of the nation. O'Connell brought together, to be an enduring theme in Irish history, the most dynamic ideologies in English, European and Irish societies: he allied the forces of liberalism, nationalism and Catholicism.

The relevance to Ireland of the principles of the French Revolution had become obvious before the abortive French invasion in 1796. The principles of English government had already been demonstrated in the Irish Parliament itself. The principles of Catholicism were embodied in the Irish Church. Broadly, the history of Anglo-Irish relations under the Union consists of the assertion of these principles, religious, constitutional, revolutionary. There was intrinsic antagonism between these principles – religio-sacred, secular reformist, violent revolutionary – but they had an aim in common, freedom from oppression. This common aim was not enough to transcend their great differences save under the magical resolution of some great personality who could, within himself, effect a harmony between conflicting principles, bring about an alliance between two of the three dynamic forces within Irish life. There is a sense in which Irish history from 1800 until 1921, and after, has been enacted under the dominance of four great personalities who were able to impose their terms, stamp their amalgam, on the energies at work in Ireland. O'Connell invented the process by linking Irish Catholicism with English constitutionalism, a tie more enduring than any other. Cardinal Cullen maintained this alliance, but reversed its priorities, placing the emphasis on religion rather than on politics. Charles Stewart Parnell continued this basic amalgam but with a difference: in harnessing Irish religious forces to English constitutional machinery, he added a dash of revolutionary bitters. Patrick Pearse was able, in death rather than in life, to combine the forces of revolution with those of religion, the most swiftly effective alignment of them all.

O'Connell's first public appearance was in 1800, his last in 1847; Cullen began his Irish career in 1850 and died in 1878; Parnell dominated Ireland from 1879 to 1891: between the fall of Parnell and the emergence of Pearse, Irish history is confusion and drift. The dynamic alliance of forces these men contrived were of their nature fluctuating and unstable, held together mainly by the singular power of the personalities in which these alliances were embodied – O'Connell, an Irish Catholic of English constitutional conviction; Cullen, an Irish-Roman cleric who sought a Catholic Ireland for religious reasons; Parnell, an Irish Protestant whose parliamentary power rested on the threat of Catholic peasant violence; Pearse, romantic revolutionary nationalist whose creed sprang from and caught a Catholic religious imagination. In large part, Irish history as it impinged on England revolved around these men and the principles they represent: the one common factor in their various amalgams was the Catholic religion.

O'Connell's great achievement was to give a constitutional political form and outlet to Ireland's Catholic religious coherence and energy. He welded an effective and enduring alliance between nationalism and Catholicism in Ireland, translating Irish grievances into language intelligible to the English. The burning grievance in the Catholic Ireland which entered the Union was the degraded position of Catholicism, seen not merely in terms of purely religious discrimination, but in terms of the host of wordly disadvantages which oppressed Catholics as members of Irish society: the Catholic question embraced all others, because all others derived from it – if, from a material viewpoint the most obvious social reality in Ireland was the gulf between rich and poor, the economic division was virtually coterminous with the religious, and stemmed directly from it. Obviously, this Irish Catholic grievance went back to the Reformation, but it was not until the end of the eighteenth century that any remote prospect of some redress appeared. Significantly, its emergence then was related both to expediency, as a measure of pacification, and to concepts of nationalism – Grattan's view that the Irish could not be one people until Catholics held equal rights. Neither of these two grounds, both secular, held much appeal to the Irish bishops, but they had great attraction to O'Connell to whose initiative the bishops had substantially lost their Catholic leadership during the veto controversy. Grattan's Parliament had shown how English principles of constitutional and individual liberty could be used against England. O'Connell demonstrated how Irish Catholics could also use these principles: the struggle for Catholic emancipation is an epitome of Irish procedure against England – a religious right demanded within the framework of English political principles.

Here it is necessary to contrast O'Connell's attitude to emancipation with that of the bishops, a contrast relevant to the relations between religion and politics thereafter. The bishops regarded emancipation as a religious matter, the attainment of a rightful and necessary public liberty for religion, a freedom necessary to religion's paramount role in human affairs. O'Connell saw religious disability as an infringement of the civil rights of Catholics, an outlook much more congenial to the English Parliament than was that of the bishops. Indeed, just how English and how narrowly political O'Connell's outlook was is often forgotten. He trained for the bar in England, adopted Utilitarianism, venerated Bentham, and read widely in the philosophy of the Enlightenment, in which England was depicted as a constitutional and political model. And all this to the extent that, for a time, he came to reject Christian belief. Succinctly, O'Connell was a liberal lawyer of the English pattern who took up and brilliantly espoused Irish causes, within an English framework. Thus, his ideals were parliamentary; specifically the restoration of an Irish Parliament similar to that of 1782. His loyalties were broadly Anglo-Irish rather than narrowly Irish: in his first public speech in January 1800 he declared that ' he would rather confide in the justice of his brethren, the Protestants of Ireland, who have already liberated him, than lay his country at the feet of foreigners ' – that is, the French.

His attitude to the Papacy was consistent with this: ' I would as soon receive my politics from Constantinople as from Rome '; ' I am sincerely a Catholic, but I am not a Papist. I deny the doctrine that the Pope has any temporal authority, directly or indirectly in Ireland. . . .' Herein lies the vital weakness in the linkage he made between the forces of religion and those of politics, and his words go echoing down the years. In 1887 John Dillon proclaimed furiously that Irish Catholics ' would no more take their political guidance from the Pope of Rome than from the Sultan of Turkey '; in 1888 Dillon laid down that ' in the conduct of our national affairs, the defending and asserting of our rights, we Irishmen – Protestant and Catholic alike – should be free from any interference; whether it comes from Italy or any other country.' This attitude to the Catholic Church, introduced by O'Connell, became a characteristic of those Irishmen who sought Irish reforms from within the English Parliament. The reason is obvious: the less blatantly Catholic Irish proposals were, the more likely it was that a hostile and suspicious anti-Catholic Parliament might entertain them. There is ample detailed evidence of anti-Catholicism in nineteenth century England, but were more needed the anxious consistency with which Irish politicians found it politic to repudiate or avoid anything which might seem merely Catholic rather than Irish or generally secular offers ample illustration. Here, then, was a radical internal infirmity in O'Connell's politico-religious structure. It explains why the agitation by the Irish in the English Parliament never had complete Church support, and why that support, at its peak on the unavoidably Catholic issue of emancipation, gradually dwindled as the century progressed. To make the point (to the degree of extremes and over-simplification) the O'Connellite compound of politics plus religion required Irish politicians to espouse Catholicism when in Ireland and deny it when in England, an exercise which however ingeniously attempted could never be a complete success. Moreover, the very attempt endangered both the politicians' support in Ireland and their objectives within the English Parliament.

The veto question was the occasion of the first abrasion between religious interests and those of politics – and O'Connell's politics won. It might be argued that this victory determined the destiny of Anglo-Irish relations. In return for emancipation, the British government had sought some control, by veto over appointment, over the Irish hierarchy. For simple religious reasons, the bishops were willing to accept this – the religious gains promised to be greater than any losses – until O'Connell raised the nationalist issue. Had his impulse been religious, O'Connell might have criticised the veto as state interference in religious affairs, but his objection was that it intruded on emancipation, which was a matter of political rights: he was to go on to rebutt Papal support for the veto as religious interference in political affairs. To O'Connell, emancipation was a political matter, which engaged the strongest institution in Ireland, the Church: the veto implied the sacrifice of this institution to British control. O'Connell was not interested in religion as such, only in its political potential. He imposed upon Irish Catholicism a nationalist political expression, so that thereafter the leaders of Irish religion were committed to taking serious account of political nationalism derived from O'Connell's liberal democratic principles. The basic unity and dynamism in the Irish situation was religious: if it had been permitted (by O'Connell, and by British willingness to concede emancipation) to pursue its religious path unhindered, the future may have been one of reasonably harmonious integration in the United Kingdom, the decisive tumult of the 1820s may not have taken place. But emancipation was not conceded, and O'Connell, with remarkable political genius, contrived a marriage of convenience between religion and national politics.

O'Connell announced in 1817, ' My political creed is short and simple. It consists in believing that all men are entitled, as of right and justice, to religious and civil liberty.' Championship of Catholic emancipation was a natural consequence of this creed, but the relationship between O'Connell's creed and that of Catholic Ireland was not one of identity. O'Connell believed in the abstract principle of religious liberty, and saw it grossly infringed in Ireland. Catholic Ireland was not interested in abstract liberal principles or general political issues. To the extent that it was intellectual it would have repudiated liberal notions of religious liberty. It was interested in its own religious grievances and its own religious freedom. O'Connell led Catholic Ireland in the direction it wanted to go, but the motives of leader and followers were different. Nevertheless because O'Connell led a Catholic movement, dramatically and successfully, to become a national hero, his principles, his English liberal principles, tended to be accepted as appropriately Irish and Catholic principles, to the frustrative delusion of almost a century of subsequent history.

O'Connell's plan was to use Irish Catholicism as the basis for mass political democracy. He assumed a natural linkage between clergy and people, with, ultimately, the general will of the people as final determinant: ' Even should any of our prelates fail, which I do not and cannot believe, there is still resource. It is to be found in the unalterable constancy of the Catholic people of Ireland. . . . The people would imitate their forefathers; they would communicate only with some holy priest who never bowed to the Dagon of power.' It is true that much of O'Connell's astonishing power lay in the fact that he embraced within his own personality the Irish duality of love and hate: as John Mitchel described him, ' hating and loving heartily . . . he had the power to make other men hate or love . . . [he] led and swayed his people by a kind of divine, or else diabolical right '. Mitchel, the Young Irelander, held that O'Connell had let the Irish astray into moderate constitutionalist, anti-republican paths, and ' would not see that the Church had ever been the enemy of Irish Freedom '. But O'Connell, however tactical his involvement of the Church in politics, saw the obvious truth that the Church must be the friend of Irish religious freedom, if only in the negative sense of wishing to destroy the exclusive dominance of the Protestant religious system. The centrality of Protestantism to the political Union, and O'Connell's contrivance of a Catholic religio-political agitation, welded together the cause of Irish freedom, and Irish religious freedom so as to make them virtually indistinguishable. Thus O'Connell identified true Irish Catholicism with antagonism to Britain and popular demands for reform, an identification which some of the Irish hierarchy accepted and those who did not found difficult if not impossible to reject. So it was that all the burdens, temporal as well as spiritual, which weighed on the Catholic inhabitants of Ireland became Catholic

burdens, somehow sanctified, however profane, by the Catholic shoulders
on which they rested. And similarly Catholic burdens were Irish ones –
he who fought for emancipation fought for Ireland: Catholicism's cause
and Ireland's seemed the one thing.

This is the setting of the mass social discontent which was a major
force behind the emancipation movement: the peasantry were convinced that Catholic emancipation would lead on to an end to grievances such as tithes and high rents. This utopian conviction was widespread in Ireland: it can be illustrated from Bishop Doyle who expected
incalculable benefits from emancipation, ' an end to those religious heats
and animosities which now prevail so generally ', ' it would tranquillise the
public mind ', encourage investment and industry in Ireland, open the
way to constructive talents, ' make us one people immediately, and I
hope in a few years, a very happy and prosperous people '. The 1830
Pastoral Letter of the Irish bishops rejoiced that emancipation had relieved them of the necessity of taking any further part in political agitation – ' It was a duty imposed on us by a state of things which has
passed. . . .'

It had not passed. The utopian belief that emancipation would be
a panacea for all the evils that had afflicted Ireland for centuries remained
unfulfilled, to become a characteristic attitude of over-expectation.
Utopianism recurs down the years in agitation for Repeal, Home Rule,
a Republic. To hostile English eyes (Nassau Senior in his 1868 *Journals*)
it appeared as a tendency of the Irish to ' select for their avowed object
an unattainable end because it is unattainable – because its mischief
cannot be tested by experience or its stimulus by possession ', but it was
rather a tendency to invest real enough objectives with prodigious curative
powers. But utopianism was not confined to the Irish: the pro-emanci-
pists in England also tended to regard emancipation as the complete,
infallible remedy for all Irish maladies.

The campaign for Catholic emancipation was the first occasion on
which this utopianism was mobilised politically, a development which
reflected the crucial role religion and the existence of religious discrimination played in Irish history and society. The religious issue was
so vital and dominant that it bred the impression that once it was removed
no other problems would remain. And indeed, perhaps this was not
entirely utopian – the matter was not put to the test, for emancipation
was yielded by Britain reluctantly, partially and with determination that
its consequences be restricted as narrowly as possible. Perhaps emancipation was the solvent of the Irish question, rendered ineffective by the
British policy to which Castlereagh referred in 1801: ' our error, per-

haps, has hitherto been yielding piecemeal rather than upon a system. In leaving an obvious ground for struggle behind, we have encouraged demand rather than attained the only end, with a view to which the concession had been made '. Certainly there was obvious ground for struggle left behind: even into the twentieth century there were Irish complaints that Catholicism had not been yet emancipated fully. Yet, so far as the political possibilities offered by the British Parliament in 1829 are concerned, hopes for a full and generous emancipation were utopian indeed, and it is remarkable that such perceptive and realistic Irishmen as Bishop Doyle should have entertained such extravagant hopes.

From the British viewpoint as well as the Irish, the failure of Catholic emancipation lay mainly in that it did not meet expectations that it would, of itself, satisfy the aspirations of the Irish people, and inaugurate peace, harmony and contentment. On the contrary, the effect was to sustain and institutionalise utopian politics in Ireland, to maintain the original religious impulse, and to further focus the blame for frustration of Irish objectives on Britain. The religious discrimination remaining at the heart of Irish affairs continued to breed the belief that once Catholicism entered into its own in Ireland, a new reign of brightness and light would begin. Anti-British utopian religio-politics were established in Ireland with Catholic emancipation.

From the time of O'Connell, the Catholic Church remained involved in popular movements, beset constantly by the problem of preserving religious interests against the demands of mass politics. But if clerical policy was restricted by the need to avoid alienating a people who had political loyalties, democratic nationalism in Ireland remained related to the Church. If the Catholic Association, founded by O'Connell in May 1823, became the prototype of Irish popular political organisation, its Catholic aspects were no less important than its political: the Association was totally dependant on the clergy and church structure for its popular dynamism and organisation. The methods of the Association – peaceful mass agitation directed by O'Connell using moral pressure and the hint of force – were not religious, but its machinery was. Its organisational units were the parishes, its local organisers were the parish clergy, its centres for fund-raising and propaganda were the churches: ' Every altar was made a tribune '. Priests and laymen co-operated in the Association and its successors; it witnessed a remarkable change in clerical political attitudes, from passivity to activity. After O'Connell had established the intimate engagement of the clergy in public affairs, even though that involvement might fluctuate from time to time, no movement aspiring to popular support in Ireland could ignore that involvement. Once religion had become so directly involved in politics it was morally impossible to remove it – that is, short of denying the wide moral claims of religion, a denial which would alienate anyone making it from the strongest source of popular opinion in Ireland. Or, bluntly, after O'Connell there was no possibility of successful secular politics in Ireland, a situation which promised, not merely the atrophy of any such Irish aspirations, but ultimately the end of British rule.

Lecky remarked that the Catholic Association ' formed a kind of Parliament which took cognisance of all political and social grievances ', a kind of alternative Irish Catholic government. Nevertheless it, and O'Connell, remained within the boundaries of the existing English constitution, treading an English path. The fact that the Catholic Association pioneered ways and means of popular agitation which were taken up within England is no doubt a compliment to it: it is also an epitaph; its framework had been absorbed into the English political system. But not its essential spirit. Its techniques of popular agitation have secured it an important place in the history of revolutionary organisations, a place acknowledged even by Russians, yet these pioneering techniques would have been useless without the energy which lay in the movement itself: Irish nationalism, as an effective force in the nineteenth century, took its mass origins in a religious issue. Because O'Connell related this issue to the political principles and phraseology of his day, he created what had the superficial appearance of ' orthodox ' nationalism, a construction which gradually gathered a pseudo-independent life of its own. Yet the basic religious context remained. What other nationalist could Pius IX describe as ' the great champion of the Church, the father of his country, and the glory of the Christian world '? Whereas other men of the nineteenth century nationalist movement earned their reputation for work towards their countries' political independence, O'Connell's reputation as ' The Liberator ' rested on his work for Catholic emancipation. Indeed by the time of the fiftieth anniversary of his death, in 1897, he was being credited with divine guidance. Archbishop Keane, preaching a panegyric in the Church of the Irish College, Rome – where O'Connell's heart was preserved – claimed: ' Clearer and clearer God was whispering in his heart, " Come, and I will send thee that thou mayst deliver My people". . . . Like Moses, he had led his people within sight of the Promised Land of Civil as well as Religious Liberty.'

The benedictions of religion which were showered on O'Connell, spoke for the nature of the movement he led rather than for his motives: he championed emancipation not for religious reasons but for liberal democratic reasons. Subtract the religious element from O'Connell's campaigns and there seemed little point or form left in them. This observation may be illustrated from the fact that European revolutionaries of the 1840s, notably Mazzini, held that Irish agitation did not amount to nationalism. Certainly it did not conform to European canons of nationalism. All that such European observers could see in Ireland was O'Connell's dominant English constitutionalism, and a tiny group of Young Irelanders: their dominant secularism, or mysticism in Mazzini's case, blinded them to the real dynamic and coherence in Irish agitation, the Catholic religion. Mazzini's contention that the Irish did not exhibit 'any distinct principle of life or system of legislation, derived from native peculiarities, and contrasting radically with English wants and wishes', nor did they claim any 'high special function' to discharge in the interests of humanity, seems absurd in the light of Irish Catholicism and its aspirations. However, it is logical and intelligible viewed in relation to Mazzini's personal philosophy which was political and non-Christian. To the Irish, their religion was sacred, to Mazzini, nationality: 'Nationality is sacred to me because I see in it the instrument of labour for the good and progress of all men'; in Ireland religion filled that role, and Mazzini was correct to exclude the Irish from any claim, on those grounds, to nationalism. To Mazzini, nationalism was born in the will of the people expressed in a moral purpose. In Ireland the people did not look to the state for morality – they believed that Britain was ample testimony to the immorality of state action – they looked to the Church. To Mazzini, the nation was the intermediary between the individual and the universal scheme, the goal of history: in Ireland the Church and clergy filled this intermediary place.

O'Connell's political genius made a very substantial impact on religious thinking: it tended to push Catholic attitudes into line with liberal-national ones. This parallelism seemed a natural alliance to O'Connell, whose outlook was that Liberal-Catholic one expressed neatly by Frederick Lucas in 1845: 'Catholicism and democracy are drawn towards each other by their natural connection and by mutual interest. If they do not acknowledge each other . . . they both are condemned to equal impotency.' However, Vatican affairs and influence being what they were, such an alliance seemed far less natural to Church authorities: to them, the marriage O'Connell had effected between Catholicism and liberal democracy was an inappropriate and dangerous liaison, and though the religious partner to the union remained to some extent constrained by its obligations, its unhappiness and disquiet rendered the union unstable and liable to dissolution. The fall of Parnell forstalled a major confrontation between political tendencies which the Church regarded as increasingly irreligious and menacing, and religious attitudes which politicians regarded as arrogant and stifling.

After O'Connell the history of Ireland is impelled by two forces, the religious and, in various forms, the liberal democratic. Both were anti-English, and in this lay their convenient or necessary unity. But they were anti-English for differing reasons, and, liberal democratic principles were only circumstantially anti-English: England happened, in the Irish context, to be the power against which such generally anti-foreign and pro-national principles were directed. Such principles were not indigenous, Irish, rooted in the soil, in the way Catholicism was. Catholicism was vigorously and fiercely anti-Protestant, characteristics rendered even more intense in the Cullenite Church of the second half of the century. Catholicism was anti-Protestant, and therefore, for deep historical reasons, anti-English so long as England could be identified as a Protestant power. It was that traditional religious disposition of the Catholic Irish which was expressed in O'Connell's 'nationalism', and gave it its fundamental strength. By mid-century this infusing of politics by religion had produced many forms of the martyr nation image. An example which stresses the religious rather than the nationalist complexion of this image is Thomas Darcy McGee's *A History of the Attempts to Establish the Protestant Reformation in Ireland* published in 1853:

> Catholicity descends into the tomb to arise again glorified and immortal; while Protestantism, like Herod, sits on its throne in gloomy grandeur, powerful to destroy, but incapable of the conquest of a single pious soul. The contrast, old as the cross, of the church and the world, in no modern nation is so boldly defined as in England and Ireland. The martyr age of the Irish church has come upon it at last. . . . That good God, who denied our fatherland domestic peace, has consecrated her to a holy war, glorious, though sorrowful. Our Lord has suffered; the saints have suffered; Ireland has suffered. If nations could be canonised she might well claim the institution of the process.

O'Connell enlisted the power of Irish Catholicism to reformist political objectives. It might be contended that this was not any remarkable achievement, or anything unusual in a country where religious wars against Britain had not been uncommon. But O'Connell's work was at a time and in a cause hardly favourable, when European Catholicism was under attack and had taken, or was about to take, political positions which, on the whole, were deeply conservative. Just how contradictory was O'Connell's politico-religious structure may be seen in the Irish support for the embattled Papal States in 1860 – £80,000 in Peter's Pence and an Irish Brigade. Moreover, there was ample evidence and argument for the assumption that Catholicism naturally favoured political conservatism: this assumption was behind a good deal of British policy in the nineteenth century, which sought by representations in both Ireland and Rome, to bring the Irish Church to the support of conservative positions. That this policy largely failed was due not merely to that Church's inherent anti-Britishism. A major factor was the Church's involvement, following O'Connell, in the cause of nationalist liberal democracy, a commitment which put strong popular pressure on the Church to reject any policy, even if it was ordained by Rome, which seemed to favour English interests.

In its British setting, Catholic emancipation was an extorted concession, given in fear, fear that failure to give it would lead to rebellion in Ireland, fear that rebellion in Ireland would lead to agitation in Britain, and fear of the consequences of emancipation itself. It is significant that its English advocates argued not only that Catholics were harmless, but that Catholicism was fast moving towards extinction. This was an endeavour to placate that Protestant conviction that Catholicism was not only false and unenlightened, but the enemy of prosperity and proper government. Cardinal Newman caught the centrality of this conviction in his comment that, ' as English is the natural tongue, so Protestantism is the intellectual and moral language of the body politic '. Forced to concede emancipation, English politicians were determined to protect their Protestant constitution from Catholic encroachment. Sir Robert Peel held that ' The great security against the possession of undue power and influence by the Roman Catholics . . . must be in the discretion of the Crown and its advisers ', but in fact, the government's protective measures were even more explicit – a drastic reduction in the Irish franchise, the replacement of the 40/- freehold by a £10 qualification, thus reducing the electorate from over 100,000 to about 16,000. The 1793 Act had given Catholics the vote, but no personal access to political position: in 1829 Catholics were given access to Parliament and offices, but were deprived of the voting basis for political power. In conceding the religious issue, at least partly, the British government created in disfranchisement a political issue – the political elimination of the peasantry, the class that had elected O'Connell in 1828.

Lecky remarked that O'Connell's Church ' entered the Constitution triumphant and unshackled – an object of fear and not of contempt, a power that could visibly affect the policy of the empire '. He saw this as O'Connell's glory, but in establishing an object of fear, O'Connell's achievement had a negative function also. It identified Catholicism, particularly that of Ireland, as a continuing threat to the safety of the Reformation State, which rested on the Revolution of 1688, that unchallengeable foundation of English political tradition. To minds committed to a Protestant constitution, and to convictions of Catholicism's insatiable lust for power and dominion, emancipation spelt the need for increased vigilance, firmer resistance.

The practical immediate consequences of Catholic emancipation were slight. Most Irish Catholics could not afford the expenses of a political career: a generation after emancipation Catholics numbered no more than a third of Ireland's parliamentary representation. Nor did it transformed what O'Connell called ' the species of *animals* with which I had to carry on my warfare with the common enemy. It is crawling slaves like them that prevent our being a nation '. The animals, the crawling slaves, had not been transformed, but they had been aroused and organised as a political force for the first time. Emancipation was both success and failure: it was a classic example of what was to become a familiar pattern in Ireland – an overdue reform reluctantly introduced in fear under threat of disorder, accompanied by attempts to render it null or reduce its efficacy: so every grievance redressed produced a new grievance. Or to put this pattern on another plane: emancipation had not been conceded as a principle but as a practical solution to the problem of governing Ireland; and the issue thus remained unsettled. The first great reform under the Union widened the religious cleavage. It gave Catholics a taste of success; it produced fear, dismay and increased resolve in ultra-Protestant circles. True, the emancipation question itself did not arouse Protestant militancy to anything like the degree to which it flared out later, say over the Maynooth Seminary grant in 1845, or over the creation in 1850 of a Catholic hierarchy in England; in 1829 the deep-rooted anti-Catholicism of English popular opinion remained largely dormant. This was because emancipation was recognised as expedient, unavoidable, perhaps just, and in any case, not conceding all that much. Lord Hutchinson, an Irish Protestant landlord, remarked, ' my mind is quite made up to fight them in defence of my property; but I don't like fighting in an unjust cause '. Many religious minds were similarly disposed: they could bring themselves to tolerate Catholics, but they would defend their property – the Protestant Constitution – against them, or rather against it – Catholicism, Popery. So it was that emancipation in fact made the Catholic question more sensitive, more acute – ' the subject on which society seemed to be going mad ' as

Harriet Martineau said of the Maynooth question in 1845. Emancipation having given Catholics a measure of freedom and equality, the
threat of priestcraft and Papal aggression seemed much more immediate.
Some measure of equality was one thing, but anything which might
seem to facilitate or favour Catholicism as a religion was another; especially – as not only the clamour of opposition to the Maynooth grant, but
also hostility to Catholic-controlled education shows – anything that
might assist the spread of Catholic doctrines and teaching.

Such was the legacy left by the age of O'Connell to Cardinal Paul
Cullen. When Cullen came, in the 1850s and 60s, to assert the claims
of Catholic Ireland, his means were necessarily political though his aims
were religious. Cullen, as E. R. Norman has indicated, had 'no political
theories, only religious and ecclesiastical ones', or as Gavan Duffy put
it, he was 'zealous for religion and indifferent to everything else'. But
following O'Connell, Cullen found that religious and ecclesiastical
policies were enmeshed in the political situation, and led directly to
conflict with the British government. Cullen saw the Irish question as
whether religious authority, or the British government should rule Ireland. He explained to Rome in October 1850: 'The real question to be
decided is whether . . . the Pope ought to rule the Church in Ireland
through the majority of the bishops, or whether, on the other hand,
the English government ought to rule it by means of the archbishop
of Dublin.' And of course, to Cullen's mind, rule of the Church in
Ireland effectively meant rule of Ireland: Duffy's comment had ample
validity: 'His idea of government was said to be simple to nudity.
Ireland should be ruled, as Rome was ruled, by ecclesiastics, laymen
having no function but to contribute a sympathetic and deferential audience.' The profound radical potential of Cullen's outlook was hidden
from most English politicians by its sheer audacity, its deep religiosity,
and the fact that much of his energy was directed towards getting a better
deal from England within the system of the Union. But the case of
Father O'Keeffe, dismissed as a school manager by his bishop in 1871,
was to make clear the distance Ireland had travelled towards one form
of independence, the spiritual: a verdict for O'Keeffe of one farthing's
damages against Cardinal Cullen vindicated the legal supremacy of
civil authority, but the moral victory lay with ecclesiastical authority.
Only the imagination of Protestant extremists could stretch to encompass
the full extent of Cullen's ambitious hopes for a Catholic Ireland,
though, of course, where they saw the abomination of desolation, he saw
the reign of goodness and truth.

Cullen's interpretation of the Irish question was a simple one, but of profound influence then and later: he saw the Irish Church struggling with the Protestant-secular English state for the soul of Catholic Ireland. The battleground was necessarily political, but what was at stake was religious: the issue which best exemplified this situation was that of education.

Prior to the 1850s, the Irish episcopacy was sharply divided in political attitudes. The division was temperamental and tactical, and related to differing assessments of the motives of the British government. Moderates, led by Archbishop Murray of Dublin, held that British legislation should be accepted gratefully for whatever benefits it might bring, and improvements courteously sought. Intransigents, led by Archbishop MacHale of Tuam, were suspicious of all legislation affecting the interests of Catholicism, seeing in it attempts to undermine Irish Catholicism by sapping its principles and fighting spirit. They regarded British concessions to Catholicism as designed to buy Church loyalty and secure its eventual enslavement to the state. Episcopal disagreement intensified in the late 1840s, under the stimulus of the British government's plans for university education in Ireland. Admitting the Catholic (and Presbyterian) grievance that Trinity College Dublin was so closely linked with the Established Church as to be unacceptable, the government set up Queen's Colleges at Cork, Galway and Belfast. Although offering minor concessions, the government stood firm on the principle that these colleges be undenominational, despite Catholic episcopal insistence that the education of Catholics should take place in Catholic institutions. The question then was – would the hierarchy accept the colleges? They were almost equally divided in 1849, but events in Britain in 1850-1 decided the issue – or rather, placed it fiercely in dispute between Irish bishops and English politicians for over half a century, until 1908, when the National University of Ireland was set up. The circumstances of 1850-1 were these. The violent Protestant reaction to the restoration of the English Catholic hierarchy was bad enough, if not surprising to Cullen (' error will always be opposed to truth, darkness to light; and we cannot expect that the world would be more friendly to us than it was to our divine Redeemer '). But it prompted the government to an Ecclesiastical Titles Act which made it a penal offence for Catholic prelates to adopt territorial titles. The Act, a token of disapproval never enforced, was received by the Irish bishops as a return to the persecution of the penal laws, and the whole affair seemed to indicate that the British government and people were impelled by a bitter and bigoted anti-Catholicism. In so far as such reforms as Britain might offer did not measure up to the highest Catholic standards, as defined by the bishops, they must be seen as

Protestant or secularist snares, dangerous, with which there must be no dalliance or compromise. The triumph of the policy of clerical intransigence, which may be dated from Cullen's succession to the see of Dublin in 1852, left very little room for any recognition of British good-will towards Ireland short of a complete British capitulation to the will of the bishops.

Cullen came to regard the ' Godless Colleges ' (as Catholics dubbed the Queen's Colleges) as the coping store of a system ' which slowly puts in the power of a Protestant Government all the education of a Catholic population.' What justification was there for Cullen's suspicions? Ample, though not precisely on the grounds he occupied. Such responses to Catholic grievances as the Maynooth Bill of 1845 and the Queen's Colleges scheme reflected little wish to foster Catholicism. Since the Reformation, a traditional British explanation of Irish unrest had blamed the alliance of priesthood and populace. A good deal of British policy had been directed towards destroying this alliance, or using it to British ends: in the nineteenth century such efforts took the form of schemes to buy over the clergy, or attempts to induce church authorities to restrain them with conservative theology. It was a common cynical view in Britain that the Irish clergy were engaged in popular agitation because they were dependent on the people for their income: they led the people because they were, in fact, their servants. Consequently, to give the priesthood financial independence would allow their natural conservatism to reassert itself and their loyalties to attach to the new source of their income. Such was a strong strand in the British reasoning which favoured increasing the Maynooth endowment, and also in the arguments, up to 1867, that the Catholic Church in Ireland ought to be endowed by the British state.

As to the Queen's Colleges scheme, it embodied precisely the hope that was Cullen's fear – that it would create a secular commonality. Peel hoped that a non-denominational secular education, if it did not liberate the Catholic middle class from the bonds of clericalism, would at least draw them away from association with the peasantry and towards a closer understanding with Protestants and Englishmen of the same class: the Colleges would weaken the clerical, religious, class and nationalist bases of Irish agitation. It is not surprising that O'Connell denounced the Colleges as obnoxious on nationalist grounds, nor that Cullen should do so later for religious reasons. Both men were right, in that the scheme was intended to undermine what they desired to preserve and strengthen.

There were also grounds for the same conclusion about the National

System of Primary Education, which embodied the principle of inter-denominational instruction. Protestants tended to support it: the Irish hierarchy condemned it in 1859 and thereafter as conducive to prose-lytism and indifference, and demanded a denominational system. The demand was firmly and consistently refused: the English government wanted to retain non-sectarian education and in any case shared the view of the Irish Catholic clergy which Cavour had expressed in 1844: ' Their profound ignorance, their numerous prejudices, their exaggerated political notions render them unfit to fulfil the task of primary teachers.' But was this all there was to it? In 1852 Richard Whately, Anglican Archbishop of Dublin, remarked to Nassau Senior: ' The education supplied by the National Board is gradually undermining the vast fabric of the Irish Roman Catholic Church . . . . I believe . . . that mixed education is gradually enlightening the people, and that, it we give it up, we give up the only hope of weaning the Irish from the abuses of Popery! But I cannot venture openly to profess this opinion. I cannot openly support the Education Board as an instrument of conversion.' The Catholic episcopacy had no hesitation in venturing to attack it openly as such.

The continuation of the Catholic education question was of para-mount importance for Anglo-Irish relations. As long as it endured as a political issue, it maintained the Irish episcopacy and clergy in a central position – an anti-English position – in Irish affairs. It also maintained religion itself in a central position: the English government's refusal to concede a Catholic university or denominational schools was taken to be a denial of the rights of conscience, and thus religious persecution. A strong element of anti-Catholicism was certainly present in the English refusal, either by way of traditional prejudice or related to the evangelical revival, but political factors were stronger. The conflict over education revealed that what was conceived in England for political reasons was received in Ireland as intended for religious reasons. This could hardly be otherwise, for the British interpretation of Irish agitation saw the Catholic religion as central to it. ' We very much doubt whether in England, or indeed in any free Protestant country, a true Papist can be a good subject,' observed *The Times* of 3 March 1853, ' but if all this had been avowed some years ago, the opportunities of Popery would never have been what they are.' Given such presuppositions, if the object of the English government was to create good subjects in Ireland, it must proceed by weakening Popery and restricting opportunities for its development. But naturally British efforts to weaken, divide or re-align Popery in Ireland so to achieve good government came across to

Irish Catholics as attempts to destroy, persecute or pervert their cherished religion.

The education issue focused this standing contretemps most damagingly, particularly as it existed through a time when the power, wealth, popularity and self-confidence of the Irish Church were growing rapidly. In 1859 O'Neill Daunt remarked that ' Whatever public spirit exists in Ireland just now is rather religious than political ': between 1850 and 1900 the Church experienced (or contrived) a remarkable development and increase in all areas of its resources. Cullen's conviction expressed in a pastoral letter of 1859 was that ' Our rulers have a great debt of justice to repay because of past wrongs and oppression '. So it was that the resentment, discontent and suspicion generated by the education *impasse* spread, via the most influential cultural medium in Ireland, to darken further the image of British policy generally. Their educational demands remained a basic criteria whereby Church leaders judged not only British ministries, but also Irish nationalist movements. Irish politicians were assessed (usually adversely) on how they measured up as champions of Catholic education. The education *impasse* invited a constant clerical activity in politics and gave politics a marked religious complexion.

It is obvious that the education issue did much to sustain the alignment between Catholic religious dynamism and popular Irish nationalism. Had this issue been settled, certainly the involvement of the Church in political affairs would have been far less close, a situation which may have had profound effects on the strength of democratic nationalist movements. And had it been settled so as to end Catholic educational deprivation, again, Anglo-Irish relations may have been very different.

On the education issue, the Cullenite policy was one of uncompromising hostility to Britain. On the tactical level of practical politics, his position was far less extreme. He was totally opposed to extremism in politics, opposing Gavan Duffy as an Irish Mazzini (and Young Ireland generally as destructive) and the Fenian movement of the 1860s as the equivalent of those Italian revolutionary movements which beseiged the Papacy. To Cullen ' those who engage in and encourage secret plots and conspiracies, may think they are patriots, but they are the worst enemies of their country.' In 1865 Cullen defined patriotism as ' a true Christian love of country, a love of country founded on the observance of the Gospel and connected with charity towards all: and let us exhort our flocks to acquire a claim to that virtue by avoiding sin and everything scandalous, by being sober and temperate, by practising the duties of their holy religion and by edifying the world with the odour of the good works which they perform.' But even such a religious definition drew Cullen into politics, not only to censure such Irishmen who acted on other definitions, but to defend his own position. In theory he might hold that bishops should be allied neither with government nor popular party, but in practice he regarded much of British policy as persecution – British administration too, as he explained to Rome in 1855: ' it seems to me an incalculable advantage to have Catholics in positions concerned with the administration of the law in Ireland, because they may do something to protect the poor and at least they will not persecute them on religious grounds, while Protestant officials often employ their influence in persecuting and perverting the Catholic poor.' From the Cullenite view (which became pervasive in the Irish Church) British government and administration were Protestant and persecuting, an interpretation which Cullen applied particularly to the Tory Party and to conservative forces generally. So, he was not only drawn into politics, but into support for the Liberals and Radicals, which in view of their basic secularism, was incongruous indeed. Though Cullen accepted the existing English political framework, ultimately he expected it to produce what perhaps it was incapable of producing, legislation and administration satisfactory to Cullen's ideal of a Catholic Ireland. The general effect of Cullen's political attitudes was to widen and deepen the gulf between England and Ireland.

O'Connell's career saw religious forces enlisted for political objectives: Cullen's career saw religion rejecting a subordinate place in this relationship. The Cardinal claimed for the Church *the* determining role in Irish society, so that even those who rejected the claim had to assert another view of the Church's role in society, a process of challenge and response which helped Cullen's case: politics could no longer abstract from religion. During O'Connell's agitation, the clergy had entered popular politics as energetic local leaders. This suited, and continued to suit, Irish nationalists who saw the Church as the only organisation that might challenge the influence of the landlords: if the landlords exerted power over men's land and sustenance, the clergy held sway over their minds and hearts. But the direct political involvement of the clergy inevitably meant that clerical standards and religious criteria would gradually percolate into Irish politics – and vice versa. Once the politico-religious structure was erected in the 1820s, its development was very difficult for either politicians or churchmen to control. After priestly behaviour degenerated to the level of the political mob, efforts such as that of the Synod of 1854, limiting the political activity of the clergy, were resented – and resisted – as in conflict with popular nationalism: any episcopal move to withdraw the clergy from politics seemed a pro-English, anti-Irish procedure, beyond popular tolerance. However, Cullen's Church did not intend to withdraw too far from politics, as this would be to abandon the populace to unprincipled demagogues. Practically, Cullen's policies tended towards the negative form of exercising over politics such moral influence as he thought imperative. In this Cullen's success demonstrated that while the Church might not be able to get Irishmen to do something positive, it could ensure that they would not do what the Church opposed. When it came to a clash between Cullen's views and those of popular nationalism, as in the stand of Frederick Lucas over the Tenant League in the mid-1850s, or over Fenianism in the 1860s, the bulk of Irish Catholic opinion went with the Church. Much of the odium in which Cullen was held by nationalists then and later may be attributed to their recognition that their power over the people was less than his and his successors. Ultimately, religion was the arbiter of Irish affairs.

Obviously, religious resistance to British policy was frontally provoked by such legislation (or its lack) which seemed Protestant and proselytising. But generally, the totality of British rule in Ireland aroused criticism on religious grounds, and from religious sources: the socio-economic condition of Ireland, for which Britain might be held at least partly if not largely responsible, was not conducive to the best interests of religion and morality; and furthermore the harshness of British rule encouraged sins of hatred and violence and revolutionary movements in which such sins were enshrined. So it was that British policy generally forced the Church to demand, and agitate for, not only religious, but socio-economic reform, in the interests of religion.

This can be seen throughout the nineteenth century, but is neatly exhibited in the 1860s. Opposition to Fenianism from the Church was complicated by the fact that Fenianism was a popular Irish response to British rule. If it were not to risk alienating its following, the Church would have to propose an alternative means of remedying the grievances which lay behind Fenianism. Cullen's reluctant entry into politics, with the National Association of Ireland in 1864, was a response to this challenge, which entailed an analysis of the basic causes of Irish unrest. Cullen and MacHale, the dominant figures in Irish Catholicism, believed these causes to be mainly three – the privileged existence of the Church of England as an established state church, the refusal of England to grant Ireland Catholic education, and, generally, poverty, particularly as associated with the land system. Remedying these grievances became the aim of the National Association, in which its natural gravitation was towards support of the English Liberal Party.

But English policy in the 1860s held even more specific provocation, in its reaction towards Italian unification. While Irish opinion supported the Pope, with money and a volunteer brigade of over a thousand men to defend his dominions, English opinion was lyrical in praise of Cavour and Garibaldi as champions of liberty and enlightenment against Papal despotism. In October 1860 the Foreign Secretary, Lord John Russell asserted that Papal government, and that of the king of the Two Sicilies, provided so ill for the welfare of their people that their subjects looked to their overthrow as a necessary preliminary to any improvement: that is, the English Foreign Secretary appeared to give his blessing to the principle of nationalist revolution against oppressive government. In the Irish view, the English government had again revealed its anti-Catholicism and had given approval to violent revolution; it had both confirmed Irish opposition to it on traditional religious grounds, and fostered the spirit of rebellion, of which Fenianism was an expression. Even prior to this, Cullen's reaction was to express the public hope, in February 1860, that Ireland ' will continue to present to the world the spectacle . . . of the masses of the people protecting the rights of property, and inculcating obedience to lawful authority, whilst ministers and statesmen are patronising rebellion, spoliation and communism, and giving an authoritative circulation to principles subversive of every legitimate government.' This response was conditioned by Cullen's belief that the possibility of Irish self-government was very remote, and, in any case, undesirable, in that he was convinced that an Irish government would be Protestant dominated, or at least worse than English rule. (Here Cullen's judgement clashed sharply with that of MacHale who saw self-government as the key to all Ireland's problems.) Cullen's conclusion that Ireland's English rulers were not only Protestant bigots but showed gross political irresponsibility strengthened his conviction that religion and the Church were the only hopes for good government in Ireland. England's dereliction of what appeared to Cullen a patent political duty forced the Church to move further into politics. The National Association was no political success, but it demonstrated the existence of some fundamental Irish political forces. Irish support for the Papacy had already shown that Ireland was no simple example of political nationalism. Had it been so, there would have been Irish support for the Italian nationalists; had nationalism and religious loyalty been factors of equal strength, the Irish might have remained aloof from what was happening in Italy; but what they in fact did was to support the Pope actively. When Bishop Moriarty said in March 1868, ' The people have no patriotism except hatred for their rulers,' he saw one side of the coin: the other was love and loyalty for their religious rulers. The National Association showed that if Irish laymen allowed their hatred to take them in political directions not approved by religion, the forces of religion would not only oppose them, but would even construct an alternative political expression. The result would be to deprive unapproved organisations of mass support. Thus, the practical limits of Irish agitation against Britain were defined: they must be at least tolerable to the Church.

However, what in fact secured results was not the constitutionalism of the bishops, but the violence of Fenianism in 1867. Violence prompted the English government to make reforms which moderates had proposed earlier as essential in order to avoid violence. Thus violence was canonised as effective, and constitutional procedures brought into contempt: reforms within the Union were granted because of agitation which sought to end the Union. The conservative potential of the Cullenite Church was disregarded, and thereby weakened as a possible support for British rule; and the efforts of the Church to render Ireland more peaceful in the interests of religion were made more difficult. However, the ever-widening breach between English policies and what was wanted by the Irish Church tended to be obscured by the appearance of W. E. Gladstone, with a positive English policy of reform in relation to church, land and education, and by the fact that the first of these reforms was that most urgently urged by Catholic Ireland – the disestablishment of the Anglican Church.

In 1861 census had shown that of an Irish population of $5\frac{3}{4}$ million, under 700,000 were Anglicans and $4\frac{1}{2}$ million Catholics: in 1869 the Anglican Church was disestablished and disendowed. The grievance had been long-standing, and Catholic churchmen regarded it as utterly crucial. In England Cardinal Manning took the view that ' The main cause of all division, conflict, and animosity is the Irish Establishment.' He told Cullen that disestablishment was imperative, ' Because it is not a Church; it is an anti-Catholic religion; it perverts the action of the civil power; it has persecuted the Catholic Faith; it insults it by lording over it; it poisons and embitters all social life; it is a badge of ascendancy.' In March 1868, Bishop Moriarty had told a Catholic M.P. (who had passed it on to Gladstone) that ' Religious equality will remove disaffection and make the Irish people contented and loyal.' Cullen stated that ' the Irish Bishops are persuaded that peace and love for authority can never be established in Ireland as long as the Catholics shall be obliged to support a Protestant establishment and to submit to a Protestant ascendancy.'

Aware of such opinion, Gladstone concluded that disestablishment would be a major step towards the solution of the Irish question. Moreover, it was acceptable to him personally, in terms of its separation of church and state and his belief that it would be a beneficial liberation of the Anglican religion; and it appeared politically possible in that non-conformists as well as Catholics wanted it – a judgement vindicated by the 1868 general election. And so it was brought about, intended as the removal of a great obstacle to the peaceful working of the Union.

But the utopian expectations of a solution to the Irish question that had gathered around disestablishment were unfulfilled. One important reason was that it was expected to open an era of sweeping reform – which never came: it liberated more dissatisfactions than it remedied. This was particularly so, in that the Act was followed closely by Gladstone's refusal to amnesty all imprisoned Fenians, a refusal which more than dispelled any credit which might attach to disestablishment. As P. M. H. Bell has written, ' The only substantial consequence of the Irish Church Act was indeed the disestablishment and disendowment of the Irish Church. . . .' In view of the claims of Catholic churchmen cited above, why was this not enough to produce peace and contentment in Ireland? Because the religious equality Moriarty wanted was not obtained, nor the Protestant ascendancy to which Cullen objected ended; and because disestablishment had the additional effect of ending any possibility of a dependant relationship between Irish Catholic Church and English state.

In its efforts to break the power of English Protestantism, Cullen's Church had allied itself with English Liberalism, whose hostility to Papal claims in Italy, and ideology generally, cut across the propositions of the *Syllabus of Errors*. As late as 1868 the Papal Secretary of State told the British government's agent in Rome that the Vatican ' could never approve or sanction the principle of the disendowment of any church – or the principle of the separation of church and state in any country '. Yet it was precisely these principles which the Liberal government, with the vigorous support of the Irish hierarchy, were to implement the following year. Papal teaching dictated Irish clerical support for the Tories who also subscribed to the principle of an indissoluble union between church and state, and state endowment of religion. But the Protestantism of the Tories made such support out of the question, and indeed, so as to break the Protestant grip on Ireland, dictated a policy of support for the Tories' opponents, though they were radicals and secularists who subscribed to propositions condemned by the *Syllabus of Errors*. So Cullen was forced to repudiate endowment of religion by the state, and support the principle that all churches in Ireland should be voluntary societies. In order to attack his enemies, he had to consort and compromise with those who were not his friends; a situation which emphasises a salient feature of Anglo-Irish relations – the inability of the Irish Church, the most powerful force making for stability within Ireland, to relate itself fully, happily or consistently to any significant element within the English political structure.

Another crucial aspect of Cullen's ecclesiastical policy needs to be related to the political situation. Before Cullen came, the Irish Church was relatively disorganised: from the Synod of Thurles in 1850 Cullen imposed a disciplined Roman unity, which made the Church into the greatest cohesive force in Irish life and established his personal dominance over it. Cullen's dislike of England derived from his detestation of Pro-testantism. Anti-Protestantism was, of course, deep and traditional in Ireland, but Cullen's influence not only greatly strengthened it, made it more vigorous and vocal, but gave it an even sharper anti-English focus: he opposed English domination because he saw it as Protestant domina-tion, and his attacks on Protestantism amounted to attacks on England. On such a premise, disestablishment could never be nearly enough. Logically the only way to end Protestant domination was to end English domination. And disestablishment had hardly touched the surface of that. Like emancipation it conceded a religious principle (again a variety of equality) to the Irish Catholics, but hardly affected the real power of the Protestant Ascendancy – at least immediately. But it did remove a religious sanction from their rule, destroyed a second line of defence, and forced them hard back on defence of property as a sacred principle; and it opened the era of positive and sustained English efforts to contrive Irish reforms.

It is no mere coincidence that the two most important Irish reforms of the first 70 years of Union – emancipation and disestablishment – were religious. The fact indicates the area of greatest Irish pressure – and also that of least English resistance: but that it took 70 years to effect even these formal, legal reforms, which left Protestant dominance still standing firmly, was disastrous for Anglo-Irish relations. The very reforming activity of the British government after 1869 attracted the hatred of the Irish people: the more the government did the more attention it drew to itself as the instrumentality and source of evils, as well as the source to be attacked for reforms. And the British acceptance of complete res-ponsibility for making Irish reforms exposed them to the damning charge of complete responsibility for their failure.

3
The Repeal Question

In large part, the Irish agitation between 1829 and 1849 for repeal of the Union with Britain was the emancipation movement adjusted and applied to a different objective: in leadership, structure, clerical participation, and mass following, the salient features of repeal and emancipation movements had obvious similarities; and indeed the one flowed on from the other. But whereas Catholic emancipation was a cause co-extensive with Catholic Ireland and derivative from it, repeal was not. Repeal, unlike emancipation, was a political issue which offered scope for both disagreement and neutrality among the leaders of Catholic Ireland.

Repeal was O'Connell's cause: he started the campaign, it waxed and waned according to his tactics, it died soon after he did. Its immense popular success, measured in terms of vast public meetings and money collected, testified not to the popularity of the cause itself, but to that of the man who championed it: it was O'Connell personally, not the demand for repeal, that captured the enthusiastic allegiance of the Irish masses and made repeal a great movement. The repeal movement was a prodigious demonstration of the creative power of popular reputation and charismatic personality, but it suffered from the weaknesses and falsities of its being so substantially merely that.

Some of the basic shortcomings of the repeal movement derive from O'Connell's own political beliefs, which, on the question of what should be the relationship between Ireland and Britain, were vague and ambiguous. He had no basic objection to the connection with Britain, but pursued reform within the Union at the same time as he demanded its repeal. His comment, in 1840 – ' if we get the justice we require, then our Repeal Association is at an end, but I know we will not get that justice ' – indicates the duality of his tactical thinking: to some extent the repeal agitation had the character of a tactic to extort lesser reforms. But at its most extreme, O'Connell's objective was the restoration of what he conceived the 1782 situation to have been – a free Ireland, with her own legislature, loyal to the British crown. Far from hating England, O'Connell admired her, and saw Ireland's future in the emulation of England's constitution, political structures, liberal aims and material prosperity. His cancellation of his projected Clontarf meeting in October

1843, after the British government had declared it illegal, witnesses not merely to his general constitutionalism, but to the particular logic of his position: violence had no place in an agitation directed towards securing that political action from the British Parliament which would allow the reappearance of an Irish parliament.

The Clontarf affair may be taken as the occasion when O'Connell's two public faces confronted each other, to their mutual discomfiture. To all his audiences, O'Connell presented repeal as a panacea: to quote his 1843 *Memoir of Ireland*, ' The Union, and the Union alone, stands in the way of our achieving for ourselves every political blessing.' In urging his case before parliament, or generally to a sophisticated audience, O'Connell's language, style and arguments were in the constitutional tradition of Molyneaux. His contention was that Ireland had been refused equality under the Union, therefore it must have repeal. This was nothing more than a demand, a declaration of determination:

> The restoration of the national legislature is therefore again insisted upon, and no compromise, no pause, no cessation of that demand shall be allowed until Ireland is herself again. . . . I repeat it – that as surely as to-morrow's sun will rise, Ireland will assert her rights for herself, preserving the golden and unonerous link of the Crown – true to the principles of unaffected and genuine allegiance, but determined, while she preserves her loyalty to the British throne, to vindicate her title to constitutional freedom for the Irish people.

Repeal was utopian not only in what O'Connell expected from it, but in his failure to confront the question of how it could be achieved if Britain refused the demand for it. To repeal meetings in Ireland, O'Connell spoke a different language, but one if anything more utopian. To meetings hung with such slogans as ' Repeal is Erin's right and God's decree ', O'Connell brought such fervid messages as that reported by Johann Georg Kohl of a Dublin meeting in 1842: ' There is but *one* means for the complete rescue of Ireland, and that is Repeal: but *one* thing on which the welfare of all depends, – Repeal! With Repeal you will be happy, with Repeal you will become rich, with Repeal you will obtain all that you deserve and strive for. . . .' In the popular imagination, O'Connell linked repeal and the Promised Land of happiness and riches destined by God's will for the Irish. It was at this primitive level, at which he drew on the hatred and hope that dwelt in the hearts of the Irish masses, that O'Connell's success lay: repeal roused again the utopian visions that had clung around emancipation, and it was these, conjured up with O'Connell's magic spell, that gave the agitation its strength – and its enduring importance. O'Connell made many great contributions to the history of Irish agitation, but probably the greatest of these was his communication to the masses of a passionate utopian hope, and a vision of a new Ireland within their grasp.

In the repeal agitation, this mass energy and hope were focused on ending the Union. O'Connell could control the practical expression of this during his own lifetime, but his fostering of mass agitation against the English connection was of its nature likely to go beyond the limited objectives O'Connell really sought. Besides, O'Connell's objective of an Irish Parliament loyal to Britain had much against it within Ireland itself. For one thing, it was patently clear that it did not offer any immediate solution to Ireland's problems: repeal did not solve the question of Irish government; it merely opened it up. Repeal, simply as repeal, was meaningless. Even Archbishop MacHale, an ardent supporter of repeal, was aware that this was the popular attitude. He publicly informed Lord Grey in 1833, ' the people of Mayo, like the people of Ireland, do not care if the Parliament were in the moon, provided they were well governed ' – so much for popular Irish nationalism. For another thing, the benefits associated by O'Connell with the ' restoration of the national legislature ' were open to very serious dispute. In general terms, O'Connell's proposal of a ' restoration ' was a step back into the past. In particular terms, after emancipation, ' restoration ' was an anachronism: Irish Catholicism had advanced past the 1782 situation; the political atmosphere of post-emancipation Ireland was radically different, for the possibility of a Catholic Ireland, both in terms of religion, and of socio-economic freedom for Catholics, had been opened up. An Ireland, in which ambitious and able Catholics could hope to rise in public affairs was not an Ireland in which the middle class was likely to reject a *status quo* so recently opened to them.

Despite emancipation, an Irish Parliament still meant dominantly a Protestant Parliament: the Protestant Ascendancy was still overwhelmingly the group with the money, leisure and position appropriate to politics. O'Connell knew this. His case therefore rested on his assumption that Catholic Irish opinion would have more influence on a Parliament in Dublin than one in London. Even more basically, his liberal, democratic nationalism led him to assume that a common Irish nationalism would swiftly overcome religious divisions, and that fears of a Protestant Parliament were misplaced. Yet O'Connell himself, for tactical reasons, stressed and played on religious divisions. Archbishop MacHale was the strongest episcopal champion of repeal, on substantially religious grounds – ' What security have we against the repeal of the Emancipation Act, if not in Repeal?' With supporters such as this, O'Connell took a religious line, as he did in writing to MacHale in December 1839: 'The mainspring of Tory hostility to Ireland is hatred of the Catholic religion. This is not to be endured. We cannot suffer ourselves to be trampled under the hoofs of the brutal Orangemen of either country. . . . My object would be, once again to organise all Catholic Ireland in an effort of resistance to all our enemies.' But Catholic views other than MacHale's were not only possible, but widely held: what if O'Connell's Catholic crusade for repeal produced a Protestant Parliament? Why should a new Parliament be radically different from that of 1782, from whose Protestantism Catholics had sought escape in the Union? Repeal raised the question – if the English government did not govern Ireland, who would? To say the least, that question did not have an automatic answer: perhaps it was better to work for reform and adjustment within the existing system, than hazard everything by throwing it away.

It is true that many bishops and priests supported repeal: it is equally true that many did not; and that if the Holy See's two letters to the Irish hierarchy, in 1839 and 1844, admonitions against clerical over-involvement in politics and insisting on obedience to constituted authority be taken into account, the situation is not one in which it can be said that the Catholic Church supported repeal.

O'Connell's argument that the clergy should support his campaign was based on the propositions that they should remain at the head of their flocks, and that it was their duty to see misery removed. Some of the clergy accepted this, on moral grounds. MacHale said, in 1843: '. . . I feel the weight of the obligation of co-operating peacefully and strenuously to free my country from the remnants of the most atrocious, the most continuous, and the most insulting system of civil and religious oppression that ever was carried on against the faith, the freedom, nay the very existence of a noble and faithful people. . . .' Others accepted repeal because O'Connell had cast his spell over their flocks and the priests felt it necessary to go with their people.

While bishops might agree on the deplorable condition of Ireland, they did not agree on whether O'Connell's proposed remedy was appropriate. The stand taken against repeal in the early 1830s by Bishop Doyle, at that time the most prominent and outspoken cleric in Ireland, famous as a pamphleteer under the pseudonym 'J.K.L.', reveals attitudes characteristic of vital, indeed dominant, clerical opinion, long after Doyle's death – and O'Connell's. Doyle took the view – which was totally realistic – that repeal was an utterly impracticable demand: England would yield it only to superior force. Consequently he objected strongly to the repeal movement as being both a delusion of the people with false hopes, and a wasting of popular strength in an impossible object, whereas it might have been applied to getting urgent possible reforms, such as abolition of the tithe. Doyle discerned what was undoubtedly the case, that popular support for O'Connell's cause derived from specific grievances about British misgovernment. What really interested Catholic Ireland in the 1830s was the tithe war against the exactions of the Established Church, an agitation which won some success in 1838. Later, the reaction to the poor law system introduced in 1842 helped the repeal cause, as did other grievances from time to time. Doyle blamed the English government's refusal to concede reforms as responsible for making O'Connell all powerful in Ireland, but he also blamed O'Connell's agitation for the English government's refusal to concede reforms.

In 1831 Doyle declared, ' I am an Irishman, hating injustice, and abhorring with my whole soul the oppression of my country; but I desire to heal her sores, not to aggravate her sufferings.' He believed that O'Connell's agitation would do just this: moreover he regarded it as dangerous to religion. If he had to choose, Doyle preferred coercion to anarchy; he feared ' the impious and seditious ' more than ' the iron rule of the constituted authorities '. O'Connell's activities seemed to Doyle to present this choice. In 1831 when O'Connell himself was becoming apprehensive of the forces he had conjured up, Doyle's sermon text seized on the heart of the popular movement: ' Revenge is Mine, I will repay '. Who were the agitators? Doyle asked: ' The most active and prominent among them are old offenders – thieves, liars, drunkards, fornicators, quarrellers, blasphemers – men who have abandoned all the duties of religion. . . .' And O'Connell's sway (' the basest tyranny ') had set these elements free in Ireland: in 1834 Doyle saw ' the tide of irreligion and multitudinous tyranny now being let loose upon us. . . . . I find a dread of the power O'C——— wields to prevail where it ought not, [i.e. among the bishops] and which is likely enough to deter weak-minded individuals from opposing in time what if unchecked may be irresistible.'

There can be no doubt that Doyle – and other bishops – saw O'Connell as a competitor for the leadership of the people. And a successful competitor: through the early 1830s Doyle was admitting that he could not challenge O'Connell's popular sway, though he thought him quite wrong. A competitor too whose arrogance had become inflated to the degree of impiety – Doyle was horrified by O'Connell's claim, before a mass audience in 1831, that he was sent by God to regenerate the country – and a competitor whose influence was turned against religious authority if it sought to curb his movement: 'Ah!' exclaimed Doyle, 'why does he seek at this crisis to weaken my influence with the misguided people whom God confided to my care? Why appeal to the passions of an excitable and ignorant multitude for the purpose of sinking me in their estimation?' The rift between Doyle and O'Connell developed after emancipation: it pointed to the weakness of O'Connell's politico-religious structure when its objectives became political rather than religious – some clergy would follow his lead, others would assert their independence and the primacy of religious objectives.

O'Connell's efforts to secure the Church's support for repeal are evident enough, and were partially successful: they illustrate his unerring discernment of the machinery which controlled popular attitudes in Ireland. But the case of his attempts to gain the backing of Father Mathew's temperance movement is a much more revealing example of the religious response than is, say, the vigorous support of Archbishop MacHale. By the time O'Connell began a new campaign for repeal in 1840, the Catholics of Ireland were being organised and mobilised in another cause, that of temperance. Between 1838 and 1843, Father Mathew preached his mission of temperance in nearly every parish in Ireland, enrolling up to five million members in his Temperance Society. He was very anxious to keep the temperance cause free from any connection with politics: his mission was to all parties and all religions. Consequently he not only refused to commit the Temperance Society to the political involvement so eagerly desired by O'Connell – to whom the vast political potential of such large and disciplined popular forces was obvious – but he also tried to stop Temperance Society members from lending their meeting rooms or brass bands for political purposes. In this he did not have complete success, nor could he prevent O'Connell from joining the temperance procession in Cork in March 1842, a manoeuvre by which O'Connell sought to give the public impression of a happy alliance between Temperance and Repeal: A 'wild joyous shout . . . rent the air as the two great men of Ireland, the political and the moral emancipators of her people, met together!' Although O'Connell did not get the formal alliance he wanted, there is much in the claim of J. F. Maguire, Father Mathew's biographer, that Mathew's temperance campaign made O'Connell's new campaign for repeal possible:

It was to Father Mathew that O'Connell was mainly indebted for the peace and good order which so signally marked those great gatherings, that inspired the apprehension of the Government of the day. . . . O'Connell cherished it [temperance] as a means to his own ends – the accomplishment of the object which required a thoroughly obedient and docile people to lead. And only in a country elevated and purified by Father Mathew's preaching, could the political tribune have found that thoroughly obedient and docile people.'

The German traveller Kohl found the temperance movement of 1842 ' one of the great moral revolutions in history ', which was giving to the Irish ' greater domestic comfort, more order and moral strength and stronger claims and hopes of " National Independence ".' But the point is this. O'Connell's political movement was substantially dependent on a quasi-religious movement over which he had no control (though he had considerable influence over its members). Mathew's biographer notes that Mathew, like Bishop Doyle, was keenly aware that O'Connell's popular influence was unchallengeable: ' he [Mathew] could not fail to be conscious of the fact that, however great and deserved was his [Mathew's] influence, and however much he was loved and venerated by the mass of his countrymen, still, if he attempted to impose restraint or check upon their free action, they would have burst the bonds of allegiance to his moral leadership, and openly disregarded his admonitions, or even his commands.' Similar situations were to confront clerics in Ireland on later occasions: they found it prudent to give popular political loyalties as much scope as they could. But failure to challenge politicians is not to be confused with support for them: O'Connell was able to draw on much of Father Mathew's support, but that was in spite of Mathew, not because of him. In the repeal campaign O'Connell failed to maintain more than a partial alliance between the forces of religion and those of politics.

All this being said, was not the decisive fact a British one, that all British parties, inside and outside Parliament, were unitedly determined to preserve the Union? Repeal lasted as long as it did because Peel feared that immediate repression might be dangerously provocative, not only of Irish opinion, but of British radicals. But it was Peel, in 1834, who put the British position very simply in contradiction to O'Connell's assertion that Ireland had been independent in 1782: ' You never had an independent Parliament, you never can have one consistently with the sovereignty of the British Crown, and the connexion with the island of Great Britain.' And in May 1843, Peel made the position quite explicit:

'Deprecating as I do all war, but, above all, civil war, yet there is no alternative which I do not think preferable to the dismemberment of this empire.' Ireland was bound to England, unless Ireland could seize her independence by force: the Young Ireland revolutionaries were more realistic in this respect than O'Connell. But England was not bound to Ireland. English politicians habitually regarded Ireland as distinct, taking the Union, in practice, as equivalent to the political subjection of a separate entity. This was made abundantly clear during the Famine when the argument that, as Ireland was an integral part of the United Kingdom, the whole kingdom should accept financial responsibility for Ireland's distress, was rejected: the government took the view that Irish poverty must be a tax on Irish property.

It is a truism that by 1847, when O'Connell died, repeal was totally irrelevant to Ireland's major problem, that of starvation. But it is even more true that the whole repeal agitation was utopian and unreal: Britain would not concede it, Ireland was not strong enough to seize it. The fundamental realities of the repeal agitation lay in its utopianism, and in the tensions between religion and politics it revealed in Ireland.

4
The Question of Survival

The ultimate test of any government is – can it, as an absolute minimum, provide the basic needs of those it governs? Put to that test by the famine of 1845-9, the government of the Union failed. The failure can be explained or extenuated: given the dependence of the Irish economy on the potato, perhaps no government, Irish or English, could have avoided the consequences of the blight; perhaps it could be argued that in the famine, Anglo-Irish relations fell victim of a terrible accident. But the government of Ireland was what it was – British. It was bad enough that British rule could not keep the Irish satisfied or happy: now it seemed that British rule could not even keep them alive. Even worse, it seemed that the British sought to let starvation rule in their stead. They had abdicated in favour of death. They would subdue Ireland by the starvation which they allowed, if they had not deliberately contrived.

The famine dealt a blow to Anglo-Irish relations from which they never recovered. It extended the Irish question, through enforced emigration, to many parts of the world, America particularly. It produced an enormous anti-British addition to the edifice of Irish historical mythology. It injected into the relationship a whole new dimension of hatred and bitterness. And it radically changed the Irish situation by destroying the old socio-economic system and revolutionising land-holding.

Emigration, and the world-wide extension of the Irish question had a profound effect on its future history. The old persecuting alternative of Cromwell's day, ' To Hell or Connaught ' reappeared in the modern forms of ' Emigrate or perish ' and ' Apostacise or die '. Materially, many – possibly most – of those who left Ireland were to be better off than they had been before. But the judgements the Irish made were on religious, moral and emotional grounds. To take first the matter of compulsion. In their view, the Irish were being forced to leave their own land, not by some natural disaster or circumstance of fate, but by the British. This impression was confirmed by the setting up by some landlords – for motives both of economy and compassion – of free emigration schemes to the U.S.A. W. Steuart Trench, who organised such schemes on the estates of Lords Landsdowne and Bath, found incomprehensible the bitter hostility which greeted his plans: surely the emigrants would be better off, and so would those left behind? It must be, he concluded, that those who had evaded rent and held land were now being forced to settle their accounts or emigrate: they could cheat no longer, and this realisation provoked their wild anger. However, to the tenants it seemed that it was they who were being cheated, dispossessed of what they had held from time immemorial, by being driven to an unknown land across the sea. To those Irish who took a wider view, emigration seemed a British policy to deprive the Irish of Ireland by simply shipping them away: denude the country of its population and there would be no resistance to British rule.

The process took on the aspect not of emigration, but of mass banishment, a vast inhumanity, made immediate to every Irishman by the destruction it entailed of family units already broken and depleted by famine. Emigration hit at the traditionally strongest unit of Irish society, the family, and so aroused the deepest and most passionate emotions, and moral anger. That fierce anger had a primitive source in the strength of ancient family ties; it also had strong religious sanctions. Whatever the constrained political liberalism of the Irish Church, its central social conservatism remained, and continued to be firmly wedded to support of the family as the basic unit of Christian society. The disruption of the family unit was, in the eyes of Irish Catholicism, a great moral evil, and as the power held responsible, Britain was again cast in a Satanic role.

Emigration was another variant on the old British theme of persecution of religion. Bad enough for those left behind. Worse, much worse, for those emigrant Irish corrupted by the heathen societies into which they were dumped, often to be submerged by vice or drunkenness, a multitude of individual spiritual destructions. There had always been a strong Irish concept of Ireland as a Holy Isle. By providing ample evidence of the destructive effects of other environments, emigration confirmed and deepened this conviction. Ireland was a Christian society: to remain within it was to enjoy all the protective advantages of a world based on faith and morality: to leave it was not only to hazard one's life and fortune, but, far more important, to gravely endanger one's soul. In this way, the traditional Irish religious objection to British rule was sharply intensified. It came to depict British misgovernment, misrule, economc exploitation as directed against a holy society. The effect of British rule, seen through religious eyes, was to disintegrate that holy society, drive its members out into distant wildernesses of infidelity, sin and corruption: British rule was, therefore, a malignant instrumentality of the devil.

Far from solving the Irish question, as some Englishmen hoped, emigration seriously retarded any solution to it, through creating a massive sense of grievance, by damning British intentions still further, and by building another Ireland overseas in which the Irish question was preserved in the desperate condition that had obtained at the time of the emigrants' leaving. The emigrants took overseas with them a picture of Irish affairs which the years, and what was happening in Ireland, did little to soften: indeed it tended to become harsher through contrast with the freedoms of their new world. Driven out in hatred and sorrow, the emigrant nurtured his anger and resentment on a static understanding of the Irish situation, derived largely from his personal experience. Ireland overseas tended to play a retarding role in the development of Anglo-Irish relations because of its anachronistic habit of deriving its own attitudes and emotions from situations long past: only the worst aspects of British policy in Ireland seemed to have a discernible impact on the American Irish. What gave this importance, was that the Irish in America coupled their venoms with means and will to act on them. Whereas the Irish of the famine period had no resources to hit back at what they saw as the causes of their ills, such American Irish as still fed on the emotions of famine Ireland had powerful resources, the immunity of distance, freedom to organise and act, and money, with which to take their revenge. Thereafter, the American Irish fed back into the Irish situation hatred, money, and revolutionary ideas and organisation – and Britain could do little to prevent this. The American dynamic is evident in the Fenian movement, and the overseas Irish generally are prominent in the demand for Home Rule. Less apparent is the fact that the Irish overseas shaped a role for Ireland that acted as a forcing ground for agitation and eventually revolution. After the famine emigration, the Irish in Ireland moved on a world stage, with an audience composed mostly of their relatives – a family which expected a vigorous performance, even when the Irish were not particularly inclined to give it. British reforms may have won more quietude in Ireland had it not been that the Irish felt it necessary to live up to an image and aspirations imposed on them by cousins overseas. The Irish American press constituted a much more unrestrained, aggressively nationalist anti-British force than did the press of Ireland itelf. And, of course, the freedom and prosperity which many Irish found in America and the British colonies provided a real point of contrast with what existed in Ireland. In indignation or patronage they fed this contrast back into Ireland unceasingly, urging that the Irish should, could or must improve their own situation so as to achieve equality of status with Irishmen living elsewhere: there can be little doubt that many of the overseas Irish felt that their homeland's subjection to Britain was an affront to their own dignity.

But to return to the famine itself: what took place and how it was interpreted was of great formative (or deformative) importance for the future. The famine provided the background for the 1848 rebellion; it was the setting for Young Ireland at its apogee – and Young Ireland produced a literature of remarkable and enduring popular power and influence. Young Irelanders were insisting in the *Nation* in 1847, that the famine and the poor law were deliberately devised to ensure that a nation 'which once numbered nine millions may be checked in its growth and coolly, gradually murdered'. The famine was ideal material for revolutionary propaganda, and the Young Irelanders' interpretation of it was given a continuing popular life by John Mitchel. In his *Jail Journal, History of Ireland* and *The Last Conquest of Ireland, Perhaps,* Mitchel enshrined the image of England as murderer: 'that million and a half men, women and children, were carefully, prudently, and peacefully *slain* by the English government.' Gavan Duffy went past this indictment to point the lesson – 'the fault is not England's, but our own. It is the right of the Irish people, and their sacred duty, to protect themselves against all aggressors on the face of the earth.' This interpretation of the famine became a component part of the Irish revolutionary tradition: a policy of deliberate starvation justified extreme

counter-measures. By the twentieth century, Irish revolutionary nationalists took it for granted, to use Arthur Griffith's words of 1913, 'that
the English Government was deliberately using the pretext of the
failure of the potato crop to reduce the Celtic population by famine and
exile.' The exultant fringe of English response was still being quoted
after 1916 – the triumph of an English newspaper: 'The Celts are gone,
gone with a vengeance! The Lord be praised!'; the grim satisfaction of
Sir Charles Trevelyan, in charge of Irish relief, that the famine was a
divine punishment on a wicked and perverse Irish people. The myth of
genocide had become part of Irish history: the English stood convicted
of an attempt to wipe out the Irish race – not, as before, Irish armies,
or Irish agitators, but the whole people. The figures could not be
denied: in 1841, over 8 million, in 1851, 6½, and so on, to 3½ million
in 1966. Those whose temper would not allow them to draw the lesson
of violent revolution, concluded that if the famine was not designedly
murderous, it demonstrated that the English government was incompetent
or criminally negligent, or inhumanly dedicated to the service of economic
laws contrived to build England's wealth: money meant more than life.
F. H. O'Donnell, in his *A History of the Irish Parliamentary Party*
published in 1910, saw the famine as 'a terrible failure of government
by England', which dealt 'the fatal blow . . . to the whole of the Conservative forces in Ireland at that period'. According to O'Donnell, the
question asked by those who lived through the famine was: 'What is
the intelligence or utility of British Government in Ireland?' It may be
doubted if many put the question so elegantly or so politely, but it is
certain that the famine united Irishmen in raising a great and simple
question mark against the record of British rule.

It cannot be denied that famine Ireland was, to some considerable
extent, the victim of British *laissez-faire* economic theory as expressed in
politics and administration. The realities of the Irish disaster were buried
underneath the bitter parliamentary wrangles the demand for Irish
relief provoked, the battle between free trade and protection. Engrossed in
the general principles at stake, English politicians neglected the actual
situation in Ireland, or disputed its extent and seriousness. One of
Trevelyan's agents said to him: 'You cannot answer the cry of want by
a quotation from political economy' – the indictment might have been
made of all Englishmen who believed that economic conditions must
be left to follow their own laws, without interference, or held generally
that the state had no responsibility or right to intervene. This concept
of the state gravely hindered any effective response to Ireland's calamity:
when the state did act to distribute food, and thus break the laws of

political economy, it did so most reluctantly. It could be argued, then, that the British cannot be held to blame: their response was within the thinking of the time and they cannot be censured for not thinking in terms of state involvement not yet contemplated. Yet, the question has been asked, would adherence to *laissez-faire* have been so firm had famine occurred within England? Distance from Ireland's famine and ignorance of it were undoubtedly factors which made it seem less urgent in England. But there was more than that. Mrs Woodham-Smith has remarked, ' It is impossible to read the letters of British statesmen of the period . . . without astonishment at the influence exerted by antago-nism and irritation on government policy in Ireland during the famine.' In the British view, the famine was caused by the potato blight. It was a natural calamity intensified by Ireland's economic situation. Trench saw the cause of all the misery as the pernicious system of sub-division and sub-letting of land, which neither landlords nor their agents could prevent: it was an Irish fault. The English who took this view saw good in the famine, as effecting, naturally if horrifyingly, the obvious solution to the Irish land problem – clearance and depopulation to effect a proper, natural, economic balance. Nor is it too harsh to say that some Englishmen who desired Ireland to remain quiet were not particularly concerned if the stillness which prevailed in Ireland was that of empti-ness and death: Thomas Carlyle wrote, ' Ireland is like a half-starved, rat, that crosses the path of an elephant. What must the elephant do? Squelch it – by heavens – squelch it.' The Irish accusation that Eng-land was responsible for the famine was met by blank incomprehension and hostility. Worse, the famine further soured the British public mind against the Irish, whose distress, mingled with incorrigible violence (as seen in the 1848 rebellion), attracted more British contempt than com-passion.

The conviction that England had inflicted the starvation on Ireland became an integral part of Irish history. That this interpretation was a political contrivance rather than a natural popular reaction may be gathered from studies of Irish folk tradition, which suggest that many ordinary Irish people took the famine to be a Divine punishment for their own shortcomings – sin, waste in days of plenty, intemperance. This is an interesting testimony to the dominantly religious rather than political cast of the popular Irish mind, but it was the political interpre-tation which had dynamic importance: it provided a simple, readily in-telligible explanation of a vast, complex occurrence (and so was an alternative to the divine punishment thesis); it drew on the deepest emotions of hatred; and it was the version promoted by popular political heroes. Besides, it linked in neatly with one aspect of popular religious emotion intensified by the famine – anti-Protestantism. For, out of Irish folk tradition there emerges, clear and burning, fierce hatred of official charity, given through Protestant stores, by degrading methods, sometimes only in return for abjuring Catholicism. Meat soup was offered on Fridays to starving Catholics by Protestant ' soupers '. Some Protestants would provide relief to Catholics only if they attended Protestant churches, schools or lectures, denied the main tenets of Catholicism, or offered insults to statues of the Blessed Virgin. The association of food distribution with proselytism burnt anti-Protestantism even deeper into Irish life. Religious conflicts and riots were common at the time, but the intangible injury endured down the years. This proposition stood proved in Irish minds: Protestant England would exterminate those it could, and convert the survivors to damnable heresy by ordeal by starvation. Here was a people that could remember savagely, Foster, a landlord's agent who used to turn away his head when speaking to Catholics, and in whom the determination to die in consecrated ground was so strong that the famished could be seen dragging themselves to graveyards. On the local level, in the everyday affairs of a starving people, the famine meant a war against death – and against Protestantism.

The famine made the Irish land question inescapable, and thus eventually involved the peasantry directly in politics. With this, the balance of Anglo-Irish relations altered, as both Catholicism and violence became more centrally involved on the Irish side. The entry of the peasantry into agitation on land issues, largely leaderless, or with no one leader, meant the appearance of a force of great potential power, not only a force which might be harnessed and used, but a force which would to some extent dictate its own terms. In the future, Irish nationalists could scarcely ignore this vast force, nor, if they wished to mobilise it, avoid contriving a popular ideology, one that made meaningful contact with mass grievances: a 1782 constitution was thereafter irrelevant. Because the peasantry was Catholic, its political emergence meant that nationalism must become Catholic, at least in some general sense. Thereafter Protestant nationalism became impossible (though not Protestant nationalists) and the Catholic Church itself occupied a much more central place in the development of Irish affairs. And because the peasantry was the peasantry, their increased importance in Ireland lent greater weight to primitivism, simplicity and violence as dynamic forces in Irish demands. With their entry onto the political stage, the possibility – never great – of a rational, ordered and peaceful solution to the problems of the Anglo-Irish relationship receded sharply. The likelihood

increased that Ireland would demand more than a settlement of grievances: it would seek vengeance as well. Yet at the same time, the
emergence of the peasantry threatened conservative interests in Ireland
itself. It was the great achievement of the Church, and the Irish middle
and educated classes, to channel much of that force away from socio-
economic revolution and towards political nationalism.

5
The Land Question

Historically, the questions of land and religion were inextricably mixed
in Anglo-Irish relations. The religious division was reflected in the land
situation – Protestant landlords, Catholic tenants. Just as religious conflict had produced economic division, so did any challenge to the
economic structure have religious implications. On a superficial appraisal,
it may seem a straining of the case to characterise the land question as
anything more, or other, than economic: at the obvious level it is
economic. Yet it would be to perpetrate an absurdity to distinguish
between the issue and the human beings agitated by the issue – and
then to go on to disregard the human beings. Agitation against an
economic structure based on religious distinction inevitably went to the
basis of the structure: to challenge the structure was to challenge its
foundations, and to repudiate its foundations left no justification for
the structure. If the land question was economic, the form it had taken
was determined by religion. Indeed the question existed on two closely
related levels – as one of the relationship between landlords and tenants;
and as one both expressing and symbolising the domination of Irish
Catholics by English or Anglo-Irish Protestants – but it is artificial to
make such a distinction. Given that the land situation combined real,
immediate, individual economic grievance, with deep religious antagonism, it was a very explosive one. For the Irish peasantry, the land
question was bound up with their identity. The land was their world,
involving their sense of self: their relationship to the land paralleled in
temporal affairs their feeling of the spiritual immediacy of God – the
church and the land provided their meaningful environment.

It was in the land grievance that Irish millennialism had sunk its
deepest roots, from which all Irish agitation drew sustenance. Ultimately,
Irish land agitation was directed not towards reform of the existing land

system, but towards its abolition. The peasantry wanted not good land-lords, but none: it wanted full control over land which it regarded traditionally as its own. How far such attitudes bred or sustained a wish not for good English government, but for complete independence is impossible to determine: given the sharp decline of peasant ' utopianism ' and agitation after the 1903 Land Act, it is obvious that there was no dependant link at that time between separatists who wanted an independent Ireland and peasants who wanted an independent peasantry. However, the close parallel is obvious, as is also the similarity of English reactions to both sets of grievances, economic and political. In the early nineteenth century, the English tended to see land agitation as the product of Irish savagery. Peel, for instance, saw agrarian disturbances as ' the acts of a set of human beings very little advanced from barbarism '. The obvious remedy was to civilise such savages, so Peel, while Chief Secretary in Ireland 1812-18, directed much of his energy to establishing a police force and magistrature. In the second half of the century, when the English were prepared to find fault with their own Irish policy, the remedies proposed remained within the boundaries of reform: such abuses as absentee landlordism were criticised, not only for themselves, but even more because they provoked the Irish to anti-British reactions. It was not landlordism that caused Irish discontent, so such reformers argued, but its abuses: it was not British rule that antagonised the Irish, but British misrule. Shelving the main question, and turning to that of the land, the situation was simply that Irish and English minds did not meet, let alone accord. What seemed to the peasant a basic natural fact – that the land was his – seemed absurd and outrageous to the English.

To return to the central role of religion, it is evident that the origins of the nineteenth century Irish land situation were historically religious – Protestant conquest and the penal laws. The removal of those penal laws – notably in Catholic emancipation – opened up the Protestant dominated economic structure to challenge: the land agitation was, in a sense, a continuation of the Catholic emancipation crusade into the economic sphere – Catholic religious emancipation led on naturally to demands for Catholic economic emancipation. Trench discerned the radical tension in Ireland as this: ' Ireland will never rise against England. *It's one half of Ireland must rise against the other half* – the Catholics who haven't the land, against the Protestants who have.' His observation was accurate, save that he failed to see that England was identified with the Protestant ' other half '.

Nevertheless, on the face of it, here is a peasants' struggle against landlords, motivated by material self-interest. Certainly the question of ownership of the land was vital, but in much more than simple material terms: the existing structure of land ownership represented to the Irish both conquest and religious persecution. However, from the landlords' viewpoint, the land question was simply one of property. Just as claims for state intervention to ameliorate the famine had challenged fundamental economic principles, so did demands for land reform challenge fundamental rights of property on which, they believed, the right ordering of society was based. To see this defence of property rights as crude self-interest is to miss its strength. The cliché phrase ' the sanctity of property ' had real meaning in describing the lynch-pin of a concept of civilisation in which property-holding was sacred, the mark of worth, and fundamental to a right-ordered hierarchical society. On such a premise, attacks or any kind of limitation or control on property were anarchic, barbarous and destructive, and indeed immoral in that they struck at the roots of right social order. Such attitudes might fairly be called a religion of property, to which England's political classes were firm devotees – firmer than they were devotees to religion as such. Landowning in Ireland had been erected on the basis of religious profession and religious debarment. There had been those who had seen that the removal of Catholic debarment from public life in 1829, made more difficult its retention in economic life; but they were utterly determined to defend their economic position, not merely because of self-interest, for survival, but because they believed that the coherence and operation of the kind of civilised society they knew and valued was dependent on property.

In England property-holders exercised enormous influence because the fundamental structures of English society were all of a piece, and were closely related to economic power and respect for economic power. In Ireland the principle of social coherence was religious. There the churches of a religion opposed to that of the landlords were the vital social centres, the points of peasant assembly, the places where public notices were posted. This religious rift sharpened the antagonism between property and democracy to an acute edge, and eventually threw the whole British political system into hazard; the anarchy of the Protestant landlords was, as the Ulster crisis of 1911-14 ultimately demonstrated, more dangerous to the constitution than the agitation of a Catholic peasantry. The democratic constitutional principle of one man one vote had no appeal to landlords, and they were tolerably reconciled to its implementation only in circumstances where they could exercise what they regarded as appropriate political influence. In the typical landlord's estimate, his status, his education and his stake in the country made it absurd and unendurable that he should have no more political power than an ignorant impoverished peasant tenant. The situation in England itself allowed a landlord to extend his constitutional powers of one vote by what he regarded as natural influence – sometimes benevolent, sometimes coercive – over his tenantry. Not so in Ireland. There the religious barrier frustrated it, to the indignation and rage of landlords. Backed by the priesthood, the tenantry often resisted attempts by landlords to direct their votes, asserting constitutional democratic rights to the alarm of the landlords already worried by agrarian unrest. It was the religious cleavage that prevented landlords from exercising in Ireland that influence which would have made the growth of constitutional democracy more tolerable to them. So they came to detest, to the point of rejection, the development of constitutional democracy because they could exercise no control over it; and they came all the more to hate, with blind fury, the religion which placed the masses beyond their influence. It was merely a matter of time before the Protestant Ascendancy staged their own rebellion: it would occur when all their defences against the tides of democracy had fallen – and this was to be in 1911 when the House of Lords was deprived of its veto powers. Meanwhile, that Ascendancy continued to attempt to wield such power and influence as it regarded natural, efforts which met increasing resistance and stronger assertions of democratic rights – and so the gulf continued to widen.

Some Irishmen drew from the famine the simple nationalist lesson that Ireland's problems lay in her subjection to Great Britain. There was another lesson to be drawn, and one of the Young Irelanders, James Fintan Lalor, drew it – that the social and economic system was the root of Ireland's evils, that the agrarian situation and landlordism were responsible. This interpretation, blaming the economic system rather than the governmental system for Ireland's ills, remained influential, obtruding notably again in James Connolly: 'No man who accepts capitalist society and the laws thereof can logically find fault with the statesmen of England for their acts in that awful [famine] period.' Given its inferiority in the field of force, Irish agitation was substantially compelled, in practice, to act on this socio-economic interpretation, seeking reform and amelioration of the existing system. Britain, faced with Irish discontent, was, up to the 1880s, totally committed to the unqualified maintenance of the existing political relationship with Ireland: consequently the only alternative British policies were repression, and social and economic reform. Such reform could pacify Ireland on two conditions only – that the fundamental and major causes of Irish unrest were social and economic, and that the extent of reform was sufficient to dispel grievances. Neither of these conditions was met.

This book is given to the argument that religion was the fundamental barrier to harmonious Anglo-Irish relations: here it is necessary to discuss the extent of the major area of socio-economic reform, that relating to the land. The land question was one on which the British attitude was particularly unyielding. Going to the heart of British conservatism, any concession towards the tenantry met firm resistance, notably in the House of Lords. It might not be too much to say that the Irish land agitation determined the Lords' reaction to the entirety of the Irish question. For them it raised not merely principles and interests in Ireland, but generally; for – as with so many Irish matters – to concede Irish demands might be to invite similar demands within England. So, incompetent, irresponsible, harsh or impoverished Irish landlords could rely on the support of English conservatism to resist what might be described as 'natural' socio-economic changes and to preserve situations conducive to agrarian revolution. Such was the general situation; the post-famine development of agrarian agitation in Ireland revealed other problems.

The first organised agitation centred around the Tenant League, founded in August 1850, which drew together Liberal politicians and local tenant protection societies that had been formed in the late 1840s, often under clerical guidance, with the aim of securing fair rents. The Tenant League aimed to build up an independent Irish parliamentary party to fight for land reform, but this party was soon destroyed by the English political situation, which made no room for a party with Irish claims. However, it is indicative of the great importance of the land issue that it was on this that the first aspirations to Irish party independence were based. Significant too is Cardinal Cullen's view that this party had Catholic aims in that it sought ' to remove all the burdens that weigh on the Catholics of Ireland '. He disagreed with its tactics of opposing any government which would not undertake such a removal: ' If all Catholics were to unite in adopting such principles, I am persuaded that the English government in self-defence would have to expel them from parliament, and begin to renew the penal laws.'

Cullen's view that this land reform party had direct Catholic relevance is further illustration of the totality of the Church's involvement in Irish affairs, and indicates his belief that any activity by Irishmen would have repercussions on religion: political intransigence on the issue of land reform would lead to revival of the penal laws. And the

Cardinal was in a position to make his opinion operative. The Tenant League depended vitally on clerical support, to the extent that Cullen's efforts in 1854 to limit the activities of the clergy in politics were seen as potentially fatal to the League. Frederick Lucas appealed to Rome against Cullen, but here religious considerations won out over the political and Irish opinion backed Cullen. In fact Cullen did not want to take the priesthood out of politics: priests were instructed to secure the election of 'men of integrity and favourable to the Catholic religion'. What he wanted was the clergy to withdraw from merely secular politics, in which their energies were used for secular ends, and take up Catholic politics, with religious purposes, standards and principles firmly in mind. He believed that the tactics of the Tenant League bred discord among Catholics, and favoured the candidature of Protestants – to which he was totally (and obsessively) opposed. It is hardly surprising that the episcopate of Cullen did not see any reduction in sectarian animus in politics. Trench remarked of the mid 1860s: 'I know of nothing more detrimental to the peace and prosperity of a district than an election for Members of Parliament . . . . The worst passions of the people are aroused to their utmost pitch on both sides, and sectarian animosity and virulence seem, demon-like, to possess the whole community.'

The Independent Irish Party and the Tenant League demonstrated the crucial importance of the Church in politics and in the land question. Their fate also laid down what was to be a law of Irish parliamentary activity, that Irish parliamentarians were compelled to substantially accept the British political structure and party system if they were to survive at all. British politics would give no recognition to an independent Irish party concerned with Irish grievances alone, and in simple political terms, perpetual opposition was absurd. Any Irish party within the British Parliament would have to tailor its demands and its behaviour to what that Parliament would tolerate, despite whatever it was the Irish wanted. Sooner or later, if the gap between what the Irish wanted and what the British were prepared to concede remained obviously unbridged, Irish parliamentary politicians would be revealed, whatever they might say or do, as tantamount to that political absurdity – a perpetual opposition. In a crude way, the Independent Irish Party of the 1850s put the crucial question – could English parliamentary procedures and structures accept and contain the realities of the Irish situation. That party assumed that a radically effective balance of power role in British politics was possible on Irish issues. It was not then, nor was it to be later: reforms and concessions might be gained by this tactic, but ultimately, when faced with the full extent of Irish claims, all divisions within the British political system drew together in a common resistance.

From the late 1840s, the swing in Irish agitation towards the land question did much more than drive landowners to dig themselves in to defend the rights of property: even more importantly it damned the Irish even further in the eyes of British opinion because it exhibited the Irish question as a peasant question. A nation of shopkeepers, devotees of the cult of progress, prosperity and industrialism, looked down with contempt and dismay at a rabble of primitive peasants. The traditional English view of the Irishman as a savage was rapidly strengthened as the industrial revolution took nineteenth century England far ahead of Ireland in those respects equated by the English with civilisation. As the agrarian agitation in Ireland became more strident, so did the depiction of the typical Irishman made by William Carleton in *Traits and Stories of the Irish Peasantry* (1830-33) become the stereotype, through constant journalistic repetition, of the accepted English image – the ape-like violent Paddy who shared the characteristics of his own pigs. And this image rapidly shed what elements of charm and quaintness it originally possessed: more and more the Irish seemed to be revealed as essentially barbarous, not only wild enemies of civilised property holding, but also prone to inhuman atrocities.

Agrarian atrocities were an integral part of Irish history, but the entry of the peasantry as a mass force into the political arena from 1850 elevated what had been a casual aspect of Irish life into something of a general principle of agitation presuming to the dignity of a political programme. By 1850, as Trench's descriptions make clear, Irish agrarian relations had degenerated into a condition resembling guerilla warfare. The famine period 1845-9 saw a great falling off in agrarian outrage as starvation displaced the landlord as ruler of rural Ireland. But after the famine, by way of reaction, and as land sale legislation attracted speculators and raised rentals, violence became much more prevalent than before. Trench illustrates the situation vividly in recounting the simple vindictive triumph of the peasantry in some petty frustration of the landlord, and in describing the celebratory bonfires lit across estates upon the death or killing of a land agent. Everywhere there was fear and the threat of violence. Trench recounts that tenants went down on their knees to him to beg a reduction in rent – ' It was fearful to see the attitude of supplication, due only to a higher power, thus mingled with a wild defiance '. Here were ' wild-looking men ', gabbling to themselves in their primitive tongue, unable to make themselves understood, unpredictable, ultimately murderous. Warned of a plot on his life, Trench found this incomprehensible: he regarded himself as a kind, liberal man

who had done nothing but his duty – he had put it to his landlords'
tenants, either pay their rent, or take a free passage to America. It
was absurd that the peasantry believed they should pay no rent at all,
that the land was really theirs, stolen by the English from their ancestors
– and it was barbarous that, in their determination to cling to the land,
they were willing to murder those who sought to evict them. English
concepts of law and property left no place for the assertion by the peasants of their own fundamental law, their only recourse, the law of violence
against what they regarded as theft and inhumanity, a deprivation of
livelihood which could lead to starvation.

On their side, the land-owning gentry never travelled alone in rural
Ireland, but in groups, with armed guards. Trials were dominated by
landlords and by the determination to obtain convictions. Executions were
public. Some English newspapers, hostile to the Established Church, had
seen the collection of tithes in the 1830s as ' the war of the parson against
the peasant ', in which ministers of religion led groups of armed bailiffs
on tithe-gathering expeditions. But few among the English saw the degeneration of rural relations after 1850 as a war of the landlord against
the peasant. No, they saw it as the reverse, though they were dismayed
by the cruelties and violence to which they were reduced in response.

The mobilisation of the peasantry for political purposes produced
hardened attitudes on both sides of the Irish Sea. To the British the
Irish peasant was both humanly repellent and representative of a
socio-economic order to which contemporary English thought was totally
opposed. The existence of a peasantry, let alone its claim for recognition,
was an affront to progressive economic theory which regarded the
peasantry as a regressive force, obstructing the course of social and
economic progress. Much English resistance to the demands of the
Irish peasantry sprang from the conviction that to give in to those
demands would be to do Ireland a disservice. However difficult and
painful it might be for those involved, eviction – so as to allow for
efficient, consolidated, large-scale farming – would be of great ultimate
economic benefit. So ran the Utilitarian argument. In such English
eyes, the emergence of peasant Ireland was a brutal reminder of just
how backward Ireland was: it was a duty to civilisation to concede it
nothing. However, the emergence of the peasant meant the establishment in Ireland of a resource of which the English hitherto had a virtual
monopoly – the threat of violence. The swing towards the land question
confirmed the pattern in which emancipation had been won and established the politics of violence: rural disorder to the degree of anarchy
became the main prompt for British policy in Ireland. The pattern

of British reform or coercion in response to violence became established. This response in so far as it produced reform encouraged violence by confirming its efficacy, and so also bred counter-violence in which landlords and their agents were drawn further into the maelstrom of atrocity, pulling the forces of government with them as far as they could. In so far as the British response to violence was coercive, the most it achieved was a lull before violence broke out again. This situation reached a peak of intensity in the so-called Land War of the 1880s, and again in 1919-21, but it was endemic, always existing, more or less.

The peculiar character of Irish peasant violence is important: it had a strong and ferocious bias towards vengeance. Its roots went deep back into Irish history – territory unknown to the English. Trench was astonished to find among the peasantry the belief that ancient Irish families would recover their forfeited estates: he was amazed to come across a map published in 1846 which professed to show land possessed by Irish chieftains from the eleventh to the seventeenth centuries. A few Englishmen – and notably Gladstone – came to recognise that Irish peasants believed that the land was theirs: most found it absolutely incomprehensible that several centuries of English ownership had not obliterated entirely even the dim memory of Irish holdings. Even if they had not, and Irish delusions of having rights to the soil remained, England could neither countenance nor recognise them – a point forcefully made by the Duke of Argyll to Gladstone in January 1870: 'I hope you will consider *very carefully* before you quote ancient Celtic usages, in a Barbarous condition of Society, as having any practical bearing upon our Legislation in the present day. If the known and admitted principles of Law on which Property and Occupation have been based for at least two centuries are not to be admitted as having obliterated "Tribal Rights" &c, &c, there can be no repose in Political Society.' But repose could not be achieved by denying ancient Celtic usages. Indeed, it was that denial which provoked turbulence, and fed the desire for redress and revenge. The prevalence of murder in Ireland shocked Englishmen. Trench pointed accurately to one of its major causes: 'In Ireland that dreadful crime may almost invariably be traced to a wild feeling of revenge for the national wrong, to which so many of her sons believe that she has been subjected for centuries.' To peasants, the national wrong was the land situation: Ireland, particularly peasant Ireland, was poisoned by this sense of wrong. Beneath the surface of Irish society, not far beneath, was a great reservoir of primitive violence which kept bubbling up in riots, outrages and atrocities. The entry of the land question into the political arena curbed and sublimated that violence, but it did not destroy it entirely nor satisfy its thirst for revenge. It merely suppressed it. As W. B. Yeats was to say of the outcry that in 1907 greeted J. M. Synge's depiction of the raw crudity of Irish peasant life in *The Playboy of the Western World*, Irish life had been dressed up by its political leaders to suit, as far as possible, English taste: in Synge's true peasantry, the buried fire burst the surface, ' an explosion of all that had been denied or refused '.

Denial and refusal of the crude violence and hatred that burnt deep in Ireland's peasant world was central to the whole Irish parliamentary movement, and, it could be argued, the fundamental reason for that movement's ultimate failure. Between 1916 and 1923 the buried violence and brutality found an outlet. But long before this, Irish pressure on Britain had developed two parallel forms, the primitive and the sophisticated. The peasantry wanted a radical change in the relationship with Britain for natural, primitive, religious and economic reasons: the peasant image of Britain was more that of a Protestant landlord than that of a foreign power. In contrast, the Irish middle classes and intellectuals sought an adjustment of the relationship for civilised, conceptualised, ideological reasons. The Home Rule movement expressed fully only the latter of the two strands: it never completely satisfied nor contained the other, though, particularly under Parnell, it did much to both harness and subdue it. In this sense, the Irish parliamentary movement was not a profoundly Irish movement. While it expressed (in an English context) civilised non-violent national aspirations, it did not satisfy the primitive beliefs and urges that impelled the peasantry. The Gaelic revival did much to bring about an understanding between civilised and primitive Irishry, but violence alone could forge real links between nationalist ideals and a mass dynamic. Fenianism began to attempt that process, but was prevented by religious condemnation. But although the Church could destroy a movement (yet its succes was not total and Fenianism simmered on) it could not prevent an unexpected explosion, such as occurred in 1916. Certainly the extent to which the Church and, in the later period, the Home Rule movement controlled, subdued and sublimated the latent violence of Ireland under the Union is remarkable. However, once violence began, its tendency was to accelerate out of control to satisfy that need inherent in its nature to take a vengeance. Whatever its origin in principles, the Irish Civil War of 1921-3 is also rooted in thwarted violence. Frustrated in 1921 in their determination to vent vengeance on the English, the Irish took vengeance on themselves.

To note the reluctance of any English government, devoted to *laissez-*

faire principles, to alter traditional land policy is to see one order of realities: to recognise that it was impossible to persuade the landlords to concede what the peasants wanted, and impossible to satisfy the peasants with less, is to see another. Did the protracted debates and discussions on Irish land reform touch the heart of the problem? It has been claimed that ' What Irish agriculture needed, above all else, was an infusion of capital '. On a modern economic view perhaps this is so – and if it is, the problem was insoluble, given the poverty and incapacity of Irish landlords, and British opposition to state subsidies or investment. Was the Irish land question (in J. C. Beckett's words) ' how was Irish agriculture to be improved to a point at which it could provide adequate support for the population dependent on it? For the next half-century this question, in various forms occupied a central position in Irish politics '. However vital this question of economic development was, however in the forefront of the minds of humanitarians and liberals, it was essentially an English question. The question which fundamentally agitated Ireland was much more simple, much more primitive – land ownership. British politicians (and Irish) spent a great deal of time and ingenuity in avoiding or diluting the harsh truth that the peasants wanted the land. Such crude simplicities obtrude more frequently in the thinking of those opposed to Irish land reform than in the minds of those radicals in Britain, like J. S. Mill, who advocated it. To postulate that Irish discontent sprang from rural poverty was natural to British radicals who saw social order as a product of economic progress. *The Times* might describe the radical economic programme as the advocating of flagrant acts of iniquity, in its trespassing on private property, but radicals and conservatives both supported the Union. The radicals' reasoning was an even more fundamental denial of any possibility of Ireland's solving her problems in an Irish way: they did not believe Ireland capable of progress if left to herself, and to them progress, not property, was the sacred fundamental law of human existence. Parallel to the traditional view that the Union was necessary for England's good, developed the conviction that it was necessary for Ireland's good also. No religious group in England, neither those who worshipped property, nor those whose God was progress, nor those whose God was Protestant, could admit of an Ireland serving any God but theirs.

So, like all Irish affairs, the land question became the victim of English politics acted out on Unionist assumptions. What emerged as land reforms were not the outcome of informed deliberation, but political decisions, the results of tests of violence in Ireland and of political strength in England: England did not produce solutions, but fragmentary political compromises. The real devilment of Irish affairs is that they split English parties and even cabinets into antagonistic groups with a consistency that thwarted the emergence of even partially aborted schemes.

If England had satisfied the peasantry, perhaps she would have held Ireland – but the speculation is unreal, for the peasantry wanted even more than possession of the land, and even that was well beyond what England was prepared to give. But perhaps there was no need for English policy to have cast the Irish peasantry so firmly in the role of social radicals, enemies of property and social order. The coercive side of English policy pressed rural agitation deep into the soil where it germinated in a flourishing multitude of agrarian secret societies and became a reservoir of anarchy. The Wyndham Land Act solved the land question a generation too late. By 1903 rural anarchy had ceased to be a way of life, but it had become an ineradicable Irish habit of mind.

Viewed in the context of the politics of Anglo-Irish relations, Gladstone's Land Act of 1870 is a momentous event, regulating relations between landlord and tenant, providing for the recognition of the principle of some security of tenure, and of tenant right to compensation for improvements and disturbance; more, its implications were of great importance – limitation of landlord power, state intervention in economic affairs. Measured on a British scale, these steps were of the greatest importance; measured on an Irish scale – that is, against what was wanted – it may have been a moral victory, but it was, in practice, a cheat. The Act failed to stop rackrenting and unjust evictions. The courts that administered the Act were expensive and landlord oriented. Consequently the Act had little conciliatory value, and in fact acted as a goad to agitation for effective reform. Moreover any measure which regulated the landlord brought the government into greater direct involvement in the Irish situation, into confronting the problems of Irish society. To embark on the reduction of landlord power, as the 1870 Act did, entailed the substitution of government power, in the form of legislation or coercion. The natural outcome was to draw Irish problems into the British political system at an accelerating pace: the bogs of Ireland were more in the nature of quicksand for legislators – and the greater the British activity, the more was Irish attention focused on the really ultimate reality of power in Ireland, that is, the British connection.

The Act of Union had been a declaration of no-confidence in the Protestant Ascendancy as governors; the 1870 Land Act was a first declaration of no-confidence in them as landlords. Though its purpose was to help pacify rural Ireland, its immediate effect, in limiting landlord power, was to weaken the traditional power structures of Irish life. A substitute had to be found to preserve the rural order: the Land Act was accompanied by a Coercion Act. The 1870 Act clearly revealed the basic problems of Irish reform. So far did it fall short of Irish demands, that it worsened the Irish temper, producing not so much disappointment as fury. On the English side it represented the most Parliament could be brought to accept, demonstrating to the Irish how little England was prepared to do, frustrating Gladstone and inducing alarm and rage among conservatives (Disraeli attacked the Act as undermining property rights) and hardening their resolve to resist further reforms. The whole affair demonstated that Irish reform would not be considered on its own merits – as Irish measures – but on the general principles it raised in English minds. Sydney Smith once remarked. 'The moment the very name of Ireland is mentioned, the English seem to bid adieu to common feeling, common prudence and common sense, and to act with the barbarity of tyrants and the fatuity of idiots.' The explanation for this phenomenon is complex, but in the political sphere one major reason for this kind of behaviour lies in Ireland's radical non-conformity with the accepted norms and foundation principles of English life: a political structure which reflected English life, and was designed to govern it, could not cope with demands both foreign to and contradictory of its own rationale. Demands that the English political system produce reforms for Ireland brought out the worst in English politicians to whom such claims were a rude intrusion, and a constant affront to their ideas of what should be. The Union implied assumptions of homogeneity which were quite unfounded. So each reform, or attempted reform, drove England and Ireland further apart – not simply because too little was conceded too late, but because the continuing process of Irish demands and English consideration of them became a mutual tutelage in, and revelation of, the basic irreconcilable differences between the two peoples.

6

The Question of a Revolutionary Tradition

As a potential seedbed for revolutionary nationalism, nineteenth century Ireland offered a contradictory environment: the relationship with England provided a most congenial soil for its growth, but the ideological climate of Ireland, its vigorous, pervasive Catholicism, was hostile to it. In Ireland, Catholicism lived in the soil together with the urge towards violent rebellion: for mass revolutionary action it was necessary that there be, or appear to be, some reconciliation (even if only to the degree of subsidence of direct opposition) between Catholicism and revolutionary movements. Until such congruity was achieved – in 1916 – it was natural that the two most dynamic powers within Ireland, the Church and the peasant masses, would merge their energies and differences in a working compromise – constitutional nationalism. This compromise was logical, but not necessarily permanent or immutable, because one of its elements, the attitude of the Catholic Church, was subject not to absolute principles, but to historical variables. The circumstances of the nineteenth century, in which revolutionary movements in Europe laid siege to both church and state, led the Church to put aside that aspect of its traditional teaching which asserted the morality, under certain conditions, of rebellion against oppressive state authority. European revolutionary movements were seen as anti-religious, and the Irish Church supported the Papacy in the defence of existing governments against all revolutionary threats. But the revolutionary movements had considerable success and became the governments with which the Church had to live and deal, and the Papacy's loss of its temporal power removed the strongest practical reason to support the principle of legitimacy: times and circumstances changed. Moreover, in Ireland, the compromise represented by constitutional nationalism had never been a very happy one, less and less so as the century came to an end. On the practical level, it had not produced the results hoped for; on the ideological level it was losing support in two crucial areas – among intellectuals, and in the Church. The alienation of the intellectuals, which took them away from the Home Rule Party and towards 1916, was paralleled by a similar alienation within the church: the development of the constitutional nationalist movement came to be seen as threatening both the religious purity of the Irish people and the sway of the Church. It is not necessarily banal to emphasise that the 1916 rebellion was directed not only against England, but against the parliamentary party as the arbiter of Irish affairs: it was a bid for a new direction and a new leadership within Ireland, and crucial to its eventual mass success was the fact that the old direction and old leadership had discredited itself in the eyes of the Church. The peculiar religious dynamic of Irish Catholicism had not found a satisfactory expression in the constitutional movement. Revolutionary nationalism was the only alternative.

The modern Irish revolutionary nationalist tradition is usually taken as beginning with the 1798 rebellion. This has some obvious truth in that what little modern ideology the rebellion had was partly derived from the French and American revolutions. But the rebellion points backward as well as forward in that the Ulster rising was Presbyterian, the Wexford rising Catholic, and that both were in rebellion against an Irish Anglican government, not an English one: the 1796-8 situation was a re-statement of the enduring importance of religious divisions in Irish history. While it is true that the modern idea of an 'Irish nation' emerged with the United Irishmen in the 1790s, Tone's assessment of 1790 was to remain valid for a long time:

> A country so great a stranger to itself as Ireland, where North and South and East and West meet to wonder at each other, is not yet prepared for the adoption of one political faith. . . . Our provinces are ignorant of each other; our island is connected, we ourselves are insulated; and distinctions of rank and property and religious persuasion have hitherto been not merely lines of difference, but brazen walls of separation. We are separate nations . . . parts that do not cleave to one another.

Of the aims of the United Irishmen – to emancipate Ireland from English influence, to reform the Parliament and to unite the people of Ireland of all creeds and races in a common bond – the first two were dependent on the achievement of the third, and that, on Tone's admission, was out of the question.

The circumstances and events leading up to the rebellion reveal some of the religious realities of Irish life and suggest that 1798 has more in common with the Ulster crisis of 1911-14 – or 1969 – than it has with 1848, 1867 or 1916. The setting for 1798 was the wish of the English government under Pitt and Dundas to grant Catholic emancipation as a conciliatory Irish reform: more broadly Pitt saw, as did Edmund Burke, Catholicism as a potential ally against the forces of the French revolution, perhaps even as a conservative element to restrain an obnoxious Protestant Parliament in Ireland. English ministers and administrators assumed that conciliation of Catholics by relaxing the penal laws would pacify Ireland and tend to unite Catholics and Protestants. To Westmoreland's astonishment, such proposals stimulated apprehension and hatred. The English assumption was that of the enlightened secular mind which believed that the elimination of religious differences and barriers must be socially harmonising: this type of mind was to drift further and further away from any deep understanding of Irish society, whose very principle was religious division, and where any attempt to reduce division was fraught with the risk of anarchy. The mind of Irish Catholicism was far better understood by those most strongly opposed to it: Fitzgibbon, later Earl of Clare, argued in the Irish Parliament, ' if any man in Great Britain or Ireland is so wild as to hope that by communicating political power to the Catholics of Ireland they can be conciliated to British interests, he will find himself bitterly mistaken. Great Britain can never conciliate the descendants of the old Irish to her interests upon any other terms than by restoring to them the possessions and the religion of their ancestors in full splendour and dominion.'

In January 1792 Westmoreland sketched to Dundas an Irish Protestant mind which could be that of Ulster in 1911-14, or 1969:

> The fears and jealousies that universally affect the Protestant mind are not confined to Parliament, but affect almost every individual and every public body. The steadiest friends of British government apprehend that indulgence will give the Catholics strength to press for admission to the State. In this they see the ruin of political power to the Protestants, and trifling as you may consider the danger – a total change of the property of the country. The final consequence will be a confederacy of the Protestants, with very few exceptions, to resist every concession. They will resolve to support their own situation by their own power. You will lose for the Catholics the very indulgence which you desire to procure. You will cause the collision which it is your object to prevent. The Catholic body can only act against the Protestant by outrage and intimidation, and you will be obliged to spill the blood of the very people whom the expectation of your indifference may have raised to a state of ferment.

The British government sought to devise, in the Duke of Portland's phrase, ' measures likely to improve the condition and satisfy the minds of Catholics, without endangering the Protestant Establishment '. Portland's own suggestions reveal his distance from the Irish Protestant mind – ' The establishment of seminaries for the education of Catholic priests; and the making of some provision for the Catholic parochial clergy . . . any mode . . . for facilitating the education of the lower ranks of Catholics, to put them on a par with Protestants. . . .' But, to improve the position of Catholics and their religion was *per se*, in an Irish Protestant view, to endanger the Protestant Establishment – which that Establishment would not allow, nor could England risk. Major Hobart put the Establishment case to Dundas:

The connection between England and Ireland rests absolutely on Protestant ascendancy. Abolish distinctions, and you create a Catholic superiority. . . . It may be said, What is it to England whether Protestants or Catholics have the pre-eminence in Ireland? It is of as much consequence as the connection between the two countries, for on that it depends. While you maintain the Protestant ascendancy the ruling powers in Ireland look to England as the foundation of their authority. A Catholic Government could maintain itself without the aid of England, and must inevitably . . . be followed by a separation of the countries. You must be aware of all the property which Englishmen possess in Ireland. It will be forfeited on the first appearance of success on the part of Catholics. Are you prepared to meet the clamours of those who have an interest in property in Ireland?

Simply, the ascendancy view was that to give Catholics the vote meant a Catholic parliament, which meant social revolution and separation from Britain. Pitt's belief was that to refuse Catholics the franchise and other reforms was to abandon them to disorder, disaffection and revolutionary ideas, and create allies for the French: he was right, but to conciliate Catholics meant the abandonment of the Ascendancy to the same tendencies, however, absurd and unreal the English government might regard ascendancy fears. Westmoreland analysed this paralysing situation late in 1792: ' The great danger is from the North, where the Volunteering spirit has gained ground from dislike of the Catholics; and if that dislike should be done away, or resentment for concession actuated them, their republican principles may lead them to any possible mischief. . . . The minds of men are in great ferment, the mob expecting to be relieved from tithes, rents and taxes by relief from Catholic laws; the Protestants alarmed and offended, and the levellers elated with the success of France.' At the centre of this ferment was the Catholic question. ' The disaffection among the lower orders is universal,' reported Fitzwilliam in January 1795, and it was speedily becoming worse. The degeneration of authority in Ireland was in large part a consequence of deadlock on the question of Catholic participation in Irish affairs – the English cabinet's urging of it, the Irish Parliament's refusal to admit it.

The rebellion of 1798 culminated a period of developing insurrection and anarchy, in some respects better described as a confused and desultory civil war than as a rebellion. In the 1790s sectarian warfare was endemic in Ulster particularly, polarising by 1795 around the Orange Society and the Catholic Defenders, who conducted bloody crusades against each other. The United Irishmen bridged, for a brief time, one religious gulf – between Presbyterians and Catholics – but their unity was a common religious hostility to the Anglican Ascendancy. The Wexford rising became a crusade against Protestants. ' God help these simpletons,' sighed a French officer confronted in Mayo in 1798 with Irish recruits who sought ' to take up arms for France and the Virgin Mary '. ' If they knew how little we care for the Pope or his religion, they would not be so hot in expecting help from us.' The historical depiction of the 1798 rebellion has derived its character too largely from that aspect of the United Irishmen's policy which sought alliance with revolutionary France and independence of England, from the revolutionary republicanism of Wolfe Tone, and from the French military expeditions. The republican nationalism of Tone was largely irrelevant to the condition of Ireland, one of deep religious division: it was this division which probably did most to foil the revolutionary plans of 1796-8, just as it was this division which lay behind so much of that eruption – as Grattan said in 1796: ' Under an Administration sent here to defeat a Catholic Bill, a Protestant mob very naturally conceives itself a part of the State ': Orangeism drove many Catholics into the United Irishmen. Edmund Burke summed up the government's policy in mid-1797: ' I see the plan is to remove, and if possible destroy, any of that religion who will not be their tools in establishing a Jacobin indifference to all religion and a hatred of the ruling one among the common people who are altogether composed of Catholics, and who, if they have not this religion, will have no other. It is all over with the peace and prosperity of that Kingdom.' General Lake rendered British policy towards Ireland more bluntly: ' Nothing but terror will keep them in order.' Nor would it, as disaffection changed under pressure to active sedition.

It was naïve to expect a national rebellion of a country which had by the mid-1790s degenerated into a condition of fitful sectarian civil war. This war was none the less real for its disconnections in time and place, and for its lack of absolute sectarian clarity – for the fact that in some cases the rebels were Catholic, their opponents Protestant, in others the reverse: if, when the campaigns of 1798 were fought, Irish rebels were crushed mainly by an Irish Protestant yeomanry and a substantially Catholic militia, Cornwallis noted the extreme anti-Catholic venom of his own officers. Notwithstanding exceptions and gradations, the radical issue in Ireland stood forth as that between Catholic and Protestant, with no other principle offering anything but a transitory prospect of overlaying that division to effect any semblance of permanent unity which might be dubbed Irish. All unifying ideologies ran aground and perished on the rocks of religion, a situation which still prevails in 1970: nationalism was to be a denominational ideology in Ireland. The Protestants were the first to give it modern formulation at the end of the eighteenth century, but after the Union the Catholics captured it and made it their own.

Sectarian division was abhorrent to doctrinaire nationalists, who had an integral geographic approach to Irish nationalism. However much these ideologies appealed to Irishmen, the religious facts were too much for such simplicity: there were two (at least two) varieties of Irishmen, and if nationalist ideologues wanted to construct an actual movement they had to contend with the actualities. Wolfe Tone's central motivation was hate: ' I was led by a hatred of England, so deeply rooted in my nature, that it was rather an instinct than a principle.' This, and his recognition of the facts of Irish life, led him to take up the Catholic cause in 1791, despite the fact that his bitter anti-clericalism made him no real friend of Catholicism. But he knew its enormous potential for a nationalist movement. He ' knew that there existed, however it might be concealed, in the breast of every Irish Catholic, an inextinguishable abhorrence of the English name and power.' Yet, to take up that Catholic cause was, as the British government had found before Tone, and as other nationalists were to find after him, to arouse the fierce opposition of Protestants.

In other countries, a secular, or non-religious nationalism did act as a unifying force, but the religious division in Ireland was too deep to allow this. Historically, nationalism and religion have often served similar or related social roles: indeed, as J. R. Talmon has argued, nationalism, in the form of political messianism, has often taken on the role of a substitute religion, most notably when religion itself has decayed as a social force. Religion had not decayed in Ireland, and consequently it was very difficult to introduce substitutes for it: the real thing thrived vigorously. In such a society, the only possible nationalism was one congenially related to religion, that would be a natural corollary to it, and would attach the sense of individual and social identity and meaning already bestowed by religion, to some appropriate political form. A nationalism not related to religion would be irrelevant, without popular roots: national identity, principles and purpose had to be linked somehow with religious identity, principles and purpose – which is why Archbishop MacHale's blending of assertive nationalist politics and religious principles made him such an immensely popular and powerful figure. (MacHale's principles could stretch to condone rebellion: in November 1832, in a letter to the *Edinburgh Review* widely reproduced in Ireland, he attacked the liberalism of the times as tyrannical, and reminded his readers that the theology of Aquinas contained such maxims as, ' A tyrannical government is unjust, being ordained, not for the common good, but for the private good of the ruler; therefore the disturbance of this rule is not sedition, unless when the overthrow of tyranny is so inordinately pursued, that the multitude suffers more from the disturbance than from the existence of the government.')

There were two religions in Ireland, bitterly antagonistic, and the logic of that was two nationalisms, not one. This seemed silly logic to doctrinaire nationalists in nineteenth century Ireland, and they gave themselves over to vain attempts to abstract from religious divisions so as to create one unifying nationalism. Their ideology committed them to the search for unity among all Irishmen. Perhaps their idealism blinded them to the fact that their cause, as a quest for totality, was already lost, that one of the two major religious groups had already found a congenial nationalism: with the Union in 1800, the Protestant ascendancy and indeed Protestants generally, had become British nationalists, and were no longer as a group open to conversion to Irish nationalism. It was natural that despite their ideals and convictions, doctrinaire Irish nationalists should be forced towards identification with the strongest potential dynamic force in Irish life – Irish Catholicism; natural too, eventually, that they should begin to give their general principles narrowly Catholic definitions.

The Young Ireland movement of 1842-8, gathered around the *Nation* newspaper, set much of the tone and provided much of the content for Irish revolutionary nationalism thereafter. The Young Irelanders – Thomas Davis, John Mitchel, John Blake Dillon, Charles Gavan Duffy, James Fintan Lalor, Smith O'Brien and Thomas Meagher – were impelled, as their name indicates, by cultural attitudes derived from the romantic phase of European nationalism. Their mission held a radical contradiction. They looked forward to and sought to attain a national movement in which Catholics and Protestants would unite harmoniously, ignoring religious affiliation: they looked back to, and endeavoured to resurrect, an Irish heritage in which Catholics and Protestants had been at each others throats. The Young Irelanders' romantic folkish bias, stressing a distinctively Irish culture, history and language, was implicitly exclusive of the Protestant, Anglo-Irish elements, which were alien. The Young Irelanders' assumption was that the revival of the past would encourage the development of a living national consciousness and unity of spirit. It did, but it also drew attention to the religious divisions of the past. To dredge the past certainly did service to the cause of revolution; it was a violent, anti-English past – but it was also a Catholic past: Thomas Davis' writings in seventeenth century history exhibit both these characteristics. Rather than establishing the validity of non-sectarian liberal democratic nationalism, the turning back process revealed the very close conjunction between Catholicism and Irish revolutionary activity, and the vital role Catholicism had played in defending a distinctive Irishness. This point was not lost on those contemporaries who took a Catholic view of Ireland's history, and it was made in criticism of the Young Irelanders in the first issue of *Duffy's Irish Catholic Magazine*, in February 1847:

> Have we not to become familiar with the men of the seventeenth century, with their Spanish fervour and loftiness, and intensity of Catholic nationality? And from our worst days of suffering what lessons may be drawn? Is not our history for ages one martyrdom? There is a halo of true glory resting on our sad annals if we had but eyes to read them right – a truer glory than is found in our protracted resistance on the field or the occasional victories that flash through the long night of disaster. Of these, the bitter result after all is, that we were conquered; but there was another, and a far higher field of battle; in which the victory was wholly ours, and the ignominy our conqueror's. Lord of land and life, and not sparing either, he sought to be lord of conscience too, and was uniformly and utterly baffled. A race, taunted with their fickleness, and too often divided, too often in other things unstable as water, were in this, in the struggle for an unseen good, the very type of resolute tenacity, of unity and unconquerable will.

Perhaps the witticism attributed to Chancellor Plunket that the tone of the *Nation* was Wolfe Tone has some limited validity, but the effect of the *Nation* movement was to revive Catholicism as well, and that much more influentially.

So in history, the same outcome resulted from the application by the Young Irelanders of their romantic values to the contemporary scene. They scorned and denounced urban life, industrialism, and the profit-making materialist ethos, and held Britain to be the epitome of these degeneracies. Mitchel puts the view vehemently in his *Jail Journal*: ' Your Anglo-Saxon race worships only money, prays to no other god than money, would buy and sell the Holy Ghost for money, and believes that the world was created, is sustained, and governed, and will be saved by the only one true immutable Almighty Pound Sterling.' In contrast, the Young Irelanders glorified the rural life and the peasant people of Ireland: to quote Lalor, ' A secure and independent agricultural peasantry is the only base on which a people ever rises, or ever can be raised; or on which a nation can safely rest.' But to rest nationalism on this base was to commit it to a necessary, even a dependant relationship with Catholicism, because the Irish peasantry were overwhelmingly Catholic. In fact, this was the situation of the Young Ireland movement in the 1840s: its alliance with O'Connell's repeal movement was an alliance with a Catholic peasant movement. And the tension between the Young Ireland ideology and that movement was immediately apparent. The Young Irelanders supported O'Connell simply because he had control of the people, but they were deeply critical of the repeal movement's close ties with Catholicism: they wanted a religiously neutral national movement, one not repellant to Protestants, but the only mass movement that did exist was Catholic. To expect to convert such a movement to religious neutrality was perhaps utopian, certainly so in the view of a member of the Protestant Repeal Association: ' Duffy is no bigot, but he must know well that he could not find ten men of his own creed in Ireland who would be as tolerant as himself. He may be enthusiast enough to believe it possible that he and his handful of allies could protect religious liberty in a Parliament of priest-selected members; but it is the dream of an enthusiast.'

The actual split, in July 1846, between O'Connell and the Young Irelanders, was provoked on the issue of their differing attitudes, in principle, to the use of physical force, but after the breach the fiercest criticism levelled against the Young Irelanders was not that they were revolutionaries, but that they were secularists and anti-clericals. This was unjust: the Young Irelanders were deeply absorbed in the Polish rising of 1846, and supported the Papacy against Austria in 1847. But they attempted to avoid religious commitment, attracting Catholic criticism of which *Duffy's Irish Catholic Magazine* of February 1847 provides a mild illustration:

Of the deep sincerity as well as the ability of the men whose work it is, [to preach the principles of national feeling] and of the good they have achieved in arousing our sense of national dignity and affection, no one can say too much. Still we think they committed a mistake in not basing their labours more on the religious feelings of the mass of the people whom they addressed. The reason of this was, no doubt, the desire to find a way to the hearts of Irishmen of all religions. Yet it was in a great degree an error, and one of which we believe they will come more and more to recognise. At all events it has left one-half, and the more necessary half, of the teaching required by the majority of our countrymen to be yet laboured at.

Much Catholic comment went a great deal further than this, insisting that what was not pro-Catholic must be anti-Catholic. A largely O'Connellite priesthood preached against the Young Irelanders, and confronted by their confused and abortive attempts to organise rebellion in 1848, urged the rebels to disperse. The more extreme of the Young Irelanders were convinced that clerical hostility had doomed their rebellion to failure: wrote Mitchel, '(what shall I call it? – the cowardice, the treachery, or the mere priestliness) of the priests'. Mitchel's bitterness – ' you would have been free long ago but for your damned souls ' – is sour testimony to the enormous, decisive influence wielded by religion and the clergy in Ireland; but Mitchel's reaction might suggest mere clerical dictator-ship. Closer to the heart and strength of the relationship between priests and people is the bond revealed in the comment made to Tocqueville in 1835 by a priest in the West of Ireland: ' The people give the fruit of their labours liberally to me and I give them my time, my care and my entire soul. I can do nothing without them and without me they would succumb under the weight of their sorrows. Between us there is a cease-less exchange of feelings of affection.'

Romanticism in an Irish setting produced results antipathetic to the liberal democratic aims of those who sought a nationalist movement of all Irishmen. Instead it fostered a nationalist movement which drew on religious roots. True, it also fostered violence and the cult of violence, adding to that tradition the rebellion of 1848, but the most important attempt to tap the vast reservoir of Irish violence – the effort to give nationalist political direction to peasant discontent over land questions – had religious repercussions. There can be no doubt that the Young Irelanders, particularly Lalor and Mitchel, were interested in the land question in terms of justice and humanity, but they also saw its poten-tial importance as a nationalist tactic. In an important aspect, the ten-ant right movement was conceived as a means of contriving an agita-tion which would be as meaningful to Protestants as to Catholic tenants, and, joint action on this issue being achieved, pave the way for an Irish nationalist movement in which sectarian distrust and animus would be buried. Ideological nationalists, not only those of the *Nation*, edited by Gavan Duffy, but Frederick Lucas of the *Tablet* and Dr. John Gray of the *Freeman's Journal*, saw the land question as a means of overcoming the cripplingly divisive effect of religion on any aspiring nationalist movement. Here was an attempt to abstract from the religious situation and stress a non-religious grievance common to all Irishmen. This com-mon factor could not be cultural or ideological – those were areas of division – it had to be material, which in the Irish economy meant land.

However, this factor too was subject to the religious rift. Certainly there were Protestant tenants, considerable in numbers in Ulster, and there were a few Catholic landlords, but the substantial situation was that of a Catholic tenantry and Protestant landlords. So simplicity triumphed and the land agitation took on a generally religious complexion, becoming subject to the sectarianism which the idealogues sought to avoid. Furthermore, these intellectuals were not willing to encourage or accept the social consequences of their stressing of material, economic factors. They wanted a basis for nationalism, but they found themselves organising socio-economic grievances. These grievances were good nationalist material so long as the socio-economic structure of Ireland could be depicted as an English infliction. However, they were potentially dangerous to any hierarchically structured society, and nationalists themselves were unsure of, and sometimes dismayed by, the forces they had unleashed – and hesitant to employ them fully. In 1848, Smith O'Brien's respect for the rights of property would not allow him to lead a peasant insurrection: doctrinaire nationalists did not want a peasant insurrection, they wanted a nationalist one.

The Young Ireland movement made another contribution to Irish nationalism – the concept of contamination. To Young Irelanders, Britain was not just an oppressing power, it was a source of degradation, its rule endangering the purity of Irish life by the destructive influence of its pervasive, alien, cultural invasion. This idea was readily adapted to religious purposes, and by the end of the nineteenth century British cultural contamination was being depicted in the religious terms of the dangers of proselytism, materialism, and depraving literature. In fact, it was in hostility to contamination that cultural and religious nationalists most readily met. Both held English influence to be evil. A good instance of such common ground was the Irish education system, planned, organised and controlled by Britain and with British content and bias. The cultural nationalists regarded this as an alien intrusion tending to destroy Irish cultural identity and thus Irish nationality: the religious mind saw it as Protestant or secular and thus dangerous to Irish Catholicism. No such common ground existed between Irish cultural nationalism and Irish Protestantism. Quite the contrary; their values were opposed.

The Young Irelanders' activity encouraged the growth of a Catholic nationalism, but this was in spite of their non-denominational objectives, and despite direct clerical denunciation. Though they became – slowly and in some ways furtively – popular heroes, they captured less leadership than popular imagination, and their actual popular influence long remained confused and uncertain. This uneasy and tentative relationship between a Catholic populace under clerical influence and a violent revolutionary dynamic is best seen in the history of the Fenian movement in the 1860s.

With the Fenian movement, the relationship between the revolutionary impulse and the Irish people becomes more simple, more primitive. The Young Irelanders were intellectuals with a fairly sophisticated programme, and plans for the education of popular opinion – and a great distance between their intellectualism and popular consciousness, save in one vital respect: a common thirst for vengeance, a common hatred. John Mitchel best expresses this element:

> The vengeance I seek is the righting of my country's wrong, which includes my own. . . . England! All England, operating through her Government: through all her organised and effectual public opinion, press, platform, pulpit, parliament, has done, is doing, and means to do, grievous wrong to Ireland. She must be punished; that punishment will, as I believe, come upon her by and through Ireland; and so will Ireland be *avenged*. . . . Punishment of England, then, for the crimes of England – this righteous public vengeance I seek, and shall seek. . . . for such vengeance I do vehemently thirst and burn.

Mitchel's theme burnt on in Irish history: on 13 May 1922 an Irish priest wrote on the last page of his copy of the *Jail Journal*, ' Re-read this Journal lest my hatred of England should be in the least diminished after 21½ years absence from my dear native land.' In the 1860s such feelings were acutely obvious even within the circles in which Cardinal Newman moved. In 1866 he remarked on ' the hatred felt for England in all ranks in Ireland, how great friends of mine do not scruple to speak to me of the " bloody English " – the common phrase – how, cautious and quiet government people simple confessed they would gladly show their teeth if they were sure of biting. . . . Every Irishman is but waiting this opportunity, and if he is friendly to this country it is because he despairs.' If this was the atmosphere among ' cautious and quiet government people ', the flavour of the simmering cauldron of Irish rural life in the 1860s needs no description.

An oath-bound secret society, the Fenian Brotherhood or Irish Republican Brotherhood (I.R.B.), was formed in Dublin on 17 March 1858, by a few men – mainly James Stephens, John O'Mahony, John O'Leary, Thomas Clarke Luby and Charles Kickham – some of whom had taken part in the 1848 rebellion, and of whom several had European or American experience. In its initial form, as the ' Phoenix Society ', its objective was ' to keep alive a spirit of hatred to the British Crown and Government ', not a particularly difficult task in Ireland. More positively the Fenian programme was prompt and violent revolution against Britain. Fenianism both nurtured and derived from that atmosphere of hatred and violence which pervaded Ireland in the 1860s. At its popular level, it gave coherent form to another of those surges of agrarian unrest endemic in Irish history, welling up from poverty, hatred and frustration, and characteristic of a society in which other outlets for agitation – most recently the Independent Irish Party – had proved fruitless.

It is indicative of the normalcy of violence in Anglo-Irish relations, that although the British administration in Ireland knew of the Fenian movement virtually from its foundation, it was not very concerned. True, open agitation by constitutional nationalists tended to give them public prominence and thus mask the growth of Fenianism. And again, if Fenianism advocated violent revolution, was republican, and had strong American connections, it was also secret and used front organisations. But the real reason why the British government did not act against the I.R.B. until 1865 was that it regarded Irish disaffection as the normal state of affairs, a permanent evil, beyond eradication which had to be tolerated up to a certain level. This attitude is reflected in the way in which the Irish Constabulary was regarded by the Irish Attorney General in 1860 – ' a semi-military force of occupation ' – and by the Under Secretary, Sir Thomas Larcom – ' It exists for civil purposes. But civil purposes in Ireland require the use of a repressive agency which verges on military action: – and happily so, as it renders the force available for defence against foreign as well as internal aggression without abandoning the purposes and objects of domestic police.' Revolutionary aspirations were too normal and too prevalent to be eradicated, but the occupation force would deal with them if they became troublesome – so ran British attitudes and policy.

The primitivism of the Fenian movement is evident in its doctrinal innocence: it had no programme past violent national revolution, and is, consequently, better understood as an emotional disposition rather than a disciplined movement. What organisational shape and conspiratorial coherence it did attain derived much more from the experience of some of its leaders in continental revolutionary movements (notably Paris in 1848) and from connections with the U.S.A., rather than Irish sources. The movement had popular pretensions, exhibited in the newspaper James Stephens founded in 1863 – *The Irish People* – but this was less in the realm of courting support, or demonstrating any really democratic character, than in the claim that the aspirations of the Fenians were, in fact, the real will and destiny of the Irish people. And, in fact, this claim did seem to have strong foundations in the atmosphere of violence which pervaded Ireland in the 1860s: conservatives as well as extremists recognised a very widespread repudiation of the existing government.

It was the reality of this climate of popular opinion which in part determined – but (and this is often overlooked) also considerably inhibited – the reaction of Church authority to the Fenian movement. The problem was this – was the strength of popular opinion such that it might ignore ecclesiastical opposition, or be provoked by it into greater extremism, to issue in alienation from the clergy and damage to Church authority? The theology of revolt had been resurrected in 1862 by Father Lavalle in a Dublin lecture on ' The Catholic Doctrine of the Right of Revolution ' in which he claimed that Ireland was so badly governed that rebellion was morally justified. This was a debatable view and though so intended, not necessarily a justification of Fenianism as the vehicle for such a rebellion. To Cullen's mind, the Fenian Brotherhood was a secret society led by irreligious revolutionaries (' disciples of Mazzini or Garibaldi ') extremely dangerous, given continental precedents, to religion. Some other bishops took this view, but the major point of ecclesiastical agreement was a pragmatic and political one – that a rising was hopeless, and that its failure would lead to British measures disastrous to Catholic Ireland. Cullen's public condemnation of Fenianism in 1865 made much of this practical argument, stressing instead the energetic use of parliament and press to demand reform.

The confrontation between the Church and the Fenian movement had some important consequences. Like the Young Irelanders, Fenian leaders wanted to avoid all religious issues. ' The main thing to all of us,' O'Leary said, ' is whether a man be Irish or not, and not whether he be Catholic Protestant or Pagan '. But this question of religion was the main thing to Church authorities; and also one of the main things to Catholics attracted towards Fenianism. So far as the Church reaction was concerned, Fenianism drove the Church further into involvement in party politics as the only alterative means of retaining initiative among and leadership of a discontented people. Indeed some bishops believed that Fenianism was a consequence of insufficient clerical activity in politics. Bishop Dorrian wrote privately in 1865, ' It was unfortunate that the priests were for a time withdrawn from politics ', – presumably in reference to Cullen's policy of 1854 – ' for people were thus driven in dispirit to combine illegally '. From this angle, the lesson was obvious: if priests did not exert themselves and control politics in the interests of religion, irreligious forces would take over.

This lesson was pressed home by the fact that ecclesiastical condemnation of Fenianism, culminating in the explicit Papal ban of 1870, although effective enough in preventing Fenianism developing into a mass movement, did not destroy it. Cardinal Manning might put it to Cullen that the Church's attitude to Fenianism ' exhibited the Church in its true light as the source of public order. I have never known a more propitious moment to make the Government feel that they cannot do without us '. But the facts remained that the government gave little evidence of any such feeling, and that conflict with Fenianism weakened Church authority in a fashion made abundantly clear during the career of Parnell.

Church censure caused Catholics committed to Fenianism to devise their own revolutionary theology, a development which had considerable future influence. At the simplest level, many Fenians argued that the Irish bishops had misinformed the Pope about Fenianism, and, that as the ban was not based on real facts, it was invalid. A related argument was that the Papacy had no right to interfere in Irish politics, and that generally the Church's authority was spiritual, not political – Fenianism being defined as a political matter. But some Fenians developed a much more positive and subtle attitude towards the relationship between their politics and their religion. Church condemnations which lumped Fenians together with infidels and the enemies of religion they would not accept, for they were in no way hostile to religion, or to the Church, or its priesthood. On the contrary, as Cardinal Manning said of the Fenians in 1867, ' They believe themselves to be serving in a sacred and holy war for their country and religion ': it had been Fenians in Pentonville in 1866 who first secured the saying of Mass within an English prison. Church condemnation forced such men to justify themselves in religious terms, which they did by forcing their political principles into a religious mould. The outcome was a concoction composed of the following ingredients: patriotism if not the greatest virtue, was certainly a true and good religious impulse which because of Ireland's peculiar circumstances was inseparable from religious aims – Faith and Fatherland; the private conscience was supreme; because Fenians sought to overthrow tyranny by the only possible means, their actions were moral; the morality of the Fenians was, in fact, a deeply religious one, and the official Church had judged it wrongly. Confronted by such attitudes, and by the obvious sincerity and religious fervour of Catholic Fenians, the Church tended not to pursue its denunciations too far, and to shy away from too precise definitions of what they meant. And as Fenians became public heroes, the Church's position became more difficult: such hero-worship implied disrespect for the Church's bans – and indeed, the Fenian period did a great deal to render nugatory clerical denunciation of revolutionary violence. Some clerics, shamed by their own church's hostility to Fenianism, were anxious to show their patriotism in relation to more acceptable agitations – which is one of the reasons for the large clerical involvement in Home Rule and the Land War.

The Fenians staged an abortive insurrection in March 1867. In September, during the rescue of two Fenians from a Manchester prison, a policeman was killed. For this, three Fenians were executed: these ' Manchester Martyrs ' became heroes in Ireland – many people who opposed Fenianism felt sympathetic. The popular reaction may be readily imagined when even Cullen described, in a private note, the responsible English cabinet as ' that brood of vipers ': they had encouraged Garibaldi's attack on the Papal States – and then executed Fenians. Generally, revolutionary violence, once attempted, attracted the sympathetic tolerance, or at the very least the mortified understanding, of influential Irishmen who themselves repudiated violence, and argued against it as a tactic. If violent men seized the initiative, even if all the rest of Ireland be opposed to their tactics, it was largely at one with their aims and general dispositions. Ultimately, on simple practical grounds, the only real difference between revolutionaries and reformers – witness even the bishops' attitudes to Fenianism – was the question of tactics. England not only failed to drive a wedge between Irish reformers and revolutionaries, its policy of dealing harshly with revolutionaries bred an increasing Irish tolerance towards them, and drove the Church into reform politics. When Gladstone came to office in 1868, moderates, many of them Liberal supporters, sought from him a general amnesty for the Fenian prisoners, as an act of clemency and conciliation. He disappointed many Irishmen who repudiated Fenianism by refusing to amnesty more than a few.

There can be little doubt that the British government's treatment of Fenians made them more acceptable in Ireland and did much to counteract the influence of the Church's condemnation. There are some obvious parallels with 1916. Perhaps this was not a vital factor in the continued life of Fenianism in Ireland after 1867: perhaps this is better explained by the continued vigour of its life in Britain, and in America, that haven for anti-British venom; or by the residual firmness of its Irish organisation. Nevertheless, the hero worship engendered by British treatment was of some ominous consequence: O'Donovan

Rossa was elected for Tipperary in 1869, defeating, from within gaol, the Liberal candidate. Fenianism remained of political consequence, always present as an alternative, even if remote, to constitutional nationalism, acting also as a goad to it, and sometimes even as its supporter.

The continued life of Fenianism may also be related to the fact that while its insurrectionary bid failed, it could claim to have produced tangible results. Fenian outrages, particularly in England itself, aroused initial hysteria, but brought home to the English public some sense of the reality of Irish grievances, destroying the prevalent complacent apathy and creating, as Gladstone discerned, an atmosphere of reluctant English acceptance of the necessity for some Irish reforms. Parliamentary acquiescence in Gladstone's reforms – disestablishment and the 1870 Land Act – was influenced by the hope that this would diminish the Fenian threat. It could be argued that to grant reforms in such circumstances was to consecrate and encourage Irish violence as an efficacious procedure. It could also be argued – and this is what was of immediate consequence – that Gladstone's reforms made an Irish constitutional reform movement possible, thinkable. Had the English government made no response whatever, by way of reform, to the Irish violence of the 1860s, a constitutional movement to press for further reform would have been an absurdity, and the result would have been that all elements in Irish life would have been pushed, probably with some rapidity, towards a common revolutionary extremism. The question now was, would the reforms be big enough and quick enough.

Obviously, the English response to Irish agitation did much to determine not only the pace of growth, but also the character of revolutionary nationalism in Ireland. For one thing it forced it to be firmly and exclusively Irish. At the level of international politics, this may be seen in the refusal of the republican government of France in 1848 to assist or even recognise the aims of the Young Irelanders: the French realised that British goodwill was crucial to the survival of the Second Republic. Spurned, the Irish revolutionaries took the lesson that, in Mitchel's words at the time, 'we must rely on ourselves'; the enunciation of a revolutionary principle which took briefer form 50 years later as Sinn Féin – ourselves alone. Self-reliance in the Irish revolutionary tradition was construed to include Irish-America as well, but after 1848 the Irish revolutionary movement had little or no contact with European revolutionary movements: for instance the interest of Marx and Engels in the Fenian movement was not reciprocated. A vital reason for this isolationism was of course the Catholicity of Ireland (that 'honest madness on the part of the people' as Engels called it) which repudiated the secularism of European revolution; but another very large reason was the attitude of European revolutionaries themselves. If they did not positively need British support, they had no wish to alienate that most liberal and democratic of governments by siding with Ireland.

There is another factor – English – which made for Irish revolutionary isolation, and also both mirrored and greatly increased the animus between Ireland and England. At no stage were English workers willing to support their Irish counterparts, regarding them as filthy and depraved inferiors, as competitors likely to lower living standards, and with all the other well-known elements of anti-Irish prejudice. That this attitude should seep from the pages of that impeccable exponent of class and internationalism, Freidrich Engels, in *The Condition of the Working Class in England in 1844,* perhaps excuses others whose progressive credentials are less obvious: Engels was revolted by the Milesian, 'his crudity, which places him little above the savage, his contempt for all humane enjoyments, his filth and his poverty' and regarded the Irish as having 'a strong degrading influence upon their English companions in toil'. In a letter of 1870, Marx described Anglo-Irish relations as they existed in English cities:

> Every industrial and commercial centre in England now possesses a working class population *divided* into two *hostile* camps, English proletarians and Irish proletarians. The ordinary English worker hates the Irish worker as a competitor who lowers his standard of life. In relation to the Irish worker he feels himself a member of the ruling nation and so turns himself into a tool of the aristocrats and capitalists *against Ireland,* thus strengthening their dominion over *himself.* . . . The Irishman pays him back with interest in his own coin. He regards the English worker as both sharing in the guilt of English domination in Ireland and at the same time serving as its stupid tool.

Engels and Marx deplored this situation because it divided and weakened the English working class. There were other consequences. It also had the effect of alienating the Irish from English working class organisations which were hostile to them, and later, of tending to stifle the very weak Irish union movement. But the major point is this, the hostility of English workers towards the Irish tended to exclude the energies of the lower classes of Irishmen from the general area of interest in, and support for movements towards democratic, socio-economic reform, and to confirm their attachment to the Irish nationalist movement, to which their intensity and weight were an enormous asset.

7
Some Questions of British Opinion

Among the major determinants of the course of Anglo-Irish relations, English ignorance, prejudice and indifference must be ranked high. Indeed to the extent that such English attitudes governed English policy – and that Anglo-Irish affairs consisted of such policy and Irish reactions to it – these English attitudes are quite central to any explanation of the relationship between the two countries.

In an estrangement that was mutual, perhaps nothing was more crucial than the prevalence of that English indifference towards Ireland, which was the normal condition of English opinion. This indifference promoted, in fact made imperative, vigorous Irish agitation because nothing less than serious and determined Irish pressure would attract English attention to Irish problems, or spur the English to devise remedies. Such English interest and action as followed Irish outbursts was always fitful and short-lived – which meant that the process had to be repeated again and again, as often as Irish grievances came to the point of being no longer endurable. Given the continuance of English indifference and of Irish discontent, Anglo-Irish relations became a history of mutual exasperation: the Irish were exasperated (to say the least) by English indifference to their grievances, the English were exasperated by the constant surges of Irish turbulence. Around the core of this English irritation grew a collection of self-justifying judgements and prejudices which compose the English stereotype of the Irish.

A host of reasons might be advanced to account for English indifference to Ireland, but the problem might be understood more fairly by reversing the question to ask, why should England be interested in Ireland, or more pointedly, why had England undertaken the government of Ireland? The circumstances of the Union explain English indifference very simply: the English government had been compelled for strategic reasons to effect the Union – and those strategic reasons were the extent of its interest, and it was indifferent to anything else. Its strategic rationale made the use of force to maintain the Union seem natural – or at least not unnatural – to Ireland's English rulers.

The use of force in Ireland confirmed England's initial indifference to any Irish problems lesser than the strategic one, and also had the effect of sealing off those lesser problems, however great, under the weight of military power. The effect of this on English opinion was vital. Repressive force in Ireland obscured and distorted the situation there in English eyes, giving them a very false impression of the reality of Irish feeling. Writing to Gladstone in 1872, Cardinal Manning made this quite crucial point: ' If you wish to know the will of Ireland, ask the Irish in our Colonies and in the United States. You will never get it in Ireland with 30,000 English and Scotch bayonets.' It is this English acceptance as real, of an Irish calm imposed by force, which explains the shocked surprise, the sense of outrage, which Englishmen felt when Irish violence suddenly broke through what they believed to be social harmony. Such apparently unprovoked savagery seemed inexplicable, insane.

Those Englishmen who saw deeper than the surface appearances maintained by their own power, found ample problems they could understand – the degraded social and economic conditions of the mass of the people, the rift between rich and poor, poverty, lawlessness. These problems might be attacked, and they were, particularly later in the nineteenth century. But whereas the English believed they were treating the Irish disease, these were only its symptoms. The Act of Union in 1800 forced Irish government on the English. It came to the English government as a new problem, that is, one without its true gravamen, its long historical context. The English government dealt with Ireland as a nineteenth century problem, but, as Mansergh says of the nineteenth century, ' The age of morality had been superseded by the age of economics '. The Irish problem was a leftover from the age of religion, the age of morality, – and even the laws of economics were against its solution under the values of the new economic age; the prospects of a solution to Irish problems within the United Kingdom of the nineteenth century were therefore not high. What the English came to regard as Ireland's disease – socio-economic problems – were in fact the symptoms of a religious malady that went back to the Reformation. That part of the Irish populace from which the turbulence of the nineteenth century derived had been demarked and degraded on the basis of its religion. It is understandable that, when Britain took over Irish government in 1800, this vital pre-history should be ignored or forgotten or simply never known on the English side, and Ireland's problems should be seen in the light of current socio-economic theory – but this issued in grave misunderstanding of the real reasons for Irish discontent.

To turn from indifference and misunderstanding to the question of prejudice. Racial and ethnic prejudice stretches far back into the history of Anglo-Irish relations. In the earlier nineteenth century it can be illustrated from such varied sources as Engels, *Punch*, and Thomas Carlyle. After the famine it grew in strength and dimensions to become, by the late nineteenth century, a widespread popular phenomenon in England: writing from Ireland to his wife in July 1860, Charles Kingsley exhibits this type of prejudice in its extreme form: '. . . I am haunted by the human chimpanzees I saw along that hundred miles of horrible country. I don't believe they are our fault. I believe there are not only many more of them than of old, but that they are happier, better, more comfortably fed and lodged under our rule than they ever were. But to see white chimpanzees is dreadful; if they were black, one would not feel it so much, but their skins, except where tanned with exposure, are as white as ours.' The ethnic and racial content of anti-Irish prejudice, and its bearing on the failure of Anglo-Irish relations, by producing stereotypes of English and Irish character, is discussed stimulatingly by L. P. Curtis in *Anglo-Saxons and Celts*. The question it raises is this: is the anti-Irish prejudice, so evident in nineteenth century England, fundamentally ethnic or racial?

Obviously, the ethnic-racial label does not get at the heart of the dispositions of English religious non-conformity or of Ulster Protestantism, or of all that variety of prejudice which is patently anti-Catholic. Is there any relationship between traditional anti-Irish prejudice on religious grounds, and the ethnic-racial variety so fashionable in later Victorian England? The relationship would appear to be directly derivative. Reformation England regarded Roman Catholicism as an inferior, degraded and dangerous religious belief: those who held that belief (*en masse*, the native Irish) were therefore inferior, degraded and dangerous, characteristics which they confirmed by their behaviour towards the English. This Reformation attitude persisted strongly in the religious sectors of English society, that is, among those to whom Protestantism still provided a meaningful belief and value structure, because in those sectors it retained its initial foundations. But what of those rapidly growing areas of English society where religion had ceased to be an acceptable intellectual position or value system? In those areas, some other – necessarily secular – intellectual basis and value estimates were required to maintain views on the Catholic Irish that had been formulated in, and were inherited from a religious age. The racial and ethnic theories that developed in the nineteenth century offered an admirable substitute for discarded or residual religious prejudices. Such theories were convenient, fashionable, and had a respectable pseudo-intellectuality, and served precisely the same function as the religious prejudices no longer tenable in a more secular intellectual world. In later Victorian society it was not the Protestant who, as a superior being, represented the paragon of virtue, but the White Anglo-Saxon, with his Protestanism a residual third of the combination. Thus, Sharon Turner, whom L. P. Curtis describes as the first of the nineteenth century Anglo-Saxon historians, characterises England as a nation ' which, inferior to none in every moral and intellectual merit, is superior to every other in the love and possession of useful liberty: a nation which cultivates with equal success the elegancies of art, the ingenious labours of industry, the energies of war, the researches of science, and the richest productions of genius '. What is most notable in this description – for a work published initially in the first years of the nineteenth century – is its strident secularism, its omission of any religious aspect or aim. The same attitude is discernible in the ethnic-racial view of Ireland. Certainly, most exponents of Anglo-Saxon superiority equated differences of race in Ireland with those of religion. And certainly the relevant pole of contrast with the White Anglo-Saxon Protestant stereotype then under construction, was the Dirty Irish Catholic stereotype. But in both cases, religion came a poor third: the ethnic-racial view of English superiority accorded the religious element the same minor subservient place in the Irish stereotype as it was rightfully accorded in the English. The Paddy/Biddy stereotype of Irish character and behaviour was built around prominent features such as simian appearance, defective intelligence, lack of hygiene or self-restraint, violence, lawlessness etc.: save for some religious externals which rated a minor mention, the religious core of the Irish person was omitted from this picture. It is not nearly enough to suggest that the prejudice revealed by this stereotype, was responsible for some of the defects of English policy towards Ireland. Far more damaging than the grotesqueries included in the stereotype (they at least bore some relation to reality) was what it omitted: the really destructive, blinding aspect of the English stereotype of the Irish was its failure to recognise the religious element, its construction of an Irishman virtually without religion, a secularised Paddy and Biddy who did not exist. To act on such a stereotype was to act on both a parody and an illusion.

But even those varieties of English opinion on Ireland that came closest to touching the religious core of Irish affairs exhibit grave blindness. Two main examples are analysed briefly here, the views of J. A. Froude and those of Gladstone, chosen because, not only can they be classified, roughly, as religious interpretations, but they exhibit a contrasting emphasis in their proposed solution to Irish problems: to

Froude, firmness to the degree of coercion would be a solvent; to Gladstone, conciliation would win Ireland over. Gladstone's opinions are particularly important, not only because of his prominence in regard to Irish affairs, but because it has been commonplace to regard him as unique among his contemporaries in his understanding of Irish problems.

It is relevant to the thesis of this book, that the sector of English (and Anglo-Irish) opinion most hostile to the native Irish was that which took its stand on religious grounds. Ulster Protestantism is considered in a later chapter, and some extremes of anti-Popery which equated themselves with anti-Irishism hold so little intellectual content and are of so great emotional intensity as virtually to defy rational analysis. However, the opinions of J. A. Froude, particularly as expressed in his *The English in Ireland* (first published in 1872), represent an interesting blend of old and new – old anti-Catholic prejudice, and new anti-Irishism based on ethnic-racial theories, and social Darwinism.

Froude's Unionism was clearly related to anti-Catholicism. The concept and structure of *The English in Ireland* are firmly anchored to the Protestant-Catholic division. That fear of Catholic revenge for centuries of Protestant rule, which is so evident in extreme Protestant circles, is also patent in Froude. He insists, in sharp contrast to Gladstone's sense of English guilt, that the Irish Catholics, Catholics everywhere, must repent for their sins: ' Not till they have done penance, all of them, by frank confession and humiliation – the Irish for their crimes in their own island – the Catholics generally for their yet greater crimes throughout the civilised world – can the past be forgotten, and their lawful claims on the conscience of mankind be equitably considered.' Both prejudice and perception are evident in Froude's comment that in Catholic Ireland, nothing thrived except the Church, to which he was an open enemy.

Around this core of religious animus, Froude built a set of justifications for English rule, derived from current pseudo-scientific theorising: '. . . the superior part has a natural right to govern; the inferior part has a natural right to be governed; and a rude but adequate test of superiority and inferiority is provided in the relative strength of the different orders of human beings.' Froude's proposition is not crudely that might constitutes right, but that ' Among reasonable beings right is ever tending to create might ' – or simply, that ' superior strength is the equivalent of superior merit '; indeed strength is the product of moral superiority, and thus the dominating assertion of this strength is essentially the rule of a greater wisdom and nobility, and of a higher degree of social organisation and intelligence – ' nature . . . has allocated superiority of strength to superiority of intellect and character.'

What of Irish nationalism? To Froude, national independence could not be based on racial or geographic differences, nor on natural rights, only on strength: the purpose of government was to ensure the rule of the weak and depraved, by the strong and noble – ' the ignorant and the selfish may be and are justly compelled for their own advantage to obey a rule which rescues them from their natural weakness. There neither is nor can be an inherent privilege in any person or set of persons to live unworthily at their own wills, when they can be led or driven into more honourable courses; and the rights of man – if such there be – are not to liberty, but to wise direction and control '. As with individuals so with races and communities: ' the right of a people to self-government consists and can consist in nothing but their power to defend themselves.' So it follows that, ' The right to resist depends on the power of resistance. . . . when resistance has been tried and failed – when the inequality has been proved beyond doubt by long and painful experience – the wisdom, and ultimately the duty, of the weaker party is to accept the benefits which are offered in exchange for submission.' According to Froude, in Ireland ' An unappeasable discontent has been attended with the paralysis of manliness. . . . Ireland should have either asserted her independence successfully or submitted gracefully.' It had done neither – which was entirely degraded and reprehensible – and this had exasperated the English into harshness.

If Froude's argument justified English rule, it also justified a violent challenge to it. There could be no middle way, and Froude contended that a situation in which ' we will neither rule Ireland nor allow the Irish to rule themselves ' was untenable. Either assert English rule firmly and effectively against Irish anarchy, or let Ireland be free: ' Between the two " impossibilities " we may be obliged to choose if Ireland is to cease to be our reproach.' On Froude's principles a constitutional agitation directed towards Home Rule was absurd, because no people could prove they had a right to independence by arguing their case pragmatically or on abstract principles. They could prove they had the right to rule themselves only by demonstrating with force their power to be independent. And the only way to prove this was by test – that is, by rebellion.

Froude's case for English rule was also related to his stereotype of the Irish character and temperament. His picture is a familiar one – unstable, passionate, sentimental, charming, and without firm manliness; untruthful, insensitive, dirty in person and habit, quarrelsome, murderous, lazy and slovenly. So far from blaming the English for the deplorable condition of Ireland, Froude's contention was that, in part, the Irish problem was the outcome of the benefits of English rule. Left to themselves, ' the Irish had killed each other down in their perpetual wars, and the children had died for want of food '. English law and order and industry had produced in Ireland a prosperity which ' enabled a race to multiply in geometrical progression, which nature, by the habits with which she had endowed them, intended perhaps to preserve only in more manageable numbers '. The very virtues of English rule had disturbed the balance of nature so as to protect an inferior species from natural destruction.

From a modern viewpoint, Froude's racialist and violent survival of the fittest theorems are totally unacceptable. So (it may be hoped optimistically) is the stereotype of the Irish which he and so many other Englishmen subscribed to. How effective as a political force was this stereotype? L. P. Curtis goes so far as to claim, ' What really killed Home Rule in 1886 and 1894 was the Anglo-Saxon stereotype of the Irish Celt.' In 1872 Lord Salisbury warned that the greatest single danger to the Union lay in the sentimental notion of Liberals that Ireland ought to be governed in accordance with the desires of disloyal and irresponsible Irishmen. Was it that in 1886 and 1894 there were just not enough sentimental Liberals to carry the day? Certainly Salisbury, and Tories generally, believed that any attitude to the Irish connection less than strict unionism was disloyal and irresponsible, but this derived less from a stereotype than from political principles and political prejudices.

One of the most interesting things about British opinion on Ireland is, that while it is possible to collect a great variety of illustrations of British ignorance, stupidity, prejudice and short-sightedness in regard to Ireland, it is also possible to find perhaps an equal quantity and range of British commentary which reveals the opposite – sympathy, perception and realism. Indeed in 1890, such a compilation of criticism of the record of the failure of English statesmanship in Ireland – compiled entirely from British or Protestant sources – was published under the title of *A Key to the Irish Question,* by J. A. Fox; and it is possible to find much more than Fox includes. The unavoidable question is, if so many eminent English statesmen and publicists were so critical of English policy in Ireland, and showed deep and logical appreciation of the nature of the problems involved, why was so little done to solve them? Gladstone is the classic example, but before turning to him, Disraeli offers another significant case.

In the House of Commons in 1844, Disraeli demonstrated that the Irish situation was potentially revolutionary: ' A dense population inhabit an island where there is an established church which is not their church; and a territorial aristocracy, the richest of whom live in a distant capital. Thus they have a starving population, an alien Church, and in addition the weakest executive in the world.' Disraeli then went on to put the acid question:

> Well, what then would gentlemen say if they were reading of a country in that position? They would say at once, "The remedy is revolution". But the Irish could not have a revolution and why? Because Ireland is connected with another and more powerful country. Then what is the consequence? The connection with England became the cause of the present state of Ireland. If the connection with England prevented a revolution and a revolution was the only remedy, England logically is in the odious position of being the cause of all the misery of Ireland. What then is the duty of an English Minister? To effect by his policy all those changes which a revolution would effect by force. That is the Irish question in its integrity.

Disraeli's argument merits analysis, as his assumptions are also those which underly a great deal of later English political thinking. He implied a distinction between Irish grievances and the English connection. That is, if the population was given economic security, its own Church, and good government and administration, it would become a placid and contented part of the United Kingdom. This conclusion entailed some very large and dubious assumptions. The first was that adequate reforms for Ireland were politically possible within the context of the Union, that is, that the English political system which governed Irish affairs could be persuaded to yield ' all those changes which a revolution would effect by force '. Even Disraeli admitted that logically the English connection could be blamed for Irish misery: if this was so, the logical Irish action would be to attempt to get rid of the Union. But instead, Disraeli was contending that the connection could be used to remedy Irish misery. Theoretically it could, but this would necessitate a revolution in English policies towards Ireland, and no government, except under the most extreme pressure, could be expected to see any call for that. Simply, Disraeli's policy proposals were not within the realm of political possibility: they were unreal. And it is interesting to note how frequently the best analysis of Irish problems came from opposition benches. Ireland was always a good stick with which to beat a government, but always an awkward and unpleasant one to attempt to handle when in power.

Even larger and more dubious was another of Disraeli's assumptions – that the English connection itself was not a major Irish grievance. English analyses of Irish problems constantly made this assumption. Why? Perhaps because England's fundamental determination to keep Ireland made irrelevant any consideration of the connection. Perhaps also because of the mentality pilloried in J. S. Mill's comment on the Irish question in 1868 – '. . . there is no other nation which is so conceited in its own institutions, and of all its modes of public action as England is. . . .'

The closer Disraeli came to the nub of the Irish question, the more inappropriate his solution is revealed to be. It is a clear consequence of what undoubtedly was a perceptive analysis, that unless English ministries pursued appropriate policies of radical reform, a potentially revolutionary situation would continue to exist, with admitted justification, in Ireland. Disraeli's solution was ' To effect by his policy all those changes which a revolution would effect by force.' Even if such a policy was politically viable, in terms of passage through the English Parliament, was it not, conceptually, a *non sequitur*? What is a revolution? Not only the securing of reformative improvement, but change effected by force and violence. In saying, ' The remedy is revolution ', Disraeli said more than he knew. Political policy cannot effect all those changes which a revolution would effect by force. It omits one vital aspect of revolutionary change, the emotional release, the taking of vengeance on the old regime, the long-awaited eruption of passionate hatreds. Five years before Disraeli's diagnosis, Gustave de Beaumont had written of the Irish peasant: ' Violent and vindictive, the Irishman displays the most ferocious cruelty in his acts of vengeance.' The desire for vengeance was central to Irish attitudes, crudely obvious in the world of the peasant, submerged or buried elsewhere. ' What did " Sinn Féin " mean?' an English journalist enquired in a Dublin hotel in 1916: ' Vingince, be Jazuz,' was the reply – one totally beyond English comprehension. All the political reforms which England might bestow would never slake that thirst for vengeance.

And Disraeli himself had already recognised the hatred. Writing to *The Times* in April 1836 he stated that the Irish ' hate our free and fertile isle. They hate our order, our civilisation, our enterprising industry, our sustained courage, our decorous liberty, our pure religion. This wild, reckless, indolent, uncertain and superstitious race have no sympathy with the English character. Their fair idea of human felicity is an alternation of clannish broils and coarse idolatry. Their history describes an unbroken circle of bigotry and blood.' The prejudice this commentary reveals – and it is notable how central anti-Catholicism is to it – does not auger well for Disraeli as an Irish reformer, and of course, he never became one.

Having in 1844, appraised the Irish question 'in its integrity', in a lifetime of politics Disraeli did virtually nothing about it. The exigencies of English party politics is a major part of the explanation. So is his imperialism. And so also is his prejudice. Disraeli is representative of that sector of English political life in which an enlightened discernment of Irish problems was negated by party and personal interests and anti-Catholic prejudice, to issue in reluctant, minimal activity in Irish affairs.

In fact, aside from Irish violence and agitation, only one factor could disturb the English tendency to do as little as possible about Ireland, and that was a genuine interest in Irish affairs developed by some powerful English politician. Gladstone alone evidenced this.

Gladstone was a singular politician, in that he was as much interested in religion as he was in politics, and possessed a peculiarly sensitive religious conscience. This is why he understood the Irish question to the extent that he did, and why he gave himself to it as a politician. Ireland seemed to him to confront England with just those political and religious questions he judged most important in the affairs of men. More than that, the situation in Ireland seemed in his view a standing affront to that moral law which ought to inspire and infuse public life, that obedience of the civil state to the law of God. Just how much this concern of Gladstone's was in conflict with the weight of English opinion may be inferred from Parnell's perceptive remark that law was to the English what religion was to the Irish. The Irish regarded religion as the foundation of society: to the English, law filled that function. The close relationship between law and morality in the mind and outlook of the English community produced a notion of law in which lawbreakers were *per se* immoral – or incapable of civilised moral choice. And of course the proposition 'Whatever is contrary to law is immoral' applied to the Act of Union and to all legislation affecting Ireland passed within the Union framework. The English connection, and the English laws that governed Ireland, thus acquired a moral status, which not only worked against any sympathetic understanding of Irish grievances, but also meant that efforts to bring about reform came up against much more than merely political or legislative resistance.

Gladstone placed the moral law first. His priorities leap out from his often-quoted letter to his wife, in 1845: 'Ireland, Ireland! that cloud in the west, that coming storm, the minister of God's retribution upon cruel and inveterate and but half-atoned injustice! Ireland forces upon us these great social and great religious questions – God grant that we may have courage – to look them in the face and to work through them.' This may seem an extravagant dramatisation, a poetic moralising, but the way in which it put Gladstone imaginatively in tune with the mood of Ireland and the temper of the Irish question, points to the fact that this was true insight: the religious man who saw politics as the struggle between the law of God and the forces of darkness and disorder, saw the total religious and moral challenge which Ireland presented to England. To men without this religious vision, Ireland conceived as ' God's retribution ' was fantastic, ludicrous. To them Ireland seemed an infuriating political problem. Or if they held a religious cast of mind, Ireland was certainly on the side of the powers of darkness, nothing Godly about her.

Gladstone's turning to championship of Irish reform has often been described as ' conversion '. The word, with its religious connotations in the realm of enthusiasm, is well chosen. His response to the summons to form his first government in December 1868 makes the point clearly. Gladstone, ' with deep earnestness in his voice and with great intensity in his face, exclaimed, " My mission is to pacify Ireland ".' The religious dedication endured: 20 years later, a Baptist minister, listening to Gladstone speak, felt that he was ' witnessing a fight for righteousness, for humanity, for God.'

Putting aside the fact that most English opinion was unregenerate, what were the shortcomings of Gladstone's religious view of the Irish question? The key problem was that his perception of the Irish question in terms of ' mission ' was not amenable to political expression: how could ' God's retribution ' be averted by human legislation? The mode of politics was pragmatic, partial, limited and specific, but on Gladstone's own reckoning, the Irish question was a great moral totality, and indeed doom-laden. That he could himself turn to grapple with this situation, to pursue what he thought was the will of God in ' the barren exhausting strife of merely political contention ', is testimony to his courage and his greatness, not evidence that what he sought was politically possible. The political system is not easily adapted to the ridding of some personal or national sense of guilt: it was not designed as a confessional, nor as a haven in which a man might quiet his conscience or banish his devils. While it is apparent that Gladstone was possessed by an urgent, driving sense of duty, it could be contended that Ireland merely happened to be the outlet for this, and that he was seeking as much personal realisation and fulfilment, as Ireland's good. In any case, the intimately personal character of Gladstone's mission was both strength and weakness. ' I do believe that the Almighty has employed me for His purposes. . . .', he remarked in 1880, expressing the conviction that he was serving God in politics, not merely generally, but specially and specifically. This made for a wonderful dedication, but also produced an opinionation in which the sense of divinely-guided personal mission mingled with the English tradition of assuming that the English alone could solve Ireland's problems. Ultimately this rendered Gladstone's reform programme down to another exercise in English domination – and this is how many Irishmen received it. He was converted to the view that the Irish were right about their grievances, but he did not accept that the Irish were the best judges of what remedies were needed: that was a matter for his decision, under providential guidance. This left little room for Ireland to pacify herself – and pacify, not satisfy, was the term in which he conceived his mission. Pacification was a term with a heavy weight and a sharp edge.

For all that he understood the Irish question as a religious totality, Gladstone did not understand Ireland. A visit of three weeks in 1877 – his only visit – did not dispel the contagion of that most common of English political diseases – ignorance of Irish conditions. He was also prey to another prevalent political malady, a ' feeling for economy as a sacred principle ' as Hammond describes it. Gladstone's conviction that, for a country's moral good, public expenditure must be restricted to an absolute minimum, did much to constrict the scope and cripple the efficiency of those parts of his reform programme he was able to implement.

Nor, for all Gladstone did for Ireland, can the reverse of that coin be ignored: the linkage of Gladstone and Ireland identified one source of division and contention with another. Dean Church remarked of Gladstone, ' There never was a man so genuinely admired . . . and there never was a man more deeply hated both for his good points and for undeniable defects and failings. But they love him much the less in the House than they do out of doors.' Lord Palmerston was reported to regard him as ' combining all the elements calculated to produce a most dangerous character for this country. . . . Enthusiasm, passion, sympathy, simplicity – these were the qualities which moved the masses; and Gladstone had them all. He would always be more powerful out of office than in it.' The implications of such a situation for Irish affairs hardly need saying. For Gladstone to make a crusade out of Ireland was to attach to that crusade all the loves and hatreds he personally attracted or generated, and to identify its destiny with the political fortunes of his own party. If there is any real meaning in the term ' Victorian England ' (and undoubtedly there is) Gladstone's alienation of the Queen, through his brilliant attacks on Disraeli, was no service to the Irish cause. Irish affairs were sucked into the bitter vortex of English politics and personalities, becoming not the occasional casualty of the English political system, but its constant victim, made the battleground for parties, passion and prejudice. Perhaps all this was inescapable, Gladstone or not, but what Irish affairs really demanded was calm non-party appraisal in an atmosphere of rational tolerance, and they had no chance of that in Gladstone's hands.

Worse still, Gladstone's unique political character – loved in the country, hated in the House, more powerful out of office than in it – bedevilled any cause which he championed. Effective legislation required, first, possession of office, second, firm control of Cabinet, Party and House; Gladstone seldom possessed all these, and his causes suffered accordingly. Actually, his role was more that of declaiming, propagandising the Irish question, rather than of answering it. And his war was wider than with those who frontally opposed him: he was fighting to awaken the English moral conscience to a great injustice and to so create a climate for reform. His was a prodigious personal performance, which though it failed to bring about the moral revolution for which he hoped, certainly inaugurated an era of reform. His failure, at this level, lay in the fact that his sense of England's guilt, so marked in his attitudes to Ireland, was shared by very few Englishmen – perhaps only by John Bright, but Bright opposed Home Rule and held that Ireland was still in ' spiritual serfdom ' to priestcraft. Even those few Englishmen who conceded, as did the Duke of Argyll that ' the diseased condition of the country is due in some measure to these old sins of England ', would have echoed the Duke's remark to Gladstone in 1869: ' I am all against sitting in perpetual sack-cloth and ashes because the Irish are violent and disaffected.' But the dominant opinion is reflected in Robert Lowe's astonishment that Gladstone should think ' that a great debt is due from England to Ireland ' and that he should talk ' of the violence of 200 years ago as if it were a thing of yesterday.'

It was Gladstone, with his moral indignation, his vehemence, who made the Irish question in British politics a continuing focus of emotion, a question of passionate intensity. From one viewpoint this may be seen as his greatest contribution to the Irish question, dispersing apathy, placing it in the centre of English politics, focusing on it a burning attention. From another view, it was perhaps a great disservice. In the final balance, the emotional forces in Britain against Ireland – the weight of prejudice – were greater than those for it. Had it been possible to make relations with Ireland a matter of rational politics, rather than of morality and emotion, then perhaps a rational political solution may have been found within the immense resources of English political intelligence. Once the issue became an emotional one, as it did with Gladstone, it attracted traditional animus and prejudice which was more vigorous, more influential, than any emotion which might be generated by liberal ideology. To set the problems of Ireland permanently adrift in a storm of emotion was to place them in great hazard of being wrecked on the rocks of violence. Passionate words lead easily to passionate deeds. Gladstone, of his political nature, must bear some of the responsibility for that atmosphere of tension and violence which built up so inexorably after 1868, around the Irish question.

Essentially Gladstone was an abberation in English politics, in imaginative grasp, in religious bent, in passionate devotion to moral principle; so far from the main stream that Hammond describes him as the most brilliant and most irresponsible member of his own party. Gladstone recognising this himself, remarked in 1875, ' For the general business of the country my ideas and temper are thoroughly out of harmony with the ideas and temper of the day, especially as they are represented in London.' Given this disharmony, what is astonishing is how far Gladstone managed to divert the political stream towards the channels of religious and moral duty through which his own energies flowed. Necessarily, this was a passing achievement. From Gladstone's conversion until his death, Irish affairs rose to the dimensions of a crusade in English politics. Neither before nor since did any Englishman lend them that stature: after Gladstone, Ireland's crusades were left to the Irish.

One hesitation. Gladstone's crusade – was it for Ireland's sake, or England's? Gladstone told the Commons that removal of Irish grievances was an English duty, ' so that instead of hearing in every corner of Europe the most painful commentaries on the policy of England towards Ireland we may be able to look our fellow Europeans in the face.' In comments like these, the English orientation of Gladstone's view comes through clearly. J. L. Hammond's classic treatment of Gladstone's concern with Ireland is entitled *Gladstone and the Irish Nation*. Yet it has more to do with the *English* nation, as did Gladstone himself. His attempts to persuade England to act stem more with concern for England's character than for what Ireland would gain: often his main focus of interest seems to have been the creation of a holy, moral English nation, shriven from the great stain of its Irish guilt.

But finally the point needs to be made with Gladstone as with Disraeli: the closer he came to a real understanding of the essence of the Irish question, the greater was the distance revealed between English and Irish standpoints. Those Englishmen who took a receptive view of the religious element in the Irish situation were very few, and that cast of mind took them a long way towards a true appreciation of its essentials. Lord Shaftesbury appraised the problem in December 1846: ' Ireland is manifestly set for our punishment, the slow but just punishment of a

ruling power that thrust upon it Popery, anarchy and unsympathetic proprietors. The nation is irreconcilable to the Saxon authority.' But Shaftesbury's evangelical Protestant solution took him far away from the realities
of the problem. ' Depend upon this,' he said, ' the difficulty lies with the
sacerdotal and monkish orders, who . . . stand between . . . the living
word of God and the dead congregation. Only allow profound security
of life and limb, with free discussion and an open Bible, and you will
cease to be perplexed in your determination how Ireland is to be
governed.' If Shaftesbury and many others departed from Irish realities
in their Protestant enthusiasm, Gladstone made his departure on his
liberal religious principles and concept of Christian unity. In 1874 he
launched, with his usual passion, an attack on the Vatican Decrees on
Papal infallibility, revealing unmistakably – and with irreparable damage
to his Irish reputation – the vast distance which separated him from
the Irish religious mind. He saw infallibility as an affront to modern
thought and a grave blow to the cause of Christian unity. In 1873, Cullen
had condemned Gladstone's proposals for University reform, another
matter with religious implications. By 1877 *The Times* summed up
Gladstone's image in Ireland thus, ' The author of the abortive University
Bill, the antagonist of Vaticanism, was better remembered in Ireland
than the Minister who framed and introduced the Irish Church and Irish
Land Bills.' So it was at the election of 1874, and so it was to continue to be in church circles – a profound distrust and suspicion, only
lightly overlaid by the later image of Gladstone, champion of Home
Rule.

In significant contrast, in England Gladstone's attack on the Vatican
Decrees appeared as a curious political irrelevance even within the
domestic confines of the Liberal Party. Joseph Chamberlain observed
acidly, ' An Ex-Minister who devotes his leisure to a critical examination
of the querulousness of an aged priest is hardly in sympathy with the
robust common sense of English Liberalism.' Here indeed is the gulf
that separated Ireland from England. For in Ireland, these politically
trivial comments on ' the querulousness of an aged priest ' precipitated a
rift between the Catholic hierarchy and their only point of really sympathetic contact in English political life – Gladstone. Nor would it be an
exaggeration to say that, English political context aside, it was Gladstone's response to the Vatican Decrees which brought to nought all his
plans for Ireland: they perished, so far as Ireland's own attitude was
concerned, on the rock of religion. Gladstone had been moving with
Ireland's wants and demands, but over the Vatican Decrees he lost contact with Catholic Ireland, the fundamental determinant of Irish life. In

immediate effect, he had alienated its leaders: they would never trust him again. In the broad, he had demonstrated publicly his opposition to Catholicism. Religious matters, in which the only real hope of meeting and understanding lay, proved as before, traditionally, the grounds for fundamental rift and conflict

PART THREE

The Question Posed
1870-1921

I

The Home Rule Question

In origin, the Home Rule movement was Protestant, prosaic and narrowly political – and also, fundamentally conservative. It never escaped from its origins. That the zeal of Gladstone, an English politician, should condition its impact on British political life, points to these realities. That the Home Rule party should be founded by Isaac Butt and reach its zenith under Parnell is often taken to signify the continuing importance of Protestants in the Irish nationalist movement: perhaps its significance is rather that Home Rule was essentially an Irish Protestant movement which gained Catholic support. If this is so, what requires explanation is not why the movement failed, but why it lasted so long and went so far towards success. If Home Rule failed because it was not an Irish Catholic solution to the problems of Catholic Ireland, its long life – nearly half a century – may be explained within a similar framework: its endurance testifies to the great strength of the English and Protestant elements that were operative in Irish life, and to the importance of English political structures as a determinant in Irish affairs.

The Home Rule movement had its origins in the perturbation of Protestant conservatives in Ireland. The Fenian disturbances, the disestablishment of the Irish Church, land reform – these were worrying things which indicated British misgovernment (and tendencies towards radicalism) and suggested that Ireland would be better off under its own legislature composed of Ireland's natural governors – the upper and middle classes. This conservative motivation is personified in Isaac Butt, who led the movement from 1870 to 1879. Butt was a patriot of religious disposition who became convinced by the late 1860s that the differences between agrarian Ireland and industrial Britain were too extreme to be reconciled in a common Parliament. He feared that the secularism and radicalism he saw advancing in Britain – to the detriment of spiritual and social values he held dear – would spread to Ireland: disestablishment seemed to prove this. Certainly, Home Rule was a political device, with political objectives – the preservation of the existing rights of property and church within the Union, by way of securing happiness and tranquillity through self-government. But its impulse was not so much political as moral, largely directed towards protecting the established moral and social structures of Ireland by the simple means of separating them from British contagion. Seen in this light, Home Rule took its origin not in nationalism, but in a religio-moral alarm that Ireland was in danger of contamination, or of decay contrived by infidels and socialists in England.

This alarm was one shared by Catholics, but to them generally the Home Rule movement founded in 1870 had the complexion of the Irish Parliament of 1782-1800. Its attraction was obvious; it sought the end of Union, and a substantial degree of Irish independence from Britain. Its repellant, dangerous aspects were no less evident; it was the domain of Protestant conservatives. However, by 1871 this had begun to change and by 1874 the Home Rule movement had become a popular one, that is, drawing increasing Catholic support. Fielded by Irish Protestants to protect their world-view and interests, the capture of Home Rule by Catholics did not merely push most Protestants out, but drove them back to the Unionist camp where they entrenched their defences even more deeply than before. The early years of the Home Rule movement were decisive in destroying, once again, any real hope for a united Irish nationalism: politics were trapped in religious cages.

Why did Catholics turn to the Home Rule movement? Because there was no other outlet for their aspirations. From the beginning, the movement had attracted nationalists who were Catholics simply because they saw in Home Rule a nationalist movement. By 1872 some bishops and a wide section of the clergy were coming to favour it for that reason: it offered a constitutional outlet for Irish aspirations. The nature of this growing Catholic support is important: it was support for an existing political device, not a Catholic solution to Ireland's problems. That is, Home Rule appealed to the political aspects of Irish Catholic aspirations. It remained to be seen if it would satisfy the Catholic aspects of those aspirations. In 1871 it was a common episcopal view to see Home Rule as a Protestant plot, assisted by some Catholics, to diminish the power of church and clergy. This view lived on, in various forms; and throughout its life the Home Rule movement also retained the image among many of the bishops of a diversion from what they believed obsessively was the most important Irish question – the need to get Britain to provide for religious education in Ireland: Cardinal Cullen thought this in the 1870s, Cardinal Logue thought this in the 1890s. But by 1872 the bishops had to face the fact of a considerable popular swing towards the Home Rule movement, a swing patent in the 1874 elections, in which the Irish Liberal party was destroyed, and Irish electors returned 59 members pledged to some form of Home Rule.

By 1874 Cullen's politicising in the interests of Catholicism had come to nothing. The Catholic Union formed in 1872 had never attracted enthusiasm. Catholic politics had failed. Home Rule was national, and by 1874, given the disillusionment with the Liberals, it had no real competitor for the support of Catholics. Cullen, however, did not like the idea of Home Rule. He feared an Irish Parliament which would be Protestant-dominated, or at least the preserve of lay persons who ' would begin to make laws for priests and bishops and to fetter the action of the Church.' This fear did not die with Cullen. Far from it. Almost on the eve of the first Home Rule Bill, the Irish bishops – unanimously, according to Cardinal Manning's account – favoured Union with England plus local provincial self-government; but not one central Irish Parliament. They feared such a Parliament as likely to weaken the influence of the Church through the operation of an anti-Christian spirit in the elected body, and of Protestantism in the Peers. To Irish politicians, the term ' Home Rule ' meant an Irish Parliament, with the widest possible powers of self-government: even to many of the clerics who supported ' Home Rule ' it meant much less, generally some form of local administration *cum* government – in which, of course, the clergy could exercise considerable influence. The reasons for episcopal misgivings about, or objections to an Irish Parliament are obvious. Under the Union, the church had become the strongest organisation in Ireland, a force of immense and popular power. Home Rule raised the possibility that this power would be curtailed, perhaps even destroyed. Dedicated to the preservation of the dominion of religion over men's lives, the Church was highly sensitive on the matter of competing authorities and allegiances, particularly when a competitor could show, as it did in the 1874 elections and on notable occasions thereafter, that clerical opposition or encouragement was sometimes not strong enough to control popular political choice. The very fact that radical Home Rulers could be elected in the face of clerical disapproval increased the suspicion in which Home Rule was held. Moreover, in Ireland, the basic fact of Church-State relations was that the Church had won considerable independent power, and great popular influence, by virtue of protracted conflict with a Protestant State. Home Rule not only raised the problem for the Church of contriving a new relationship with a new government structure. It also raised for both churchmen and Home Rulers the contentious question of whether the Church's power, independence and influence would be the same – or greater or lesser – in the coming new order as in the old.

Why then did the Church, bishops and clergy, apparently come to support Home Rule? For many, the support was genuine – leaving open, of course, the very important question of what they meant by 'Home Rule'. But for others – and the point may be made in relation to the Irish bishops acting as a body – they became involved with the Home Rule movement because they could not avoid doing so. The movement became popular in a way and to an extent which dragged the Church in after its members, and silenced clerical misgivings through fear of alienating the flock. It would be an error to assume that the bishops favoured what the politicians meant by 'Home Rule'. Their calling on the Irish party in October 1884 to champion Catholic educational claims in Parliament was a test of that party's Catholicity (one which it notably failed). The bishops' statement of February 1886, that, 'it is our firm and conscientious conviction that Home Rule alone can satisfy . . . the legitimate aspirations of the Irish people', was a reluctant, delayed recognition of political facts which avoided the question of what Home Rule meant, but attempted to relate the Church to a movement which had proved its great popular appeal.

Part – a very large part – of the Irish success of the Home Rule movement can be explained by the hostility with which the movement was met in England, and by Irish Protestants. Being amenable to religious interpretation, this hostility tended to arouse religious zeal around the Home Rule cause. Writing in 1889, Monsignor Bernard O'Reilly – in his biography of Archbishop MacHale, the first episcopal Home Ruler – asserted that 'the one great reason why Englishmen refuse to Ireland the boon of self-government in dependence on the British Crown is not so much because the majority of Irishmen are aliens in race, as because they are aliens in religion. Were the Irish all Protestants, they would tomorrow repeal the Union, and restore to them their native Parliament.' O'Reilly held that 'The Irish bishop or priest is by the very force of things compelled to be an active politician, for the simple reason that the agitation and advocacy of the simplest political reforms or improvements means, for priests and people, the agitation and advocacy of measures essential to the religious interests of the nation.' Assessed on these grounds, the long fight for Home Rule became another religious crusade, and the refusal of England to grant it, a continuing religious persecution.

On a general Irish view, a movement which provoked bitter English resistance, must be, just because of the testimony of that opposition, in Ireland's best interests. And indeed the majority of Englishmen rejected Home Rule as revolutionary, Roman Catholic, and an unacceptable reflection on the quality of English government. It was revolutionary in that it sought a fundamental change in the relationship between the two countries, destruction of the old Unionist regime; it was Catholic in that its support was mainly from Catholics; and it was trumpeted out that English rule was intolerable. As Sir William Harcourt told Gladstone in December 1883, referring to the extension of the franchise, the greater the expression given to Irish opinion, the more obvious it would be 'declared to the world in larger print what we all know to be the case that we hold Ireland by *force and by force alone* as much as in the days of Cromwell. . . . We never have governed and we never shall govern Ireland by the good will of its people.' Manning had told him the same thing nearly 20 years before: '. . . we hold Ireland by force, not only against the will of the majority, but in violation of all rights, natural and supernatural – that is, of political justice and religious conscience.'

This analysis of Anglo-Irish relationships was anathema to Gladstone, and indeed most Liberals: as Mansergh puts it, 'it was not so because it should not be so.' The Liberal conscience rejected the notion of government by force. Yet it was committed to Union. Home Rule was a lot more than Gladstone's personal conscience: it was an attempt to pursue a *via media* or reconciliation between imperialism (the needs and facts of power) and liberalism: Home Rule would consolidate the Union by winning the Irish to its support. Perhaps this was a delusive attempt to erect an inconsistency. When Gladstone argued that the concession of autonomy, on the Canadian model, would reconcile Ireland to the Empire he was on dangerous ground. Modern Imperial precedents and situations were misleading when applied to Ireland, as Ireland's relationship with Britain, in its origins and nature, was very different. All sides, Irish and English acknowledged this. When Cardinal Manning confided to the Pope in 1885, 'I consider a Parliament in Dublin and a separation to be equivalent to the same thing. Ireland is not a colony like Canada . . .', much opinion on both sides of the Irish Sea would have agreed with him. Yet Home Rule, for all its modifications and limitations of dominion status, amounted to a pretence that a form of dominion status was appropriate to Ireland.

Much more decisive politically than the inconsistency or delusion of the Liberal approach were the facts that the Liberals were not often in power, and that the Tories (and the Queen) disagreed with them: the

British were split on the question of what to do about Ireland, and, particularly after 1886, the Liberals were not the really decisive force in English politics. At crucial moments in the development of Anglo-Irish relations, conservative Unionists held power: at other times they had enough influence to cripple Liberal plans. The Unionists translated 'Home Rule' as meaning 'Dismemberment of the Empire' – the Conservative slogan for the 1880 elections. The first Home Rule Bill was debated in an atmosphere where 'Imperialism' had already been established as (to use Koebner's phrase) 'the shibboleth by the use of which one section of the nation expressed its low opinion of the political morality allegedly possessed by the other section'. Despite the fact that both Unionists and Home Rulers wanted to preserve the Empire, the Home Rule issue convulsed and divided British opinion because it asked the basic questions – what sort of Empire, and how should it be maintained?

Moreover, the very defects and shortcomings of British rule in Ireland militated against English acceptance of Home Rule as a solution. Surely the obvious thing to do was to remove the grievances that had produced the Home Rule movement? This had been Gladstone's own view until he had accepted Home Rule as an inevitable necessity. To those who remained in the position he vacated in 1886, Home Rule was a hazardous experiment and an abrogation of England's duty – which was to make the Union work well. In this view, the vital Irish grievance was not who governed Ireland, but how Ireland was governed, perhaps not even at the level of new measures, as of a new spirit and methods of administration. The prevailing English reaction to Home Rule ignored whatever content of Irish nationalism that movement held and moved very little past an understanding of its early stages, when it was a reaction to unpalatable English legislation and administration. The most positive English responses tended to remain at the level of conceding that English rule needed to be improved: even Gladstone's adoption of Home Rule merely meant an admission that the improvement of English government might entail perhaps a drastic limitation of its scope.

However, as an Irish demand, Home Rule had a dual nature. Besides its declared programme, it had become a vehicle for dynamic forces within Irish society, forces not so much expressed in particular demands as in temperament and disposition. W. B. Yeats criticised the Home Rule movement under Butt as lacking in 'hereditary passion', and remarked that Parnell, seeing that this lack made Butt's party powerless, sought to draw on the peasantry's tenacity and violence – which he did. What had the emotions and objectives of the peasantry in common with Home Rule?

– essentially nothing. The ' success ' of the Home Rule movement under Parnell contained a deception : it was not the constitutional agitation that was succeeding, it was the primitive power behind it. Butt was a natural leader of the Home Rule movement, as was John Redmond later. The temper and style of these two men were in harmony with a gradualist constitutional objective within an English structure. They not only led the Home Rule party, they symbolised it; whereas Parnell's leadership, vitally related to a surge of violence, had the contradictory effects of achieving great power for the Home Rule movement, and of assisting to bring about its eventual failure. Ultimately, Home Rule's failure as an Irish cause lay in its prosaic nature. It failed to satisfy dreams, imagination, emotion, hatreds. Under Parnell it came somewhere near to doing this, and the result was that thereafter, when the movement returned to its real self, that reality seemed a weak dim shadow, not even a pale ghost of what Parnell had conjured up. Parnell and the dramas that swirled around him gave the Home Rule movement a popular status beyond its own reality. After Parnell, Home Rule became a dramatic illusion to which the Irish paid homage because it was a familiar traditional goal which had once been magnificent, a great cause. To that illusion, Gladstone with his concept of Home Rule as a sort of crusade, made a substantial contribution. If the illusion dazzled the Irish, it also blinded the English. Absorbed in this great solution, Gladstone had no interest in local government reforms which may have been of great practical value, would have had the support of the Irish bishops, and had some hope of political passage.

What it all comes down to, however, is that the great obstacle that lay in the path of Home Rule was that England would not allow it. Home Rule was antithetical to the English spirit and values in a time of the growth of imperial sentiment, imperial convictions and attitudes. To a majority, Home Rule involved a risk, if not the certainty, of the disruption of the Empire, and that was sufficient to make it totally unacceptable. What was astonishing was that English politics tolerated the debate for so long. Part of it was having to, in terms of the strength of Parnell's party; part of it was Gladstone personally; part of it was mere party; part of it was the troubled conscience of men engaged in arguments of empire – the Home Rule debate offered both English sides the opportunity to proclaim in public their virtues and self-justification. If the imperialists' proclamations now sound absurd or bombastic, is it idle to wonder how many supported Home Rule knowing it would be defeated, the first Bill in the Commons, the Second in the Lords? How many conspired in a liberal pretence which Gladstone took seriously? Was Home

Rule a luxury of principle which the Liberals could easily afford, if others could be relied on to ensure its defeat?

Very little of what was purely political or genuinely imperialist was intelligible to the Irish Catholic mind. It saw the situation as religious, as always. In 1887 an anonymous pamphleteer on 'Ireland and the English Catholics' explained, 'Let this matter be clearly understood. The balancing power which has beaten the Bill is – hatred of Catholicism and contempt for the Clergy. Were the Irish people faithless to the pastors they would win the support of the English Atheistic poets and Dissenting Politicians. The price they pay for their fidelity to Heaven is still, as much as ever it was, the refusal of English Protestantism to think " Papist rats " fit for Freedom.' The Irish bishops looked at Home Rule from other religious angles. Suspicious of Home Rule and hostile to Gladstone as the enemy of the Papacy, some bishops regarded Gladstone's taking up of the Home Rule cause as proof of the dangers of both. So deep was distrust of the Liberals that it could issue in the reasoning revealed by Bishop Nulty in 1887: ' Our Religion and perhaps our liberties are *safer* under a Tory Government as the Whigs are sure to be on our side against a Tory Govt. but the Torys w[oul]d not back us against a Whig Govt. no matter how hard it was.'

The question has been asked earlier – if England would not have it, if it was a very partial expression of the major currents within Ireland, if decisive sections in Irish life neither liked nor wanted it, why did the Home Rule cause survive so long? Some particular answers have already been suggested: some general ones remain. The Home Rule agitation acted as a profound test of the realities of the Anglo-Irish relationship. It was neccessary for the movement to prove, with some degree of finality, firstly whether or not Ireland's governors, English and Ulster Protestant, would accept it; and secondly, the related matter of whether or not it was what Ireland really wanted. Of its nature, this was a long drawn out experimental and educational process, confused by partial successes (in the form of gaining reforms) and by apparent progress towards the objective. But, crudely, the Home Rule movement (that is, a movement within the political ways and means which the English offered the Irish) had to exist in order to prove that it was ultimately futile and unsatisfactory as a vehicle for the dynamic forces at the centre of Irish life. It was necessary to prove with reasonable certainty that Irish demands would not be conceded within the constitutional structure and methods of English politics – necessary in practical terms (in that rebellion, as an acceptable majority movement, must be a last alternative); necessary in moral terms (in that violence, ethically, must be a last resort). It was also necessary

for the English themselves to arrive at decisions about the extent of
concessions they were prepared to make to the Irish. By its pressure, the
Home Rule movement achieved a great deal, short of its full objective.
Its forcing of British legislation did much to set Irish life in a British
mould. Modern Ireland may be in many ways an Irish construction, but
it is also in many ways an English one – and for that the Home Rule
movement is substantially responsible.

2

The Question of Land War

The 1870 Act had not solved the Irish land problem. In the following
decade, depression and bad seasons forced the economy of rural Ireland to
crisis point, offering a firm basis for a popular national movement of great
strength and passion: the misery and resentment endemic to peasant
Ireland had been screwed to desperation point, and would burst out spontaneously if it was not harnessed and organised. To tap this energy
Michael Davitt, a Fenian whose major hatred was landlordism, contrived
a working agreement between himself, Parnell, and the American Fenian
John Devoy, which was followed by the establishment of the Land League
in October 1879. The League's aims were to end rack-renting and evictions, and promote occupant ownership. Parnell was its president, and it
had American Fenian Support. It thus expressed the alliance between
an organised mass peasant movement, the new aggressive phase of the
Home Rule movement led by Parnell, and the mood and money of
American Fenianism.

This co-operative venture became known as 'the new departure' in
Irish politics. Departure it was, but for where? It went back deep into
the primitivism of peasant Ireland. The new departure mobilised
peasant desires and emotions and organised them into a national movement. Davitt, cast adrift as a peasant boy by eviction, maimed in England
by the industrial revolution, had a patriotism fed by harsh experience of
the Irish land system and first-hand knowledge of its victims. Parnell
epitomised resentment: detestation of the English had drawn him into
politics. From America, Irish revolutionaries who had fled from English
law, and the exiles of emigration, looked back with hatred, and romantic
dreams of a peasant paradise: their political objectives often went beyond
Home Rule to republicanism.

The Land League was not a movement for land reform, it was a wholesale crusade for the establishment of a peasant Ireland. As such it was not – despite Davitt's personal advocacy of land nationalisation – a forward looking socialist solution to the problem of Irish freedom and identity; it was a backward looking peasant solution. The Land League marked the popular beginnings of that massive fit of historical introspection and reaction which achieved cultural respectability in the Gaelic revival: it was a fundamentalist movement which drove Ireland back on its past as a source both for mass nationalism and Irish values. Davitt's view was that ' The struggle for the soil of Ireland involved a combat for every other right of the Irish nation.' In practice, ' the recovery of the soil of Ireland ' from the ' buttressed, feudal garrison ' meant the resurrection of nothing but peasant Ireland. Davitt's own contention was that England had deliberately destroyed the industrial life of Ireland: what remained – a peasant economy – was an inflated vestige, a distortion. Yet logically, inevitably, a free Ireland meant freedom for a dominant peasantry, for their economy and for their social values. To make the peasants kings of Ireland was to enthrone a very powerful force, certainly one too powerful to be controlled to their liking by theorists or politicians. Whatever the Land League's ultimate ideals, or the politicians' assumptions, the immediate consequences of mobilising the peasantry must be to hand the dominance of Irish life over to the peasant, and to establish his world as a pervasive tyranny.

Religion – Catholicism – was integral to the peasant world, and an inevitable consequence of the turn to the peasantry as a basis for a national movement was the strengthening of the sway of religion in Irish political life. The pervasive influence of the Church in Irish life in the late nineteenth and early twentieth centuries is closely related to the rise of the peasantry to political power – a point which seems to have escaped many Irish intellectuals who made a cult of the peasantry but who were hostile to Church power. The peasant was coming to rule Irish life, and the Church was his culture. Urban intellectuals, to whom many other cultural structures and belief systems were accessible, did not suffer peasant Catholicism gladly. Their angle was the romantic one that the peasant embodied noble and distinctive Irishry at its best. This chimed in harmoniously with religious opinion, and it was on this matter of the tillers of the soil that religion and romantic nationalism, as well as hard-headed political power-ism, met to their joint benefit. There was the deep religious conviction, stretching back to Christian antiquity, that the rural life was more conducive than any other to Christian belief and practice. In Ireland this had been reinforced by the growth of urban life and industrialism in Protestant England, contrasted with the agricultural village life of Catholic Ireland. The land war of the 1880s embedded the concept of the superiority of rural life much deeper in both the religious and the national outlook, because that way of life was then identified, in violence and in spectacular political agitation, with the national cause and the Irish value system. True Ireland, holy Ireland was the Ireland of farm and village, the domain of a free God-fearing peasantry. The city was English, its values were English. It was *per se*, naturally, the product and genèrator of iniquity: its destiny was to spawn Protestantism or secularism. In April 1888 the Irish Catholic monthly *Lyceum* could see no remedy for Dublin's slums until something was done ' to check the current which flows towards the city centres, and leaves naked of human life the soil on which man should labour and find his home.' The *Lyceum* dreamt of a land of peasant farm owners, free of both landlord and state. The way in which Gaelic romanticism merged with values derived from religion is illustrated by the hope, in 1890, which Bishop O'Donnell of Raphoe entertained for a revival of ancient Ireland: he had found in Donegal a few vestiges of such unity of patriotic feeling and oneness of practical sympathy between the tiller of the soil and its owner, as ' remind one of the close ties that bound each local chieftain and his clan together.' In terms of such visions of a reversion to an idyllic past, the future was to be disappointing. Land reform there was to be, but as rack-renting and evictions diminished, so did the new problem of mortgaging emerge: however successful the peasants were in throwing off the landlords, they still had to contend with the capitalists.

Who roused and organised the peasantry of the 1880s? Who urged them to resist excessive rents and eviction, throught boycotting and rent-withholding? Who were the generals of the peasant army which took the field against the landlords and the forces of English law and order to engage in land war? It was the nationalist politicians, who sought to use this mass force to back their political agitation directed towards land reform and ultimately Home Rule. However, once mobilised as a basis for the new departure, the natural momentum of the peasant movement could not be controlled for long by those who did not share fully its objectives and values. Its natural tendency was not towards any new departure or any sophisticated political objective: it wanted to depart back into the realm of that which was lost – the old Irish world of peasant ownership and peasant community. In fact, its natural tendencies implied the destruction of those who had liberated it: in turning to the peasantry for support, Parnell ensured immediate and immense popular power for himself and his party, and also the eventual extinction of that power.

The natural tendencies of the peasantry to seek the construction of an Ireland which suited it but not necessarily the politicians, was fostered by the Church, both because it was identified with peasant values, and because it sought to retain mass allegiance. The peasantry as a mass were incapable of intellectual nationalism. When Church and nationalist politicians came to contend for possession of the peasantry, the Church would win.

Russia provides illuminating historical commentary on peasant revolution. The Irish situation, if less vivid or extreme, also points the problem: if an agitation is undertaken with peasant support, and necessarily embracing peasant aims, success means success for the peasantry. If the tyranny of the agitation's leaders or idealists is impossible or unthinkable, then the subsequent governmental situation must be, if not rule by peasants, certainly rule for peasants. The very substantial identification of nationalist movement with peasants' revolt means that nationalist victory will entail the triumph of social conservatism. The natural product of such a nationalist agitation carried to success would be a conservative, agricultural state expressing peasant values; that is, hostile to anything other than the traditional orthodoxies in politics and religion. Applying this argument to the Ireland of the later nineteenth century, there were reasonable grounds for the belief (productive of fear) that drove Protestants into opposition to Home Rule – the belief that a Home Rule Ireland would be dominated by Catholic peasants.

Even in the short term, mobilising a peasant revolt to sustain a constitutional movement for self-government had obvious dangers. Davitt is an extreme case, but the type of statement he was making in the land war situation of the 1880s, made the realities explicit: 'Unless the Liberal party did something to ensure confidence, some of the nationalists would feel compelled to fall back on means and methods not constitutional. . . . If the people did not defend their hearths to the death, they would never prove themselves worthy of getting their country to rule. A race that would allow their homes to be tumbled about their ears were unworthy of any sympathy.' In so far as Home Rule politicians accepted violence as the real power behind their movement, or as a means of demonstrating that the Irish were worthy of self-government, they were digging the grave of their own constitutional movement: they, the constitutionalists, were accepting violence and revolt as the measure of national strength and stature. And they were making their own task of securing progress and harmony by legislative reform very much more difficult. The turbulence that lay behind the political agitation seemed to many Englishmen a disqualification of Ireland from any claim to self-government, a very dangerous threat to the established social order, and conclusive evidence of retrogressive barbarism. Gladstone incorporated into his 1881 Land Act the basic demands of the Land League – fair rents, determined by arbitration; fixity of tenure; and freedom for the tenant to sell his occupancy. *The Times* expressed a very common English view when it held that these ' three Fs ', in establishing a form of dual ownership, were an absurd economic regression into the feudal past.

If the Land League agitation produced the 1881 Land Act, it had also produced the Coercion Act which immediately preceded the Land Act. The land war, harnessed to a parliamentary campaign, polarised English reactions, producing both conciliation and coercion to the effective frustration of both modes of dealing with Ireland: they cancelled each other out. At one end of the spectrum of English reaction, the government sought to devise measures and policies which would conciliate the Irish. It is indicative of the governmental recognition of the accuracy and critical importance of the Church's opinions on Irish affairs that this search for knowledge of what lay at the bottom of Irish disturbance, and for methods of remedying it, took the British government towards a closer relationship with Church authorities. Cardinal Manning who had acted since the 1860s as an intermediary between the Irish hierarchy and the British government, became, in the violence that marked the 1880s, tantamount to the government's Irish adviser, giving advice and warnings, always available for consultation. As well, the government made energetic and constant efforts to engage spiritual authority on its side, mainly by discreet diplomatic attempts to get the Papacy to condemn Irish agitation and to make conservative episcopal appointments, as in the case of the Archbishop of Dublin in 1885. Such efforts produced, or helped to produce, Vatican intervention – in 1883 a condemnation of clerical involvement in Parnell's National League, and, much more importantly, condemnation of the Plan of Campaign and boycotting in 1888. The consequence of the 1888 Rescript was that the Irish bishops awoke to the fact that they had lost control of Ireland to the politicians. The popular reaction in Ireland to English attempts to engage the weight of Papal authority against the Irish national movement was hostile to the degree of frenzy – but it expressed itself not only against the English, but also in part against the Pope and in repudiation of Church authority. Faced with this, the Irish bishops inevitably – if only eventually – chose to support Papal authority, and their own, against the national movement. To the extent to which the British government's relations with the Vatican initiated the development of this situation, it had tacitly acknowledged where the true forces of authority in Ireland lay. It would be wrong to think that British manoeuvres contrived the conflict between Church and politicians: the British encouraged and provoked a confrontation already latent and unavoidable.

At the other pole of English reaction to the land war and parliamentary agitation, was the resolve of conservatives to meet coercion with coercion, and to resist and obstruct change, particularly such change as appeared subversive of the sacred rights of property. So it was that the land war between rent-withholding tenants and evicting landlords that ebbed and flowed in the Ireland of the 1880s divided not only Ireland but England, where it became a test of political strength. Such was the balance of political forces that the outcome was virtual deadlock. Such reform measures as were passed by Parliament without major evisceration were negated and contradicted by measures of coercion. Other reforms, and ultimately Home Rule, were defeated or destroyed, if not in the Commons, then in the House of Lords. The outcome amounted to the paralysis of English policy-making for Ireland, a kind of governmental abdication. Any kind of planned policy of reform was impossible, because the forces operating within Parliament rendered it so. To have any hope of passage, reform legislation was required to be either partial and ineffective, or wedded to coercive measures that negatived its conciliatory intention.

Obviously, from one Irish viewpoint, this situation tended to discredit constitutional and legislative methods as potential solutions to Irish problems. And in so far as the British political situation strangled, blocked and constricted the channels of reform, it handed Ireland over to the governance of violence, physical force. At the same time, the dramatic excitement of the parliamentary battle over Irish questions did strengthen the impression in Ireland that there was much to be gained in that arena: the fact that reforms, even to the extent of Home Rule, were being proposed in the British parliament, the very heat and evenness of the political contest, encouraged the impression in Ireland that if only the Irish pressure were stepped up that little more a breakthrough would occur.

However, particularly among English conservatives, the vigour and prolongation of the Irish agitation had the effect of subordinating the question of Irish reform to what were regarded as much larger and important issues. At the parliamentary level, Irish demands pressed through assaults on procedures, and provoking such bitter internal divisions, resulted in an increasing absorption with the structural and functional problems of English constitution, Parliament and politics which Irish pressure had revealed or created. Then there was the question of whether the acceptance of Irish demands amounted to a general encouragement of extortion by violence, and social and political revolution. Randolph Churchill denounced the 1881 Land Bill as a first step in a social war, an attempt to raise the masses against the classes. Lord Salisbury characterised it as a ' violent innovation prompted by temporary passion '. Suggestions that the powers of the House of Lords be curbed to enable the passage of Irish reforms seemed to the Tories a frontal attack on the very constitution. In fact, to the Tories there was no such thing as Irish land reform, only the threat of Irish revolution. It would be going too far to say that the Tories created a revolutionary situation in Ireland where before only demands for reform existed. Nevertheless they did foster the growth of a revolutionary situation where it was latent, and they did help to destroy all hope of reform by treating it as tantamount to revolution. Home Rule – and much less besides – perished on a whole reef of rocks, but one of the sharpest was the Tories' refusal to regard it as anything less than revolutionary and destructive. Against this, it can be said that in the short term Tory intransigence assisted in giving the Home Rule movement its long span of life: the bitter opposition of the Tories helped foster the prevalent illusion that Home Rule was a great cause, and the real matter at issue between Ireland and England.

The 1880s exhibit a familiar political situation – a reform agitation driving governors and governed further apart. Such reforms as were conceded were inadequate from an Irish view, far too great in the view of the English Tories: such reforms as were rejected were still a matter of agitation, division and animus. Each new reform proposal became another matter for contention and conflict, and thus became a further step away from an atmosphere of conciliation. Every inch gained by the Irish made demands for further ground more pressing and vociferous, while at the same time stiffening further the resistance to its concession. The extent of concessions already made, and the violent nature of the campaign for more, produced a progressive hardening of English attitudes. The logical end of this process was a position from which the British would retreat no further, while the Irish continued to agitate and demand more. Seen thus, it might seem that it was merely a matter of time – and not much time – before an eventual impasse was reached which might be disturbed only by violence. Why did it not come to this in the 1880s? In part, the answer lies with Parnell, in his unwillingness to use violence as more than a threat, and in his extraordinary ability to control the natural acceleration of violence within the movement he led. Partly the answer lies in the situation. The Irish cause was making some progress; the times were exciting; and the future seemed to hold the promise of eventual success.

Patently, the land war involved economics and politics. What was religious about it? Can it be seen as another expression of the violent religious conflicts that began with the Reformation? The question of the morality of the Irish land war campaign is dealt with in a later section: here the concern is the nature of the English campaign.

Matters of economic justice aside, the landlords' most powerful weapon – eviction – raised three major religious issues: it destroyed the social fabric to which religion was related; it appeared to be an instrument of Protestant aggression; and it occasioned and provoked serious sin among the people. Socially, the era of evictions tended to produce the same effects as had the Famine: the people were driven from the land and into emigration. The reactions noted in relation to the Famine were duplicated – the same bitter anger at the deprivation of property and destruction of traditional life, the same religious fear that religion would be damaged by the disruption of the families and communities on which religion rested, and that emigration would lead to loss of faith and morality. The Famine was not the only precedent that sprang to the religious mind. Archbishop Walsh observed to Cardinal Manning in April 1888 'that the seventeenth century had not passed away, that the people were still struggling for their religion and their land, and that the permanency of the one depended to no little extent on the possession of the latter.'

Eviction seen as a Protestant plot was a Catholic interpretation widespread in the North particularly. In Cardinal Logue's observation of Armagh in 1889, most of the evicted farms were being taken up by Orangemen: 'I fear it is only the beginning of a Protestant plantation in several parts of the Country. I fear many of our poor people will be swept from the country.' The reaction of Catholic authority is made very clear in what Archbishop MacEvilly of Tuam told a friend in 1889: 'We are engaged in a new Association for *the defence* of our poor Tenants. It is a matter of absolute necessity for the preservation of our Catholic people. There is a *manifest* determination of Landlords to get rid of them and plant the country with Godless Emergency men, and Protestants of the worst type. I regard it as a sacred & solemn duty, as a Catholic Bishop and in view of future judgement to give it every encouragement and support.' MacEvilly's attitude makes clear the religious – as distinct from the political, or socio-economic – element in clerical involvement in the land war, and clerical support for the Land League and Parnell's party needs to be interpreted in this light. Seen thus, it is not nationalism which is at stake in the land war, but the survival of the Catholic religion: eviction is seen as another manifestation of Protestant persecution. Though prevalent there, such religious interpretations were not confined to the North – nor to the clergy. The lay editor of the *Irish Catholic* argued a variant of the religious theme in May 1889, when he contended that eviction was a device intended to frustrate Home Rule. Eviction would secure the banishment of the traditional Catholic tillers of the soil and the substitution of Ulstermen or aliens in their stead. The consequences of this would be that the Home Rule movement would lose its impetus, or, if it continued, issue in Protestant Home Rule. This contention makes evident the *Irish Catholic*'s firm conception of Home Rule as a Catholic – as opposed to a Protestant – movement, and points up the popular Catholic crusade aspect of the Home Rule movement.

Generally, the view that the land war amounted to a bid for Protestant supremacy produced the obverse opinion that the defence or assertion of tenant rights amounted to a Catholic religious duty. The Land League and Parnell's party thus took on the appearance of a religious crusade, becoming another variation on the Irish theme of holy war. From the outside, Catholic clerical support of tenant resistance and agitation seemed aberrant – ' The unnatural alliance at present subsisting between Rome and Communism ' the Anglican Archbishop of Dublin described it in 1889. On the inside also, many Catholic clergy were seriously disturbed to find themselves involved with an agitation which tended towards morally questionable methods, and to escape from their control. However, the over-riding consideration was the preservation of the Catholic religion, and to many priests this seemed to be an issue – if not *the* issue – involved in the land war. It was this belief that allowed the Land League and Parnell's party to build up their enormous popular power, either with clerical support, or with clerical neutrality. Had it not been for the religious complexion ascribed to the land war, it seems highly likely that the Church would have checked the power of the politicians long before it did.

There was another religious aspect to the land question: it produced unrest and disorder, violence and crime. To secularists these things appeared as brutality or social malfunctions, but to those of religious disposition they were simply sin. To religionists, the situation in Ireland in the 1880s bred sin, breaches of God's law. It is common to regard the 1880s as having killed respect for law among the Irish peasantry. At the end of the decade the *Irish Catholic* remarked ' " Respect for the law " is a wholesome maxim to inculcate in a self-governing country, but one adherence to which, in Ireland, would have only tended to secure the annihilation of the Catholic Faith and the ruin and degradation of our people. We must judge of the morality of every national effort outside the provision of alien laws or the prohibitions of Castle proclamations.' This point had perennial application in Irish history, but it had a special weight in the 1880s, and that particularly, and very importantly, in the evaluations made by the clergy. In the 1880s British law and rule in Ireland became morally indefensible because it encouraged sin, widespread and on massive scale. The equation between law and order was gravely damaged because British land law meant Irish disorder. So law, the public emanation of British civil authority in Ireland, rapidly lost much of the active and even the passive sanction of religious authority in Ireland: the real authority structure in Ireland – the Church – no longer tended to support the formal authority structure, that of Britain. Not that the Church encouraged rebellion, or ceased to discourage it, but it was tending to abstract from civil issues to concentrate on their religious aspect: the rule of Britain and of landlords had become a positive menace to personal salvations. Writing to Archbishop Croke in 1889, Bishop O'Donnell hammered this point:

> Eviction in Ireland has been the fruitful parent of an evil brood. It counts starvation, anguish, hatred, revenge and crime among its progeny. . . . It has blurred the image of the Creator in thousands of His creatures, whom it consigned to the most squalid quarters of large cities at home and abroad, and who, had they been permitted to remain where their fathers toiled, would have continued models of industry and uprightness. It has robbed the poor, fostered secret societies, and provoked outrage.

And again, later, ' . . . what we find hardest to forgive the evicting landlords is the moral waste they have wrought in our people.' In addition to this, the situation had direct repercussions on the growth of the priesthood: in 1890, Bishop McGivern of Newry attributed a sharp drop in vocations to the plight of the farming class.

Hatred and the urge to vengeance, those emotions so central to Anglo-Irish relations, had been given by the land war a new injection of life. This twist of mind was evident even in the *Irish Catholic*, which observed in October 1889: ' The Union, it is true, is lost, the day of its destruction is nigh, but who will ever be able to make amends to Ireland for the bloodshed, the misrule, the corruption, the sorrow, and the suffering it has caused. . . . No human power can ever blot out the memory of these things.' The political potential of such emotions and memories was enormous, but it was their potential for spiritual destruction which worried priests. Bishop Nulty of Meath recalled of the 1880s: ' He remembered being called at two o'clock one Winter's morning to the bedside of a dying man, and he told him that he was about to go before his Maker. The man said: " I will say to God Almighty when I go before Him that I call for vengeance against the villain who evicted me " . . . He had to appeal to such people over and over again to banish from their hearts feelings of vengeance and hatred. . . .' Such appeals had limited success. Britain and the landlords were held to blame both by those who hated and sought vengeance, and by those who saw hatred and vengeance as evil.

Without a conception of the religious implications of the land war, it is impossible to understand fully why the land agitation convulsed Ireland as profoundly and for as long as it did, or why Parnell's party commanded in the mid-1880s so much of the dedication and talent of Catholic Ireland. On a simple economic view, the 1880s might be explained as demonstrating that economic factors are the fundamental determinant in men's affairs. But to put these economic affairs in their religious context, to see their deep religious consequences and repercussions, is to see their true dimensions in Irish society. The plight of the peasant's body was a matter which involved the plight of his soul. The entire quality of his life was threatened by eviction, not only his livelihood. Had the land war been motivated on the Irish side only by material considerations, the Church would have stood arrayed against it: its course would have been short, its roots in Irish life shallow.

3

The Question of Parnell's Ascendancy

The crucial importance and real genius of Charles Stuart Parnell lie in the fact that he was able to contrive the harnessing of the wild horses of Irish violence to the sober chariot of parliamentary agitation. This remarkable feat was not his alone. Michael Davitt was essential to it. So too were the Irish circumstances: fundamental forces were seeking an outlet. Because British power was always superior, and the Church was hostile to violence, these forces which boiled below the surface in Ireland took secret forms, as in Fenianism, and sought open expression where it offered. Parnell was able to offer this mood of violence and rebellion an outlet in constitutional politics. That this was possible and successful testifies not only to Parnell's extraordinary ability (and enigmatic duality) but also to the inability of the revolutionary temper, in the face of British strength and Church disapproval, to adopt a more flagrantly violent form and objective. However, the linkage lay in Parnell personally, and when he fell in 1890 it snapped, leaving the forces of constitutionalism and those of revolutionary violence to gradually assume their natural polarity.

Parnell's success in Ireland derived in the main from two sources – his success in English politics, and his creation of a mass basis for the Home Rule movement. In both cases his success held the seeds of his failure.

Parnell made his Irish reputation in England. When he entered the House of Commons in 1875 his position was very different from that of O'Connell in 1829: O'Connell was by then the tribune of the Irish people; in 1875 Parnell was nobody. Parnell's road to the uncrowned kingship of Ireland began in the House of Commons, where by his aggression, he proved that he could seriously embarrass England, thus winning the reputation he took back to Ireland. He deliberately sought popular support, but it was given because he earned it by his performance in politics: Parnell's success is entirely explicable in terms of the public prominence of the political element in Anglo-Irish relations – hence the narrowness, superficiality and instability of that success, as well as its stark dramatic quality. In very large part, Parnell won his reputation by an aggressive and masterly exploitation of political procedures and forms; the use of obstruction of various kinds to bring political life to a halt and to paralyse Parliament, the heart of the English political system. This was a negative, destructive tactic, reflecting a determination to compel Parliament to attend to Irish affairs or be rendered incapable of attending to any business at all. The tactic had great popular appeal in Ireland, not so much for any results it produced – which were inconsiderable – but because of the English indignation it provoked, because it was something of a sophisticated rendition of the Irish urge to take vengeance, and because it had a bit of the savour of discomforting the English and beating them at their own game of politics.

For a while, Parnell forced English politicians on to the defensive. But what were they defending? Their own political machinery. In fact Parnell's tactics tended not only to load his campaign with a new burden of English animus, but to divert attention away from Irish reforms towards English political and constitutional questions. The result was to draw the attention of the *ad hoc* world of politics to an extensive range of large political and constitutional principles and questions which seemed to be (and often were) related to questions of Irish reform. No doubt there were plenty of English politicians who would have highlighted such relationships anyhow, but the tactics of Parnell and his party made it particularly easy and effective for them to do so. Large general questions were at stake: Parnell's tactics helped greatly to make their confrontation inescapable, and thus swung attention away from the detail and reality of the Irish situation.

There is another way of looking at the moot point of whether Parnell's mode of agitation ultimately did his cause more harm than good. The Irish onslaught on the efficiency of the House of Commons, their apparent contempt for this venerated English institution, aroused a very deep English anger. Gladstone himself reacted very strongly, and there were those English politicians, John Bright among them, who never forgave the Irish parliamentarians for their treatment of the House of Commons. It was Cardinal Manning's belief, by July 1881, that the behaviour of her parliamentarians had ' unspeakably damaged the cause of Ireland '. It is impossible to measure how much the Irish assault on the sanctum of English political life prejudiced the affairs of Ireland thereafter. As Gladstone's career demonstrates, the closer Irish questions came towards the centre of the English political system, moving from the country, to the Commons, to the Cabinet, to the Lords, the stiffer the resistance they encountered. At least part of this seems to have been a reaction to what was regarded as a crude and barbarous raid on the centre of English political civilisation. Though Parnell's tactics brought Irish affairs to the attention of ignorant and apathetic English politicians, they did so in such a way as to radically antagonise them. It seemed that the Irish parliamentary party was engaging in some political equivalent of the warfare that was taking place in the Irish countryside, and of course the party's intimate involvement in that land war was an additional reason for detesting it. The Irish land agitation repelled not only English politicians, but the ordinary Englishman as well, creating a climate of public opinion which provided ample support for the resistant reaction of English politicians.

It is generally agreed that the source of Parnell's power, both in Britain and Ireland, was his ability to maintain around him a penumbra of revolution. Some of the liabilities attached to this asset have been considered. There are others. Parnell created the impression in Ireland that his party and methods could achieve changes which would satisfy Irish aspirations: this diffused, in both Ireland and England, exaggerated expectations of the true potential of the Home Rule movement. The inability of this movement after Parnell's fall to live up to the anticipations he had manufactured is often taken to reflect the lesser stature of the men that followed him. It is also, perhaps even more, a comment on his gross inflation of the potentialities of his own policies. As early as 1882, in the so-called 'Kilmainham treaty', Parnell capitulated to the demands of a constitutional political system. He accepted an amended 1881 Land Act as 'a practical settlement of the land question', and agreed to collaborate with the government in efforts to calm Ireland and secure further reform. This, and his appalled reaction to the Phoenix Park murders in 1882, revealed an identification of Parnell's party with the general spirit of English politics, and also instanced its willingness to co-operate with the English government in pacifying Ireland through reform. The identification went much further in 1885 when, after dalliance with the conservatives, Parnell's support put Gladstone into office, thus aligning the Irish parliamentary party with a major element in the English political structure, the Liberal Party.

The consequences of this were profound. It placed the actualities of the political commitment of the Irish party in contradiction to the disposition of its popular social backing, which was that of agrarian agitation bearing on rebellion. It committed the Irish party to be an appendage of the Liberal Party, and to accept what the English political system was willing to offer.

Whatever the immediate validity of the political reasons for taking this action, it set the limits of the gains from Irish parliamentary agitation as British limits, what the British Parliament would concede. It could be contended that if Parnell wished to remain formidable in politics he had to accept eventually the rules of the political club he had joined. He had to use the system that prevailed: if he did not use it, he would be rejected or become ineffective: his Irish reputation rested substantially on his power in English politics and if he lost the one he endangered the other. He had to accept the facts of British political life or risk oblivion. Yet it could also be argued that his acceptance – particularly his conjunction with the Gladstonian Liberals – effectively destroyed Home Rule as a political possibility before it was tested in Parliament. Up until Gladstone's conversion to Home Rule became known in December 1885, many Tories believed that Home Rule was inevitable, and were, in consequence, giving their minds to considering schemes for limited forms of it. Lord Randolph Churchill, who was totally opposed to Home Rule and very perturbed by Tory hesitation over it, greeted Gladstone's conversion with the comment: ' Surely the Lord has delivered him into our hands' and almost immediately began organising the dramatic 'Home Rule is Rome Rule', 'Ulster will fight; Ulster will be right' campaign he launched in Ulster in February 1886. The effect of identifying Home Rule with the politics of the Gladstonian Liberals was to split the Liberal party (to an extent decisive in defeating the bill in the Commons) and to ensure that the Conservatives adopted opposition to it as a front line plank of their platform. As a bitterly contested party issue, which it became from January 1886 on, the question of Home Rule was more vulnerable to attack than tenable for defence, because while its justice or its practical necessity could be urged or admitted in rational argument (even by Tories and Irish administrators), the strongest emotional forces in Britain – party and personality at the political level, prejudice at that and at the popular level – were decisively opposed to it. Parnell's political genius was for short-term manoeuvre, not for long-term perception. He never appreciated the reality of the anti-Irishism that was so much a part of Britain's emotional climate: he thought it a pretence, or contrived. Could some alternative action by Parnell have preserved Home Rule from the storms of prejudice which the Conservatives unleashed against it? Not entirely, when men like Churchill were willing to propose in Cabinet the simultaneous arrest of all the Irish nationalist parliamentarians on a charge of high treason. The 1885 election and Gladstone's acceptance of Home Rule made a Liberal-Parnellite alliance completely natural, but whereas what the Home Rule cause needed most was the political isolation and popular attenuation of the Ulster Tories and those of Churchill's ilk, what resulted was a *rapprochement* between Churchill and those he had denounced in November 1885 as 'foul Ulster Tories who have always ruined our party', the establishment of the Churchill-Ulster Tory axis as the pivot on which Conservative policy turned thereafter, and a deliberate and intense campaign to arouse popular prejudice against Home Rule. From 1886 on, the Conservatives erected their anti-Home Rule platform on no-Popery, anti-Irishism, and imperial sentiment. Some of this was genuine, some was manufactured, very much was unearthed and organised simply for party purposes. So, before Gladstone had attempted to settle the Home Rule issue on the basis of a high-minded and generous rationality, it had been degraded to the lowest levels of prejudiced emotionalism, vested interest and plain bigotry. Gladstone's task was not merely that of pleading an unwelcome case, it was also that of redeeming a cause already lost to political faction and popular emotion.

Given that Home Rule became a matter of party contention, if it was to be resolved it would have to be in a party political way, that is, by way of compromise based on the strength of the political forces. Because Home Rule had become a Catholic political cause it was likely to provoke anti-Catholic resistance. When Home Rule became a party matter in England, the potential religious division became actualised in the English party situation. Since Home Rule had become a Catholic cause, it was doubtful if it could have produced a co-operative solution to the problem of Irish government unless its religious teeth were drawn: perhaps only the Tories could have done that. In fact the identification of this cause with the Liberal sector of the English party system invited in reaction anti-Catholic politics which accentuated the religious divisions within Ireland and England; thus ensuring that Parnellite Home Rule must fail as a total solution for Ireland and that whatever solution was reached would be determined by the play of the bitterest sectarian politics. The Home Rule cause as organised and directed by Parnell led with doomed logic, to the partition of Ireland on the basis of religion.

Nor was that all that was disastrous in Parnell's legacy. His fall left behind a shattered party – and what was of more importance, bequeathed disillusionment with parliamentary politics: the central forces in Irish life lost confidence in party politics as a panacea, or as a true expression of their aims, but the myth of a powerful dramatic leadership was strengthened It is a curious and significant fact that it was Parnell the potential revolutionary, not Parnell the constitutional politician, who caught and held the Irish imagination, in his lifetime and thereafter. However much his parliamentary heirs insisted that he belonged to them and that they could complete what he had begun, the revolutionary tradition claimed him for its own. It had every right to do so, for although Parnell had been committed to constitutional politics, he had built a bridge between those politics and the forces of violence and rebellion, and crossed that bridge himself from time to time. It was this that was unique about Parnell, this that gave him his popular appeal and power. Once that bridge collapsed with Parnell in 1891 it was never re-erected.

In fact, even under Parnell, the master builder, it was a very flimsy structure. And so, despite its size, unity and efficiency, was the parliamentary party he had done so much to create. Parnell had – though he disguised this superbly – built a remarkable political machine of great power on weak and shaky foundations, flawed by contradictions which went to the centre of the structure. It was the momentum of this powerful political machinery which kept the party going for so long, until the grave contradictions it embodied were exposed by alternative action.

As leader of both Home Rule party and National Land League, the logic of Parnell's position was to campaign for a series of greater and greater reforms and concessions from Britain until the objective of Home Rule was achieved. However, this logic was politically hazardous to pursue, as Parnell saw clearly, for instance in relation to the 1881 Land Act, when he played for time. The problem is even more clearly revealed in Parnell's direct refusal to press for some measures demanded in Ireland – a Catholic University, for example – on the ground that if such measures were secured, it would weaken support for the ultimate objective of Home Rule because supporters of particular measures, becoming satisfied, would then drop out of the movement. The problem was simply that if too much were secured by way of reform before Home Rule was attained, then enthusiasm for Home Rule itself would wane: if all important measures demanded in Ireland were obtained before Home Rule then perhaps there would be no need for Home Rule, or at any rate, no popular support for it. This line of argument was still being used long after Parnell, by John Dillon for instance, in relation to land reform in 1903. It was a problem accentuated by the fact that the two areas of support which the parliamentary party most needed – the peasantry and the Church – were the areas most open to pacification and satisfaction by particular reforms, in land-holding and in education. The party could not afford to be too successful in gaining reforms in those areas or it might put itself out of business. On the other hand were the party not to bestir itself to press for such reforms, it would also endanger its support, this time on the ground that it was not attempting to gain what its supporters wanted and needed: it would open itself to the charge of betraying Ireland's demands.

The obvious party tactic was to try to steer some middle course, providing its supporters if not with partial satisfaction, at least with the appearance of activity, the meanwhile holding their support as a weapon to extort the ultimate concession. Certainly one of the reasons why Parnell and his party were so critical of English reforms was because they believed these reforms inadequate, but it was also because they had to adopt political postures pleasing to their Irish supporters and because they had to create the impression that the totality of desired reforms and the Home Rule cause were inextricably linked. Put bluntly, inadequate reforms by the British government were in the Irish party's interest, as a Home Rule party reliant on retaining Irish support. Against this, the impression that the party sought to create in Ireland that Home Rule would mean all that Ireland desired, did much to harden English interests against Home Rule, not for what it was in itself, but for what it might lead to. In any case, the party's unwillingness to prefer immediate reform to the ultimate objective of Home Rule was a tactic very much subject to the attrition of time. Much of Parnell's success lies in the fact that his were early days. As time went by, particular reforms, such as the Wyndham Land Act of 1903, did diminish the energy of the party's basic support; and its failure to secure other reforms – most notably in Catholic education – became inescapably obvious, so as to produce the alienation of those committed to such reforms. To a considerable extent the Irish parliamentary party's attitudes towards its supporters, or potential supporters, were based either on an inflated view of its own power and prestige, or on the view that as there was no political alternative to itself, it could act as it saw fit, despite the desires of important sections of Irish opinion. The danger of this was that the dissatisfied would not only desert the party, but would seek to cripple the party and construct political alternatives of their own.

Parnell's genius only partly reconciled those who wanted reforms and those who wanted Home Rule: Church opinion was a notable exception to his grand design. In addition to this rift, there was another complication – the party was, in the nature of things, virtually committed to a policy of self-denigration, even self-destruction. Its aims and political situation dictated an attitude of constant and aggressive dissatisfaction with anything less than Home Rule, and even with diluted versions of that. This had gravely detrimental effects on the party and forced it into contorted political positions. It bred a habit of rejecting anything less than its ultimate objective. Parnell's rejection of Chamberlain's 1885 scheme of National Councils for Ireland, in favour of Gladstone's offer of Home Rule was entirely natural, but was it politically wise? Worse still, from the viewpoint of its own health, was that the achievement of unsatisfactory reforms was as much as the party, throughout its long history, could ever claim. It constantly rejected legislation as totally unsatisfactory, or criticised it as inadequate: even the great advance embodied in the 1881 Land Act was subjected to this treatment. In so far as the party was responsible for advances, it was, on its own claim, responsible for unsatisfactory advances: indeed the nature of its position forced it into deliberate attempts to belittle the achievements won at its own insistence. It is difficult to estimate the consequences of this tactic in maintaining and extending dissatisfaction in Ireland and creating a popular appetite for results which the Home Rule party eventually could not produce. Instead of claiming the credit for British reforms, the Home Rule party tended to disown them – which amounted to a policy of discrediting itself and its own methods: it could not allow itself to be judged by its actual political performance, that is, by the practical results it had achieved. It chose instead to stand on its ability to achieve its objective – Home Rule. The revolutionaries were to criticise the Home Rule party for its gradualism, its pragmatism, but essentially the party was a millennial one: it was not a party with a policy, but a movement with an ultimate objective. In consequence, the viability of the party depended not on the extent of gains won in the normal partial modes of politics, but on whether or not it achieved Home Rule. Eventually the success or failure of the Home Rule party must be total. It had an inbuilt time limit on its career. Unlike the English political parties with which it lived, it was not a potential administration with a day-to-day policy: it was an instrument, a means to an end. Its continued popular existence depended on the major determinants in Irish life agreeing on what the end was, and that it was desirable, and on the party's ability to demonstrate convincingly that it was an appropriate and efficient means to that end. Under Parnell, the issue of agreement was skirted, but the demonstration of efficiency seemed dramatically made. This was a mechanical illusion, contrived in part by Parnell's spell-binding genius, and his organisational ability, but utterly dependent on a transitory situation – novelty, the fact that the first steps were the easiest to take, the surge of popular enthusiasm, the existence of Gladstone – which masked the fundamental contradictions and defects of the whole approach.

The Home Rulers were committed to perpetual political dissatisfaction until their millennium dawned. A natural consequence of this was a high degree of political irresponsibility among the Irish members: their constant endeavour was to make sure that the British, not themselves, would carry the responsibility for what came out of Westminster. But while they refused to take the blame for British misgovernment, they also refused the credit for anything which might be good that the parliamentary system – of which they were a part – produced. Since they were intimately involved in that system, they were bound to attract much of the odium it continued to generate. Instead of counteracting this process by celebrating real achievements and progress, they made the system seem even more odious. Dedicated to constant political dissatisfaction, they communicated this to their constituents, and time produced no Home Rule millennium. The argument that whatever reforms Britain conceded were unsatisfactory could be applied to the objective of Home Rule itself. Of its nature Home Rule was no obvious political absolute: a national republic was. Under Parnell, the Irish parliamentary party adopted tactics which were to raise up its own executioners. This was so at the political level and at the religious. When Parnell erected his party on the support of the Catholic masses he both recognised and accentuated the political facts. This determined the party's immediate strength. It also assisted if not determined its eventual destruction, for the parliamentarians in claiming the leadership of a Catholic people, failed to measure up to the criteria for Catholicity demanded by Church authority.

4
Religious and Moral Questions

Behind the dramatic events taking place on the public stage of Irish affairs from 1886 to 1891, a crucial confrontation was developing on the question of who should lead the Irish, and where and how should they be led. The Cullenite assumption that a religious people should be led religiously had been implicitly challenged and denied as the 1880s progressed, to such an extent that the militantly Catholic elements in Irish life were coming to believe that the most vital Irish question was that of social leadership. The Land League – Parliamentary party activity of the 1880s altered the content and balance of ordinary life in Ireland. The broadly political element in that life was inflated dramatically to an extent which diminished, if it did not conflict with, attention given to the demands of religious duty, which the clergy tended to equate with pursuit of the traditional rural life. As a competitor for popular attention and loyalty, political agitation aroused clerical suspicion. Expansion in the extent of popular agitation and political involvement presented a challenge to the dominion and authority of the clergy. As the non-religious concerns of the Irish populace increased, so did their susceptibility to the influence of those who were appropriate leaders in those concerns: as politics and agitation grew in popular importance, so did the sway of politicians and agitators. Clerical involvement in Irish politics is often construed as an aggressive interference in an area irrelevant to religion: it is much more intelligible as a natural defensive reaction to what they saw as threats to their traditional popular power and religious interests. The problem of competition or conflict between the claims of politics and those of religion had not risen so acutely in that earlier upsurge of popular politics that had centred around O'Connell from the 1820s to the 1840s. The problem was present, and occasionally obtruded, but O'Connell was a Catholic; he recognised the vast strength of the bishops and clergy, and generally of Catholic sentiment and attitudes, and worked as closely as he could with these forces; his major triumph was on a specifically Catholic issue, emancipation, pursued by an organisation openly called the Catholic Association. In contrast (and it was made at the time privately, by Church leaders), Parnell was a Protestant who had no affection for the Catholic Church; his relations with the central forces of Irish Catholicism were shrewd, but distant; his causes were political, social, economic, not religious.

At first, indeed until the late 1880s, the popularity of the new departure phalanx drew the clergy to it. In 1887 a parish priest looked back to describe this impulse to his bishop: ' the fumes of popular applause carry many of us astray . . . we allowed ourselves to be swayed in our action and judgement by the expediency of the hour.' That is, the local priest was under strong community pressure, even if he felt personally reluctant to join an immensely popular movement: it was easier to join than to find reasons not to. Besides, there were cogent practical religious reasons for involvement – better for the priest to follow the people than to risk losing control or influence over them. So it was that the same parish priest justified his own membership of the National Land League: ' I am in the League to guide a poor, unthinking and confiding people and prevent them from forgetting for the time, the teachings of the law of God.' It is clear that this priest's involvement was based not on support for the League, but rather on the conviction that it was – or was potentially – a spiritually dangerous environment in which he needed to be present in order to protect his flock.

Many priests neither analysed nor rationalised their motives for supporting the Land League and Irish party. Many strongly supported the agitation for nationalist reasons, or from their desires to secure socio-economic improvement, or on the religious ground that the work of the Church was hindered by the conditions that prevailed in Ireland. Misgivings did not surface at all widely until the Papal Rescript of 1888, nor consolidate firmly until the Parnell crisis of 1890-1. However, before that, what was to become the dominant clerical attitude by 1891 was held firmly by Bishop O'Dwyer of Limerick, and Dr Healy, coadjutor-Bishop of Clonfert. O'Dwyer and Healy were commonly regarded as pro-Unionist, or ' Castle bishops '. That their interpretation – a strongly religio-clerical view of the political and land agitations – did not gain acceptance in Church circles earlier is due very considerably to their unpopularity among nationalists, or rather among those prelates, notably

Archbishops Walsh and Croke, who equated the good of religion with the nationalist agitation.

The O'Dwyer-Healy attitude rested on two judgements; that the Irish parliamentary party was not Catholic, and that the methods of the Land League were a potential menace to religion and its values. The first of these points was made clearly by one of Bishop O'Dwyer's lay correspondents in 1886: 'while the National party contains many excellent Catholics, it is not Catholic in its spirit or aims. . . .' To some of those whose paramount interest was the religious quality of Irish life, this characteristic could seem a grave defect in a party dedicated to the national cause. Was it enough that the party should contain excellent Catholics if it also contained Protestants, secularists and atheists, and its ethos was religiously neutral? No. The party must be Catholic in both personnel and ethos, run by Catholics, motivated by Catholic principles, seeking to establish a Catholic state – in all, a holy party working towards a parliament of saints. This quasi-theocratic political vision was not often explicit in Irish affairs, at least in the 1880s, but it was widely prevalent, usually in a passive form: if it did not rigidly dictate actualities, it conditioned the formation of ideals. In the case of the Irish parliamentary party, if the theocratic ideal did not issue in a direct attempt to create a holy party, it certainly was an important source of opposition to a party that came to be regarded as unholy. The assertion of theocratic criteria, ominous for the future of the Irish party, is evident in the private correspondence of the Rector of the Irish College in Rome, in April 1887: ' During the agitation of the past few years, it often occurred to me that too much confidence was placed in the number & ability of the Irish members as advocates in & out of Parliament; and scarcely any mention made in their speeches or other public acts, of God, the supreme ruler of nations. . . . Could it be that God now wishes to shew the futility of their efforts to build the house of their independence without him?'

The land agitation took its most effective form in the boycott, from 1882, and from 1886, the Plan of Campaign, that scheme whereby the tenants of individual estates were encouraged to decide on a reduced rent, offer it to the landlord, and if he refused to accept it, withhold it for payment into a fund to assist those evicted. All this raised religious issues which Bishop O'Dwyer set out early in 1887 in a letter to a fellow bishop:

. . . the spirit of general resistance to civil authority . . . has been growing in Ireland, and if encouraged will produce the same results to religion that the revolution has produced in every country in which it has triumphed. In my humble opinion we are abandoning the principles of . . . reverence, and of Charity that were the traditions of our predecessors, and for the sake of mere [popularity?] allowing the people to follow methods of violence and disobedience. As long as the priests of the Church are useful political agents of the leaders of this system they will be applauded, and appear to hold influence: but when the time comes as come it must that we can no longer pander to popular passion I fear the reaction will show that our power has been undermined.

O'Dwyer's prediction was vindicated the following year in the popular reaction to the Papal Rescript, and later, in relation to the fall of Parnell, but the principles on which he entertained fears – the preservation of traditional religious and social values, the maintenance of the power and influence of the priesthood, the avoidance of sin – needed no vindication among his colleagues. Those bishops who disagreed with him rejected not his principles, but his tactics, and were reacting against what they believed was his motivation – subservience to the British administration. Walsh and Croke were also trying to defend religious values and priestly power, but whereas O'Dwyer reacted directly to the spiritual degeneration he discerned among the Irish, Walsh, Croke and ' nationalist ' bishops and clergy generally, took the view that this problem was induced by destructive British policies which must therefore be strenuously opposed. This belief enabled them to adopt popular nationalist postures, whereas in fact they were impelled by religious considerations, not nationalism. There is ample testimony to this in episcopal correspondence in 1887 – and also abundant evidence that these bishops believed Britain was deliberately seeking to push Ireland into rebellion. Thus Bishop MacEvilly of Tuam: ' My own impression is that the shocking Coercion Bill which is to be permanent has for object to goad our people to extremities & outrage and thus secure an opportunity or pretext for shooting them down. . . . I am greatly afraid that this Coercion Bill will drive our people notwithstanding all our vigilance into the arms of the Secret Societies.' And Bishop O'Callaghan of Cork: ' we fear the blind bitter hatred which drives those who rule the destinies of the country to terrible extremes.' Archbishop Walsh: ' There is very little room for doubt that the present Government are pursuing a deliberate plan to drive the young men of the country back into the old lines of secret societies.' The majority of the bishops shared Walsh's conviction – which amounted almost to obsession – that the major danger to Irish religiosity came not from within the

Irish, but from British policy. They believed that 'to save our people' they must not stand aside from nationalist agitation, but join it. Walsh justified this conclusion as follows: by joining the nationalist movement the clergy had restrained the people from violence and the sins thereof, had kept the leadership, confidence and loyalty of the people and protected them from falling under the influence of secret societies, and had deterred the British government – because of its dread of episcopal power – from implementing its determination to attempt to crush Ireland by coercion, an attempt which would provoke rebellion. Privately, Walsh contended that those priests who refused to participate in Land League activities left their congregations ' in the hands of a few local politicians utterly unfit to take the lead in any political or social organisation, with the usual disastrous results.' He went so far as to attribute the disturbed state of Ireland and its related sinfulness to the failure of such priests to do their duty: ' so exceptional a state of affairs is in large measure the result of his [such a priest's] own neglect of the opportunity that must at some time have presented itself, of taking, and keeping, things in hand, and so of saving the country the discredit which is brought upon it by the crime and lawlessness which undoubtedly prevail in a few exceptional districts.' Walsh's position was that British policy was designed to destroy Catholic Ireland: therefore the clergy must join the populace both in order to avoid forfeiting their confidence, and in order to control the situation, as was their duty.

This justification of clerical ' nationalism ' applied mainly to their support of the Land League. However, from the Irish parliamentary party, the episcopacy expected positive achievements favourable to religion, and believed they had a practical right to expect them. The bishops were convinced that their support determined the party's electoral success. Referring to the nationalist triumph in the 1886 elections, Archbishop Kirby observed to Cardinal Moran, ' Let us trust that some good will result to the poor people & to the cause of education from the victory, as it is due, in great part, to the support given to them by Dr Walsh & the other Bishops.' Kirby was sceptical of such results, but there is no doubt that the Walsh policy was determined by the belief that the Irish party existed on the basis of clerical support in return for the party's championing religious causes – notably Catholic education. Of course the party did not see itself in such terms but it took care to disguise this from its episcopal supporters by pleading the exigencies of its political position, by contending that the Home Rule cause left room for nothing else, and by claiming that once Home Rule was achieved all else would follow.

To clerical minds such as Walsh's, to condemn Irish agitation was to play Britain's game, a conclusion hardened by British efforts at the Vatican to get a Papal pronouncement against Irish resistance: such intriguing seemed patently an attempt to pervert religion for political ends.

After the Holy See had sent a representative, Monsignor Persico, to examine and report on affairs in Ireland, in April 1888 a Papal rescript was issued condemning as immoral boycotting and the Plan of Campaign. The demands of Irish politics, and the pronouncements of the Papacy were thus in open conflict. What followed was an uproar in Ireland of such passion and dimensions as to indicate that Ireland's two most important loyalties were involved. Of the vast public meetings in May and June, the *Irish Catholic* remarked that they were the most important held for ten years and rivalled in numbers the largest ever associated with the national movement. Popular feeling ran to cursing the Pope and throwing his picture out of homes. From the outset, Irish parliamentarians rejected the rescript. A meeting of almost all the Catholic members challenged the rescript's factual basis, implied that the Papacy was politically partisan, deplored its failure to condemn the evils of British policy, and repudiated any Papal interference in Irish politics. The Lord Mayor of Dublin spoke of the party's duty to Protestants: ' we owe it to those of our countrymen, who are Protestants, to show that their liberties as well as those of Catholics are safe in the hands of an emancipated Ireland.' John Redmond maintained that if the Catholics of Ireland acquiesced in Roman interference in their civil and political affairs, ' the English people would be absolute fools to concede or restore their Parliament.' Tim Healy pronounced, ' With regard to his approval of the manifestations known as the Plan of Campaign and boycotting, he remained, in the face of the Roman circular, a wholly unregenerate and unrepentant sinner.' Michael Davitt, long under suspicion of having heterodox views on property, denounced Bishop O'Dwyer's support of the rescript as the worst form of clerical dictatorship. John Dillon took it on himself to declare that the Plan and boycotting were not sinful, and boldly suggested that if it came to a divorce between the Church and politics, it would be the Church that would suffer: ' Woe to the Church if the priests were driven from politics; woe still more if it was done at the bidding of a hated English minister, and if, as would be the inevitable end – if the ministers of religion were to be turned into policemen for the Government.' As to William O'Brien, Bishop Woodlock at Athlone found his conduct in the affair ' simply atrocious – unworthy of a Catholic, and especially of one who is said to be a practical Catholic.' And as to the popular reception of the politicians' pronouncements, the *Irish Catholic* summarised the position in noting that ' all over Ireland, meetings were held to express approval of the declarations of the Irish members and to make clear that in the management of the political affairs of Ireland the Irish people must be supreme.' The *Irish Catholic* itself defined the morality of the situation:

> Our leaders have declared that a life and death struggle is being fought out between the Irish nation and the felonious landlords and that there are no other available weapons wherewith to save the people from destruction or a miserable dying existence, except the Plan and boycotting. It would be very difficult to maintain that in such a struggle the preservation of the people should not be the supreme law. . . . These weapons are not of themselves unjust or immoral, and cannot become unlawful when their use is rendered imperative by the supreme law, the safety of the Irish people.'

The *Irish Catholic* went on to argue that the very fact that the national movement had prospered showed that it was morally good: success ' could not have been secured by a movement which was itself unholy or un-righteous, by politicians who were unscrupulous or unjust.'

Archbishops Walsh and Croke regarded the rescript as a gross tactical blunder which gravely embarrassed the Church, disagreed with its inter-pretation of Irish facts and its specific condemnations; and Walsh par-ticularly was almost in a frenzy to excuse and minimise it and to explain it away. But the Irish reaction to the rescript exhibited general charac-teristics which made the bishops' previous attitude to the national move-ment no longer tenable. Defiance and contempt of Papal pronouncements, ridicule and abuse of clerics, lay definitions on moral questions, assertions of the moral supremacy of the popular will, claims for the superiority of political judgements and considerations above all others, and the wholesale popular desertion of the world of religious authority for the world of politics – these things were gravely alarming to all Irish bishops. They saw themselves confronted with a powerful and direct challenge to religious authority, and with the inescapable question – was it the poli-ticians or themselves who were to determine ultimately the character of Irish affairs?

The rescript affair forced the Irish party to reveal itself in a way it had hitherto avoided. Bishop O'Dwyer once referred to the party as one ' to whose care the Irish Bishops have confided the Catholic cause.' The comment was apt enough: many of the clergy looked forward to the achievement, under Home Rule, of a Catholic Ireland and a few politicians – Charles Dawson for instance – did so also. But the Irish party, in the British political context, was under strong pressure – which accorded with its inclinations – to avoid any Catholic commitment: it could not afford to give countenance to the charge that Home Rule meant Rome Rule. Yet at the same time its electoral support was overwhelmingly Catholic. The party's rebuff to the Church over the rescript had popular support, so that was not endangered immediately: on the contrary it was strengthened. But it revealed to the Church that not only was the party itself quite willing to flout the Church's wishes, but it was capable of mobilising popular opinion against Church authority.

This situation soon revealed itself to the bishops as one of wide extent, considerable strength, and grave implications: it prompted Bishop O'Dwyer to say in June 1888, ' To my mind there has never been in Ireland since St Patrick planted the Faith here, a greater scandal or more injury done to religion than this most deplorable agitation.' He went on to predict, with uncanny accuracy, the outcome: ' unless those who are in opposition to it [the rescript] hope to trample on the consciences of the ecclesiastical teachers of Ireland and terrorise them into revolt against the Pope, I cannot see what they expect to gain from their present agitation. I said it before, and I repeat it, that the result for them will be the wreck and ruin of their political organisation, and the putting back of Home Rule for Ireland perhaps for a generation.' The Irish parliamentary party signed its own death warrant in 1888, though it was to be a long time dying. After the height of the rescript crisis had passed, even Archbishop Walsh publicly admitted that ' Men's minds were strangely troubled. It seemed almost to be the opinion of some that all the ancient moorings of our Irish Catholicity had been disturbed, and that our nation was in danger of drifting away upon those shoals where many another nation, once as Catholic as ours . . . had made shipwreck.' He referred to ' the fearful narrowness of their escape from disaster in which . . . that faith might have been brought to ruin.' And when the crisis was at its most intense, privately Walsh was almost in despair that ' any sort of respect for ecclesiastical authority ' would be ' saved out of the general wreck.'

Despite his personal unpopularity, O'Dwyer's view of the dangers revealed by the reaction to the rescript spread rapidly among the bishops. Many of them came to believe, as Bishop Donnelly put it as early as May 1888, ' that if the movement is allowed to go on unchecked much longer, it will be too late to interfere.' What was the basic problem? Bishop McCarthy of Cloyne summed it up in March 1889:

We have a state of affairs which of its very nature is calculated to withdraw our minds from the consideration of heavenly things and to fix them on the affairs of our country, or in other words, to substitute patriotism for religion as the chief object of our thoughts and aspirations. This state of feeling exposes us to another danger in the efforts we make to advance the affairs of our country, and that is in the means we employ for that purpose. We are apt to have regard to the efficacy of these means rather than to their lawfulness or morality.

The Irish episcopacy set its face against two evils – the substitution of patriotism for religion, and immoral political methods. The practical consequences of their growing determination to fight these evils depended on the actual power of the Church over the people.

That power was very great. Even those who challenged it on the rescript issue, gave it general support. The *Irish Catholic* held, in July 1888, that, ' None is placed in a better position than the Irish prelate to know how his people stand. He knows exactly what they need. He is at the head of a body possessed of the full trust of the people. The Irish priest has the confidence of almost every peasant home in the land.' This comment was occasioned by the Irish Bishops' resolution urging land reform, resolutions which paralleled those of the Irish party and demonstrated that the party had a major competitor for social authority in Ireland. The *Irish Catholic's* exaltation of lay-clerical solidarity is typical of the platitudes aired when bishops or clergy supported the nationalist movement. The tactic was to identify newer political causes with traditional religious loyalties, and it had the effect of calling a blessing on politics when Church and nationalists were in accord. However, its overall effect was to acknowledge implicitly that political authority and judgement were somehow subordinate to that of the Church. Churchmen themselves held that view, sometimes to the extent of claiming a degree of political infallibility for the episcopate, based both on personal religious enlightenment and on its representing the religious disposition of the nation: in October 1888 Bishop Nulty of Meath referred to

> the more enlightened and more experienced political wisdom which has never abandoned and can never abandon, the great majority of the Irish Episcopate. Further, the whole Irish nation stands sympathetically and approvingly at its back; and, without making any claim to a Divine promise or a Divine guarantee, the enlightened instincts of a thoroughly Catholic nation like Ireland will always preserve it from going wrong.

And of course priests constantly played a day-to-day politico-social role. In relation to an incident in his own diocese of Armagh in 1888, Cardinal Logue explained to Archbishop Kirby in Rome: 'I telegraphed to Chief Secretary that if he kept the police quiet, I would get the priests to keep the people quiet. He assented to this. . . . A military officer . . . said the people seemed more afraid of the umbrellas of the priests than of the rifles of his men.' On some occasions the clerical will did not prevail, but that was usually because it was deemed prudent not to make an issue.

Ultimately there could be no avoiding the fact that the Church sought to pull the parliamentary party in a direction different from that desired by the politicians. The party's reaction to the Papal rescript called its attitude to religion into serious question. European Catholic journalists dubbed the party 'revolutionary' in the European anti-religious sense, claiming that the leaders of the Land League, from Parnell down, had shown themselves more ready to make use of Catholicism than to serve it. Such allegations that Irish Catholicism was being committed to a revolutionary cause were difficult to rebut in the light of comments such as that of Edmond Leamy, M.P.: 'If the Irish tenants took arms, and in the martial ranks faced their enemies, their banners would be blessed and Te Deums would be sung upon their victories.' Nor could the Irish clergy answer the English *Tablet's* question: 'Is the Irish Party in politics Catholic or anti-Catholic?' The *Irish Catholic* correctly answered that the party was neither: it was Irish. 'With its Protestant leader it aims at being the representative of the nation, within which Catholicity has a free home and a full scope for its efficiency, but within which Catholicity does not claim anything but equal rights before the law and sets up no exclusive privileges.' This situation became tolerable to the Church by 1921, but in the 1880s it fell far short of clerical ideals for Ireland's future.

The fact is that the episcopal concept of Ireland as a nation was wedded to a concept of Catholicity. What the bishops sought to defend, assert, and eventually realise in practice, was not fundamentally Ireland as a self-governing political unity, but Ireland as a distinct Catholic community, uncontaminated by the secular world. This concept of a holy Ireland was closely linked with political nationalism in that self-government seemed necessary for its realisation, and in that the political overlord – England – was also the spiritual enemy, purveyor of Protestantism and secularism, and provocateur, through misgovernment, of sin; but the value structures and priorities of the two movements, religious and political, were very different. The Papal rescript affair made this clear, drawing such comments as Bishop MacEvilly's in July 1888 that ' merce-

nary, would-be local Patriots are doing much mischief in estranging our
people from religion ': the contrast was between the selfish worldliness
of politicians, and the holy claims of religion. The tendency had certainly
been to confuse the nationalist movement and Ireland's religious grievances. The *Irish Catholic* illustrates this clearly in December 1888 in its
denunciation of

> the system of government which had struck a terrific blow at one of
> the chief centres of Catholic Faith in Europe, which has resulted
> in the wholesale banishment and which has even attempted the
> extirpation of the only truly devoted Catholic people to be still
> found in this hemisphere. . . . These are the kinds of thoughts which
> nerve the resolve of Irishmen to never make peace or pact with the
> most diabolical system of government which has produced such evils.

The very strong popular reaction to the Papal rescript was partly due to
a genuine indignation that the Pope had found moral fault with his most
Catholic people: it was seen as an unmerited insult to the Faith's most
devoted children. The Irish commonly looked upon the Catholics of other
nations with at best sorrow, at worse contempt. They regarded English
Catholicism as contaminated by aristocratic anti-Irishism, and saw
European Catholicism as effete – why didn't those continental Catholics
do something about their irreligious governments? The fear that Irish
Catholicism might be degraded to the level of its European counterpart
was a major factor in persuading the bishops that they must recapture
Ireland from the politicians. As Archbishop Walsh wrote to Archbishop
Kirby in Rome in July 1888, ' the people of Ireland, Catholic as they
are, might easily enough be brought into the same state of mind that now
so manifestly prevails throughout the peoples of Italy, France, and other
so called " Catholic " countries. The same influence is at work, which
has wrought such mischief there '. Walsh feared that Ireland might be
lost to clerical influence: ' When it becomes necessary for us to act
directly in opposition to some popular movement the situation will become
fearfully critical.'

By 1890, before the Parnell divorce case, the Irish bishops had
arrived at the conclusion, some of them very reluctantly, that as Cardinal
Logue put it to Walsh, Bishop O'Dwyer's analysis of the conflict between
politics and religion was correct: ' however intemperate he may be he is
right at bottom '. Logue summed up the situation. Some of the Irish
parliamentarians were seriously compromising the bishops. To avoid
dissension the bishops had remained silent when parliamentarians had
said or done ' unbecoming ' things. Now these men were depicting such

silence as approval. Furthermore, Logue complained, having climbed to power on the shoulders of bishops and priests, the politicians were now neglecting anything that might be Catholic, notably the bishops' education schemes, but also a proposal, emanating from the Vatican, that the party move in the House of Commons in favour of the Pope's temporal power. ' My impression,' Logue wrote, ' is that they have fallen into the position of a mere tail to the Radical Party in England and that any question that would displease that party they will not touch.' Logue was very suspicious of apparent anti-Catholic moves within the party: there had been expulsions of Catholics in the South, while in the North the party was sacrificing principles in order to win Protestant adherents.

Logue was also very incensed by the contrast between John Dillon's apparent impunity in making ' unjust and unwarrantable ' charges against Bishop O'Dwyer, while the Bishop himself was subjected to a howl of public abuse. This aspect of the rescript legacy worried and angered all the bishops: Bishop Coffey of Kerry saw men ' calling themselves the leaders of our people, and calling themselves Catholics, making use of language – in and out of Parliament – which is naturally calculated to subvert ecclesiastical authority and bring it into disrepute.' His brother bishops were probably not aware that O'Dwyer had received an assassination threat which revealed a crude but alarming mixture of confused religious primitivism and democratic assertions: '. . . you must submit to the people that is keep you up. . . . Don't go out . . . you will be done away with if you go into the chapel to say Mass you will be shot for there is men going from Dublin to send you to atternity for your conduct you are not a Catholic . . . how mutch money did Balfour give you. the next thing we will here is your turning a protestant . . . you Rotton Orange Man.'

In November 1890 the O'Shea divorce case produced an undefended verdict against Mrs O'Shea and Parnell as co-respondent. Its effect was to drive home with inescapable force the lessons of the reaction to the rescript; it opened the eyes of all the Irish bishops to what they saw as a grave moral crisis within Irish society. ' We all feel intensely and are alarmed at the dangers that have been revealed to us ', wrote Bishop O'Callaghan of Cork, privately. ' The people seem to have gone mad and lost their reason. What is most singular is that even good pious people who frequent the sacraments are in some instances carried away by the fury.'

The episcopal reaction was unanimous, profound and of decisive importance for the future. Revulsion against Parnell personally was total. Some bishops, like Walsh, merely regarded him as a profligate, others, such as Bishop MacEvilly, saw him as an agent of the devil, a ' *Lucifer 2nd* who would fain drag the whole Irish race down to perdition and trample on the clergy & Catholic people.' A number of bishops regarded the turmoil into which the Parnell affair had thrown Ireland as a divine punishment for Ireland's sins; as Bishop Donnelly described it, ' a kind of retribution for the hostility in some quarters & indifference in others, with which the Holy Father's injunctions were met, for the conduct employed by some of our political men towards the Bishop of Limerick for daring to enforce those injunctions, & for the general disregard of both the 7th and 8th Commandments which was allowed to pass unchallenged during the whole course of ten years agitation.' The Pope himself, as Archbishop Kirby reported to Cardinal Moran early in 1891, hoped ' that the present crisis may bring about in the end a wholesomer state of things, & break down the lay dictation of the past years & restore the Bishops & the clergy to their proper influence with the people, which the past agitation has been gradually undermining.'

What of politics? The consensus of episcopal opinion, from every part of Ireland was that the Parnell scandal was providential, a divine blessing, revealing the true nature of the political situation before Home Rule had been achieved. Bishop McCarthy's comment was typical: ' It is almost providential that this should have happened before any measure of Home Rule was granted as otherwise the country would have been at the mercy of a bold unscrupulous despot who has shown by his acts that his own exaltation & not the interests of his country was his prime object.' Bishop MacEvilly's belief was that Parnell would have been a ' detestable persecutor of [the] Church '. Archbishop Walsh took some consolation in pointing out that there was no other country on the face of the globe ' where a people have risen up, as our people rose, at the call of their Bishops to cast aside a profligate leader even at the risk of wrecking all their National hopes.' Walsh regarded the fall of Parnell as a triumph for the influence of the Church and particularly that of himself and Archbishop Croke. To support this view, Walsh invoked Lord Salisbury's comment that while the British government had been unable to destroy Parnell, Archbishops Walsh and Croke had deprived Parnell of popular support ' with as much ease as a man turns aside a boat in the current by simply putting his hand on the helm.' Both Salisbury and Walsh chose to ignore Gladstone's role, and that of non-conformists in England, and members of Parnell's party in Parnell's destruction: they ignored too the substantial section of Irish opinion that still supported Parnell.

In fact, their episcopal colleagues were sceptical of the efforts of 'nationalist' bishops to control the situation in Ireland: Bishop Healy wrote to Bishop O'Dwyer: 'They made the idol & worshipped it; now let them unmake it, *if they can.*' O'Dwyer's view – that the people had been demoralised by Parnellism – had become prevalent among the bishops. O'Dwyer was quick to point out that Parnell himself was only one aspect of the problem: 'the authority of the Holy See even within its own sphere of moral teaching has been repudiated by that very section of politicians to whom we now look for the alternative to Mr Parnell.' Several bishops held that neither Dillon nor O'Brien would be any improvement on Parnell as party leader. Many, like Bishop Woodlock, viewed the future despondently: 'I confess I am very anxious about the future and I fear 20 years will see a great change in the religious dispositions of our people.'

The general clerical conclusion was expressed by O'Dwyer: 'If we had less politics and more religion the church in Ireland would do better.' The opportunity had arisen to destroy the dominion of politics, stop the drift towards a secular social system and redirect Irish energies again into religious channels. Those clerics who regarded the fall of Parnell as providential, saw an opportunity to achieve great good – 'The result will be to bring them [the people] more under the guidance of Catholic and moral principles than hitherto they had been', observed Bishop McCarthy in May 1891. This providential chance had, of course, to be seized: it was a clerical duty to assert a decisive political initiative. Bishop O'Callaghan observed of Cork politics in 1891: 'A great deal will depend on the action of the priests, in fact it is altogether in their hands.' That one Parnellite had gained election to the Board of Poor Law Guardians he attributed to the indifference of a few priests. 'This will be efficiently remedied and it is not likely to occur again', O'Callaghan assured Archbishop Kirby in Rome. Such vigorous and direct political intervention was justified as necessary to preserve Ireland, as O'Dwyer put it, 'from the dominion of dangerous men'. Its primary aim was the destruction of the residue of Parnell's political support: by 1892 even Archbishop Walsh was convinced that Parnellites were the Irish representatives of an international conspiracy against God, religion and social order. But naturally this negative function had positive implications: an unholy party must be replaced by a holy one. As the lay editor of the *Irish Catholic* wrote privately to Rome in 1893, 'What we want in Ireland is what the Holy Father is endeavouring to secure in France, namely that the will and conscience of the Catholic people shall rule the country.' The kind of men clerics hoped for in political life may be gathered from Bishop O'Callaghan's description of the candidate he supported in the

Cork election of November 1891: 'Mr Fluoin is a good catholic well known in the city. He is Vice President of the Confraternity of the Sacred Heart and during the week before his selection as candidate he was not present at the political meetings but was in attendance at the retreat of the society at St Vincent's Church.'

Parnell's fall led on to a declared policy of clerical socio-political leadership. Its central propositions were set out in the *Lyceum* in August-September 1892. The influence of the Irish priest was due to his labouring for his flock's temporal as well as spiritual welfare. The priest could retain his beneficent over-all influence in men's lives only if he retained not only interest in, but active leadership of, their temporal affairs: such temporal leadership was requisite to the proper spiritual work of the priesthood. At the same time only such leadership could protect Ireland from the dangers of social conflict and disorder so prevalent in modern irreligious life.

However, such a conception of clerical duty did not mean that clerics took over the leadership of the nationalist movement. That had turned to ashes in their mouths. They had given it their support and it had revealed itself corrupt. There could never be the same enthusiasm for the national cause again, among the clergy, particularly as the Parnell split left them exposed to bitter anti-clerical attack from the Parnellite residue. There was more in the clerical reaction than disillusionment with the party and politicians: deep-rooted and long-standing misgivings now surfaced and spread rapidly. Was Home Rule desirable? Would it establish lay power in Ireland to the detriment of the religious realm? Even Croke's 'nationalism' was far from anti-British. In 1888 he had

> no hesitation in saying that if we had guaranteed to us the full measure of national autonomy to which we are plain entitled I should far prefer British protection to that of any other nation in the world. It would in my opinion best secure for us an orderly existence, whilst safeguarding us, besides, as far as possible, from those wild and latitudinarian views in Church and State that are so widespread and have proved to be so destructive in Continental countries.

There was another danger. It was widely believed that Home Rule would bring Ireland prosperity. But was this, from the church's standpoint, a good thing? In 1889 Archbishop Walsh's secretary, Denis Pettit, was hoping in private correspondence that 'an era of prosperity will do as little harm to the faith of our people as many centuries of poverty and persecution.' Early in 1890, the *Lyceum* had no doubts on that point: 'we do not believe that temporal prosperity, when carried beyond certain limits, reacts favourably on Catholicism, or, indeed, on any form of revealed religion. The fact seems constant, however it is to be explained, that when a people rises above a certain level in education, wealth, refinement, liberty, religion loses its hold upon their beliefs and moral conduct.' Even before the Parnell split shattered the nationalist movement, this strong element of clerical conservatism was becoming more and more apparent. In January 1890, the noted Jesuit intellectual Father T. A. Finlay, speaking at the consecration of the Bishop of Waterford, took a very pessimistic view of Ireland's religious future: ' The long struggle in which fidelity to the Church and fidelity to the nation were identified in the Irish mind is drawing to an end. We are approaching the time in which the motives and impulses, the prejudices and the errors which have affected the peoples of other lands through the stages of their calmer histories will prevail amongst ourselves.' To minds such as these, the Parnell split came as a blessing, opening the opportunity to reverse irreligious trends, or at least of postponing their day. The outcome was a vigorous reassertion of Catholic conservatism in Ireland. Before the split, Catholic journals such as the *Irish Catholic* and the *Lyceum* had painted visions of a Christian Democracy in Ireland: these were a total casualty to the Parnell affair. Now freed from the necessity to adjust itself to the directions taken by a powerful and popular political movement, the clerical preference for conservatism reasserted itself.

What followed was either clerical hostility or opposition to any political agitation, clerical apathy or indifference to an ineffective political machine, or a clerical search for a suitable political vehicle for their own policies. The result was fragmentation of both clerical and political forces as various clerical groups supported or opposed various political factions; but the general situation was one of a dominant clericalism as politicians contended for the clerical support they believed necessary to reconstruct the shattered party. But no one was able to bridge the great chasm between church and party riven by the Parnell affair. It was this failure, at bottom, which led to the party's slow drift away from the common people, the dying of its roots in the soil of Ireland.

Clerical domination of politics took no single form, nor produced any concerted leadership or policies: it amounted rather to setting the temper and determining the character of political life. The consequences of this were, aside from party disintegration, a drift away from practicalities towards political idealism. A Limerick priest told a fellow priest in Rome in 1887: ' I am afraid if the history of political Priests were written it would show that they are advocates of the wildest and most untenable political doctrines.' The substantial truth of the observation may be seen even more clearly after 1890. Priests lacked political realism and inclined strongly towards the doctrinaire – in their case, the creation of the kingdom of God on earth. They were irresponsible, in that they exercised political power and influence without having to account for its use, could retire from political activity at will into the realm of the priesthood, and tended to act negatively in that they sought not so much to create their own party, as to hinder or destroy any party which did not measure up to their religious ideals. This atmosphere was hostile to pragmatism and compromise, favourable to visionary idealism: it was the atmosphere in which the Irish parliamentary party withered and died, in which revolutionary dreams and ambitions grew and flourished.

Gladstone's second attempt, in 1893, to secure Home Rule for Ireland was overwhelmingly defeated in the House of Lords. The major importance of this attempt was to further harden and entrench Unionist, particularly Ulster Unionist, opposition to any departure from the existing union relationship. In Ireland, public opinion had grown apathetic and cynical about a cause championed by a divided, wrangling party: worse still, for the future of cause and party, clerical enthusiasm had vanished, to be succeeded by suspicion and hostility. Bishop Coffey put his opinion to Archbishop Walsh: ' I believe Dillon, O'Brien, Healy and their following are much more dangerous to the Church & future of this country than Parnell '; Parnell was a Protestant – and was thus an obvious danger – but the others purported to be Catholics. Bishop O'Dwyer held that the anti-Parnellite factions could not be supported by men of religion as these factions contained bad Catholics and atheists. Certainly not all the episcopacy would have agreed, yet when Bishop Healy told a bishops' meeting that the anti-Parnellite group were ' men not of Catholic but of revolutionary principles ', several bishops openly sided with him, and none ventured a defence. By 1891 some bishops could still tolerate Dillon and O'Brien, but none could muster any enthusiasm for them. Not all Irish prelates agreed with Bishop O'Dwyer that given ' the evil tendencies' of many of the politicians ' it is a merciful providence that delays Home Rule ', but many did, and perhaps all, to some extent, had misgivings. Writing to Cardinal Moran just before the defeat of the second Home Rule Bill, Archbishop Kirby reflects a typical clerical outlook:

> Whatever may be the final result, this simple fact [of the Bill being debated] is a wonderful event, all things considered: & it would be a good omen in all human appearance, for our poor country if we had a body of true catholic patriots to utilize it. But those that are at

present to the front, do not seem from their antecedents to be such. It may be, that divine Providence may have so disposed, to teach us that he does not wish us to place the hopes of our catholic nation in political greatness, but in the greater attachments to our holy faith & to the centre of her unity, carrying out more and more the words of our Lord . . . not that political improvements are not to be desired, if attainable without danger to faith, but that our main hopes should be placed in the divine Protection & continual prayer . . . to obtain it thro' our great advocates the Blessed Virgin & Saint Patrick, whose blessing is happily, so visible in the country.

The influential importance of political conservatism deriving from religious principles is such as to merit some extended analysis: a letter from Aubrey de Vere to Bishop O'Dwyer in June 1893 provides a suitable text. De Vere was dismayed by what had happened in Ireland since the 1880s. Moral indifference and religious coolness were commonly the sins of the rich, but in Ireland, according to de Vere, they were corrupting the poor: ' When a chronic political agitation, especially if it be for unworthy or illusory objects, draws unto itself all a nation's ardours, nothing but coldness remains for nobler things. When ' Socialism ' becomes a people's ideal the great Christian Ideal vanishes away. . . .' De Vere's contention was that ' The recent agitation in Ireland is the first one that ever rested on *Jacobinism* which O'Connell abhorred. Jacobinism is, in its spirits & interior meaning, the exact opposite of Catholicism & of course destroys it.' The conclusion that the Parnellite-Land League agitation was socialist and Jacobin was of great importance for the political future: its effect was to link these evils with the Irish party and its policies, predisposing conservative minds towards tolerance of such future movements as would challenge this tainted party. De Vere's belief was that the swing towards Jacobinism was real, subtle and insidious: ' One of our chief dangers is that our priests so often do not observe this change, because the people still frequent the Sacraments oftener than their pious forbears were able to do. When they see it fully it may be too late to cure the mischief, for their spiritual influence will have declined & ' Jacobinism ' which begins its work by a war against Civil Authority, & property always proceeds to its more serious business, the war against religion.' De Vere related this observation to the 1880s and 1890s, and thus to the Irish party. As to the immediate prospect of Home Rule in 1893, de Vere was eloquent on its potential for utter disaster – the people of Ireland were as yet totally unfit for it: ' I feel confident that the passing of such a measure now, or soon would simply place Ireland in the position occupied by France during & subsequent to the first French Revolution: — that she too would have her " Reign of Terror "; & that that would be the *least* part of the evil. Religion, Honour & Happiness all would go: — and if God's mercy accorded a remedy one day it would be a painful one indeed.' Ireland needed to be pulled back from the abyss of revolution and secularism, and only the priesthood could do that. But de Vere had always been opposed to Home Rule: of what significance are his views on it? The basis of his opposition is crucial — ' not so much because of *its dangers* as because I regarded it as a *low ideal.*' Here, from a conservative, was the terminology of the revolutionary: Home Rule was not enough. To both religious conservative and political revolutionary, Home Rule appeared a piece of shoddy pragmatism, offering nothing to ambitious imagination, starved idealism or messianic fervour. It threatened to reduce Ireland to irreligion, to establish the realm of seculardom, the reign of the crude and material. Antagonism to Home Rule and the Irish party brought conservatives and revolutionaries into a kind of spiritual conjunction which was the true basis of revolution in Ireland.

As far as the 1893 Home Rule Bill was concerned, none of the hierarchy was happy with it. The widespread suspicion of Gladstone and his motives which had prevailed since his attack on the Vatican Decrees in 1874 flared up again. Even Archbishop Walsh, the episcopacy's most vigorous Home Ruler was privately convinced that ' it will be disastrous as regards Catholic Education.' Cardinal Logue held the Bill generally unjust to Catholic interests, to embody inequality, and to deprive the Irish legislature of power to redress such grievances. The bishops as a body submitted their criticism to Gladstone privately, but their intervention was little short of a gesture. They were perfectly aware that the Bill was certain to be thrown out by the Lords, so they refrained from making a public protest against its treatment of Catholicism: ' The Bill will not pass ', wrote Logue to Walsh, ' and it would not be wise for the Bishops to take upon themselves the odium of defeating it.'

The judicious silence of the bishops was particularly appropriate in view of the very strong popular reaction in Ireland to a public protest against Home Rule in June 1893 by a number of prominent upper class Irish and English Catholics. This protest, based on grounds similar to those of de Vere, discussed earlier, claimed that ' The agitation which has been carried on in Ireland since 1879 has been based to a great extent upon principles which are manifestly identical with those of the European Revolution so often and so authoritatively reprobated by the Holy See . . . Many of the teachers who helped to indoctrinate the Catholic people of Ireland with these anti-Christian tenets now stand high in the Home

Rule Party.' On this basis, ' It seems to us certain that Home Rule must inevitably lead to speedy and progressive development of the revolutionary spirit. . . . We believe that under these circumstances a section of the Irish people must ultimately be brought into conflict with the Church, and we cannot look forward to such a struggle without great apprehensions.' This statement provoked vigorous predictable denials in Ireland. The clericalist *Lyceum* took the line that ' Were Home Rule the danger for Irish Catholic interests which some would have us think, it would not have been left to laymen to discover such a vital fact and proclaim it.' The episcopacy had indeed discovered this vital fact, or at least this dangerous possibility. They chose not to proclaim it, because they believed that Home Rule was certain to be defeated without any statement from them which might damage their popular reputation – but by and large they shared the views of those lay Catholics who protested against Home Rule in June 1893.

The *Lyceum* believed that it had exposed an absurdity: ' " Home Rule means the triumph of Catholicism; therefore we will have none of it," say the Orangemen and their anti-Catholic abettors. " Home Rule means the ruin of Catholicism; therefore we will have none of it," say the Irish and British signatories to the anti-Home Rule Catholic addresses!' Absurd perhaps, but these propositions, in their opposite ways, explain much about the fate of Home Rule, not only in 1893, but thereafter. The period between the first and second Home Rule Bills saw a sharp sensitising of the religious issue in Ireland. With such supporters as the Irish episcopacy, the 1893 Bill hardly needed enemies, though these were overwhelming. A situation had arisen in Ireland, where the effective weight of both Protestant and Catholic religious leaders was thrown against Home Rule, though in one case opposition was strident, in the other muted and disguised. After this period, the Home Rule issue ceased to embody for the Catholic episcopacy their religious cause in a political form. As a consequence it gradually lost the character of politico-religious amalgam that had been its main strength.

5
The Question Avoided

Between 1885 and 1905 Conservatives held office in Britain for over 16 of those 20 years. Dedicated to the maintenance of the Union, their Irish policy was the twin one of coercion and conciliation. Coercion was nothing novel, but 'killing Home Rule with kindness' was a new and positive approach to Irish unrest and agitation.

Conservative policy derived from four major sets of assumptions – that Irish agitation was an assault on property, wealth and social hierarchy, a destructive, revolutionary levelling movement; that a Home Rule Ireland would gravely weaken England's defences and be a major step towards the disintegration of the Empire; that Home Rule would produce a Catholic parliament of persecutors, unenlightened, an instrument of Rome, hostile to Protestants in Ireland and to Protestant Britain; and that what the Irish really wanted was not Home Rule but practical, material reforms.

The programme of positive reform carried out in Ireland by Conservative Unionists was based on this last assumption. The Conservative evaluation of the Irish did not provide scope for the existence of any real nationalism among them. Men such as Lord Salisbury and Arthur Balfour believed the Irish to be, in mass, a primitive peasantry so far inferior to the British in the arts of civilisation as to render them totally unfit for self-government, indicating that Irish nationalism, as expressed in the demand for Home Rule, was not genuine, not a sense of independent corporate identity such as the English themselves possessed. What purported to be Irish nationalism was in fact something else masquerading as nationalism under the manipulation of a few politicians, something else which must be more simple and primitive. Conservatives diagnosed this something as socio-economic discontent: the economic interpretation of Irish history is a conservative no less than a radical contrivance. Conservatives – Unionists generally – set out not so much to kill Home Rule with kindness, in any sense of buying the Irish away from their principles with material bribes, as from the conviction that by attempting to solve the land question, establishing industries, remedying poverty, and generally improving living standards, they were dealing with the real causes of Irish agitation. Remove these material grievances and the empty edifice of so-called nationalism would collapse.

That Conservatives could take up such a reforming policy points to the strength of their determination that the Union must be preserved. Imperial integrity and the self-interest of the propertied classes were under threat in Irish agitation, therefore that agitation must be ended. In 1887 when he was Chief Secretary, Balfour summed up the Conservative Unionist approach – hitherto English governments had 'either been all for repression or all for reform: I am for both: repression as stern as Cromwell: reform as thorough as Mr Parnell or anyone else can desire.'

Up to 1905, when they lost office, the Conservatives had passed a spate of legislation aimed at removing Irish socio-economic grievances. But Ireland was rid neither of its discontent nor its nationalism. This has been commonly explained as due to Irish nationalism having assumed an existence independent of the grievances that had produced it. The Conservative reforms were too late: nationalism, the demand for some measure of self-government had taken on a separate life of its own which the remedying of subsidiary grievances did not diminish. Further, mixing repression with reform negated the potential of both to act as solvents. All this holds truth, but the failure of Conservative policy demands more complex explanation.

In part, that policy was successful. Culminating in Wyndham's Land Purchase Act in 1903, the Conservatives' land policy did much to alleviate peasant discontent by making land available for purchase. Thereafter the peasantry was no longer a revolutionary factor in Ireland. Indeed by 1903, Bishop Sheehan could speak of a ' " silent revolution " going on in our midst that must alter things for the best for our long-suffering people ' and expressed ' gladness, that the dawn of that long night of misery and suffering for this land of ours is at length approaching '. The total effect was quietening and markedly conservative. Looking back from 1911 George Russell observed, ' When the State decided on turning tenants into proprietors it set up a barrier against socialism which will last, I fancy, for a couple of hundreds of years yet. An Irish farmer would pour down boiling lead on the emissaries of the State who tried to nationalise his land, the land he sweated sixty years to pay for.' However, from the standpoint of Conservatives, strengthening the socio-economic conservatism of the Irish peasant was to prove a mixed blessing. To conserve and strengthen the peasant economy entailed the preservation of the peasant value structure – dominant in which was a politico-religious antagonism to Britain. To achieve their fundamental purpose, British Conservatives needed to bring about a revolution in attitudes, to effect a positive acceptance of the Union. However, all they succeeded in doing was to reduce or remove those grievances through which Irish peasant venom and hostility had traditionally been channelled. The basic venom remained. To remove those channels would be enough, only so long as new channels were not provided. So the Conservatives succeeded, very largely, in removing anarchy and agrarian unrest from Ireland, but they did not remove the elements of rebellion. No longer did the peasant pot boil, but it simmered still.

Conservative reform in Ireland had a series of contradictory effects. In meeting peasant grievances it confirmed the existence of a class long hostile to Britain. The very reform policy itself, in testifying to Britain's willingness to remedy grievances, nourished hopes which the reforms were designed to kill. The reforms did nothing to satisfy either the major conservative force in Ireland – the Church – or the major new elements in Ireland – younger intellectuals and urban workers. In fact, the reform policy instead of conciliating these groups aroused their more intense suspicion and hostility.

The major flaw in the policy of killing Home Rule by kindness was that it pandered to Irish pockets and stomachs, but ignored Irish religion. The Conservatives left office with the university education question, agitated by the episcopacy for nearly half a century, still unresolved. In a published letter in February 1899 Bishop O'Dwyer put his view that a measure granting a Catholic university would lay a foundation for true conservatism within Irish public life. Instead, the policy of killing Home Rule by kindness had killed its own friends – by that he meant the landlords as well as the bishops – and had entirely neglected the one question from which only advantage could come, ' the one of all others in which they might render the greatest amount of service to Ireland and give intense satisfaction to the great majority of people, and touch those deeper springs of feeling that feed the national life, without taking anything from anyone '.

The failure of the Conservatives to reach an accommodation with the Church on the university issue was of the utmost importance. Not only did it leave that particular matter unsettled, it suggested very strongly that the Conservatives were motivated by anti-Catholic religious prejudice. They thus confirmed and strengthened a reputation for Tory bigotry which adhered to all their measures, largely dissipating any credit which might have attached to their reforms, and causing those reforms to be viewed with the greatest suspicion as potential Protestant snares. The general effect of this was to saddle the Conservatives with such a reputation for Protestant bigotry as to vitiate, in Catholic eyes, their moral authority as a government. Cardinal Manning commented privately in the early 1890s, ' The present Government would fall tomorrow if it were not upheld by this Protestant party. Law, order and authority may be maintained, but at the cost of violating the moral justice by which alone nations are governed.' The Conservative image in the Irish Catholic world in 1900 may be gauged from Bishop MacEvilly's private comment: ' The temper of England towards us is very bad. Indeed we are suffering persecution. In the present temper of England they only want an opportunity of showing their contempt for Catholicity.' The Irish party was powerless in the face of this. ' They all hate Ireland ' T. M. Healy observed of the ministry in 1897, going on to concede, ' our Party can't make it feared or respected.'

The particular effects of the Conservatives' reputation for bigotry may be seen in the intense suspicion with which the Irish episcopacy viewed every piece of their legislation. Reforms designed to remedy poverty were looked upon as attempts to somehow buy and corrupt the poor: where half a century before it had been Protestant soup, it was soon to be Protestant pensions. Reforms aimed at producing wealth and prosperity touched that clerical fear that economic improvements might act against the interests of religion. Even the Local Government Act of 1898 which did much to transfer local powers from Protestant land-owners to the Catholic middle class seemed to Cardinal Logue, firstly an evasion of the possibility of a Catholic Home Rule, secondly a device which would be exploited ' to preserve as much as possible the old Protestant ascendancy '. And of course the fact that this Act specifically excluded clerics from membership of local bodies became an immediate religious grievance.

Outside the official religious sphere, the Conservatives' reforms were no more welcome. All varieties of Irish opinion were opposed to this legislation, either because it was too radical, too expensive, potentially dangerous to Irish values, or merely English, or some combination of these. The new, growing dynamic in Irish affairs – younger intellectuals – were untouched by the practical down-to-earth reforms of Conservative Unionism. Indeed, Gaelic revivalists saw in these reforms a deliberate British attempt to destroy Irish character and will-power. By 1911 the *Irish Review* was arguing that British reform legislation – both Conservative and Liberal – had forced Ireland onto an extravagant, champagne living standard which it would find impossible to maintain when independent: in consequence it would fall into economic dependence on Britain, which would mean political dependence as well. Furthermore, the policy of accepting sops from the British government was degrading, accustoming the Irish to state handouts and thus depriving them of the power of self-help. And of course the reforms sought to Anglicise Ireland. The *Irish Review* feared that the policy of killing Home Rule with kindness would succeed through undermining Irish character and moral fibre. For all this the *Review* held the Home Rule politicians to blame, because their total disposition was that of looking to London for the solution to Ireland's ills. In fact Home Rule politicians, such as John Dillon, were also very unhappy about these reforms – on the ground that they distracted attention from Home Rule and weakened its support.

The Boer War demonstrated the failure of Conservative policy in Ireland. The *Irish Times* reported in October 1900 that 'while all England is ringing with one question – the greatness of Empire – that question is almost forgotten here in the turmoil of insular politics'. In fact, the situation was much worse. A Transvaal Committee was organised in October 1899 to oppose the war. The nationalist party and press was predominantly anti-war. By early 1900 Irish radicals had resurrected the traditional adage that England's difficulty was Ireland's opportunity. In January the *United Irishman* asked. ' Great possibilities are opening up. Will the last days of the 19th century see Ireland regenerated and redeemed? Shall we blind ourselves to the fast approaching opportunity?' Comments like those of Father P. K. Kavanagh in the *Enniscorthy Guardian* in 1903 were typical: 'this war against the Boer is nothing but organised murder promoted by the insatiable greed of the vampire Empire.' He claimed that Irishmen fighting in British armies were guilty of homicide because the war was unjust.

Conservatives themselves eventually recognised and admitted that they had not solved the Irish problem. In 1913 Balfour conceded that Ireland still claimed separate nationality. He still maintained that this had no real justification in facts, but was a produce of ' the tragic coincidences of Irish history '. Balfour could not see that Conservative reforms had increased Irish suspicion and hostility and had avoided or ignored the basic grounds of Irish antagonism. He argued that only time would cure the Irish question, time for the programme of reforms to do its work.

6

The Education Question

Measured by the usual yardstick of political importance, the question of education in Ireland – if of long continuance – seems a minor one, narrowly constricted to the issue of Catholic university, effectively conceded in 1908. This appearance was deceptive, for the education question was central to the religious view of Ireland's future taken by the Irish Church. Abrasion between Church and British government views on education went back to Peel's establishment of Queen's Colleges in the late 1840s, becoming a confirmed pattern under Cardinal Cullen. By 1868 Lord Mayo was writing of the problem, ' Are we to continue this struggle for ever? I am absolutely in despair about Ireland. If a Catholic says Yes, the Protestant says No!' In fact it was usually the Catholic

– in the person of Cardinal Cullen and the Irish bishops – who said No
to the various proposals for an Irish university, scenting in every plan
the danger of ' Hegelism and infidelity '. Gladstone's good will and ingenuity were unequal to the power of the bishops, as was shown by the
destruction of his 1873 Bill, a parliamentary vote which he described as
' the most extravagant compliment ever paid ' to the bishops' political
influence. Extravagance was also a characteristic of episcopal denunciation of the projected measure: its tone and religious content may be
illustrated from the pastoral letter of March 1873, of Bishop Nulty of
Meath. Nulty contended that Gladstone's measure was an example of
English persecuting ' fanaticism ';

> the wealth, the power, and the vast influence of England are once
> again – and under the guidance of her ablest statesman – set in
> motion against us, and that the undisguised object of the movement
> is to extirpate, not now by a bloody persecution, but by a gigantic
> scheme of Godless education, the Catholic religion out of Ireland.
> What England failed to effect by the rack, the dungeon and the
> scaffold, she now hopes to accomplish by the more insidious agency
> of Godless Colleges, Godless Model Schools, and Godless Uni-
> versities.

Such attitudes were never far from the surface, and when Home
Rule entered the realm of practical possibility, together with the religious and moral questions that became obvious from 1887 on, the
education issue again became one of great religious sensitivity.

Clerical reasoning is typified in the *Lyceum*, that monthly published
with the approval of the Irish bishops, of November 1887:

> Irreligion and anarchy go hand in hand. If the masses cease to
> be imbued with Christian principles they must become material-
> ists. . . . They will live for the day; comfort will be holiness; might
> will be right; and the family ties will bind no longer. . . . The res-
> ponsibility for such a state of things, if it should ever come to pass,
> will lie at the doors of those primarily who have laboured to divorce
> education from religion: and of those in the second place who have
> ground the faces of the poor and made their life a misery against
> which they are prompted to rebel.

On both these counts, the English were guilty, and herein is revealed
the true dimensions of Catholic interest in Home Rule. Would not Home
Rule produce a vitally necessary improvement in Irish government, by
changing a state of society which injured religion? But the simple equa-

tion of Home Rule equals Catholic Irish government came under increasing clerical doubt from 1887: would Home Rule produce a situation favourable to religion; worse still, might it not be dangerous or
hostile to religion?

In judging religious education crucial to Ireland's destiny, the
bishops went to the extent of holding it to be decisive for the future
beyond all other considerations. Indicative of this, is the nature of
Archbishop Walsh's fear of the consequences of Papal condemnation of
Irish agitation. He believed, in 1887, that the area where a predictable
mass reaction would express itself to most devastating religious effect
would be in popular attitudes to the bishops' education campaign:

> Our people who have hitherto stood so loyally by us in the cause of
> religious education will simply be turned against that cause, and
> thrown bodily into the open arms of the English Radicals. In fact
> I do not know any other way in which it will be possible to turn
> the present Irish movement into a movement like the modern revo-
> lutionary ones of Italy and France over which neither priests nor
> Bishops nor the Holy See itself can pretend to exercise the faintest
> control.

Walsh's proposition was that if the bishops lost control over the key area
of education, they would eventually lose all influence over popular life
and attitudes, which would become governed instead by irreligious forces.
In its European form, this irreligious bogey was represented by various
revolutionary nationalist and socialist forces, in its English form by the
Radicals. In terms of its political principles and attitudes, English
Radicalism might have been expected to approve, if not champion, Irish
causes. To some extent it did, but the secularism of the Radicals conflicted sharply with the religious claims of Irish Catholicism, to produce
mutual suspicion and hostility.

The influence of the unsolved education question on Anglo-Irish relations was continuous and malign. It both added to and was nourished
by the deep wells of Irish religious suspicion of English intentions. To
the English it served as a continual irritant and a constant affronting
reminder that the Irish were unwilling to bury religious differences in
some secular compromise. Bishop Gillooly's sentiments, expressed
privately to a brother bishop in 1892, could have passed for a medieval
supplication for deliverance from the Turks: 'Pray that God in His
great mercy to Ireland, may defeat the evil designs of English Infidels.'
Any proposed educational reform instantly aroused the clerical fear that
it was another English scheme to destroy religion. In January 1890 the

Irish Catholic noted that the Irish education system had been crippled by denominational hostilities prompted by every attempt to take a step forward: the newspaper's conclusion testifies to the dimensions of the problem and the intensity of the sectarian feeling that accompanied it – it declared itself against compulsory education as this would raise the denominational issue. There is ample evidence of the gravity with which some bishops viewed the proposal of compulsory education, seeing it as soon leading to the destruction of Irish religion. Cardinal Logue, though aware than many priests and some bishops favoured compulsory education because they thought they could use it to religious advantage, feared privately in 1891 that it was 'only the thin end of the wedge for the purpose of completely secularising the schools. I believe that on the day on which the Queen signs a Compulsory and free Education Act for Ireland the influence of the clergy in the schools is doomed.' And what would be the consequences of this? Bishop McAlister confided to another cleric his catastrophic predictions: 'If it comes Ireland will soon cease to send her children or missionaries to carry the faith into other lands and she will lose the only glory she possesses.' So decisive was the field of education, it could see Irish faith placed in jeopardy and the religious imperialism of Ireland in ruins. As English educational reforms came under debate, Irish bishops resorted to prayers for divine intervention: thus Cardinal Logue in March 1892 – 'I am hoping that it may please God to bring the Ministry to smash before the Bill is carried through.' Within Ireland, the efforts of lay school teachers – a profession distrusted by the clergy since the late 1850s when many of its members were prominent in the Fenian movement – to better their conditions and claim some say in school administration met a similar episcopal response, verging on the hysterical. In 1894 Cardinal Logue was convinced that the teachers wanted complete control of the schools, and that Parnellites were at the bottom of teacher agitation, inciting unrest in order to destroy the power of the priesthood.

Given their evaluation of the education issue as utterly vital to the interests of religion, the bishops made it a test of virtue – and by that test, the Irish parliamentary party showed up very poorly. Generally, the party held that the Home Rule cause left no room for the education question. Episcopal pressure occasionally forced the party to depart from or equivocate about this attitude, but it is nicely summed up in Davitt's objection late in 1899 to any tendency to 'drag the University red herring athwart the course of the Home Rule cause'. Its subordinate position aside, as a specifically Catholic and therefore potentially divisive demand, the university cause had little appeal to the Irish party. The bishops' recognition of this response increased their misgivings about the whole Home Rule movement: in their order of priorities the university issue was more important than Home Rule – which ought, in any case, to be Catholic-oriented. In fact the bishops suspected that the party had unacceptable views on education. Early in 1889 – before the Parnell split had opened the floodgates of clerical criticism – Cardinal Logue regarded as ' very ominous ' Irish party support for the Queen's Colleges. Any expression of opinion on education from politicians, which did not accord completely with that of the bishops, the Cardinal felt to be ' dabbling in matters they knew nothing about '.

What did the bishops propose? The Irish party had an excellent excuse for not pressing the university question – the failure of the Irish bishops to agree on what they wanted. T. M. Healy put it to Bishop O'Dwyer in 1897. ' Unless & until the Bishops as a body agree on a line, I don't see how we can start any plan which has not their complete sanction ' – a very reasonable stand from the party's viewpoint, if also very convenient. But, as it issued in total inaction, it displeased all the differing episcopal and clerical groups. Much of the party's unpopularity in the 1890s is traceable directly to its failure to take up and press through a university education measure. True, no agreed episcopal policy existed in detail, and even if it had its religious complexion would have made it a political impossibility in an English situation governed by the Conservatives. Such objections did not weigh with the bishops. Their minds did not work in this way. Writing to Archbishop Walsh in 1897, the requisites for Catholic university education seemed simple to Cardinal Logue – one ' really respectable ' University equal to Trinity College, not a university consisting of local fragments, and this a university over which the bishops would have ' effectual control ' though of course the actual working would be largely in the hands of laymen – that is, laymen who were ' real Catholics '. This solution seemed self-evident to Logue. He paid no heed to the fact that some bishops did want ' local fragments ', and that a blatantly episcopal university was out of the question in the English political context.

Logue and Walsh still related their hopes for a university to what might be secured by the efforts of the Irish party in the British Parliament, but as early as 1895, Bishop O'Dwyer, one of the most energetic advocates of a Catholic university, was opposed to seeking the party's support for that cause. Instead, he contemplated a national campaign organised by the Church that would arouse tremendous popular interest in and enthusiasm for a Catholic university: what gave him pause was his profound suspicion that the parliamentary party would attempt to take over and pervert such a campaign to their own designs. O'Dwyer did not need his friend Lord Emly to point out obvious facts about the party's performance on the university question. For all his convinced – or prejudiced – unionism, Emly's biting sarcasm held much truth:

> Why didn't [the] Irish Party take up [the] cause of Catholic Univ. when they held the late Govt. in the hollow of their hands . . . What became of the Catholicity of that devout Catholic party. The holy cause of the evicted tenants, the thrice holier cause of the dynamitards was espoused by our own newspapers and blessed from our altars. Catholic University Education was left severely alone. Mr Morley must not be embarrassed. Now that 'the Party' see an opportunity to embarrass a Unionist Government, the tender shoots of Nationalist Catholicity are beginning to sprout out in all their verdant loveliness.

Such acid cynicism could have been pressed further: the party avoided Catholic causes when it did not need the church; after Parnell's fall, when it – or its various factions – desperately needed church support or approval, it turned to Catholic causes. It did so with little or no enthusiasm and by then it was too late. The bishops had lost confidence in the party as a means to achieve the Ireland they desired. The superficial appearance of some linkage between nationalism and religion remained, but in fact the conjunction was at an end.

By 1899, when the hostility of English feeling towards a Catholic university again became evident, Cardinal Logue had so moved from any vestige of dependence on the party as to suggest that the bishops might use the party as a weapon to extort a university. He told Archbishop Walsh he favoured a bishop-led Home Rule campaign:

> I would declare that the spirit in which the Univ. proposals have been received and the spirit of bigotry it has aroused clearly prove that it is hopeless for the great body of the Irish people to expect justice and fair play from the English Parliament. I would declare moreover that if the Irish members abandon their disputes and fight as one man for Home Rule, they will be supported unanimously by all the material aid and influence the Bishops can give them. I believe such a declaration, boldly made, would do more to push forward the Univ. Q. than all the coaxing and knuckling down to the Tories we have witnessed of late.

The implications of Logue's outburst are unmistakable: only the education issue was of sufficient moment to move him towards suggesting church support for Home Rule, support which would be a device not for getting Home Rule, but a Catholic university. He reasoned that such an episcopal declaration would blackmail England, in order to avoid a massive Home Rule agitation, into giving the bishops their university, whereupon, presumably, the bishops would drop their Home Rule campaign. The episcopal priorities are clear in Bishop Comerford's remark to Archbishop Kirby in 1892: 'I confess I would much prefer seeing Catholic Education triumphant than having Home Rule with its doubtful advantages carried.' Some Home Rule enthusiasts argued that its great advantage would be that it would open the way for Catholics to get university education. A layman asked Archbishop Kirby in 1893, 'Why is it so many of our present leading public men are so badly instructed as Catholics? Because higher education in Ireland can be had by Catholics only at a sacrifice of faith'. Such an argument was double edged, for it could justify the episcopal conclusion that it would be better, in such circumstances, to postpone Home Rule until the leaders of public affairs in Ireland were properly instructed in sound Catholic principles in a Catholic university.

Both the episcopacy and the shrewder politicians had no illusions about the practical political significance of the university question. Writing to Bishop O'Dwyer in 1899, Arthur O'Connor reminded him of the fate of a Catholic University Bill O'Connor had drafted in 1890: 'Mr Parnell told me at the time that he would not accept the Bill on any terms . . . he thought that if the priests got their University they might not be such good Home Rulers.' Parnell thought right, and his tactic was a sound political one – if it could be maintained. Its danger was that the party should appear to be deliberately frustrating the desires of its clerical supporters, and this is what happened. Cardinal Logue's 1899 proposal revealed that the power relationship was, or at least seemed to Logue to be, reversed: instead of the Catholic university cause being dependant on the inclinations of the Home Rulers, the Home Rule cause had become dependant on the bishops' feelings about the university question.

In fact, Logue's whole reaction – and that of most of his colleagues – was that of an ideologue. T. M. Healy spent a good deal of his correspondence preaching to bishops about the realities of political life. In one of his epistles of 1903 – to Logue – he tried to explain that:

A Ministry is like a company of actors, or corps of ballet girls – whispers of fame, doubts about public applause, threats of withdrawal effect them more than principles or the calls of justice. The anxiety of a yawn of a tired supporter, the growl of a doubtful friend, are

portents of greater moment in Westminster, than the voice of conscience, which commands no votes. . . . It is not ethereal or elevated
politics, but we are dealing with 'vulgar fractions' or at least I
am. . . . We must therefore in the wretched plight in which Catholic
Ireland is placed, work in the conditions and with the instruments
that come to our hands, so long as they are not soiled.

Healy's explanations were in vain. The situation he sketched was not
acceptable to religionists, a disposition and characteristic they shared
with the new group of idealist intellectuals which was growing in Ireland.
Neither religionists nor politico-cultural intellectuals could abide the
world of compromise, of bargaining and partial gains, and they were
contemptuous of those politicians who engaged in such sordid work. Both
the world of religion and the world of revolution were that of principles,
purity, and the striving for full achievement of theoretical ideals. To the
inhabitants of both these worlds, politicians seemed depraved, and England corrupt.

The anti-English animus of the clergy, centred on the university
question and of great popular influence in the late nineteenth and early
twentieth centuries, was anchored firmly to the conviction that English
policy was determined by anti-Catholic bigotry generally, and by the
Orange faction in particular. There was ample evidence suggesting that
this was so. The resolution of the 1903 General Assembly of the Irish
Presbyterian Church was typical in its strong protest against a Catholic
university ' as detrimental to University education, as tending to the
perpetuation of divisions and animosities amongst the young of different creeds, and as practically involving in a very objectionable form a
State endowment of religion '. Typical too was the current jibe that an
Irish Catholic university would be an ' institution for the preservation
of dead languages and undying prejudices '. Irish politicians, particularly
Healy, fed the episcopal interpretation with comments such as ' Balfour
& Co have been utterly swept aside by the wave of No Popery fury ' and
' Balfour is quite well disposed (as I am towards bumble-bees) but he
has an 18lb Orange shot shackled to each ankle '.

It was the British government's failure to solve the education question, not its failure to concede Home Rule, which deeply alienated men
of religion in Ireland from that government, and gravely weakened their
respect for it. Nothing could be clearer than Bishop O'Dwyer's statement in an 1895 pamphlet that ' If that [Imperial] Parliament is so
dominated by English bigotry that, in the great matter of education, it
can take no account of the religious convictions of the great majority of

the nation, then no one can deny that it has forfeited all right to legislate for us. Such a Government is a cruel tyranny '. O'Dwyer continued to ventilate this theme as in his claim in 1899 that the ultimate obstacle to the concession of a Catholic University ' is simply the bigotry of a section of what are styled political nonconformists ', that it was unreasonable ' to blame Catholics if they retaliate ', and that the ' fate of the country ' was being determined ' not by the wisdom of the best, but by the prejudices of narrow-minded sectarians '.

To the British government, the Irish bishops gave the appearance of quarrelling clansmen unable to agree on what they wanted, at the same time as being irresponsibly and unrealistically critical of anything they were offered. British impatience with this is understandable, but it merely increased the salient bond of unity that did exist among the bishops – profound distrust of Britain. In 1896 Cardinal Logue was indignant that an Irish Education Bill should contain no conscience clause, and very angry when, in response to representations, the Lord Lieutenant intimated that the bishops might take the Bill or leave it. ' This seems to be the fixed principle of the Government now in dealing with Irish Questions ', observed Logue to Walsh – in a remark which, significantly, generalised from the particular education instance. The process of arriving at a general estimate of British government on the basis of a reaction to the education question was common among the Irish episcopacy. Late in 1898 Logue was agreeing with O'Dwyer that ' it is intolerable that four fifths of the Irish people should be put under the feet of a few ignorant Orange bigots [sic] here in the North. The longer we submit quietly to such treatment the worse our case will be. I still think that if the Irish Bishops . . . boldly joined the people in contending for our national rights, they would be more respected by the Government and would have the full sympathy of their own people '. Fighting words – sparked by the education grievance. The relationship between that grievance and Ireland's total situation was direct and immediate because the bishops would not allow that the animus against Catholic education had anything sincere or religious in it. As Bishop Foley told Bishop O'Dwyer in 1899, ' The real motive which, I believe, lies at the root of the existing opposition is the apprehension that Protestants cannot retain their practical monopoly of the positions of emolument in the Country, if the Catholics be granted higher Education '.

By the end of the century, the leading bishops had arrived at a position of deep distrust of everybody except themselves, and of dissatisfaction with any solution to the university question other than one which ensured their complete dominance and control. British efforts to

devise a politically possible solution to the problem by taking into account
the major elements of sectarian contention seemed to Logue a bigoted
revival of the penal laws. In the 1899 Bill he regarded the exclusion of
the subject of modern history as merely ludicrous, but the exclusion of
clerics as a gross concession to English bigotry. Nor was the Cardinal
satisfied that the bishops had any control over the character of university
teachers: as there was no religious test, it was conceivable that an
infidel professor could be appointed. Haldane had told the bishops that
the British government would give a private undertaking on this point,
but Logue would not accept this. He told Archbishop Walsh, ' our past
experience of Gov.[ernment] appointments and Gov. action, warns us
of the imprudence of taking too much on trust '. Profound distrust had
become the episcopal rule – which extended to its own laity. The
proposal that the Catholic university have a governing body of Catholic
laity filled Logue with anxiety and foreboding. His mind is sharply
revealed in his reaction, in 1906, to the even more alarming prospect
of local control in primary education. He told Walsh:

> Important as the Univ. Q. is, I am more anxious about the future of
> Primary Education because the faith of the great body of our people
> will depend on it. It is very ominous to find some of our politicians
> going through the country advocating *thorough local control*. I
> find that even some of the priests who have attached themselves to
> that party are going in for local control. Why they ask, can we
> not trust our own people? Are they not Cath[olic]s? God help
> Irish Catholic education in this country if it is put under local
> control.

By this stage, as the bishops had made clear in their 1900 Synod, they
had contrived, through the device of clerical management of schools, a
National System of education which was ' as denominational almost as
we could desire '. This capturing of a system designed to be non-
denominational had attracted, since the 1880s, criticism from such politicians as Joseph Chamberlain – which in turn provoked Catholic criticism of British secularism which could go as far as Cardinal Logue's
advice to Catholic voters in a British by-election in 1906 – ' Wherever
you see the head of a Radical or a Nonconformist, hit it '. By 1911
criticism of the clerical domination of Irish schools was still at such
a volume as to call for the issuing of a pamphlet, written at episcopal
direction, to defend it. All criticism was branded as anti-clerical and
secular. In 1900 the bishops had made it clear that they would relinquish
none of their complete control, exercised through clerical managers, as

any such change would be 'so injurious to the religious interests of our people'. The 1911 pamphlet set out the basis for this conclusion: 'We must not forget that we are still living under a foreign and Protestant Government, in a Catholic land to be sure, but one in which Protestant-ism dominates every public department of the State. The spirit of hos-tility to our holy Faith is still there. . . . there is a new spirit abroad with which our rulers and their supporters are impregnated – an agnostic, atheistic, socialist, secular spirit'.

Judged by the expectations and requirements of many of the episcopacy, the National University of Ireland established in 1908, was too little, too late. They had become soured with a Britain that had denied for so long what they regarded as their rights in a crucial matter, and in any case the National University by no means fully satisfied the bishops. Given the delay of over half a century in granting a university, there was ample room for episcopal speculation on what religious harm might have been prevented had this reform been made earlier, much earlier; and on what religious damage had been done, particularly to the middle and upper classes – Ireland's natural leaders – by deprivation of a Catholic university, and their attendance at secular or Protestant Institutions. The satisfaction which the clergy took in the National University was an aggressive, not a grateful one: Archbishop Walsh was elected the first Chancellor and Cardinal Logue declared that despite English intentions, the university was a victory for Catholic exclusiveness.

Almost immediately this concept of the university was challenged from within Ireland. From 1908 the Gaelic League promoted an agita-tion for compulsory Irish within the University, a vigorous and candid campaign taken up by three nationalist newspapers, *Sinn Féin, The Leader* and *The Irish Peasant*. It was marked by harsh criticism of the bishops, often by their own clergy writing anonymously. Much of this criticism was wider than the language question, arriving at such broad conclusions as 'where simple national issues are at stake, they [the bishops] are not necessarily wise or safe guides for the people. . . . History certainly teaches the lesson, that on national issues the judge-ment of the people is, on the whole, much more likely to be sound than that of their Lordships'. These echoes of the age of Parnell at its height brought a sharp reaction from the bishops, which made very clear that the episcopal aim was not an Irish university, but a Catholic one: they defended their stand against compulsory Irish on the grounds that such a regulation might debar deserving Catholics from the university.

Britain had again failed the bishops. The 1908 Act had not created explicitly a Catholic university, only the possibility of one, leaving the bishops the task of attempting to realise that possibility in practice. The 1908 Act bequeathed to Ireland the problem of determining the nature of its new university. The bishops' intention of making it exclusively and rigorously Catholic incensed the champions of Irish Ireland. They asked of the university ' Is it to be Irish, or it is to be West Briton?' and accused the bishops of flouting national opinion, outraging national sentiment and degrading the national language. They claimed that the Senate of the University was not Ireland's choice: ' It is the choice of the British Government, or its agents '.

So it was that the National Univerity of 1908, Britain's answer to demands that went back to the 1840s and before, brought Britain no gratitude. In so far as it was a concession to the continual demands of the Irish bishops, it was not nearly enough to satisfy them, and too much to satisfy the new wave of Gaelic nationalists.

7
The Question of Irish Nationalism

It has been common to trace the growth of that phase of Irish nationalism which issued in the 1916 rebellion back to the formation of the Gaelic League in 1893, and to identify its development with the ideas, activities and organisations of a tiny coterie of intellectuals. So Patrick Pearse, in 1913, related the movement of which he was a part directly to the Gaelic League: ' when the seven men met in O'Connell Street to found the Gaelic League, they were commencing . . . not a revolt, but a revolution '. John Eglinton made the claim that ' Yeats, and the literary movement in which he was the commanding figure, may be said to have conjured up the armed bands of 1916 '. Yeats himself asked the question: ' Did that play of mine send out/Certain men the English shot?'

The work of intellectuals, vital though it was, was merely a facet − a narrow if brilliant facet − of a much wider and deeper revival which was taking place in Ireland. From the late 1880s Ireland experienced an accelerating popular religious revival. Devotion to the Sacred Heart of Jesus had been established in Ireland since the early nineteenth century, with minor success. But from 1887, under the leadership of the Jesuit priest James A. Cullen, the devotion swept Ireland in various organised forms, notably the Apostleship of Prayer. The explosive success of this movement is typified by the single church which enrolled 8,000 Apostleship members in the first four months of 1888, and by the instant success of the *Messenger of the Sacred Heart* first published in January 1888. By 1894 this pious magazine, by doubling its circulation annually, had reached a circulation of 47,000: by 1904 it was at 73,000 and still climbing. Father Cullen was an ardent temperance crusader, and he used his *Messenger* and the Apostleship as the vehicles for a temperance crusade which he began in 1889. Again the success was prodigious – over a quarter of a million total abstinence pledges, permament or temporary, taken within the first two years. Cullen's Temperance Catechism sold out its first printing of 60,000 in 1892. His organisational work developed in many directions, most importantly in the formation in 1901 of the Pioneer Total Abstinence Association which spread world wide. From 1905 the Capuchin Fathers conducted a parallel temperance movement which claimed a million pledges taken by 1912. The monthly *Messenger* appeared in January 1888, the weekly *Irish Catholic* appeared in May, issued by the M.P., T. D. Sullivan. The *Irish Catholic* mirrored and encouraged the Catholic evangelical revival of which it was a part: it was dedicated to the realisation of a Christian Democracy, gave much of its space to the temperance crusade, and professed belief in the superior Christian worth and potential of Ireland and Irishmen.

The religious revival of the late 1880s combined militant ascetic Catholicism with aggressive emotional nationalism. While the religious and spiritual aspects of the temperance crusade – in terms of the sin of drunkenness, its related moral evils, the virtues of self-denial, and so on – were central to it, no less prominent in the crusade were its temporal, politico-nationalist aspects summed up in the popular slogan. ' Ireland sober, Ireland free '. As reported in the first issue of the *Irish Catholic,* the temperance preacher Father John O'Mahony typifies this nationalist angle to the crusade:

As you love your race, as you love your country and its freedom, as you would restore again its ancient glories and bring back its long-lost wealth, persevere in the path you have chosen. You will not have long to wait, and in other times it shall be written of you that even in the darkest hour of cruel and cowardly despotism, the hour preceding the dawn, you were true patriots – proudly free. . . . There is but one thing needed to make our proud freedom perfect. . . . It is the emancipation of our grand and historic race from the degrading slavery of drink.

So religion, culture and politics were emotionally merged in the one crusade which both drew on and strengthened the latent power of all three; it exalted discipline, dedication and self-sacrifice; it nourished a sense of national pride which often swelled to arrogance. In all, the temperance movement was providing, by the late 1880s, much of the emotional mood for revolution – even down to the terminology: speaking in October 1899 at a commemoration of the birth of the great temperance advocate, Father Mathew, in Cork, the Very Rev. Father Arthur Ryan told his audience,

> You are here to show that rebel Cork glories in this her greatest rebel – the revolutionist who shattered the tyranny of drink . . . you are in one thing, at least, rebels like myself, aye rebels like Father Mathew, in open rebellion against one, at least, of Ireland's foes, and determined to keep the flag of that rebellion flying as long as there is a hand in Cork, or in Tipperary, or in all Ireland, to uphold it, determined with God's help to plant it triumphant over an emancipated people.

The sermon notebook of one of Father Cullen's co-crusaders, Father Michael Kelly, shows that in the late 1880s he was preaching throughout Ireland the thesis that Irish intemperance was a deliberate English contrivance: 'With fell design England suppressed our commerce, our factories, our mines, our industries, and left us only the distillery.' The jargon of nationalist violence remained a feature of the temperance crusade. A handbill of March 1911 enjoined temperance forces

> to show forth the number and strength of our battalions, to set before the public gaze the enthusiasm, the noble generous resolve, the ardent panting desire of a vast army of priests and people ready to besiege the enemy's camp, willing to do battle for God and Erin, prepared to storm the citadel of Bacchus, and deliver their native land from the cruel tyranny which has oppressed and degraded our people for centuries.

The religious revival had its real temperamental links with the emerging cultural rebels, not with the Home Rule movement. Sensing the power of the temperance crusade, some Home Rulers made haste to support it. In October 1889, John Redmond M.P. declared that ' as soon as Home Rule was carried this country would witness a temperance movement such as had never been seen in Ireland before, or perhaps in any other land.' Three years later, in July 1892, Archbishop Walsh, in private correspondence was linking the two evils of Parnellism and the liquor interest: ' It is well known that the whole *publican* interest is on the

Parnellite side. In fact that is the only definite point of organisation they have now. The money expended is all publicans' money.' Despite this, and Redmond's promise (or threat), the Irish parliamentary party remained unable to shed its image of involvement with the liquor interest – an image which did it great harm among the ascetical revivalists of religion and nationalism. A correspondent of Bishop O'Dwyer's wrote late in 1915 that ' The only influence Redmond and the so-called Nationalist party have now in England is the influence of the Trade, the Brewers, Distillers & Publicans who through the centuries have been the bitterest foes of Ireland and her cause.' Furthermore, it was natural that a campaign for improvement of individual habits and behaviour should bring the lives of Ireland's politicians under harsh scrutiny. Not that the parliamentary party was any scandal of intemperance, but some of its members were not above criticism, particularly from zealots to whom the consumption of even small amounts of alcohol represented weakness and degradation. Count Moore asked a Dublin temperance audience in 1903, ' why do we tolerate drunkards in public life? Well may the English Parliament deny our rights and refuse a just measure of equality, bargain and haggle over education, when it sees a people send such men to legislate for the Empire, to govern millions. . . . Do you think you will ever be masters in your own house while you are ruled and roped by a majority of publicans?' This kind of questioning had very radical implications because it assumed the necessity to sweep away the old political system and its representatives before true Irish freedom could be gained: it assumed, in the traditional mode of revolutionary thought, a thorough cleansing of public life to make way for new men, dedicated ascetics.

However, nothing illustrates more clearly the close links between the temperance cause and the new nationalism than Father Cullen's speech in June 1914 to the National Catholic Total Abstinence Congress – at which Patrick Pearse was present. ' Ireland is a nation, whose history though written in tears and blood, has never bartered honour for gold, nor Faith for spurious freedom. She is a nation which, though long insulted and down-trodden by superior force, never yet was conquered: a nation that in her darkest night of suffering never doubted but that the morning of triumph would follow.' To this rhetoric Cullen added, as temperance advocates commonly did, economic nationalist arguments:

> While at the moment we stand on the threshold of our legislative independence, and while thoughtful Irishmen are puzzling over the difficult problems of financing successfully our Home Rule Government, they see the Irish nation brought to the very verge of bank-

ruptcy by the mad, profligate expenditure of thirteen or fourteen millions sterling, paid annually for the licensed sale and consumption of strong drink. . . . Now if I were to ask how the Irish nation, the men, women and youth of Ireland, were to effect this great peaceful revolution which means so much for Ireland, and without which Ireland can never be prosperous, I would answer . . . convince them that strong drink is a drug.

To Cullen, Total Abstinence was a complete economic panacea, its utopian revolutionary potential vital not only in the moral order but the economic. As to the political order, Cullen had misgivings about the dependability of the Irish parliamentarians – 'we ask anxiously, will they, like so many of their countrymen in the past, wilfully shut their eyes to the magnitude of the Drink Evil in Ireland?' About the newly formed Irish Volunteers – that irregular army so central to the rebellion in 1916 – he had no misgivings whatever: there he saw a moral crusade akin to his own.

Here again a new and wondrous light is beginning to fall on the past clouded picture of our country, for amongst some few other influences for our young men, we recognise and hail with joy the advent of the Volunteer movement. We believe it will supply muchneeded recreation to our boys and young men. It will give an outlet to their youthful energies, it will give them a manly and soldier-like bearing, it will make them exact, punctual and enduring, it will teach them that labour is necessary for success in life, but above all it will make them love the Old Land, whose rights they will learn to uphold and defend even to death.

For a temperance congress, Cullen's were strange words, but the similarity in atmosphere and disposition between the moral and religious revival, and the political one, made them seem totally appropriate. Cullen's ideal – and prayer – was that all Volunteers would enrol as Pioneers. As another priest told the Congress Demonstration in which Volunteer units participated, ' They had united with this great temperance movement that energy and devotion, enthusiasm and heroism, which was represented in what was, to his mind, the greatest and most striking movement of modern times – the Irish National Volunteers. . . . It was a movement of their own; it rose up from the very heart of their people.'

Going back to the late 1880s, temperance was not the only religiocultural issue to be given a sharp nationalist point. Protestant proselytism had been a traditional occasion for Irish Catholic anger, particularly in relation to Protestant orphanages. The British evangelical movement of the nineteenth century turned some of its energies towards Ireland, provoking, in 1888, a massive clerical-led agitation against proselytism. From this the *Irish Catholic* took, in September 1888, the nationalist lesson ' That in vindication of our national and constitutional rights, we again resolve to continue the struggle against Irish landlordism and British misrule as the radical source and occasion of this abominable system.'

But it was in the central formative area of the new Irish nationalism – the Gaelic revival – that religion and the new nationalism found their most natural meeting ground, because Irish culture was thoroughly religious. Long before the formation of the Gaelic League in 1893, the Gaelic revival in its literary form was receiving strong support from clerical sources. The episcopally authorised monthly *Lyceum* summed up the reason in May 1890: ' the English literature which has come to us is essentially Protestant. . . . The daily and weekly journals, the reviews, and all the lighter literature preach Protestantism with a hundred tongues.' But as to ' the literature of ancient Ireland . . . there is about it all a glow of the spirit of faith, warm and genuine as among the early Christians . . . we find everywhere the spirit of that Faith which was the life-breath of the nation.' From the religious viewpoint, the Irish literary movement, in spurning English publications which were ' infidel and licentious for the most part ', was not so much a cultural-national revival as a religious one, a moral cleansing process, a rejection of the corruption and filth dumped in Ireland by the English: to go back to the literature of ancient Ireland was to return to the pure unsullied well-springs of the old faith. So patent had the vital linkage between religious and national-cultural interests become by the late 1890s that T. M. Healy could tell Bishop O'Dwyer that the church was to blame for endangering both causes through its neglect of the Irish language: ' if the Church here had held by the Irish language, & not helped to bring in English, there need now be no such outcry against vicious literature which is Anglicising as well as de-Catholicising youth.' Clerical condemnations of British publications were no passing fad: in 1907 Cardinal Logue listed the two greatest dangers to Ireland's religion as, first, ' unsavoury ' literature from Britain, second, an unbelieving, atheistic, anti-Christian spirit. The conviction that British literature was spiritually destructive is the main reason why the priesthood played such an important role in a movement whose popular linguistic basis was erected so largely on the book of one priest – Father Eugene O'Growney's Irish Grammar. Certainly the priesthood had the training and leisure for literary or scholarly pursuits, but their strongest motivation and interest sprang from their own profession – religion. The intimate connection between the Irish revival and religion was obvious to both: Eoin MacNeill remarked that 'When we learn to speak Irish, we soon find that it is what we may call essential Irish to acknowledge God, His presence, and his help, even in our most trivial conversation.' To outsiders the linkage, being not so apparent, had surprising consequences. The Italian cleric Father Buonaiuti, visiting Ireland early in the twentieth century saw what he regarded as 'the curious fact that the language revival is accompanied by an intensification of missionary zeal, a re-awakening of that ardour for winning converts to the Faith.'

It was a linkage which swung religious attitudes into sympathetic alignment not only with the contemporary cultural revival, but with major elements in the Irish revolutionary tradition. This was apparent in the *Lyceum*'s review in August 1890, of Gavan Duffy's life of Thomas Davis.

> While our peasants say their beads, and meditate on the Mysteries of the Rosary, they can never come wholly under the sway of the doctrine that men were sent into the world to be happy and to make money . . . [this] moral poison that flowed after the triumphant chariot wheels of utilitarianism as embodied in English power. . . . He [Davis] would have his countrymen not merely politically free of the English Parliament but he would have them morally and intellectually free of the English Gospel. . . . He wanted the social organisation of Ireland to be based upon the Home, and he thought he saw in the process of the aggregation of men in huge cities and in the industrial system which dragged the father and mother away for the greater portion of each day, the destruction of the Home. . . . He saw in the factory system a monster that destroyed this ideal life, and he was its foe. He would have Ireland a nation of peasant owners. We could find no better proof of the spiritual-mindedness of the Irish people than the readiness with which they appreciated Davis's teaching and the permanence of its influence over them. There was nothing in it that appealed to sordidness, selfishness, or sensuality. . . .

Gone was Davis's image among religionists as one of the dangerous revolutionaries of the 1840s: the religious revival of the late 1880s accepted him as a spiritual hero and saw his ideas as pure and moral long before he became the romantic idol and intellectual arbiter of the Pearse generation.

A fundamental point of linkage between religionists and cultural nationalists was their idealised image of the peasant: to cultural nationalists he was the essential, undefiled Irishman, to religionists he was the true, pure Catholic; both nurtured the myth that he was noble and holy. The Protestant Douglas Hyde, founder of the Gaelic League, wrote in 1895 in his *The Religious Songs of Connacht*: ' The Irish Gael is pious by nature. He sees the hand of God in every place, in everytime, and in everything . . . unbelief is alien to his mind, and contrary to his feelings.' And to his dismay Hyde was soon to find that the outcome of the League's work, avowedly non-sectarian, was to foster Catholic Ireland above all else. He complained to Lady Gregory in 1901, ' we cannot turn our back on the Davis ideal of every person in Ireland being an Irishman, no matter what their blood and politics. . . . It is equally true, though that the Gaelic League and the *Leader* aim at stimulating the old peasant, Papist aboriginal population, and we care little about the others.' Nevertheless, neither Church nor intellectuals wanted an uncontrolled mass movement in Ireland: both believed their leadership necessary, for a popular movement might mean the reign of ignorance. After the land war and Parnell the Church viewed the peasant with a mixture of suspicion and great hope – suspicion that he might desert to ' Jacobinism ', hope that his spiritual qualities might be made the basis for holy Ireland. Similarly, the intellectuals had no taste for the crudity and violence of peasant life, but yearned to see realised only that which was noble, beautiful.

In the late 1890s, Catholic Ireland produced a novelist of popularity and power – the priest, Canon P. A. Sheehan. There were many other popular writers who glorified the religious life of the people, but Sheehan's work illustrates strikingly the merging into the one integrated outlook of the values of religion and the values of the new cultural nationalism of his time.

Sharp hostility to Britain – on religious grounds – is implicit in all Sheehan's novels. *Luke Delmege* (1901) contrasts the base ideals of England with the spiritual ideals of Ireland, productive of the heights of moral beauty and heroism. Dialogue from *Geoffrey Austin: Student* makes explicit the basis of Sheehan's contrast. Two Irish boys talk as they walk in London: ' We are standing in the world's centre, Charlie.' ' Or in the vestibule of hell!' ' The very air is redolent of culture and civilisation!' ' It smells rankly of sin!' ' These are the world's conquerors!' ' Or the devil's slaves!'

Much more remarkable is the way in which the work of this priest-novelist embodies the key principles of those who led the 1916 rebellion.

In *The Graves at Kilmorna*, the story of an old Fenian, written in 1912-13 and published in 1914, Sheehan idealises the Irish revolutionary tradition, and is bitterly critical of the supine worldliness of contemporary Ireland. He contrasts a noble Fenianism with a degraded parliamentary representation and with a corrupt contemporary Ireland that had apostasised from its national duty. Ireland of the Fenians had kept the ten commandments: modern Ireland had sold out to vice, avarice and materialism. Sheehan, through his characters, denounced democracy: 'the reign of democracy set in with the French Revolution; and its elephantine hoofs have been trampling out all the beauty and sweetness of life since then. . . . Democracy has but one logical end – Socialism. Socialism is cosmopolitan – no distinction of nationalities any longer; but one common race. This means anti-militarism, the abolition of all stimulus and rivalry.' Sheehan's closeness to the spirit of the new nationalism is evident from the views of *Sinn Féin* 11 November 1911: 'Imperialism and Socialism – forms of the Cosmopolitan heresy and in essence one . . . have offered man the material world – Nationalism has offered him a free soul. . . .'

Even more striking is Canon Sheehan's exposition, in this work written in 1912-13, of those theories of revolution and blood sacrifice which Pearse was to promote from 1913 until his death. The characters in the *Graves at Kilmorna* anticipate the words of Pearse. Thus:

I have never thought of anything higher or greater than to strike one smashing blow for Ireland, and then lie down to die on some Irish hillside.

But, if I were certain that our movement was to be as futile and profitless as that smoke, I would still say, Go on! . . . The country has become plethoric and therefore indifferent to everything but bread and cheese. It needs blood letting a little. The country is sinking into the sleep of death; and nothing can awake it but the crack of the rifle. . . . We may also have to teach from our graves! . . . the political degradation of the people which we have preached with our gaping wounds will shame the nation into at least a paroxysm of patriotism again! . . . it is the fools that do all the world's great work. Then the world calls them heroes.

. . . if no blood is shed, the country will rot away . . . nothing can stop the dread process of national decomposition except the shedding of blood. I shall not trespass on the sacred principles of religion to illustrate my meaning. I shall only say that as the blood of the martyrs was the seed of saints, so the blood of the patriot is the sacred seed from which alone can spring new forces, and fresh life, into a nation that is drifting into the putrescence of decay.

The beliefs, value judgements and disposition of this priest-novelist are scarcely less important than those of Pearse the activist, because Sheehan both formed and reflected the clerical and popular mood and conscience in Ireland, and, obviously, he had accepted the redemptive necessity for a rising long before it came. Sheehan's novels, widely read from the 1890s to the 1920s, suggest that at least a part, perhaps a substantial part, of thinking, religious, non-revolutionary Ireland dwelt imaginatively in the realm of rebellion well before 1916. Sheehan's attitude to Irish nationalism, as revealed in *The Graves at Kilmorna*, exhibits clearly that strong self-purifying element which made nationalism acceptable to many of those who would otherwise have baulked at the idea of repudiating the English connection. But Sheehan's message, chiming in with that of the new nationalists, was that England was corrupt and was corrupting Ireland, and that Ireland must take upon itself the responsibility of its own salvation.

I tell you, [says the hero of *The Graves at Kilmorna*] that in building up a Nation, it is not to Acts of Parliament you must look, but to yourselves, because no material gain can compensate for moral degeneracy, and I doubt if Ireland ever sank lower in the sty of materialism than in this present age. . . . I speak . . . in sorrow, to see a great race, with all the elements of moral and intellectual progress, failing to rise to the level of its opportunities, because it will not see that it is from itself, and not from foreign influences, its redemption must come. Let us cease from being a nation of slaves, begetting dictators and tyrants.

This introspective, self-critical aspect to the new nationalism was of profound importance, not only because its spiritual and moral dimension held great appeal to those concerned with Irish religion and morality, the quality of Irish life, but in making Ulster's stand and partition, such an an intolerable affront to nationalist Ireland. Partition was unthinkable not only because it destroyed the integrity of the geographic nation, but because it would prevent Ireland's internal moral revolution from being total and complete: the religio-nationalist urge to purify Ireland, so that it might be born anew, amounted to a rage, and Ulster's refusal to co-operate in this rejuvenation was a gross frustration which high-lighted the very degeneracy which the idealists sought to purge.

The cult of the peasant had a natural corollary in that denunciation of the city and industrialism common to both religious and cultural-nationalist opinion in Ireland. Again the *Lyceum* (of November 1891) may be cited to illustrate the close linkage between religious, nationalist and cultural values, in its warning that emigration and the drift to the cities were endangering the real Ireland: ' Rural Ireland contains most of the elements essential to Ireland's life as a nation. Rural Ireland is Catholic too, in larger proportion than the general people. Economic causes threatening its existence threaten the existence of that entity which men point to when they speak of the Irish nation . . . whatever the way out of the danger, those who wish to preserve the old Ireland as a moral and spiritual force must be wary and alert.' The *Lyceum*'s particular stimulus for concern was fear for Catholicism – Ireland was becoming less of a Catholic country: in 1861 Catholics were 77.6 per cent of the population, in 1891, 75.4 per cent. But this concern lived on vigorously, even being built into the prayer life of the Irish through such media as *The Irish Messenger of the Sacred Heart*: the issue of August 1895 proposed a Morning Offering which concluded with the supplication ' that Thou mayst especially bless our toilers in the fields, that remaining in their country homes, by their labours, simplicity and holiness they may counter-balance the corruption and irreligion of towns and cities.' The religious desire to preserve rural culture could even issue in economic antiquarian-ism as exhibited in Archbishop Healy's plea, in 1915, that the peasantry learn again to live, as their ancestors had done, on the simple fare which they could produce from their own fields, by the labour of their own families.

This religious outlook had much in common with that of Gaelic revivalists who feared Ireland was becoming less Irish. As typical nine-teenth century romantics, these revivalists repudiated the industrial and commercial worlds as depraved and vulgar, and, like their Catholic countrymen, rejected Britain on moral grounds. Where the English took pride in their industrial society and commercial supremacy, respected wealth and held the economic virtues in the highest regard, Gaelic roman-tics regarded these things as depraving. To the romantics, Irish society was morally superior to the English; a conviction they shared with the spokesmen of Irish Catholicism. The Irish romantics, like romantics elsewhere, rejected modern civilisation which they anathematised with a vehemence worthy of the *Syllabus of Errors*: to them Britain epitomised that civilisation. They turned to the imaginative construction of an idealised Irish community, some wonderful land of heart's desire. For romantics, as for religionists, Britain represented the evil modern world.

Perhaps it was that neither group could cope with that modern world, with all its complexities and problems, and that their rejection of it testifies to a fearful inadequacy, a flight from reality, a vain attempt to recreate a past – beautiful, simple, holy – that had never existed. Certainly the misery and degradation of Ireland was an atmosphere conducive to a flight from reality, the romantic creation of a nobler Ireland than ever was; conducive too to belief in myth rather than reality. Or was it Catholicism itself which, as Alexander Herzen observed of the Poles, ' has developed that mystical exaltation which keeps them perpetually in the world of dreams.' Perhaps it was that both religionists and romantics saw in their different ways that the modern world threatened all that was valuable in their concept of human life, and sought not so much escape, as the assertion of a right to refuse to conform to its decadence. However the motivation be construed, this movement of assertive rejection is a vital element in Irish nationalism. Far from being a ' progressive ' movement, it was a reactionary one, a moral reaction against modernity as exemplified by Britain. To the extent that this was so, Britain had no chance of controlling the growth of Irish nationalism because that nationalism was substantially a reaction not so much against what Britain did, but against what Britain was – a vast industrial, commercial, imperial, urbanised power. It was simply, as Bishop Kelly put it in 1919 that ' the industrial system does not promote earthly or heavenly happiness ', and, as the focused strength of Parnellism in Irish cities and towns showed, the city destroyed Christian life and values. So, against the evils of the industrial system and the degradation of city life, Irish romantics and religionists asserted the virtues of the rural community; against commercialism they asserted spiritual values; against imperial power they asserted a morally superior nationality.

In this assertion, religious and secular elements blended into a cultural whole, which even sported some trappings of racialist ideology. To quote a contributor to the *Irish Review* in December 1912:

> Let no one imagine that the ideals of the Celt and the ideals of whatever Latin or Teuton races have inherited from the Empire of Rome can co-exist in the same people. The one is absolutely destructive of the other. The ideal of the one race is beauty, whether in the mould of life or the spirit of action, the ideal of the other is power. There is only one kind of power that does not destroy beauty, and that is spiritual power – that the Celts once possessed, and on that was their Empire founded. The power of the Latin and the Teuton is material power.

It was possible to build on such theories a concept of Irish imperialism in which the Irish would emerge as rulers of a world-wide spiritual empire. A writer in *Sinn Féin*, 15 April 1911 contrived such a possibility:

> . . . the Irish. . . . fought for a civilisation, a great civilisation, a noble civilisation – a civilisation in which pure materalism could find no place. They fought for it against not only England but the whole world. They held it intact until three hundred years ago – and they hold the idea of it still. That is why they have failed in a world where Julius Caesar is still the King of Kings. If they hold on to it long enough it may make them rulers of a world which has really buried Julius Caesar. . . .

The vision of spiritual empire was based on the conviction that, to quote the Gaelic Leaguer, Father P. S. Dineen in 1904, ' The influence of a people on the world at large is in no way commensurate with their wealth or even with their intellectual power. National character counts for far more than national affluence or national genius.' All this was secular thinking, but its intimate linkage with concepts of Ireland's religious mission is unmistakable.

None of this kind of anti-modern thinking seems to have rejected those aspects of the industrial revolution which were a major convenience, railways, fertilisers and so on. Between 1850 and 1880, the growth of railways in Ireland contributed more than any other single factor towards westernising the Irish interior, promoting its contact with the outside sinful world, contributing towards rising material expectations and perhaps partly explaining why distress before 1850 could be accepted with primitive resignation, but the recession of 1877-80 led on to the land war. No one preached against railways.

The religious and cultural revivals nourished and sustained one another, but of the two, the religious had a more forward looking, or at least more ambitious dynamic. The religious revival was related to a firm conviction of Irish holiness, and, indeed, of Irish religious superiority over all other races. This assumption became strident in the late '80s and early '90s and remained vigorous thereafter. Bishop Brownrigg's evaluation of intemperance in 1890 makes the typical point: ' With this one stain removed from Ireland, no nation can approach her in everything that is good and religious.' Cardinal Logue expressed this view even more clearly in 1914 when he told a Total Abstinence Congress that ' Ireland would be not only the most virtuous nation on the face of the earth, as, indeed, she was at present, but also the most sober nation '. Others spurned such quibbles. To an Irish laywoman writing to Archbishop Kirby in Rome in 1892, the Irish were ‘the evangelisers of the English-speaking world. A people whose persecution by England was turned into a blessing for almost the whole world, for they were a religious people, a noble people, a brave people, and wherever they had to fly to from the persecutions, they carried the lamp of faith shining untarnished. . . . the Irish are the most intensely religious and practical Catholics in the world. . . . no other people make even a distant approach to them’. Such judgements were proclaimed throughout Ireland, and Ireland’s religious world: Cardinal Moran informed the Second Australasian Catholic Congress in 1904 that ‘the sons and daughters of Ireland are, beyond all question, the most enlightened, the most progressive, and the most virtuous people of Christendom at the present day’.

That the clergy were particularly vocal in the making of such extravagant claims is explained, at least in part, as a reaction to assertions that Ireland was decadent and backward because it was priest-ridden. The clerical response was to argue, as Moran did, that no country in the world, during the nineteenth century, had made greater progress than Ireland – material, intellectual, industrial, political and religious progress – and that this had been achieved because of the harmonious alliance between priests and people. On inspection, this argument, as expounded by Moran, tends to equate ‘progress’ with ‘victory’ or ‘triumph’ over the forces of established Protestantism and British rule. The proposition on which everyone agreed was summed up in 1904 in Sir Horace Plunkett’s *Ireland in the New Century* : ‘In no other country in the world, probably, is religion so dominant an element in the daily life of the people as in Ireland, and certainly nowhere else has the minister of religion so wide and undisputed an authority’. Plunkett was critical of this as repressive of individual initiative, and as leading both to extravagance (in church-building) and economic stagnation. Coming after the numerous books of the bitterly anti-clerical Michael J. F. McCarthy (most notably *Priests and People in Ireland* in 1902) Plunkett’s comments sparked off a major clerical counter-attack spear-headed by Monsignor M. O’Riordan’s 510 page *Catholicity and Progress in Ireland*, which went to several editions in 1905-6. This controversy was not a dispute about the major extent or importance of clerical influence in Ireland – that was agreed – but about whether its effects were good or bad. It exhibited not only the power of the clergy, but also their firm conviction that their dominant social role was a proper and beneficial one.

It was natural that such a high self-regard should produce that belief in national destiny mentioned earlier. In 1892 the *Lyceum*, from a religious standpoint, confessed itself among those 'who dream that Catholic Ireland has a mission in the world '. A similar sense of mission can be found among Gaelic revivalists. John Eglinton was convinced that though Ireland was denied the opportunity to become a political force, she would find her role as a source of moral regeneration. Minds like those of Yeats and George Russell saw the Irish as somehow chosen people, instruments of the divine will in history, the preservers of noble and heroic spiritual ideals. Douglas Hyde distilled Irish Ireland's conviction of the approach of a great destiny in his translation from the old Irish:

> *There is a change coming, a big change!*
> *And riches and store will be worth nothing;*
> *He will rise up that was small enough*
> *And he that was big will fall down.*

The time was coming when the old order of wealth and power – epitomised by England – would be overturned, discarded, and when other, spiritual, values would enter into their own. This conviction was intuitive, or if it had any basis in reasoning, it was in the belief that ultimately moral superiority would triumph, even in the world of power. Ireland's messianism could take grotesque forms – George Russell, preaching to a crowd from a sea wall at Bray, about the return of the pagan Irish Gods: it could also seem grossly inflated even to some of those who had helped to create it. By 1913, some of Ireland's own intellectuals, like Ernest Boyd, were speaking of Gaelic jingoism, accusing Ireland of being infected with a spirit of overweening nationalism similar to Britain's imperialism, revolting, in their imaginations, from ' the intolerable slavery which would result, were Gaeldom suddenly enabled to realise its ambitions '.

At the core of the self-image of this new messianic Ireland was the belief that the Irishman was, by nature, innocent: the Irish could do no serious wrong of themselves; whatever evil might exist in Ireland had been imposed on the Irish; Irish faults were what the English had made; their shortcomings were not their own, but those of an oppressed people. Such assumptions were prevalent across the whole spectrum of Irish life and are neatly summed up in Maud Gonne's catechism: ' What is the origin of Evil?' Answer: ' England '. This disposition bred an outlook in which, somehow, Irish actions were above, or immune from, the operation of the ordinary moral or human laws – English provocation justified whatever form or degree of response the Irish felt compelled to make, an Irishman's shortcomings were as nothing when measured against his virtues, his corruptions were not his own, but imposed by England, evil was not part of Ireland's national identity. Given such beliefs, violent rebellion against Britain might appear as a holy necessity in that it would rid Ireland of the source of evil, and thus clear the way for progress towards perfection and national sanctity. Measured against the pursuit of sanctity, surely extreme means could be justified? In this way, Irish hatred of England could be justified, dignified and intensified as a hatred of the source of all evil. Dedicated nationalists developed a strong sense of moral superiority. ' Could you mix among average ordinary Britons as I have done & listen to their uncouth animalism in discussing womanhood – and their jibes at " the superstitious priest-ridden Irish ", perhaps it might generate a wee spark of Nationality in your mind ', a correspondent told Bishop O'Dwyer in 1915. Detestation of the English fed on the conviction that the English hated them. This belief was not complicated by any reservations prompted by the existence of Catholicism in England: in 1893 H. Grattan Esmond expressed, privately, the common Irish view when he said, ' The aristocratic English Catholics . . . hate us, though we emancipated them '. Nor were any other potentially common bonds sufficient to mitigate such hostile emotions: when put to the acid test in 1913, the brotherhood of the working class was demonstrated not to apply – British workers were unwilling to support Irish.

It was over the matter of Ireland's righteous self-image, that the literary intelligentsia fell out of popular favour. So long as that intelligentsia was producing or strengthening laudatory myths, its popular influence was strong, and indeed seminal, but as it took on a less idolatrous attitude towards Holy Ireland, and veered towards realism, it fell out of favour, and, with Synge's unflattering portrayal of the peasantry and Irish womanhood in *The Playboy of the Western World*, into popular execration. To the extent that in the twentieth century, notably with James Joyce and Synge, later with Sean O'Casey, the literary renaissance became a candid self-appraisal, a search for real Irish identity, a revelation of the shams, the pettiness, the crudity, greed and violence of Irish life, it aroused a howl of popular contumely. Popular Ireland – and revolutionary Ireland – much preferred to live with a self-image of noble, holy beauty than with the reality. It was from within this dream world that the *Irish Review*, to which so many of the 1916 leaders contributed, was able to insist in March 1911: ' We must believe in all Utopias '. Deserted by popular opinion in Ireland, the main function of the literary renaissance after its myth-making phase was to acquaint world opinion with Ireland and its claims and causes.

The secular strand in the new cultural nationalism went back to the scholarly work of Petrie, O'Donovan and O'Curry in the 1830s and 1840s, but it was not until the 1880s that Standish O'Grady began widening the popular knowledge of Irish history from its bitterly preserved memories of Catholic Ireland to embrace the mythical grandeurs of pagan Ireland, dominated by the epic legends of Cúchulainn and his peers, and the Fianna. Here was the secular compliment to the glories of Christian Ireland, a world of ferocious yet chivalrous heroism, vast and magnificent, violent, war-like and moral. The world of Ireland's ancient pagan heroes, and that of Ireland's battle for Catholic faith, had so much in common that Father Stephen J. Brown, S.J. in his *A Readers' Guide to Irish Fiction* (1910) felt it necessary to make a disclaimer: ' I have, however, no wish to pretend here that Cúchulainn and his peers are nobler models to set before our youth than the heroes of Christian chivalry . . . to say nothing of times more modern '. Models they did become. Patrick Pearse saw in Cúchulainn heroic violence sanctified, and had inscribed at the entrance to his Rathfarnum school: ' I care not if my life have only the span of a night and a day if my deeds be spoken of by the men of Ireland '. Resurrected in the present, Ireland's past glories, pagan and Christian, gave birth to a messianism which looked forward to that future time when a new Ireland would rise equal to the old. To the Irish mind in its Catholic aspect, Ireland had a glorious religious mission to the whole world, to that mind in its secular aspect, it had a destiny in the world of nations. Given that habit of making all history present politics, the revival of the myths and legends of heroic Ireland was dangerous indeed, particularly after 1891 when the dazzling edifice of Parnell's party came crashing down in ruin, chaos and disillusionment. Repelled by the sordid realities of Irish political life, now enfeebled, petty, torn by dissension, the best young minds in Ireland turned in their quest for Ireland's identity (and their own) to dreams and imagination. The Gaelic revival of the 1890s was possible as a popular movement because politics were in ruins: there was now time and space for other things. But the revival of a great past entailed rejection of much of the present, all that was foreign, non-Irish, English – which meant almost everything except the peasantry, their culture and religion. A thorough Gaelic revival called for a profound social revolution – destruction of the existing tainted order, and the building of a new Irish Ireland centred on the Catholic peasantry. Moreover, it was the revivalists' thesis that Ireland had not only been conquered from without, it had been betrayed from within by those who had accepted English ways: in the forefront of those traitors were the politicians who were part of the very system that had destroyed what Ireland should have been.

On such conclusions as this, and generally in its determination to pursue a national examination of conscience, the disposition of the Gaelic revival coincided with that of the Catholic revival. Sharing a common disposition of mind, temper and attitudes, both had their ideosyncratic expressions. Ultimately, the Gaelic was to be the more aggressive and activist, but the Catholic was no less determined. Why should a group of Catholic laymen, with the blessing of the bishops, form a Catholic Association of Ireland in 1902? They explained:

> The reasons may, indeed, be well compressed into one grand reason, which is, that while the Protestant Ascendancy is nominally dead in law, it is vigorously alive in fact. . . . the Protestants of Ireland have largely maintained the same spirit of exclusiveness as animated them in the Penal Days, when the laws . . . encouraged them to be arrogant . . . the spirit is essentially [still] there, deeply resident in that series of castes, landed, official, professional, and higher commercial, which form a powerful network of hostile influences, always operating in restraint of the Catholic, Celtic, and therefore genuinely native element in our country. It is evident that this network must be at least broken, if not destroyed.

The sponsors of the Catholic Association asked, ' How can our own country develop from within, save upon Irish and Catholic lines?' To submit any longer to Protestant dominance would be ' only endowing intolerance '. And the aim? – ' to close up Catholic ranks, and so encourage amongst our people the principles of mutual help and organised action . . . we feel confident that if this be rightly done, the balance of forces will be rectified in Ireland, and for the first time since the Reformation, real tolerance will be established '. Like that of the Gaelic revival, this Catholic programme implied the necessity of bringing about a social revolution – and the Catholic Association was to be linked to the Irish Ireland movement by its support for Irish language, literature, art and industries. In February 1903, the *Irish Catholic* began an editorial, ' Slowly but surely the Catholic forces of this country are uniting for the achievement of the natural material supremacy of which an artificial social and legal system has so long deprived them '. The winds of change in Ireland, both Catholic and Gaelic, were, by the early years of this century, blowing harshly and in concert, on the edifice of the established order.

8

The Ulster Question

In a private audience he gave to Cardinal Moran in October 1902, the old Pope Leo XIII said of Ireland: ' Those who oppressed her of old are now ashamed of their dealings with her; & they desire to make amends by beneficent & friendly legislation '. Such was the vision of a man who saw the relations between England and Ireland as the entirety of the Irish question – and who looked for the best in human motives. It omitted entirely the massive sectarian problem that was built into the very structure of Irish life. Hartley Coleridge's witticism that Ireland would be a delightful country if it was not for the Catholics and the Protestants avoided the inescapable fact that Ireland, as a human situation *was* Catholics and Protestants. Augustine Birrell, Chief Secretary from 1908 to 1916, could not make up his mind ' which of the two has been Ireland's worst enemy '. The question was very misleading, for there was no Ireland (save some disembodied model in the minds of detached liberal administrators like Birrell) other than that composed of Catholics and Protestants: in a very real sense their enmity *was* Ireland, and the Irish question.

The Home Rule movement was the occasion for the clear emergence of the Ulster question. Its essentials were very simple. Ulster Protestants feared that Home Rule would mean Catholic rule, which would destroy their world, a world erected on the religious distinction between Catholics and Protestants. Abolishing this distinction would be bad enough, but the dominant Ulster view was that it would not be abolished but upended, with a Catholic majority ruling a Protestant minority with all the exclusive intolerance they had themselves dispensed. The intensity of Ulster fears springs from the belief that Home Rule amounted to nothing less than revolution, in which the Catholic mob would rule their Protestant masters even more harshly than they had been ruled, for the Catholics would take vengeance on the old regime. The *Irish Catholic* in January 1889 caught the spirit of this nightmare, when it observed that very many Unionists believed of Home Rule ' that the opening of a College-green Parliament would mean the inauguration of an era of revolutionary activity which would find its climax in the establishment of a Red Republic, the despatching of an Irish Armada against England, the storming of London by an Irish army, and the decapitation of Queen Victoria by an Invincible specially hired by means of " American dollars ".' It is only in the light of the existence of such extreme beliefs that the extravagance of the Unionist reaction to Home Rule can be understood: Lord Randolph Churchill described Gladstone's Bill in June 1886 as ' a conspiracy against the honour of Britain and the welfare of Ireland . . . base and nefarious . . . this trafficking with treason, this condonation of crime, this exaltation of the disloyal, this abasement of the legal, this desertion of our Protestant co-religionists, this monstrous mixture of imbecility, extravagance and hysterics.'

In 1912 and 1913, the *Irish Review* analysed with keen perception, the elements of Ulster sentiment:

> The hydra-headed monster which North-East Ulster dreads consists of the Pope, the persecuting Catholics, the unscrupulous Nationalist politicians who, when they get the chance, will levy specially heavy taxes on industrial Ulster. . . . Back of all the protestations on behalf of civil and religious liberty is the racial intolerance of the planter towards the native whom he had supplanted. Back of all the practical sounding talk of undue taxation is the conqueror and exploiter's subconscious fear of those who, however successfully they may have been exploited, yet remain unconquered.

Perceptive Protestants recognised this no less than Catholics. In 1829 Henry Montgomery had said of his own Presbyterian Church, ' our Church is now in a melancholy condition. Political and religious bigotry have mingled together; and those who foment the persecutions amongst us have made it their policy so to conjoin the two principles that scarce an individual is now held orthodox who is not also an enemy to the civil and religious rights of his fellow-man '. As it was in 1829, so it was in 1886 and thereafter in Ulster.

Derived from self-interest and a wide range of fears and prejudices, Ulster emotion was focused on the ' Papish ' as the symbol and epitome of its hatred. The *Irish Review* commented:

> the average uneducated Ulster Protestant (as well as many who are supposed to be educated) believes that Catholicism is a colossal system of fraud and organised iniquity, which places the laity entirely in the power of an immoral, selfish and intolerant priesthood. . . . The ' Papish ' *is* looked down upon by his Protestant fellow-countrymen, and half the ire raised by the idea of Home Rule is due to the fact that the despised ' Papish ' will be on terms of absolute equality. It

is to him as if the Kaffir in the Transvaal were to dominate at the polling booths, and the Africander be bottom dog. . . . 'Never trust a " Papish " ' ' He has a " Papish " face on him ' ' A low " Papish " name.' ' You can tell he is a " Papish " – he has the mark of the beast on him.' These are remarks which you may hear from the lips of respectable Ulster Unionists.

The real religious content of such attitudes was often very slight. An 1853 comment on Presbyterian bigotry in Glasgow might be applied to many in Ulster: ' Ignorant of the first principles of religion, they nevertheless suppose they are right, simply because they hate their Romanist neighbours.' As to the supposed enormous power of the Pope in Ireland, even Protestants who were not bigots regarded the Pope as intimately and decisively influential in Irish affairs. (In 1917 some priests sought permission from a British official in Dublin to travel to Rome. ' Are you gentlemen going to see the Pope?' he asked. ' We hope to.' ' Will you do me a favour?' ' If we can.' ' Look, when you see the Pope will you get him to issue an encyclical or something condemning these bloody Sinn Féiners.' The official told the priests that life in Dublin was becoming intolerable: only that day as he was coming in from Celbridge in his pony and trap, there was a tree across the road. ' Outrageous! Get the Pope to do something about it.')

William Bulfin's analysis of Belfast bigotry in his *Rambles in Eirinn* (1907) highlights its lack of true religious content and its irrational complexity: ' underlying all this commercialism, all this thrift, and all this cult of the main chance, there is a cast-iron bigotry – a cruel corroding, unfathomable, ferocious, sectarian rancour '. Bulfin held that

> Orange hostility to Catholicism is largely due to sordid political enmity, or, in other words, to hard cash. . . . sectarianism is being used for a political end. . . . It is not religious zeal. It is merely inherited spite. . . . There are Catholics ready to take their lives into their hands on St Patrick's Day who may not have complied with their religious duties for years. There are Orangemen ready to cry ' To Hell with the Pope ' who have not been inside of a church since their boyhood. They are born to it, brought up to it. It is an inheritance, this blind, unreasoning hatred. . . . When self-interest gets tangled up with human pride and a tradition of conflict you have an imposing congestion of vexations all knotted together. . . . People have been born into a fight for over a century. They will have to be born out of it. Time will heal the evil – time and common sense and a broader conception of tolerance and nationhood.

Of its nature, this situation was inaccessible to change by logical argument: to attempt to explode the Ulster Protestant case was both very easy and totally irrelevant. The *Irish Review* remarked on its absurdity: ' The composite picture of Ireland which is being circulated by the Orange faction is a very curious one. It may be summed up thus: Ireland is a sham nation, very prosperous and contented, of murderers and moonlighters, who would all be Unionists only for the paid agitators and agents of Rome who hope to fatten on plundering Protestants '. On no subject were Irish nationalists of all complexions so sweetly reasonable as on the Ulster question; but to confront deep and bitter emotion with argument was futile. In 1912 the Anglican Bishop of Down observed that there was never a time when Irish Protestants had harboured so deep a dread of Roman aggression or so firm a conviction that Rome aspired to a complete subjection of Ireland. Protestants loathed Catholics and were convinced that Catholics loathed them. The *Irish Review* could ridicule ' the minute proportions of the " physical force " element in Ulster, behind which the whole conservative party has hidden its lack of arguments against the principle of self-government.' It could dismiss the anti-Home Rule Covenant of September 1912 as ' signed by some 250,000 men of Ulster among whom there are the widest imaginable differences upon all subjects (except, perhaps, the wickedness of " Rome ") and, not least, upon the meaning of the Covenant itself.' But the exception – that agreement on the wickedness of ' Rome ' – was utterly crucial and the core of Ulster solidarity. Chief Secretary Birrell made the same point from another angle: ' It is the Mass that matters: it is the Mass that makes the difference so hard to define, so subtle is it, yet so perceptible, between a Catholic country and a Protestant one, between Dublin and Edinburgh ' – or, he might have said, between Dublin and Belfast.

Bulfin appreciated that what existed in Ulster was better described as a fight than merely the existence of Protestant prejudice. He saw that emotions were polarised on both sides: ' The very intensity of the anti-Irish feeling which prevails among so many of the people fans the flame of Nationalism in the breasts of men and women who hold to the Irish ideal. In no part of Ireland have Nationalists more to lose, in a material sense, than in Belfast, yet in no part of Ireland will you meet Nationalism of a sterner school, nor of a more daring hopefulness and faith '. This was, of course, to take a pro-nationalist view of such emotions. To what extent were Ulster Protestants correct in believing that Catholics loathed them and intended, after Home Rule, to carry out a Catholic revolution in Ireland? The episcopal evaluation, at least in Ulster, may be illustrated by Bishop O'Doherty's remark to Bishop O'Dwyer in 1897: 'So vile a set of bigots does not exist in creation as the Protestants of Ulster. They want not the wish but the power to re-enact the penal laws of Queen Anne'. When bishops held such views, it is hardly necessary to illustrate the attitudes of the mass of ordinary Catholics.

Furthermore, it was a self-evident fact that Home Rule must have some transformative implications. It simply could not mean that there would be no change at all in Irish affairs, and any change must be detrimental to the interests and beliefs established in Ulster. As William J. Flynn observed in 1907, commenting on Balfour's allegation that Irish County Councils were being dominated by nationalists: 'The minority in Ireland cannot expect, in the long run, to come off any better than minorities in other countries'. Even parliamentarians had some radical ideas about the necessity for post-Home Rule purges. T. M. Healy told Bishop O'Dwyer in 1905: 'Official Ireland is a hot bed of Freemason ascendancy' – and he added – '& no tinkering can cure it'.

And there was also the matter of the Catholic revival, from the late 1880s. From this grew, in more aggressive Catholic quarters, the view that while there was no question about Ulster being part of Ireland, the position of Ulster Protestants was less clear. The same doubt prevailed in relation to Ulster's economic character. Recognition of the economic necessity for the industry and commerce of the North East to be integrated into a Home Rule Ireland often co-existed with the opinion that the industrialism of the North, accelerating particularly at the end of the nineteenth century, had placed it and its culture on a level with that of Britain, meriting the same kind of condemnation: Ulster's corruptive materialism, lust for wealth, and degrading urbanisation were the antithesis of all that was holy, peasant and Catholic. There was much in renascent Catholic Ireland that was vigorously intolerant, repudiated industrialised Protestant Ulster, denied diversity and sought religious homogeneity. There was a strong element in Irish Catholicism which saw the achievement of Home Rule as a signal for a crusade for conversion of the North. A writer in the *Catholic Bulletin* of March 1912 put this objective without equivocation: 'The time has arrived for action. The day of Ireland's missionary heroism is at hand, and to be utilised first of all in our own country. . . . To bring into the bosom of Holy Church the million of our separated brethren is a most attractive programme, and there is in it enough of the heroic to engage and to claim the hearts of Irish Catholics.' The attraction of this programme was less obvious to Irish Protestants: in Ulster their heroism was to be engaged in ensuring that it would not be implemented. Acording to Father Patrick Boylan speaking in Dublin in 1914 on ' Catholicism and Citizenship in Self-Governed Ireland ', Protestant fears of Catholic intolerance were totally unfounded. That such fears and hatreds were entertained was because of the ' well-known fact that a man can seldom forgive one whom he has injured '. Then Father Boylan went on to cite the self-restraint and self-effacement demonstrated in the Land War as proof of the Irishman's fitness for self-government – reasoning which held little appeal or comfort for Protestants. He claimed that the differences between North and South were soulless and artificial and would vanish ' when the men of North and South meet as honest, stern men to do the best for Ireland '. Where would they meet? In ' an Irish Parliament, conscious and proud of its Catholicism ' engaged in legislation based on Catholic social teaching and the Gaelic revival. It is difficult to see how Protestants could have warmed to such a prospect. When, eventually, partition became an issue for debate, much of Ireland cared more about it as a principle, and as a continuing symbol of the endurance of British and Protestant power, than about its practical consequences. This Ireland denounced partition not because it violated Ireland's geographic integrity and deprived it of a section of its people, but because it denied the possibility of complete tribal unity to the Catholic Irish, and of complete tribal possession of the tribe's ancient lands, and – probably above all – cheated them of the triumph of complete victory over the Protestants and English.

Irish nationalists of all complexions consistently failed to understand or properly evaluate the Ulster question. Their common assumption was that it was really no question at all, but at worst a mere contrivance, a nuisance: they believed that there would be little or no difficulty in solving it internally after Ireland, as a whole, had achieved political autonomy. There can be little doubt that this assumption worsened the situation, both in further alienating and infuriating Ulster Protestants, and in misleading nationalists into over-simplification and under-rating the seriousness of Ulster's stand. Such misconceptions derived from the fact that nationalists tended not to take religious differences seriously. Some were not religionists, others were intellectuals tolerant themselves and assuming tolerance in others, others were so devoted to nationalism – that aspiring religious substitute – as to see religious differences as inconsequential. Their assumptions were essentially political, leaving no room for religious determinants in public affairs. Ireland's leaders from Parnell to Pearse – and even to de Valera – had erected their nationalist ideologies on the assumption of a cultural one-ness which in fact did not exist in Ireland, particularly in North East Ulster. Their lack of any real

Ulster policy (other than the unthinking expectations that it posed no real problem) reflects their belief that their nationalist idea of Ireland automatically dispelled sectarian divisions; that is, their attitude to Ulster was an aspect of their utopianism, not a real appraisal of the situation. Regarding sectarianism as unenlightened, divisive and destructive, they made the often related error of grossly under-estimating its strength and importance. John Redmond's refusal to regard Ulster's threat to take up arms against Home Rule as anything more than bluff is an example of such an under-estimation. As late as 1915 Eoin MacNeill, in an Irish Volunteer pamphlet, was still maintaining that the British government and the landlord party had manufactured the Ulster reaction, and that the Catholic mob and nationalist leaders had played into the hands of these skilful manipulators by accepting the empty rhetoric of Ulster Protestants as a genuine expression of their racial and religious spirit, and by returning bigotry with bigotry. So, MacNeill contended, by accepting this hoax, nationalists themselves provided 'proof' that Ireland was divided and must be denied autonomy. 'We see this cause of politico-religious division not arising from any ingrained "common hatred for centuries" but operated from above and without for the deliberate purpose of preventing good feeling between the two sections of the nation.': this manipulation was motivated by the lust for power and wealth. MacNeill concluded that the 'victory of a practically united Ireland over British spoilation', by cutting off the manipulation, would dispel all division. His interpretation was nothing new. John Mitchel had written in the *United Irishman* in 1848: 'In fact, religious hatred has been kept alive in Ireland longer than anywhere else in Christendom, just for the simple reason that Irish landlords and British statesmen found their own account in it; and so soon as Irish landlordism and British dominion are finally rooted out of the country, it will be heard of no longer in Ireland. . . .' Given such premises, there was no real Ulster question to consider: cut the connection with Britain and it would cease to exist.

This was a neat solution, if it could be applied: the problem was that Ulster Protestants were determined that it would not be; and meanwhile, the nationalist interpretation that their feelings were false, contrived and baseless remained an affront and a continuing confirmation of the threat they felt. No less offensive to Ulster was the other main Irish nationalist response to Protestant expressions of profound distrust. This response tended to explain the Ulster reaction to the prospect of Home Rule as mere bigotry or in terms such that it was natural that someone who has done his neighbour an injury should suspect that neighbour of awaiting an opportunity for revenge. These very explanations, discreditable to Protestants, fostered the emotions and suspicions therein condemned: to denounce Protestant bigotry increased, not eradicated it.

Under Conservative governments, Protestant fears in Ireland remained largely latent. Yet, even under the Conservatives, the position of the Protestant Ascendancy was being constantly eroded. Killing Home Rule with kindness entailed concessions to the native Irish – in land ownership and local government and so on – which weakened the power of the Ascendancy and strengthened that of the Catholic majority. The outcome was a further hardening in the Protestant resolve to cling to the Union as their last protection, one which compensated for their minority situation in Catholic Ireland. The advent of the Liberals to power in 1906 did little to disturb Unionists: the Liberals were independent of Irish support, had lost the Gladstonian crusading passion, and were obviously unwilling to revive the issue of Home Rule which had deprived them of office for so many years. But the events of 1909-10, centring on a dispute over the veto power of the House of Lords and issuing in an election which made the Liberal government dependent on Irish support, transformed Protestant Unionist unease and concern into a militant open refusal to accept a threatened Home Rule.

Even the most liberal elements in Britain had always partly accepted the Ulster Protestant case against Home Rule, by their recognition of the Ulster fear of Catholic discrimination and their willingness to be swayed by this. If Home Rule was to be a viable practical solution to the problems of the relationship between England and Ireland, it required the British government to repose trust and confidence in the Irish to manage their own internal affairs harmoniously. Yet, such was the importance conceded to the religious division, that even the foremost champion of Home Rule in British politics – Gladstone – was unwilling to grant that full trust and confidence. In proposing his 1886 Bill, Gladstone made it clear that while he would not permit the Ulster minority to call his Irish tune, he was open to any sensible proposal whereby ' Ulster itself, or perhaps, with more appearance of reason, a portion of Ulster, should be excluded from the operation of the Bill ', or by which minority interests be protected. The actual Bill contained no such protective or excluding provisions. If such omissions fed Ulster's fears of what Home Rule would mean for itself, they recognised the other political fact – that Catholic and nationalist Ireland would not tolerate any special treatment for Ulster.

Of course Ulster's influence on British politics went far beyond inducing hesitation and perplexity in Gladstone: the Ulster stand against

Home Rule had a firm base in British public and political opinion, which was strongly Unionist, anti-Irish and anti-Catholic – in some quarters to the degree of fanatic passion. By contrast, support for Home Rule was feeble and constricted. Ulster was much more than a geographic area: it represented and symbolised a religious position – Protestantism – and a conservative social order. The fierce passions that were associated with these issues were given immediate political point and power – and a vital added dimension – by the linking of the Irish question with the constitutional question of the role of the House of Lords. By 1912 the possibility of Home Rule was no longer remote, but real and immediate, with Ulster's determination to resist it the last line of defence. The Commons had rejected Home Rule in 1886, the Lords had killed it in 1894 – and could have been relied on to continue to kill it, had it not been for the Parliament Act of 1911 which replaced the Lords' veto with delaying power only.

The Conservative Party believed this Act to be tantamount to a revolutionary overthrow of the constitution. In their view the political situation was one in which the Irish party had helped the Liberal government to destroy the House of Lords in return for the Liberals' undertaking to destroy the Union by conceding Home Rule: the Irish and the Liberals were united in a vile revolutionary conspiracy to destroy Conservative Britain. As Bonar Law put this interpretation late in 1912: 'We regard the Government as a revolutionary committee which has seized by fraud upon despotic power. In our opposition to them . . . we shall not be restrained by the bonds, which would influence our action in any ordinary political struggle: we shall use whatever means seem most likely to be effective.' Lord Escher advised the King in 1913 that 'the constitution is for the moment abrogated and that the House of Commons is, in point of fact, a " Constituent Assembly " of a revolutionary character, and not a Parliament '. Any methods – even civil war – were justified in repelling this revolutionary assault on the English constitution.

Bonar Law's standpoint has been generally regarded as illustrative of a dimentia peculiar to the period of Ulster crisis 1911-14. In fact it represents a theme recurrent in Ulster history – which is why the Conservative Party-Ulster Protestant alliance is much more than some tactical arrangement: it was a substantial union of minds and hearts. Brother W. J. Gwyn of the Orange Lodge told a great Protestant demonstration in Belfast on 30 June 1867, called to oppose Irish Church disestablishment:

We have – I should rather say we had – a Protestant Constitution.

The guardianship of that Constitution was committed to the King, Lords and Commons, the rulers of this Protestant kingdom. So long as they discharged their trust as honest men, there was no necessity to seek to withdraw it from their charge, but as soon as these guardians betrayed their trust and commenced, step by step, to assail that Constitution, break down the most precious bulwarks, and seek to destroy the Protestant faith, then it became a duty, and an actual necessity, to take upon ourselves the duty which they neglected to perform – to do the work that belonged to the Government of a Protestant land, for the Protestant subjects of that land.

The Conservative Party was convinced, in 1912, that this had occurred, that the Liberals had betrayed their trust and thus the duty of protecting the true constitution devolved upon the Conservatives. Bonar Law's endorsement of Ulster's Solemn League and Covenant to take up arms, if necessary, so as to prevent Home Rule, might seem to his opponents an attack on constitutional government: to him it appeared a defence of it; to him the threat of armed rebellion against Home Rule legislation was an assertion of true loyalty; to him the Liberals must be destroyed as traitors, a menace to the state.

Ulster's stand, supported by the Conservative Party, confronted the Liberals with the insoluble problem of how Ulster could be coerced into Home Rule. In Ireland Birrell believed that Ulster loyalty was a fraud, masking their bigoted determination not to be ruled by a Catholic parliament, cloaking that old hatred, suspicion and contempt of the Church of Rome. But what could he do? The ultra-loyalty of the North defied unmasking and censure as rebellious, because it purported to be a defence of the true constitution against a threat to destroy it and implicitly claimed that whatever Ulster did, because Ulster was loyal, must be right and lawful. Besides, this was a situation in which Birrell could not rely on the Ulster police, and after March 1914, when in the so-called 'Curragh mutiny' 58 British army officers said they would prefer dismissal to acting against Ulster, the Liberal government could not rely on its own army.

Ulster's stand against Home Rule drew too much British support for the Liberals to do other than capitulate. Men not otherwise interested in Ireland were moved to defend what seemed to them a danger to the integrity and greatness of the Empire. That great imperialist, Lord Milner, was the organising centre of opposition to Home Rule from within England: he regarded it as a 'horrible nightmare'. And he also had the utmost contempt for the democratic process and the parliamentary system. Public opinion he dismissed as 'rotten'; parliament itself he detested as 'this rotten assembly at Westminster'. To preserve itself from Home Rule, Ulster drew on the last energies of an England confidently and proudly imperialist, respectably Protestant, and sternly aristocratic.

To the Catholic Irish, Ulster's ultra-loyalty – the willingness to take up arms against England so as to compel England not to cut it adrift – seemed absurd, a matter for derision as well as extreme vexation. Yet Ulster's stand had a genuine logic – the logic of the Reformation: that if those who held power were perverting, weakening or corrupting the institution, it was the duty of the pure, the elect, to bring it back to its original principles. For all its hard core of self-interest, the Ulster cause, as such things as the Covenant witness, was steeped in Protestant history, which heavily featured old religious injuries. As Catholic and nationalist Ireland harked back to their own pasts, so did Protestant Ulster: it sought to preserve the old England it knew – the England in which it had a logical and favoured place – which is why that old England responded so strongly to Ulster's appeal for support.

But Ulster's attempt at counter-revolution, to stem the tides of historical change, was only partly successful. Protestant Unionists in Ulster had a total objective – the retention of the Union unchanged: their tactics were based on the belief (shared by many Irish nationalists) that Home Rule could not function without Ulster, and that Ulster's refusal to co-operate would destroy Home Rule entirely. It did, but not in the way Ulster expected. Nationalists had as total an objective as Unionists – one Irish nation, naturally including Ulster. To neither was partition conceivable initially, but, given that to concede the total demands of either Unionists or nationalists was to court rebellion in Ireland, partition was a natural political consequence, the only possible compromise, and, as Asquith saw in 1914, the only way to avoid civil war. The relative readiness with which Ulster Protestants settled for partition suggests that they were much less interested in Union as a constitutional principle, as in any contrivance which protected their interests and maintained the social order they had constructed for themselves.

The Ulster agitation gravely damaged Home Rule as an objective and discredited parliamentary activity as a method of determining policy. It made quite clear that violence or its threat was more effective than argument or entreaty, and the outcome demonstrated that it was naïve to expect an English government to satisfy the demands of Irish nationalism. By its actions, or lack of them, the government had handed initiative in the Irish question to those in the field – firstly the Ulster Unionists, later the Irish Volunteers. As it became obvious that the

British government would not or could not defend the rest of Ireland against potential Ulster aggression, the Volunteers rose from 10,000 at the beginning of 1914 to over 100,000 by May. Ulster looked forward to a general election which would destroy the Liberals and end any prospect of Home Rule.

From 1913, in British political circles, partition was coming to be accepted as the only practical solution to the Irish question. Obviously, however much Ulster Protestants cherished the idea of total Union, partition gave them the essentials of what they wanted – freedom from Catholic rule. Despite the violence it did to ideas of national integrity, partition might have been seen in the South (as some see it now) as ultimately for the South's good in removing a source of serious friction and difficulty, had it not been for the fact that a Catholic minority existed in Ulster: no partition could be clean-cut. From a Catholic viewpoint, partition was totally unacceptable, much more repugnant than British rule, because it would place the Irish Catholics of Ulster under a rule they feared and hated far more than that of Britain. In June 1916, in relation to an offer of Home Rule to Redmond, an offer which excluded Ulster, Bishop McHugh, on behalf of the Catholic bishops of Ulster, condemned the proposal because of 'the perilous position in which religion and Catholic education would be placed' in the area excluded from Home Rule. The bishops expected active persecution of Catholicism, deprivation of what rights it had already won and an end to any prospect of improvement. McHugh had no doubt that it was 'better to remain as we are for fifty years to come under English rule than to accept these proposals.' That the Irish party should receive, let alone consider and eventually accept partition placed it in a position of violating both nationalist feeling and the Catholic religious conscience. To purchase Home Rule at the cost of partition may have been politically realistic, but it was a gross assault on nationalist idealism, and to religious minds amounted to selling a section of Ireland's Catholics into the slavery of religious persecution.

9
The Question of the Irish Party

From the viewpoint of Catholic Ireland, participation in British politics was fraught with great religious dangers: the Conservatives were under ultra-Protestant influences, the Liberals were under radical and secularist influences and the Irish parliamentary party had to treat with one or the other. This was obvious long before the defeat of the second Home Rule Bill in 1893-4, but that reverse marked the clear emergence of a new relationship between the Church and the Irish party within Irish affairs. Where before the Church had been on the defensive, absorbed in and worried by the potential dangers of an imminent Home Rule, assuming without much question the closeness of its implementation, now the Home Rule cause seemed lost, at least for the foreseeable future, and the formerly dominant politicians seemed discredited. Instead of political leaders calling the tune, they were coming cap in hand to Church authorities appealing for guidance, assistance and support.

In the new situation, the clerical reaction was at best withdrawal of interest, at worst acid contempt for such as ' the high-stepping gander Dillon or the vain windbag O'Brien '. The reactions of the two most ' nationalist ' members of the hierarchy, Archbishops Croke and Walsh, testify to what changes had swept through even the progressive section of the clerical camp. Croke wrote privately to Rome in March 1894: ' Politics in this country are at a discount. I have ceased to mingle in the fray. Home Rule will, I dare say, come, sooner or later, and to a greater or lesser degree; but it will not come as soon as it is expected, nor will it come, I fear, in my time.' In July 1895, Walsh confided to Cardinal Logue, ' As regards the elections generally, I cannot see any ground for thinking that we have anything to gain by what the I.[rish] P.[arliamentary] Party would consider as a victory.' Walsh's cynicism was in the context of a situation in which the politicians were actively seeking to submit their differences and problems to Church leaders, pleading for a clerical resolution of the party's factional divisions, and competing for clerical patronage: Walsh had telegraphed Logue early in July, ' Irish Party prepared to leave settlement of differences to the four Archbishops and abide by their decision. Immediate action necessary to save election.' No action was taken. Meanwhile John Dillon was trying to get some token of Papal approval. Acting on her husband's behalf, Mrs Dillon sought a Papal audience for him in 1895. She made no disguise of the reasons: ' there are political considerations which would give . . . [a papal audience] a most especial value in many ways at this particular time.' The following year, Dillon was angling for a Papal Blessing on his political work. Other politicians, notably T. M. Healy, were attempting to ingratiate themselves to bishops, by seeking (and agreeing with) episcopal opinions on politics. This was all to no avail. In 1897 Cardinal Logue was still convinced – and it was a general, if privately held, clerical view – that 'politicians who call themselves Catholic' were attempting 'to effect a complete separation of the people from the Bishops and priests'.

This was one major problem: despite the politicians' energetic efforts to jump through clerical hoops, the clergy were quietly spurning the party – as a Catholic cause it had gone very sour. The other great problem was that of the party's continuing factionalism and lack of concerted policy. From 1891 the potential members of a Home Rule government were engaged in a protracted public demonstration of their unfitness for such office: if these were the men who would conduct Home Rule, surely Ireland was better without it. Even as advocates for Ireland's interests they were useless or worse: Cardinal Logue concluded in 1898 that 'The country would be just as well unrepresented as being in the hands of the present squabblers.'

To those who had a serious and intelligent interest in both the national and the religious movements in Ireland, this was an undesirable situation, needing remedy. In April 1895, the Catholic clerical *New Ireland Review* took a hard look at what it saw as the facts. The national political movement had become almost exclusively Catholic. In previous great Irish movements, Protestants had taken a conspicuous and often a leading part. No longer did they do so: they had been frightened away from what was much less than a truly national movement but rather a wild and irrational eruption of indiscriminate protest and rebellion, which, if Catholic in personnel, was not Catholic in spirit. Now this movement lay in fragments, none of which held valid national policies. The Parnellites offered no future whatever, save anarchical and exhausting combat. The section of nationalists grouped around John Dillon had no future either, in that it was anti-clerical, opposed to official Church policies, and wedded to an impossible alliance with the Radical party in Britain. This faction was a sort of Liberal Catholic party of the continental kind. The *New Ireland Review* regarded attachment to British Radicalism as absurd and un-Catholic: 'A Catholic Radical is a contradiction in terms . . . the Dillonite conception of hitching Catholic Ireland on to the Radical-Socialist party in Great Britain is an outrage on the nature of things and must prove barren and mischievous.' The *Review* correctly believed that the Radicals were not really converted to Home Rule, but in any case Home Rule would be purchased at too great a cost if it meant the dissemination of irreligious radicalism in Ireland. (A. J. P. Taylor has described Dillon as 'a key figure among the Home Rulers and a great British Radical into the bargain': from the contemporary religious viewpoint, it was a very bad bargain indeed.)

What then, according to the *Review* was the proper course for Irish politics to take? A Conservative alliance. The facts demanded it. ' Sooner or later a country of Catholic peasant farmers, secure in their tenure, and many of them proprietors, must become Conservative.' Furthermore, if Home Rule was to work, it must be cheerfully given by England and unanimously accepted by Ireland. ' Hence a policy that would tend strongly to reconcile Irishmen among themselves, and all Ireland with " the predominant partner " could not in any way impede Home Rule, and under favouring conditions might even smooth the path to its accomplishment ' – the *Review's* belief was the common one of the time that Home Rule was now a very distant goal, with its own rider that, so far, it had been pursued in very much the wrong way. What would this policy of reconciliation consist of? The *Review* claimed that ' many thoughtful minds are forced to consider whether in a Conservative and temperate clericalism, Ireland – after a century of fierce contention and fruitless controversy – might not find satisfaction, dignity and repose.' The inference, clearly indicated, was that this Conservative and temperate clericalism (bearing in mind Cardinal Cullen's dictum that ' if the Church was attacked in Ireland it would be in a Home Rule Parliament ') favoured amelioration of Ireland's grievances within the Union. Given popular nationalism, the Church could not conduct an active campaign for this cause, but it could, and did, cease to support the Home Rule movement and engage in sharp private criticism of it and its members. This position was not difficult to occupy in a prevailing atmosphere of public disgust with, distrust of, and apathy towards a party torn, in Healy's words by ' the ravages of vermin ': indeed the politicians them-selves were to the forefront in public denigration of their own party as ineffective, degraded and a disgrace to Ireland.

The emergence of John Redmond as leader of a united parliamentary party in 1900 made little difference to the clerical estimate. Cardinal Logue regarded Redmond as an anti-clerical and wished to have nothing to do with him. None of the bishops could stomach Dillon: those of them that supported him did so because they regarded him as the strongest man in the party, and, given popular opinion, judged it prudent to go along with him as far as they could. As to Michael Davitt, when he died in 1906, a relative of Cardinal Moran's wrote to him, ' I am glad he is gone. His acquaintance and constant meetings with Tolstoi made him dangerous in many ways to the interests of Faith.' Simply, the re-united party contained the old factionalists, and they carried their previous odium into it. However, the party's revived popular fortunes after 1900, and the suggestion that if it had taken wrong courses it was for the want of a lead from the bishops carried some weight in clerical circles. At least the party was now a force to be reckoned with, and Cardinal Logue, for instance, was very much of the opinion that as clerics now had the support of the bulk of the people, they had a serious duty not to let 'their legitimate influence slip through their own slackness'. He sought some basis for a united episcopal support of the Irish party. But the old problems still obtruded: as soon as the Irish party regained its unity, and thus some of its independent strength, it dropped its posture of deference to clerical wishes and opinion. In 1901, the Cardinal admitted bitterly that he could not 'influence in any way the votes of the Irish members'. In 1904 a party candidate in the Gateshead election publicly declared himself opposed to a Catholic university, 'and still', Logue noted, 'Irish Catholics are being pressed to vote for him contrary to the religious interests of themselves and their children.' In all, Logue observed, the revived party was showing 'pretty clearly that religion must take a back seat'. The most that T. M. Healy could give Bishop O'Dwyer in 1906, by way of assurance of the religious integrity of the 'ruck of our own M.P.s' was his opinion that they would not 'consciously tolerate anything hurtful to the Church'. In the clerical estimate, this was not enough, not nearly enough, and the fact that the four archbishops and nearly all the bishops sent subscriptions to the Irish Parliamentary Fund was a gesture for the benefit of popular – and British – opinion, not an expression of trust.

Then there was the matter of the party's continued association with the most radical elements in British politics. In 1906 William Redmond, in a letter introducing Ramsay Macdonald to Cardinal Moran in Australia, could say easily in a context where Catholics were aligned with the Australian Labor Party, 'I need hardly point out to you that Mr Macdonald's colleagues in Parliament are staunch friends of the Irish movement, and there is much in common between the British Labour Party and the Irish Party as both work together in the interests of the people.' But in the Irish context – and the British – this was a damning alliance. In 1910 the *Irish Catholic*, now fiercely religious, greeted the Liberal government as 'the motley and shabby horde of Radicals, Socialists and Secularists who will now claim to be the supreme rulers of the once proud British Empire': this was the dangerous and degenerate group which the Irish party maintained in power in return for Home Rule. The party continued to be judged, very adversely, by the company it kept. From Sydney in November 1914, Archbishop Kelly expressed to Bishop O'Donnell of Raphoe a very common clerical conviction: 'The leaders in Parliament should stand out from a policy of secular administration, harmonising with Non Conformists etc. With myself some great names have long been regarded with apprehension because of utterances and action less Catholic in principle than St Patrick would wish, I think.'

The Conservative swing notable within Ireland was, to some extent, marked by a sympathetic movement within English Conservatism. The situation described by the *New Ireland Review* had substantial logic – Ireland was, of its nature, a country inclined towards social conservatism, and its posture of political radicalism was merely circumstantial. Yet any rapprochement between Irish and English Conservatism was impossible: Ireland's problems were trapped in the prison of British political structures (and the Irish Party's long-standing relationship to them) and even more decisively governed by religious bigotry. In November 1910, T. M. Healy gave Cardinal Logue his opinion of changes in British Conservative attitudes: ' Fear of an Irish settlement has now almost ceased to terrify the leading Tories, and as compared with the Socialist terror, we are regarded as lambs by the rich. I have again and again had evidence that the conservatism of Catholic Ireland appeals more and more to (what used to be) the " governing families ", and that there is a big change of tone among the younger Tories too.' Healy believed that it was the religious issue which frustrated the natural Tory gravitation towards seeking an Irish alliance: ' If the narrow-minded little Orange clique moved by Londonderry bigots . . . had only kept decently quiet, there would have been some sort of settlement.' No doubt the possibility of a Conservative response to the Irish question was stifled by religious bigotry, but it seems very doubtful whether this response, even had it not perished on religious rocks, would have extended to Home Rule. A writer in the *Irish Review* said of the third Home Rule Bill in March 1912, ' the present Bill is coming from the wrong side of the House, if the Conservatives had been responsible for it, Ulster would have realised the impossibility of resisting, and would have made up her mind to grin and bear it.' This was very true, but totally unrealistic. So was the same writer's comment that had the Conservative party won the 1910 election, ' the immense change that has taken place in Ireland since 1893 would beyond doubt, have brought forth a Conservative Home Rule movement.' However natural and desirable such a movement would have been, the forces and factors militating against it – religious animus, imperialism, Ulster, and so on – seem such as to render it impossible, if not inconceivable.

But if it was a possibility, then the Irish party itself contributed greatly to rendering it void. In its 1895 plea for a Conservative alliance, the *New Ireland Review* had seen ' the alliance of Irish Catholicity with

English Radicalism ' as ' the great obstacle to such a policy '. It has been common to criticise the Irish party after the fall of Parnell as having lost touch with the mood of Ireland – meaning that it was largely unaware of the development of a revolutionary temper. The criticism is also valid in relation to the party's failure to appreciate the growth of conservatism in Ireland. Ireland had lost much of its enthusiasm for Home Rule, but the party continued to act as if nothing had changed. The established laws of its political existence demanded that as a Home Rule party, it must continue to pursue Home Rule – whether Ireland wanted it or not. And, by and large, Ireland – thinking, intelligent, religious, opinion-forming Ireland – did not. Thus, to Britain and the world, the Irish party projected a very distorted image of the dominant opinions and convictions within Ireland, an image greatly exaggerated in the direction of a particular form of political radicalism. Those British Tories who discerned Ireland's intrinsic conservatism could also not mistake the radical posture – and radical alliances – of Ireland's parliamentary representatives who were the politically operative Irish reality.

In fact the Irish party was rapidly losing contact with all the dynamic forces within Irish reality, an isolation achieved by such a deliberate policy of rebuffs as to convey the impression that the party had reached that stage of invincible self-absorption immediately antecedent to self-destruction. The party's reputation in Church circles has already been described. It was vigorously critical of beneficial British reforms. Dillon opposed land reform in 1903 : his view was that the real importance of land reform agitation lay not in securing immediate improvements, but in keeping Ireland in a state of unrest until Home Rule was secured. The party would brook no organisations not subordinately related to itself. Redmond condemned the Irish co-operative movement in 1904, declaring that ' the real object of the co-operative movement . . . is to undermine the National Party and divert the minds of our people from Home Rule, which is the only thing which can ever lead to a real revival of Irish industries.' The whole Irish-Ireland movement was regarded by the party with suspicion and hostility.

After Parnell's fall, the Irish party perpetuated, for its own interests, an objective for which most of Ireland had lost enthusiasm, or even belief. It drew on old loyalties and habits to sustain it where, in fact, a true basis of genuine convinced support was lacking. Its policy of radical alliances continued to alienate British conservatism, and be of benefit only to British radicalism: the Irish party gained very little for Ireland, but was of great assistance to British reform. It was, in fact, after Parnell's fall, a political anachronism of great destructive influence. In repelling conservatism in Ireland it denied political expression to what was probably Ireland's dominant temper; in repelling it in Britain, it induced a political situation much more polarised and intolerant than it otherwise might have been. In attempting to impose its own narrow Home Rule straitjacket on the new wave of radicalism in Ireland and in refusing to adjust itself in any way to new dynamics, it failed to contain these forces, and indeed drove them out of the Irish constitutional political framework of which it demanded exclusive possession. The party's attitudes, both to conservatism and to any other brand of radicalism than its own, led on to – and produced – a situation wherein violent rebellion was the only natural solvent. As A. J. P. Taylor has observed, 'Ultimately the Home Rulers hoped to be a new version of the Garrison – more enlightened, Roman Catholic of course in sympathy, but a British Garrison all the same.' This hope evoked no real support in an Ireland whose conservatism rejected the Home Rulers' brand of enlightenment, where their brand of Catholicism was rejected by the leaders of the Church, and where the Irish Ireland movement rejected the whole idea of any British Garrison. The party had always been subject to those influences discerned by the Earl of Charlemont as early as 1815: 'Let it not be said that Ireland can be served in England. . . . The Irishman in London, long before he has lost his brogue, loses or casts away all Irish ideas, and . . . becomes, in effect, a partial Englishman. . . . He may enrich himself as a courtier or gain applause as a patriot. He may serve his party. He may serve himself. But Ireland must be served in Ireland.' This was the point D. P. Moran was making in 1903 when he said that the Gaelic movement denied that the party was composed of any real Irish influences and asserted that it was an artificial self-contrivance: 'the politicians themselves . . . instinctively feel that the only way of keeping up any difference with England is by hysterical and artificial stimulation of racial hatred . . . the hatred that is raked up in us is merely personal spite and a desire for vengeance.' This very serious charge held very substantial truth: the party did a great deal to keep old hatreds alive, as necessary to its own political existence and purposes. Yet at the same time, the party's Britishism was very evident. John Redmond's leadership represented a clear return to the Isaac Butt tradition of veneration for British institutions and the British Empire, into which Home Rule would tie Ireland even more closely. Redmond saw the first World War in the British way – a crusade for freedom against German tyranny, in which Ireland must, in honour, engage: this interpretation was incomprehensible to those Irishmen who saw the war as a further instance of the British imperialism that had tyrannised Ireland. Redmond's vision fell victim

to Kitchener's prejudice: the War Office refused to recognise the distinctive Irishness of that contribution to Britain's forces that came from
Catholic Ireland. In this identification with Britain, Redmond epitomised
the disposition of his party: so did his aloof and proprietorial air, so
resented by Ireland's younger generation – ' he thought Ireland was his
private cabbage garden,' Joseph Plunkett's sister recalled.

To cap it all, the Irish party was entirely at the mercy of the British
political situation, as well as driven by the internal necessity of having to
appear to be making progress towards Home Rule. In November 1910,
T. M. Healy observed of the party in these circumstances, ' the danger
is they will snatch at any crumb and call it the whole loaf '. From both
conservative and radical standpoints the third Home Rule Bill seemed
just such a crumb. From the first, Cardinal Logue described it as ' a
skeleton on which to hang restrictions ', but as, by 1914, the possibility
emerged that it would not apply to Ulster, he took a different and totally
antagonistic tack: ' It will leave us more than ever under the heel of the
Orangemen.' By the time of the third Home Rule Bill those Irishmen
whose main interest was internal reforms and development had become
thoroughly cynical about the traditional ' Wait until we get Home Rule '
slogan of the party. The utopian aura which once hung around Home
Rule – the impression that it would be attended by a miraculous and
virtually instantaneous removal of all Ireland's ills – had been well and
truly dispelled. The attitude of radical nationalists is neatly summed up
in Arthur Griffith's comment that the Bill merely established ' an Advisory
Committee to the British Government in Ireland.'

Griffith's description was accurate enough. So was the *Irish Review*'s
observation in March 1912 that the Bill was not a natural outgrowth of
Irish affairs, but an accident of British politics: the ' Irish Question has
been prematurely forced into the front place just now, not by anything
that has happened in Ireland, but by the condition of British political
parties resulting from the 1910 elections.' The *Review* lamented that
the ' Irish Question ' should have been ' forced upon the country just
now, while the men of the Eighties are still at the head of their political
forces.' This was unfortunate not in terms of any personal or generation
tensions and jealousies, but simply because Home Rule no longer fitted
the Irish situation: it was an irrelevant anachronism. The *Review* believed
that Ireland was on the verge of a great change: ' Today we are living
through the first years of an era in which the English have begun to build
up what they formerly pulled down, and, what is of far greater importance, to allow the Irish people the opportunity of self-development.'

The third Home Rule Bill came to Ireland at a time of hope, which it did nothing to satisfy. In itself it was a mean and very limited concession, but in any case the whole cause had gone stale and the goal seemed hollow. In 1913 Ernest Boyd outlined what had happened. ' The Home Rule fetish no longer dominates the prostrate bodies of the faithful. Some English writers have mistaken this for an indication that Ireland no longer desires a measure of self-government, whereas it merely represents the displacèment of an obsession by more powerful interests. The Home Rule movement has long been a dogma; it is now reduced to the natural proportions of a political idea, which must take its place with a host of others in the life of a nation.' The waning of popular enthusiasm for Home Rule did, as Boyd states, convince some Englishmen that nationalism was dying in Ireland; some Irishmen also – George Russell bemoaned ' the tragedy of the decline and fall of the human will in the people '. The effect of this in Ireland may be seen, partly, in the determination of the new cultural nationalists to redeem Ireland from this tragic fate. In Britain, it had the contradictory effect of assisting Ulster's crusade against Home Rule by helping to convince influential Englishmen – for instance, the King himself – that all the Irish really wanted was more money and continued prosperity and therefore Ulster's demands could be countenanced with a degree of safety from any extreme Irish nationalist reaction.

But is this picture of an absence of popular enthusiasm for Home Rule in accord with the facts of public response? – Redmond's statement that it would end forever the disharmony between Britain and Ireland, Asquith's tumultuous and enthusiastic reception in Dublin in July 1912, all the verbiage of the Home Rule press. The professed enthusiasm for Home Rule among the Catholic Irish populace rose in intensity in direct relationship to the expressed determination of Ulster Protestants to prevent it. Redmond and his party rode for a brief time on the crest of a popular anti-Protestant wave, a wave that broke swiftly as the possibility of Ulster's exclusion became real. In the long run, such a wave of anti-Protestantism could do Redmond's party no good, only grave harm. It ultimately derived from a rock-hard and militant Catholicism which was much more powerful than the party, and basically opposed to it; and it also provided an atmosphere and circumstances which liberated the potential violence of the South which was eventually to sweep Redmond's party into oblivion. When the Irish Volunteer movement was initiated late in 1913, as a vigorously successful response to the example of the Ulster Volunteers, the exigencies of his political position and popular standing forced Redmond to support this armed organisation – whose whole rationale horrified him – if only as a first step towards bringing it under control. That the Volunteer movement, Ulster and Irish developed at all was evidence of the extent to which the Irish situation had escaped the confines of constitutionalism and parliamentary politics. Redmond's partial success in capturing control of the Irish Volunteers was in the upshot a total failure, for those who refused to accept his control were centred around the Irish Republican Brotherhood and were the key factor in the 1916 rising.

10

The Question of Rebellion

After the turn of the century, if not before, the cultural nationalist movement began to harden, narrow and simplify. It moved towards the adoption of an aggressive political stance against Britain, and towards the moulding of actual revolutionaries as practical expressions of a rebellious mood. The movement shook off its non-political literary fringes, among them W. B. Yeats. Yeats was repelled by a transformation which he was to see so vividly again in the years prior to 1921: ' The best lack all conviction, while the worst/Are full of passionate intensity.' The early years of the century were witnessing the emergence of the classic revolutionary syndrome. The rulers, the old hierarchies, the thinkers, were losing their unity, and their confidence in themselves and in the existing order, and losing control over the movement of events, even their understanding of what was taking place. No better example exists than Augustine Birrell, the Chief Secretary himself, who spent a good deal of his time, so he confessed, ' wondering what the real Ireland, the new Ireland, the en-franchised Ireland, was thinking about and witherwards it was tending.' That such should be matters of wonderment and perplexity to Britain's chief executive in Ireland illustrates the extent to which the real Ireland, the new Ireland, was escaping not only from British control but from British comprehension. Certainly Birrell was in touch with one aspect of the new Ireland: he frequented the Abbey Theatre. There he saw, so he told the 1916 Royal Commission on the Rebellion in Ireland, merciless fun made of mad political enterprises, and aspects of Irish revolutionary history savagely satirised.

Birrell did not see that mad political enterprises were becoming as much part of the real Ireland as was the Abbey itself, and that the popular mood sided with the idealistic assumptions of such enterprises in hostility to the Abbey's artistic realism. That this was so, was demonstrated by the riot provoked by the staging of J. M. Synge's *The Playboy of the Western World* in 1907, and by the fact that in the forefront of the denunciators of Synge's degenerate slander on the noble Irish peasant and the purity of Irish womanhood was Arthur Griffith, founder of Sinn Féin – that epitome of the Irish-Ireland movement. That the Abbey was very critical of some aspects of Irish life seems to have blinded Birrell to their reality and power. Art mirrored life: the Abbey's productions reflected the growing crescendo of violence. In reviewing the Theatre's work in February 1913, Ernest Boyd saw that ' The most striking feature of more recent plays has been their unrelieved brutality ': in the wings life was waiting to imitate art.

Outside the tiny artistic world, the search for national identity, the painful dissection of a complex Irish reality, was being rendered down to the popular level in a few slogans – Sinn Féin, Ourselves Alone, in a sense embraced them all – and a few small organisations whose major characteristics were intolerance and arrogance, were claiming to have discovered the true path to Ireland's destiny. In 1913 Ernest Boyd described this process of hardening, narrowing and simplifying as the ' gradual extinction of political thinking. . . . In the prevailing intellectual apathy political dogma has been substituted for political thought.' Thus distilled, concentrated, dogmatised, the ferment of post-Parnell Ireland was a fierce heady brew productive of the extreme of passionate exaltation in those few with a thirst for it. These men were marked by their youth, their obscurity and their stern asceticism. Take Denis McCullough, a key figure in the Ulster section of the revolutionary movement. Joining the Irish Republican Brotherhood in 1903, McCullough was affronted by the fact that he was sworn in to the organisation in a hotel, and that most of the members were old and effete – with many addicted to drink. (His impression was shared by the police who, in 1908, regarded the I.R.B. as ' monstrously ineffective ' and energetic only in the ' consumption of porter and whiskey '.) When McCullough later became a controlling member of the I.R.B., together with Tom Clarke, Sean MacDermott and others, they insisted that only men of known sobriety and character be admitted: this was not only a protection against loose-tongued betrayal, but a measure designed to free the reputation of militants from any suggestion of personal weakness. How effective this was may be gathered from a pamphlet biography of Pearse published late in 1916: ' He scarcely knew the taste of intoxicating drinks, never used tobacco, and was entirely free from the foibles and vices of young men.' By the early twentieth century, the island of saints and scholars had produced new – revolutionary – varieties of both.

Nationalist, revolutionary intoxication took a variety of forms, all of them distasteful to those who remained sober. That it was akin to intoxication is confirmed by the excitement of Pearse, that total abstainer, who, by December 1914, was finding meetings of the Dublin officers of the Irish Volunteers ' as exhilarating as a draught of wine '. Perceptive observers saw that the mainspring of this delirium was not only idealism, but hatred, ' maiming hatred ' as O'Casey was to describe it later. The duality is nicely expressed by a writer in the *Worker's Republic* in March 1916: ' There is the great tradition of love and hatred, love for Ireland and hatred for her enemies. . . . There is the inborn craving for vengeance for over seven centuries of insult and rapine and wrong. There is the glory of fighting for an ideal and dying for its achievement.' These sentiments could readily be expressed in religious terminology, as the Commandant of the Hibernian Rifles demonstrated in the same month: ' There is a God in Heaven – Be sure that his vengeance will strike the tyrant and traitor alike, in His Own Good time. Who knows but that time is even now? The Clock of Doom has struck – one tyrant will lie low, and then shall at least one small nationality have the right to breathe, to live, to expand! Oh God! How long! How long!'

Hatred, idealism – and also messianism. In January 1914, as its staff became more and more involved with the Irish Volunteers, the *Irish Review* published ' The Messiah – A Vision ' which sketched imaginatively Ireland's coming Redeemer, still living in obscurity, young, Irish, a combination of statesman, philosopher and apostle, to be a radiator of dynamic force, the man who would deliver Ireland from her thousand years of sorrow, a man who in history would rank with the Teacher of the Galilean shore. Even before the Rebellion the messianic aura had gathered around Pearse: Cathal O'Shannon wrote of him in the *Worker's Republic*, 5 February 1916, ' is it not today as one of the Apostles of Revolution, Insurrection Incarnate itself, that we love him best and need him most?'

From the viewpoint of what was rational and moral, the revolutionaries, their ambitions and actions, were absurd. Writing just after the 1916 Rising from a convent in Wexford, an Irish nun described the rebellion as ' that terribly mad act . . . All for a nothing, aiming at impossibilities '. If it seemed mad when it happened, the rebellion in its germination seemed merely silly. The funeral of the old Fenian O'Donovan Rossa in August 1915 was a decisive event in the development of the revolutionary atmosphere and inspiration, marked as it was by a graveside oration by Pearse, which ended: ' The Defenders of this Realm think that they have pacified Ireland. They think that they have purchased half of us and intimidated the other half. They think that they have foreseen everything, think that they have provided against everything: but the fools, the fools, the fools! . . .' Birrell saw the whole affair as futile, grossly unreal, and engineered to prop up a sham revolutionary sentiment. The whole thing seemed to him to reek of posturing and play-acting. It did: but here were men prepared to stage their revolutionary play with themselves in the leading roles. Pearse labelled himself as ' The Fool ' who ' squandered the splendid years . . . In attempting impossible things ' and asked ' O wise men, riddle me this: what if the dream come true?' Then, as his graveside oration had predicted, the world's wisdom would be proved foolishness.

For the dream to come true, the revolutionaries first needed to be able to launch a rebellion, and thereafter secure popular support for it. These were the stern practicalities, and they received attention. But the real dynamic lay within the psychology of that ' little isolated circle ', as Darrell Figgis described them: ' The men who planned the rising had brooded so long on that event that it had come to pass in their minds, and they avoided contact with other minds in which that finality had not occurred. They had, in a very real sense, passed into a world of vision.' The peculiar intensity of Pearse was only one aspect of the thirst for revolution for revolution's sake. A writer in the *Worker's Republic* of December 1915 asserted, ' I agree that it is not worthwhile to fight against conscription any more than it is to fight for Home Rule. But to have a revolutionary aim and purpose and to declare that purpose and to fight for it, that is the only thing worthwhile ': by February 1916, the *Worker's Republic* was looking forward to ' the Great Adventure of our generation '.

The revolutionaries' prodigious heroic ambitions were erected on the assumption, made with the arrogance of any group which regards itself as a vanguard embodying the real will of the people, that popular support would erupt as response to their act of rebellion. So it did, though slowly. Nevertheless for Ireland to accept the rebellion Ireland had not only to accept the act, but also the actors – the rebels themselves. Had the rebellion been made, say by men of Jim Larkin's socialist stamp, or led solely by James Connolly, its popular reception may well have been very different. True, the odds were strongly in favour of popular acceptance of any rebellion made in Ireland's name. Any rising was, in a sense, a gigantic piece of blackmail of the many by the few, with the virtual certainty that Ireland's pride would pay. Those interpretations which see the 1916 Rising as a magnificent gesture underestimate the perception, the intuitive knowledge of the popular mood, of those who led it: they knew, with emotional certainty, that their rebellion could not fail to gain popular acceptance, that Ireland could not disown it. But would Ireland's pride, and its feelings of guilt and shame that its honour had been left to an obscure few to assert, would this have been sufficient to produce the glorification in death of these few had they not been acceptable to Ireland's religious requirements? Hardly so.

The fact was that these few were acceptable – or nearly all of them – to Irish Catholicism, most notably Pearse, the most prominent. In his own personality, Pearse appeared to reconcile all the contradictions of Ireland – Paganism and Christianity, love and hatred, violence and peace, pride and humility. Pearse's unconscious genius was to sum up all the major themes of Irish history in his own self: Pearse was a hero for everyone and thus could be a rallying point for an effective nationalism. Judged by society's normal criteria, Pearse's personality seems pathetic, infantile, obsessive, irresponsible, vain; but reflected in the distorting mirror of a revolutionary mood and situation, he had something to appeal to everybody. The strongest appeal lay in his combination of violent rebellion with religious dispositions, a feat never performed before. Superficially, Pearse was a Catholic, in the orthodox sense, indeed involved in the religious revival through its Temperance wing: with his brother Willie, and Joseph Plunkett, both of whom died with him, he was a Pioneer. A salient characteristic of Pearse the revolutionary was his absorption with Christian models, or rather, *the* Christian model, the blood sacrifice of Jesus Christ for the salvation of the world: ' One man can free a people as one Man redeemed the world ' declares MacDara in Pearse's play *The Singer*. Pearse saw himself as Ireland's Christ, its Redeemer. The Christian references and symbols appear, disguising Pearse's death-wish and lust for violence. His wedding of violence to the Irish situation took on a Christian complexion because he gave it one. But Pearse's Gospel reversed the Christian message. It was not Christ who took up violence, but those who opposed Him. Pearse's mingling of Christian values and symbols with the violence of pagan heroic Ireland was both an expression of and a strong stimulus to that doctrine of a holy violence, a sanctified hatred, a just vengeance that hung heavy in the very air of Ireland.

Again, Pearse's concept of martyrdom in a great cause – and his and his comrades' actual fate – seem to have much in common with the deepest well-springs of Christianity, and so it appeared in Irish Catholic evaluations after his execution. In fact, Pearse's quest for a famous death, on the Cúchulainn model, was the converse of Christian martyrdom: he sought death from vanity and the desire for immortal fame, he courted it so as to satisfy an ego in which ordinariness and obscurity meant futility, meaning-lessness and frustration. He craved death not as spiritual fulfilment, but as an enduring posture before men. To apply the criteria of Camus, Pearse was merely another event in the prodigious history of European pride.

To put the superficial appearances aside, Pearse and his ideas made little accord with the basic values of Catholic Ireland. Why then did Catholic Ireland accept and indeed canonise him and his rebellion? To answer, because the rebellion was successful, reveals part of the truth – the Church swiftly adjusts itself, as far as it can, to political facts. But this answer takes no account of the strong and compelling argument that the rebellion would not have gained popular acceptance had it not been accepted by the Church. And here it is that those 'superficial' appear-ances of congruity between what was religious and what happened in 1916 cannot be put aside. The congruity was real in the way in which a play may appear to be real and indeed offers an aspect or level of reality, though not its totality. Gradually, in the years that followed Parnell, Ireland, thinking, feeling, praying Ireland – of which the Church was such an integral part – became obsessed with grandiose dreams and images, spiritual and religious certainly no less than political and national. The attempts of the revolutionaries, particularly those most romantically visionary, Pearse MacDonagh and Plunkett, to break out of the prison of reality into the world of hopes and dreams, caught the imagination of a people whose quest for identity, and yearnings for self-realisation, both tormented and exalted them. Here, totally, was the world of Yeats's contradiction, 'a terrible beauty': the violence and hatred were terrible, the sacrifice, the idealism, the vision, were beautiful.

In part, this world was that of the Gaelic revival, but it was the world of the religious revival as well, and here lay that congruity of mood, emotion, temperament and disposition that linked religion and rebellion, two aspects of the one visionary reality. And there are cruder links. So intense was the religious vision of Holy Ireland – always latent, but, from the 1880s an increasingly sharp and aggressive projection – that every-thing that Ireland actually produced had either to be utterly banished from that picture or somehow squeezed into it. In holy Ireland, every-thing, even a rebellion, ought to be holy. This is not quite the same as saying that the 1916 rebellion was a Catholic one and succeeded because it was. It is to say that, in appearances, the rebellion was amenable to reconciliation with the Irish Catholic religious world, and was heir to, and indeed an aspect of much of Irish religious tradition – that tradition which took aggressive pride in holiness, hated the enemy (the origin of evil) with a holy hatred, and pursued, without counting the cost, holy sacrifice and holy death. It was not only a poet who saw a terrible beauty in what had happened: a nun wrote to Bishop O'Dwyer in June 1916: 'It is very pleasant to see how the hearts of the people are turning towards the poor fellows who fell in Dublin. Their deaths have touched a cord of religion and nationality that were hardly ever more beautifully united.' But this was after the event. What of the Church's role in its prelude?

Disillusionment both with the Irish party and with what British governments were prepared to do for Catholic Ireland was deeply entrenched within the episcopacy by early in the century: the consequence was that the official Church – the strongest single force in Ireland disposed to side with law, order and conservatism – was alienated from the political realm and tended to withdraw from it in disgust. 'How utterly corrupt is the government of this country' wrote Bishop O'Dwyer – that reputed conservative Unionist and 'Castle bishop' – to a clerical friend in April 1907: this judgement, and its source, illustrate how little support Britain's government in Ireland could expect from the Irish bishops. As small radical groups, such as Sinn Féin, began to emerge in the early years of the century, their anti-British, anti-Home Rule party orientation was one they shared with the bishops, if the principles on which it was based were often very different. Many clerics actively supported such groups, believing them an aid to true religion: witness Father Cullen's eulogy of the Irish Volunteers. Certainly there was a good deal of religious criticism of radical groups – it was claimed that Sinn Féin was anti-Catholic, there was a bitter clash with Gaelic Leaguers over the question of compulsory Irish in the National University, T. M. Healy tried to convince the bishops that the Ancient Order of Hibernians was anti-clerical and irreligious, and so on. Some conservative churchmen, such as Cardinal Logue, were worried by these aspects from time to time, but by and large the Church did not intervene to attempt to check the growth of organisations which were to play a vital part in creating the climate for rebellion or in the rebellion itself: the simple fact was that these organisations and the Church shared common detestations – of Britain and the Irish party. There was also the fact that the smallness of such organisations suggested that their importance was commensurate, beneath serious concern. Besides, the clergy were largely unaware of the work of the real revolutionaries, the I.R.B., and the extent to which they had penetrated and controlled such organisations as the Irish Volunteers. In the late 1850s and early 1860s priests generally were very well informed about the existence of I.R.B. groups, and not only vigorous in their denunciation, but also prompt in informing police and officials. Such intimate knowledge was possible in the rural Catholic situation, but the new wave of the I.R.B. was substantially an urban based one, tending towards much greater discipline, smaller groups and stricter secrecy than the Fenians – and also unlike the Fenians, working in and through other quite acceptable organisations.

Perhaps even more important in explaining the apparent clerical blindness to the violent revolutionary tendencies of nationalist groups is that, at a crucial time, clerical attention and concern were diverted by what appeared to be a much more dangerous threat elsewhere – the danger that all that was valuable in Ireland, most notably religion, would be destroyed by socialist revolution.

Horror of socialism stretched back half a century into Ireland's religious past, where the term had, largely from observation of the continent, accumulated connotations of gross irreligion, violent revolution, expropriation, and anarchic destruction of lawful authority and order. To clerics, all these characteristics seemed to be embodied in the socialist gospel preached from 1907 in Ireland by the militant and flamboyant James Larkin. Larkin's efforts to organise Dublin workers led to a major industrial struggle which began in August 1913 and continued for five turbulent months, marked by demonstrations, violent clashes with the police, and the formation by some of the strikers of the Irish Citizen Army, dedicated to revolutionary socialism. Clerics, and Catholic commentators generally, denounced the Larkinite doctrines of socialism and syndicalism as totally at variance with both religious and national principles. Thus Bishop O'Dwyer, though sympathetic to the workers, saw syndicalism as ' one of the most un-Irish programmes ever tried on Irish people '. The *Catholic Bulletin* of November 1913 summed up Larkin's ideology:

> An entirely material concept of life, from which every idea of God, the soul, moral obligations, and even intelligence was carefully eliminated was constantly insisted on. A full stomach was put before the people as the one thing in life worth striving for – the next life did not count. . . . the worst passions of our nature, and these alone, were appealed to: pride, cupidity and selfishness. . . . The upright spiritualised Irishman for the time disappeared, and all of the brute that was in him was drawn out and fed.

Given such an interpretation of socialism, small wonder that religious opinion was so obsessed – to the degree of hysteria and outrage – by its potential threat to the religious vision of Ireland.

The *Catholic Bulletin* went on to link its religious revulsion with nationalist nausea: ' For the past twenty years the Gael has been crying

– oftentimes a voice in the wilderness – for help to beat back the Anglicisation he saw dragging its slimy length along – the immoral literature, the smutty postcards, the lewd plays and the suggestive songs were bad, yet they were mere puffs from the foul breath of paganised society. The full sewerage from the *cloaea maxima* of Anglicisation is now discharged upon us. The black devil of Socialism, hoof and horns is amongst us.' ' But the crowning shame remains to be told', lamented the *Bulletin* – and that was that hungry Irish strikers had accepted food and money from English workers.

> When English Socialists succeeded in filling the heads of Irish workmen with half-baked paganism, as a reward and a tie on their future allegiance, they proceeded to fill their stomachs with bread. They would not only load a ship but an armada if by doing so they could loosen the stronghold Christianity has upon our people. The sight of what was once a proud and self-respecting people, whose grandfathers gladly died on the roadside rather than accept the poorhouse taint, crunching the beggar's crust thrown by English Socialists . . . that sight was the most sickening spectacle witnessed in our generation.

It was this which also burnt into Bishop O'Dwyer, this ' humiliating memory . . . of rations and strike-pay from England '. Irish pride was riding much too high to stomach English hand-outs. What the few Irish socialists regarded as an example of class solidarity, of internationalism, seemed to non-socialist nationalists a degrading and compromising acceptance of English charity, and to Irish religionists even worse, an attempt to buy Irishmen's souls.

Beneath the vehemence of the clerical reaction to the 1913 strike was a strong undercurrent of fear. Since Parnell, the spectre of the loss of their influence over the populace to irreligious forces had haunted the thoughts of the clergy: now this nightmare walked again. Nothing could be more explicit than Bishop Donnelly's anxious comment to Bishop O'Dwyer: ' Larkin has got our entire working population in his hands and *out of our hands* & he is working hard to accentuate the separation of priest from people.' Rumours circulated that Larkin was the devil in man's guise, complete with cloven hoof. In some ways, the situation of agitation and organisation contrived by Larkin's energies resembled what Parnell had created in the 1880s: indeed Archbishop Walsh explicitly linked the two situations and saw very strong similarities between them. Larkin's magic, though limited in its spell to workers, was of the same charismatic quality as Parnell's, if not more forceful: the clerical fear was that it would have the same outcome – a massive popular alienation from the authority and values of religion, a reversal of the priority of the spiritual over the material.

One effect of the spectacular and violent social conflict that centred around Larkin's activity was to divert clerical attention away from the growth of revolutionary currents in nationalism. The other major consequence, in a situation where socialism seemed to have become a threat of great destructive power, was to dispose bishops and clergy favourably towards nationalism: they believed that a proper Irish nationalism would kill socialism – an Irish nation would be a Catholic nation. Bishop O'Dwyer held that 'Had the healing influence of native rule been felt for even a year', the 1913 strike would not have occurred. Socialism would swiftly die in an Ireland which managed its own affairs. The lesson was obvious – the clergy should support and encourage true nationalism. This meant, not the spiritually untrustworthy Irish party, but nationalism in its Gaelic form. The *Catholic Bulletin* made the point: ' In the Gaelic League we possess the one natural weapon that constitutes our hope for a clean and spiritual Ireland. Shall Gaelic Ireland perish and a godless monstrosity rise in its place?' The violent eruption of socialism in Ireland in 1913 did the cause of rebellion a great service: it swung Catholic opinion even further into commitment to the ideals of cultural nationalism as expressive of a religious crusade.

The radical vanguard of the cultural nationalist movement was also vitally interested in the effect of religious beliefs and attitudes on the movement. It was an immediate practical problem: I.R.B. organiser Diarmuid Lynch recalled of the period 1911-12 that frequently a man deemed suitable in every other respect as a prospective I.R.B. member, turned out to be totally unwilling to join because of ' religious scruples in the matter of joining a " secret organisation ".' This was one aspect of the religious problem; the other was the religious chasm that divided Ireland, ' the paltry quarrel of Protestant and Catholic, which so far has prevented Ireland from realising either its political or literary ideals ', as the *Irish Review* put it – a paltry quarrel but with paralysing consequences for nationalism. Nevertheless, the *Review* group, drawn from Ireland's intellectual and political *avant-garde*, however impatient they were with religion as divisive politically, was keenly aware of realities: a contributor remarked that Thomas Davis's proposal to unite Ireland by means of a national culture which would ignore the ' religious question ' was a little like proposing to act *Hamlet* without the prince – it was this apparently insurmountable obstacle which prompted the invocation ' We must believe in all Utopias '.

The *Review* group perceived clearly the importance and character of the religious question: John Eglinton observed that in religious matters Ireland had not yet emerged from the seventeenth century; Ernest Boyd testified that ' in most cases, religion is the touchstone by which every Irishman is tested '. Its Protestant members particularly saw clearly the extraordinarily powerful and pervasive influence of Catholicism in Irish life. Evaluating this a *Review* contributor asked, ' Is it any wonder that Protestants in this country should think that their Catholic countrymen do not really understand patriotism – that, in fact, the Catholic Irishman's idea of patriotism is simply the apotheosis not of his country, but his Church?' This did not fall too far short of the truth, though it missed the tension between popular Catholicism and hierarchical ambitions. In June 1912 F. Sheehy Skeffington contended as self-evident ' that the clerical power is stronger than ever in Ireland ', that there was ' a sleepless subterranean pressure by which the tremendously powerful clerical organisation has managed, in each case, to turn the tables on its opponents ', and that there was indeed ' a clerical party in Ireland, comprising nearly all the older ecclesiastics and bishops, who entertain the most outrageously arrogant views of their mission and authority'. Skeffington, a sceptic in religion, deplored this situation, but he did not believe it could be changed.

A very different interpretation of the ideal relationship between religion and nationalism may be seen in an article in the *Review* of January 1913, by Captain J. R. White:

> a State . . . [should] guide itself to its true destiny with . . . the foundation of a religious purpose. Religion should be the wedded wife of politics, always inspiring, never interfering. . . . In Ireland the Church and the National and Democratic movement may almost be said to be one. . . . I hear the spirit of Catholic Ireland crying to the spirit of Liberalism: ' Give us some of the Freedom you have won, and we will give you some of the Reverence and Beauty you have lost.'

White's attitude is typical of the new religious brand of nationalism, acceptable to the Church, which avoided the religious question by the simple assumption that Catholic Ireland was all Ireland: it proceeded as if by definition (to quote Arthur Griffith) Ireland was the part of England where the Catholics lived. White's views are also typical of a new phase of that old shrewd nationalism which had tried, successfully enough, to tie the Church to its own coat-tails. To assert that the Church and the national and democratic movements were one was to commit the Church in advance to whatever adventures nationalism might embark upon.

The outbreak of war in August 1914 created that difficulty for England which was Ireland's opportunity in the eyes of aspiring revolutionaries. Outside the Irish parliamentary party, ultra-nationalists held no brief for Britain's cause. Some contended that the war had been precipitated by the Liberals in order to relieve themselves of internal difficulties – Ulster, suffragettes, the labour movement, the need to capture German trade and so on: Belgium was mere pretext. Others were openly pro-German: *Sinn Féin* on 8 August 1914 said of the German people, ' If they fall, they will fall as nobly as ever a people fell, and we the Celts may not forbear to honour a race that knew how to live and how to die as men '. Redmond was execrated as a political prostitute who had no influence with the government and who, by his recruiting mania had betrayed Ireland, and split the Irish, in the face of their enemies.

The same revulsion against the British cause, and Redmond's championship of it, may be discerned in religious circles. As the prospect of Home Rule – placed on the statute book in September 1914 – grew closer, tension between Church and Irish Party increased: the Church feared for the future, and so did the Party. In the discussions taking place between Redmond, Dillon and Devlin, and the British administration in Ireland, Dillon particularly was insisting that the administration was bequeathing to the future Home Rule government a situation of too much clerical power throughout Ireland. The formation of a British Coalition government in May 1915, including Sir Edward Carson and other Unionists, seriously damaged the reputations of both Irish Party and British government. The damage was political in that anti-nationalist Ulster rebels seemed to have triumphed in the halls of British power, religious in that these rebels represented Protestant bigotry. The Coalition seemed evidence that the hopes of Catholic Ireland were at an end, despite Home Rule on the statute book. ' Home Rule is dead and buried and Ireland is without a national party ', Bishop Fogarty of Killaloe wrote to Redmond.

There were also explicitly religious matters involved in the further alienation of the Church from Britain and the Irish party after the outbreak of war. A meeting of the Irish bishops in January 1915 was told that the Holy See had asked Redmond to nominate an Irish Catholic M.P. to represent Ireland at Rome. Redmond refused, presumably, the bishops thought, because he was unwilling to risk an anti-Catholic reaction of the Home Rule Rome Rule kind – a reason not acceptable to the bishops. In August 1915, Bishop O'Dwyer asked Redmond publicly to support the Pope's attempts to end the war by a negotiated peace. Redmond refused, on the grounds that the German powers were the aggressors and had shown no sign of wishing to repair the wrongs they had inflicted – upon Belgium. The weight of clerical opinion was strongly with O'Dwyer, strongly of the view that ' The National Party have sunk very low. They are afraid to mention the name of Ireland or the Pope lest they should offend " our allies ".' And the negative British response to the Papal appeal seemed, in Irish religious opinion, to confirm their conviction that Christianity did not count for much in Britain.

Moreover some clerics had erected on Catholic religious premises, a position hostile to the Allies' cause, and to Ireland's involvement in it. Canon Dunphy, parish priest of Kilkenny, put it to Bishop O'Dwyer early in 1917 that while the position of the Catholic Church in the British Empire was tolerable, ' what about her Allies France and Russia? I cannot understand how any Catholic priest or Bishop can wish to see these Countries triumph in this war, to see the noble and powerful Catholic body in Germany humiliated and discomforted, to see Austria the only great Catholic power in Europe dismembered, and a Russian Pope enthroned in Constantinople'. Dunphy's argument was that Germany and Austria were friends of Catholicism, England and France were not: Irish allegiances should be placed accordingly. His contention was by no means unique: other of Bishop O'Dwyer's correspondents were also refusing to ' cut the throats of our brave Bavarian and Austrian co-religionists'. Irish clericalism harboured a strong and undisguised anti-French bias. Writing on the war in the *Catholic Bulletin* of March 1915, Monsignor Hallinan described France's rulers as ' a Freemason infidel gang of anti-clericals'. In his view, English patriotism was ' national arrogance and self-glorification'.

Bishop O'Dwyer's own interpretation of the war hit the headlines in November 1915 when some Irish emigrants, passing through Liverpool, were mobbed by an English crowd that claimed they were shirking their duty to join the army. O'Dwyer wrote to the newspapers: ' Their crime is that they are not ready to die for England. Why should they? What have they or their forbears ever got from England that they should die for her?' O'Dwyer then turned to hit at Redmond. ' Mr. Redmond will say a Home Rule Act is on the Statute Book. But any intelligent Irishman will say a simulacrum of Home Rule, with an express notice that it is never to come into operation. The war may be just or unjust, but any fair-minded man will admit that it is England's war not Ireland's.' This last jab enraged Ulster Protestants, though given their view that it was a Protestant war they should have had no objection to O'Dwyer saying it was not a Catholic one. Few of the bishops would go openly as far as O'Dwyer, but if their Lenten pastorals of 1915 be any indication none were prepared to back Britain with enthusiasm: where the pastorals referred to the war, they saw it as ' a manifestation of Divine anger ' at the sins of those involved. The pastorals of the Archbishops of Dublin and Cashel were devoted to the evils of objectionable literature from England.

It is scarcely surprising that, from the British viewpoint, there was ample justification for regarding the Irish situation, despite Redmond's assurances, as dangerous. After all, the war had absorbed the actively loyal Irish elements into the army, leaving behind the apathetic and the disaffected. Concentration on the problems of war tended to push Irish affairs into the background of British political attention. About to go to Ireland in March 1915 Birrell remarked ' There ought to be a jack-daw in the Cabinet Room trained to say Ireland at stated short intervals '. In fact, it was not so much that cabinet forgot Ireland as that, under the pressure of war, it tended to concentrate on the simplest and most superficial Irish policies. One was to treat the Irish party as Ireland, natural enough in terms of future Home Rule government, but conducive to the formation of impressions substantially irrelevant to what was really happening in Ireland. In some conflict with this policy, the war also prompted the British to tighten their physical grip on Ireland, as the simplest and most effective means of ensuring that a traditional source of trouble would behave itself during a general emergency. Extended powers were given to the military, officials of doubtful loyalty were sacked, there were deportations without trial, several nationalist newspapers were suppressed, and so on. Coming on top of unemployment and a rise in the cost of living, this strong-arm policy produced what the *Catholic Bulletin* described early in 1915 as ' a general feeling of insecurity '. This intensified throughout 1915 as the threat of conscription created a highly emotional atmosphere throughout Ireland, which was relieved but not dispelled by the exclusion of Ireland from conscription in January 1916. Birrell, as Chief Secretary, tried to tone down this tension, notably by resisting the constant pressure of Unionists and army officers to apply severe coercion to destroy any sign of Irish disaffection. Birrell tried to be cool and calm, and to avoid provocative aggression against Irish feeling, such as, what was often demanded, the disbanding of the Irish Volunteers. Several Irish revolutionaries, notably Piaras Beaslai and P. S. O'Hegarty, later testified to the effectiveness of Birrell's policy in weakening the revolutionary impulse, but all that Birrell could do to mute British policy could not disguise the fact that its most strident notes were irrelevant, in so far as they were related to the Irish party's tune, or belligerent, in so far as they had a sharp repressive edge, discordant in the new Ireland.

To come at the central problem again: why, in this Ireland pervaded by conservative Catholicism and clerical power, did a revolutionary movement develop and succeed? It was born of necessity, because from the early 1890s the parliamentary party ceased to satisfy the imagination and emotional needs of a new ' Young Ireland '. It grew and developed because it shared many of its values with the religious revival of the same period, had close parallelism with religion, and was a semi-secular version of the enthusiasms and visions that marked Irish Catholicism. It survived because of what it had in common with Irish Catholicism: what it held in difference went largely unnoticed by the Church. This oversight was partly due to the attractive strength of the religious parallelism and value-sharing; partly to the fact that the dominant and dishonourable existence of the Home Rule party blinded religious eyes to the growth of revolutionary elements. The party did the revolutionary cause the basic service of providing a discreditable image of reform, and its public prominence effectively screened the revolutionaries from the serious notice of both the British and the Church. Had the parliamentary party not existed, the secret revolutionaries of the I.R.B., like the Fenians whose successors they were, would have found themselves much more obvious on a political terrain where they alone stirred. As generals who prepare for the war just ended, the Irish bishops, after the upheavals of the period 1887-91, were obsessed by the dangers of the Home Rule movement, and thus failed to see the negative aspects of the new nationalist movements. Besides, the Home Rule and Land League organisations were mass popular ones, whereas the revolutionary movement was that of a tiny minority: the bishops were concerned with the disposition of the mass of the people, and, even under stress, there was nothing eagerly revolutionary about that – witness the initially hostile popular reception to the 1916 rebellion. The 1916 revolutionaries were, before the event, comparative nonentities who would scarcely have rippled the surface of Irish history had they somehow vanished in 1915. Trinity Provost Mahaffy's haughty reference to ' a man called Pearse ' is not an unfair reflection of Pearse's public standing in 1914. The public generally and those interested in, or responsible for the public domain, were concerned with the big names, the men who constantly made the headlines and appeared to be determining Ireland's affairs – which explains their astonishment when confronted with the 1916 rebellion. Outside its own narrow circle of revolutionary cultists, it was totally unexpected, and thus initially seemed insane, a tragic farce.

It was in this totally unexpected finality that the eventual popular success of the rebellion lay. The major problem of all Irish nationalist movements, moderate or extreme, cultural or political, had been that their pursuit of their objectives had always ended by creating further divisions and fragmentation. The main reason for this was that Ireland was not a practical unity, it was an idea, a concept which meant different things to different people. The difficulties of winning united support for any movement from all sections of the Irish population – even the Irish Catholic population – were immense, even perhaps insuperable, once the movement appeared in the public domain. Once it emerged, it was subjected to the critical evaluation of these sections and as, inevitably, some sections would like or dislike it more than others, it became some sectional possession, the object of contention and controversy, subject to the pressure of the existing power factors in Irish affairs.

The 1916 rebellion by-passed all these hazards by presenting Ireland not with a revolutionary movement, but with a revolution. 1916 was a fact, not a movement in the process of becoming, which could be opposed, diminished, frustrated or modified, but something which had already become actual, an unchangeable fact. After the fact, the question simply was whether Ireland should accept it or reject it. Having occurred, the rebellion could not be undone or altered in any particular, and it thus represented a very clear choice – for or against. However much either support or criticism might be qualified, or hedged with reservations, the fundamental choice, whether to accept or reject, confronted every Irishman inescapably – which is why, no doubt, complex and subtle minds, like those of Yeats and George Russell, long brooded and agonised over the rising, trying to cope with the brutal assault of this contradictory simplicity, both terrible and beautiful.

This choice was made all the more clear-cut, not so much because the 1916 leaders could be viewed as martyrs, as simply because they were dead. The event, after the executions, was rendered incapable of further development. The executions were a major British error, in that they made martyrs – and because they put an end to the rebellion situation. Had the leaders lived, the patterns of previous Irish history suggest that the effect of the rebellion would have been blurred, weakened, perhaps quite dissipated, by clashes of personality, regrets and recrimination, and policy fission among the people, the interests and the aims that had coalesced for that week in 1916. Had the leaders lived, the probabilities are that the issues of the Civil War which was to come, and conflicts such as that between nationalist and socialist groups, would have been fought out in words in the months following Easter 1916, to the destruction of all heroes and heroism, the disintegration of all unity, and the burying of the rebellion as a failure under the weight of dispute and quarrel.

As it was, the rebellion stood out stark and static, irrevocable, artistically complete, executed by men virtually without a public past and deprived by death of any living public future. They had risen up briefly to confront Ireland with a choice of terrible simplicity – would Ireland support this rejection of British rule, or would it not? And they had asked this question with all the imaginative trappings of a poem, a historical epic, which had irresistible romantic appeal. Could Britain have prevented that question being asked then and there? Formally, it had already taken action which would have prevented the rising: on Easter Sunday the Irish administration had determined on the arrest of known extremist leaders, but rebellion occurred before – a day before – the decision could be implemented. That British authority had so narrowly missed forstalling the rebellion can hardly be seen as some disastrous accident: it seems rather to be further testimony to the fatality of a situation at last moving, if tragically, towards some hopeful solution.

How would Ireland – and England – adjust to the inescapable facts of 1916? The total dynamic of the revolutionary movement had been thrown into making this event. Once the event had gathered around itself a popular movement, the revolutionary stimulus had nothing more to offer: Lord Dufferin's 1917 witticism had much point – 'The Irish don't know what they want and won't be happy until they get it.' The Irish revolution of 1916-21 fed on that one event, the Easter rebellion, to the extent of passionate obsession, as the Civil War shows. The rebellion and the men who led it offered very little as a practical programme to the men who faced the problems that followed. After the Civil War, the revolutionary movement had no developing dynamic to offer, no impetus which would take Ireland past the simple fact of political severance from Britain – a situation very much related to the fact that, because of partition, the severance was not complete. The rebellion had not fully succeeded in its aims as set out in the proclamation of the provisional government in 1916, a proclamation of total Irish independence, asserting a republican government ' of the whole nation and of all its parts, cherishing all the children of the nation equally, and oblivious of the differences carefully fostered by an alien government, which have divided a minority from the majority in the past.' So, much of rebellious Ireland's energies and ambitions were concentrated on that appalling rent in the seamless cloak of Irish nationality, and thus not available for the task of revolutionising that part of Ireland the rebellion had eventually freed. In consequence, Ireland entered on to a period not so much of stagnancy, as of suspended animation, dominated externally by partition and the residue of the British control over the Free State, and internally by a reversion to her former self in which British influences in politics and society had been so important.

Against this, had the rebels of 1916 possessed any strong, concerted, detailed, constructive ideology, some precise blueprint for the republic they declared, this might have hindered, or even thwarted, public acceptance of the rebellion. From one angle, the failure of the 1916 leaders to conceptualise, let alone provide, a realistic plan for a new Ireland may seem irresponsible or naïve: from another viewpoint it can be seen as a great advantage. Acceptance of 1916 did not commit anyone to other than the vaguest of possible ideologies – Irish freedom – and so it avoided the divisive contentions which an explicit ideology would have produced. Support for the 1916 rebellion demanded much less any commitment to a formulated intellectual position, as the common sharing of an emotion, an attitude, an outlook: as Joseph Plunkett's sister put it, ' We traced all our evils, big and small to England. . . .' – and that was that. The rising did not – save, crucially, for the republican tradition – become a living continuum in Irish affairs: almost immediately upon its occurrence it became a historic event, innocent and venerated.

II
The Question Changes

In Catholic Ireland, political and religious activity expressed two moods of the one mind. The 1916 rebellion opened a new era in Irish nationalism by changing the Irish question from that of Home Rule to that of full independence: 1916 also saw an amazing outburst of missionary zeal, the initial manifestation of a new era in Irish religious imperialism.

In China, in the years between 1912 and 1916, Father Edward Galvin from Cork, had found, with that curious assurance that saw the face of Ireland reflected everywhere, old Ireland once again: ' China, in many respects, reminds me of conditions in Ireland. There are practically no industries. The whole population live on the land, and every available acre is under cultivation. They work hard and live on the plainest fare. . . . They are now in very much the same position as our own people were during the famine years in Ireland.' Whether or not such apparent similarities moved him much, the challenge to Ireland's Catholicism certainly did, and Father Galvin conceived the idea of an Irish priestly mission to China. On the principle that ' when the people are suffering they rise to heroic heights' he put this proposal to the Catholics of Ireland in the months following the rebellion.

Galvin's plans, beginning with the project of founding in Ireland a missionary college to prepare priests for China, met an immediate enthusiastic response. Galvin, and men like Father John Blowick who left a professorial post at Maynooth to join his cause, visualised their movement as a kind of national spiritual resurrection, a new crusade in which Ireland would recapture the glories of her missionary past. In promoting his campaign, Galvin himself was prone to engage in flights of messianic religio-racialism: 'We will write the Irish Mission to China across the world, wherever an Irish heart throbs or a drop of Irish blood flows in Irish veins. We will re-unite the scattered sons and daughters of St Patrick into one great missionary army to fulfil again in our age the divine destiny that God has entrusted to our race.' The Irish bishops responded warmly to Galvin's proposal. For them, it seems, it dispelled the uncertainty and disquiet about Ireland's religious health which the shock of the rebellion had engendered. Galvin's campaign and its immense popular success restored their shaken confidence, and substantially strengthened it. Bishop Fogarty of Killaloe told Father Blowick in November 1916: 'I heard of the China Mission with feelings of joy and gratitude to God. It dispelled a fear that was increasing, that St Patrick's children had lost St Patrick's ideals and that the apostolic graces lavished on our early Christian forefathers were because of our sins subtracted from us.' Similarly, in his 1917 Lenten pastoral, Bishop McKenna of Clogher rejoiced ' to know that Ireland has not fallen away from her high and holy ideals. We thank God that Irish minds are still guided by the light of Faith, and Irish hearts are aglow with the ardour of the sublimest charity.'

The episcopal reaction was in the light of the campaign's popular reception. The newspapers most co-operative in publicising the China Mission were those most firmly dedicated to an Irish Ireland. The first priests who joined the missionary society were young, in their twenties and thirties, contemporaries of those who had died in the rebellion, and were themselves enthusiasts for Irish Ireland. Father Blowick testified to the fact that his mission had been helped by the rebellion:

I am strongly of the opinion that the Rising of 1916 helped our work indirectly. I know for a fact that many of the young people of the country had been aroused into a state of heroism and zeal by the Rising of 1916 and by the manner in which the leaders met their death. I can affirm this from personal experience. And accordingly, when we put our appeal before the young people of the country it fell on soil which was far better prepared to receive it than if there never had been an Easter week.

Post-rebellion Ireland, priests and people, received the China missionaries with a spontaneous enthusiasm and generosity that astonished them: in practical terms, the first year of the appeal raised a group of priests – and £33,000, with only half of Ireland's dioceses then visited.

This national missionary campaign, following on the heels of the rebellion, had two important effects. The response evoked by the campaign convinced the leaders of Irish religion that popular religious impulses and zeal were as strong, if not stronger than before the rebellion. In sharp contrast with what had occurred in relation to Parnell, or Fenianism, or Young Ireland, the aftermath of the 1916 crisis seemed to be an intense religious revival, exhibiting a popular response to the exhortations of clerical authority and all the virtues of which the priesthood approved. The success of the China mission appeal was not the only evidence of this: those seeking to found a magazine, the *Little Flower Monthly*, devoted to the religious example of the new French saint, Thérèse of Lisieux, were told ' People won't read anything nowadays unless it is about the war or the rebellion ' – but the magazine was an instant success from its first issue in July 1916. Its purpose was pious, not political, but still it carried some material on the rising: its more politically oriented religious contemporaries, the *Irish Rosary* and the *Catholic Bulletin*, carried a great deal. Evidently the rebellion's effects had been the reverse of spiritually destructive and the clergy could therefore feel safe in accepting and indeed blessing the rebellion. Ireland, it seemed, had energies enough for two crusades, one ' to bring the light of Faith to the countless millions of a mighty Empire that still sits in the darkness of Paganism and the shadow of eternal death ', the other, with a more political edge, against that nearer Empire which sat in the darkness of Protestantism and the shadow of materialism.

The other effect was more diffuse. The five young missionaries who preached the appeal were frequently asked, as they toured Ireland, if they were Sinn Féiners: they invariably answered that they had no concern with politics. Yet the fact remains that they were personally sympathetic to the rebellion, and that they were conducting a mission which called on Ireland's national religious tradition and spiritual resources in the aftermath of a rebellion which had asserted related forms of idealism. It seems highly likely that these parallel idealisms nurtured each other to their mutual benefit, rendering both popularly more acceptable.

The way in which British military authorities handled the immediate post-rebellion situation in Ireland has often been criticised. What actually occurred, in terms of executions of the leaders, martial law, mass deportation of suspects to English detention camps, was a much diluted dose of the medicine some military men wanted to administer. That military intelligence attempted to get MacNeill to implicate Dillon and Devlin in the rebellion plot is evidence of desire to obliterate the Irish party: that Sir Henry Wilson, Director of Military Operations on the Imperial General Staff, should attempt to persuade General Sir John Maxwell, British military commander in Ireland, to have Birrell, Chief Secretary and British cabinet minister, arrested, tried and executed suggests that Ireland could make some Englishmen lose their reason. The context was of course the public depiction of the rebellion as having German connections and objectives: in the face of the passions unleashed by this impression, Birrell's efforts to diminish the importance of what had happened to the level of a minor disturbance, no rebellion, had no chance of success.

The strong military reaction, dragging behind it a reluctant Asquith, was based on the pre-existing assumption that the Birrell policy of non-repression had been the wrong policy. It seemed self-evidently wrong: rebellion had occurred. The Liberals' Irish policy had, of course, many long-standing enemies, not only among the military, but now, because of the Coalition, within the Cabinet itself. What had happened in Ireland gave Asquith and the Liberals no choice but to capitulate to the demands of Tory policy on Ireland, in order to save the Coalition. Conservative 'I told you so's' were almost triumphal: the Catholic Irish had proved themselves traitorous, violent and disloyal as Ulster Protestants had always contended. There could be no question of Home Rule for Ulster now. The political situation of war-Coalition even made it possible – indeed necessary – for the Conservative Unionists to shed whatever guilt they may have felt, or seemed to bear, for the Ulster crisis of 1911–14: the Royal Commission on the Rebellion in Ireland had terms of reference which were so defined as to exclude consideration of the Ulster rebellion, and its explanations of what occurred in 1916 were innocent of any linkage with, or mention of the earlier activities as an Ulster rebel, of Sir Edward Carson, then First Lord of the Admiralty, previously Attorney General in the Coalition.

That British policy should be reversed in response to the rebellion was natural enough, but it was a mistake to assume that the rebellion had occurred because of Birrell's policy of non-repression: in fact it occurred in spite of it. To a considerable extent the internal momentum of the Irish situation was such that any British policy was irrelevant. The abandonment of the pre-1916 policy as bad, and ineffective in pacifying Ireland did not mean that the alternative of coercion would be good and effective. It was worse. Superficially, the rising seemed to demonstrate that a British policy of conciliation had failed. So it had. But much more basically the rising confirmed the Liberal view that there was such a thing as Irish nationalism, which had to be dealt with; whereas the rising bluntly contradicted the premise on which Conservative Unionism erected its attitudes – that Irish nationalism was a sham, did not exist or had no real force. It took some Unionists a very long time to recognise this, and some never did. The effect of the rising was to push the Irish question to its natural extremes – was it to be Union or separation? If for no other reason that it was a *via media* – though there were many other reasons – Home Rule had no place in the new situation. The extreme Irish answer to the question of English rule – violent rebellion – prompted an extreme English response – open military rule. Having avoided this for the whole period of Union, indeed since the seventeenth century, Britain was reduced to a policy, largely dominant down to 1921, of regarding the Irish situation as a military problem, a question of finding the best means of applying superior force to the subduing of the Irish enemy. At last British rule had been stripped to the gaze of all – Ireland, Britain, the world – to reveal the naked reality of force which had formerly been respectably, if sometimes scantily clothed.

How outrageous this was in the eyes of the Church is a vital factor the importance of which in the Irish situation, is seldom appreciated. British military rule swiftly alienated Church authorities for whom it showed scant respect and sometimes overt hostility. When the bishops of Ireland met in June 1916 they discussed the question of whether they should authorise a church-door collection for sufferers in the rebellion, but came to no decision, ' lest they might incur the imputation of favouring in any way the authors of that unfortunate attempt '. The imputation had already been made – by the military. That the bishops should discuss such a question at all, and that they should come to no decision rather than an adverse one, reflects their sympathies, their appreciation of the public mood – and awareness that while the rebellion was one thing, its aftermath was another. The bishops held no brief for violence – on either side. The rebellion was unfortunate, but it was over: British policy was continuing, it was violent and provocative. And that British policy was informed by the assumption, both tribute and affront, that priests had been substantially responsible for Irish unrest, and that in restoring order, the Church was the key to the situation. Accordingly General Maxwell called on Cardinal Logue to ask him to keep the younger clergy in particular under restraint. Logue reacted very sharply to the request and its implications, denying – as the body of Irish bishops had asked him to do – that there were any grounds for complaint against the activity of priests, and taking Maxwell sternly to task for 'the mistake the authorities are making in keeping the whole country in a state of excitement by their wholesale arrests'. Logue's position, and that of the Irish bishops generally, had ample historical precedent: it was the traditional religious reaction against British policies deemed provocative of Irish crime and sin, and detrimental to social conditions in which religious values could be preserved.

Maxwell experienced an even more vigorous rebuff from Bishop O'Dwyer to whom he wrote in May 1916 regarding two Limerick priests whom he considered 'to be a dangerous menace to the peace and safety of the Realm'. Pressed for details, Maxwell revealed that his case rested on these priests speaking against conscription, having assisted in organising Irish Volunteers and blessing their colours, and having been present when 'inflammatory and seditious speeches' were delivered. O'Dwyer not only refused to take any action, but told Maxwell that he regarded his rule as 'wantonly cruel and oppressive', the executions merciless, in cold blood and an outrage to Ireland's conscience, the deportations an abuse of power both fatuous and arbitrary, and that 'altogether your regime has been one of the worst and blackest chapters in the history of the misgovernment of this country.'

If there had been any chance of co-operation between the Church and British authority in dealing with the post-rebellion situation in Ireland, it was promptly lost by Britain's handling of the situation, the government's failure to contain the military reaction within reasonable limits. The rising had been the work of a very small group, but the British reaction was of a kind and dimension which implied that all Ireland was to blame, that Ireland as a whole was guilty of treason. This shocked and outraged that majority of Irish opinion which, like Britain, had been taken by surprise by the rebellion: the response of Logue and O'Dwyer to Maxwell was, in microcosm, the reaction of moderate and conservative Catholic Ireland to a British policy seen as embodiment and revelation of hatred and injustice. So British policy brought about what was its most imperative need to avoid – a general Irish sympathy towards the rebellion. British tactics, even at the crude level of military rule, depended for success on isolating the rebels. Britain could not undertake a total reconquest of Ireland: it was a military impossibility in a war situation, and a political impossibility in the prevailing climate of opinion, within Britain as well as outside it.

Within a month of the rebellion, there could be no doubt that the Church was generally sympathetic to the rising and certainly would not condemn it. The new nationalists were greatly comforted by this decisive development. Of Bishop O'Dwyer and other priests whom the British regarded as ' sources of disaffection ', Dr. Patrick MacCartan, a member of the supreme council of the I.R.B., wrote late in May to Joseph McGarrity in America, ' They have redeemed the Catholic Church in the eyes of Nationalist Ireland of the stain caused by the attitude of some priests and bishops in the days of Fenianism.' There would be no return to the anathemas of the 1860s. In fact, the *Catholic Bulletin* went to the other extreme – a kind of canonisation – in its monthly featuring of brief biographies of the Irish rank and file who fell in the rebellion. James Quinn – ' So ardent did he grow in his religious duties that he became a most devoted member of the Confraternity of the Cross and Passion at Mount Argus.' George Geoghegan – ' An earnest and almost lifelong member of the Dominick Street Sodality of the Holy Name, he received Holy Communion on Easter Sunday morning.' Patrick Doyle – ' a prominent member of the Milltown Temperance and Sacred Heart Sodalities. Every evening regularly he visited the Milltown Chapel to say the Rosary.' And so on. The message was loud and clear: Catholic Ireland had fought in Easter week; pious blood had been spilt for Ireland.

Such was, it seemed, the religious quality of those nationalists who had died. What of those who still lived? The rebellion confirmed what many had previously thought, that the Irish Party was irrelevant to the real Ireland, and it unleashed on that party an avalanche of abuse. A typical example is F. Hugh O'Donnell's printed letter of June 1916 to the leaders of Irish affairs, clerical and lay, which asserted that the Irish Party was a ' sordid aggregation of Bosses, Nominees and Dupes . . . ridiculous . . . uneducated, thoroughly corrupt and scandalously negligent dictators of Irish politics.' All sorts of rumours of party corruption were circulating – for instance that the party had a secret agreement with the Liberals to destroy Irish industry in return for lucrative places in the Irish administration. In contrast, the new men, and notably de Valera, were emerging in the minds of responsible observers, as men of real worth. Sir James O'Connor told Cardinal Logue in November 1917: ' De Valera is a high-minded and sincere Catholic . . . he does not want physical force – nor do his colleagues, John MacNeill & Arthur Griffith & men of that stamp. But we have reason to fear trouble from other quarters.' These other quarters were the socialists and physical force extremists. In the new situation, the Irish Catholic establishment's hostility to such irreligious and potentially disruptive forces, disposed it to support whatever it could in the new Sinn Féin which emerged early in 1917 as the political wing of the revolutionary movement. The importance of de Valera's survival as the sole living commandant of the rebellion is very great. He was a Catholic and a very pious one, not open to denigratory criticism from Catholic religious extremists. De Valera embodied the two dominant forces in post-rebellion Ireland – religion and separatist nationalism – demonstrating in himself (for he was a man of forceful integrity) that the two could be harmoniously reconciled. Only the social revolutionaries remained out of religious step, a situation which increasingly committed the Church to the new nationalism, not only for itself, but as a defence against the threat of social revolution.

Bishop O'Dwyer's statements continued to enhance the nationalist reputation of the Church. The popular response to his comments suggests that their effect was very great. This effect is best described as an easing of the conscience of Catholic Ireland: O'Dwyer dispelled that long-standing tense confrontation between religion and revolution which, under Cardinal Cullen, had done so much to hinder the popular gravitation towards violent revolutionary movements. O'Dwyer's pronouncements, delivered from a position of immunity from arrest, are of immense significance in freeing the revolutionary cause of its traditional religious stigma. Coming from the bishop who had supported the 1888 Papal rescript against the popular nationalist tide, the impact of his analysis of the 1916 rebellion was profound.

Bishop O'Dwyer's speech in receiving the freedom of the city of Limerick in September 1916 set out his views for all to see. What of the young men who had died in Dublin? 'Was I to condemn them? Even if their rebellion was not justifiable theologically, was I to join the gang of renegades who were throwing dirt on Pearse and MacDonagh and Colbert, and the other brave fellows whom Maxwell had mercilessly put to death. Was I to join in the condemnation of the men, and women too, who, without trial, were deported by thousands.' Simply, the rebellion and the British response to it, had created sides, and it was impossible to occupy the British side. O'Dwyer was prepared to concede some truth to the British case that the rising was a hopeless folly, but given that it was the British case, it could be given little weight. ' The Irish Volunteers were too few for the enterprise, but that perhaps is the worst that is to be said against them. Rebellion to be lawful must be the act of the nation as a whole, but while that is true, see the case of the Irish

Volunteers against England.' O'Dwyer saw the English government as self-condemned. 'What is that ghost of Home Rule which they keep safe in lavender on the Statute Book, but a confession of the wrong of England's rule in Ireland.' England had been guilty of 'tantalising perfidy' in the case of Home Rule: its concession was mere pretence, it sought to partition the country by religion. O'Dwyer held that the young men of any nation could not be expected to bear this treatment patiently. He went further to declare that these young men were 'the true representatives of Ireland, and were the exponents of her Nationality', thus attributing to the rebels an unimpeachable status as the only real nationalists. The Irish Party O'Dwyer denounced as forgetful of the national spirit, as having misplaced its faith, as bankrupt of future plans: 'Sinn Féin, is, in my judgement, the true principle, and alliance with English politicians is the alliance of the lamb with the wolf.' O'Dwyer continued to express views of this kind, and when his letters, such as that of 1 May 1917, were refused press publication, they were printed as handbills. To him the 1916 rebellion was 'a reaction against weakness and stupidity, and corruption. But hopeless as it was, it has not been fruitless. It has galvanised the dead bones in Ireland and breathed into them the spirit with which England has had to reckon.'

Bishop O'Dwyer's approach to the ethics of the rebellion set the dominant tone of Church reaction. Its more general premises are discernible in a sermon on St Patrick's Day 1918 by Monsignor O'Riordan, Rector of the Irish College, Rome:

> . . . for Catholics, love of country and loyalty to civil government are not a mere natural sentiment . . . They are a religious obligation, which binds in conscience; and hence, with Irish Catholics, the national watchword has always been Faith and Fatherland, not Fatherland and Faith . . . force does not consecrate its deeds. Wrong is not less a wrong because it is decreed by a legislature; and illegal resistance or evasion became the natural protection against immoral laws. And so the Catholics of Ireland rightly disowned what force made them endure.

In this last proposition lay the justification for 1916. Was the rebellion made by the Catholics of Ireland? Essentially, yes, was Monsignor O'Riordan's position. Because, with the Irish 'their supernatural life has become also the mainstay of their national life. The soul of a nation can never die, except of moral corruption. Brute force may grind to powder the material elements that compose it, but if it rests on the moral law it will revive and put out its activity again. A nation that lives in God, lives by purity, by justice, by fortitude, by hope.' This Godly nation was rising again. Few within the Church tried to swim against the current of such arguments. The only major attempt to do So was Rev. Walter McDonald's book, *Some Ethical Questions of Peace and War with special reference to Ireland*, published in 1919, which argued, on grounds of Catholic principle, that most of the typical claims of the new nationalism, backed by the Church, were not ethically justifiable. As McDonald himself, noted, his book was favourably received by Protestants, Unionists and the English press: the great body of the Catholic clergy were hurt and hostile. To his disgust, Professors, Editors, Politicians, Bishops, Canonists and Theologians continued, in their devotion to Sinn Féin, to use ' rotten arguments, bogus history, indefensible ethics '.

The 1916 rebellion was the apogee of Ireland's escape from the realm of politics into the realm of myth and idealism. By the middle of 1917 the revolutionary movement, united and strong after tutoring in that ' university for revolutionaries ', the English detention camp, was right down to earth again, with questions of manoeuvre and tactics and organisation the main concern of the I.R.B. The claim for Irish representation at the Peace Conference to follow the world war was recognised as hopeless, but 'good politics': it would help to put the Irish question before world opinion and would divert Ireland's attention away from the attempts of the Irish party at Westminster to re-establish themselves. It was a first political necessity to destroy the Irish party and secure mass support for Sinn Féin. Any possible ally was investigated: the I.R.B. decided to negotiate with the new provisional Russian government for its support, later, a treaty was proposed with the Bolsheviks. On his release from prison, in June 1917 de Valera had said that he knew nothing about politics and did not like them: his was precisely the cast of mind that fitted the new spirit in Ireland, the politics of the anti-political.

But the major politicing was against Britain, taking the form of a shrewd and concerted effort to place Britain at a moral disadvantage. This was not difficult to do, as the executions of the rebellion's leaders had provoked a British reaction also: before they were completed, the *Manchester Guardian* warned, ' The executions are becoming an atrocity '. The rebellion, after the initial censorship blanket, attracted a great deal of attention to itself and generally to British policy in Ireland. To radicals, liberals and humanitarians in England, the fact that there had been a rebellion in Ireland suggested that there must be something wrong with

English policy there. This in itself diminished the certainty and self-confidence characteristic of English attitudes towards Ireland. Ireland demanded attention, but what many English observers saw when they looked, shook them, undermining their sense of moral superiority as they saw Englishmen committing what seemed to be patent atrocities.

The executions were one blunder: their alienation of awakened liberal opinion in England was no less important than their effect on Ireland. Under the pressure of Germany's March 1918 offensive, a further major blunder was made – a revival of the threat to extend conscription to Ireland. The result was an extraordinary set of manifestations of Irish national solidarity, this time lifted, by the proclamation of a national novena – nine days of prayer – to the level of spiritual exaltation. Aodh de Blácam described it: ' together leaders and people turned to spiritual sources of consolation and strength that the stranger could hardly understand. Ireland became a land on whose air prayer was almost audible '. So Britain further welded together religion and nationalism in Ireland.

By 1919 the Irish situation was degenerating into warfare that became open in 1920. But already Britain had suffered moral defeat. Lloyd George justified the use of British forces as necessary against ' a small nest of assassins ', ' to hunt down the murder gang ', but already world opinion saw Ireland as wronged and oppressed, rebelling in the name of a rightful self-determination against foreign government. That Britain, with her Black and Tans and her Auxiliaries, should attempt to defeat the guerilla warfare of the Irish Republican Army by using atrocity against atrocity was a situation from which Britain inevitably derived by far the greater odium and much of it within Britain itself – a reaction of eventually decisive importance.

Given the degeneration of Irish affairs into the reign of violence, murder and atrocity, why did the Church not intervene? Early in 1920, Sir Horace Plunkett – not a Catholic – drew Archbishop O'Donnell's attention to the ' inevitable progressive demoralisation of a people by the tyranny through which we are now passing '. He pointed to the great moral truism of the Anglo-Irish war: ' many more suffer spiritually from the absence of moral sanction from the law than are exalted by the righteous indignation and Christian resignation such a tyranny evokes '. Some bishops were aware of this, and gravely alarmed by it. Writing to a friend in Spain early in 1919, Bishop Kelly in Skibbereen observed ' Things in Ireland are most dangerously unsettled. The mind of the country is a shaking bog. I have heard basic principles denied and ridiculed; and hopes held that I regard as lunacy.' For those who perceived this accelerating moral disintegration, the problem was – how could they prevent or control it? Some, like Bishop Kelly, gave way to pessimism verging on despair. By the middle of 1921, he thought Ireland had gone mad: the women were going off their heads, there had been a great crop of miscarriages, Ireland had been caught up in the vortex of those social-ist and revolutionary ideas that had engulfed the whole world, daily the Irish situation grew blacker and more tangled.

But for many Irish Catholics, no less their clergy and bishops, their conviction of moral and religious superiority was too strong to entertain the idea that there was fault among them. Late in 1919, as the tempo of violence increased, Bishop Fogarty of Killaloe replied to a censure from the Bench that the people of Clare had fallen to the depths of moral degradation. He defended his people as of ' pure and intense religious life ', to be contrasted with ' the filthy compound of burglary and murder, sodomy, bigamy and infidelity, child murder, divorce and sexual promis-cuity that covers the standing pool of Saxon life '. In his Lenten Pastoral of 1921 Bishop Fogarty wrote, ' Religion is insulted, convents raided, divine service interrupted, priests beaten and murdered. . . . Nothing is spared, nothing is sacred, no one is safe '. In Fogarty's mind the Anglo-Irish war consisted of the struggle of Holy Ireland against the filth and sacrilege of persecuting Saxons: no censure of the Irish could be expected from such a quarter. In its abodes high and low, Catholic nationalist Ireland would brook no criticism, nor would it tolerate any truths but its own. The denunciation of Eimar O'Duffy's novel of the 1916 rebellion, *The Wasted Island*, which dared to question the awful chastity of con-temporary Ireland, illustrates the usual response: it was condemned as being no Irish book, but English literature of a debased order.

Besides, in what Carlton Younger has described as ' the most devasta-ting single-handed stroke of the Anglo-Irish war ', the most intense religious fervour and sacrificial ardour seemed happily and luminously united with the ultimate in revolutionary dedication. This was the 74-day hunger strike – to the death – conducted by the Lord Mayor of Cork in Brixton prison from August to October in 1920. Terence MacSwiney's ordeal in the cause of Irish freedom attracted the attention and sympathy of the world, and further gravely undermined the reputation of Britain's policy in Ireland. MacSwiney's death was no mere political act, it was firmly and consciously a religious one, and herein lay both its true significance as an expression of Ireland's spirit and the reason for its astounding impact on public opinion. From prison, MacSwiney issued, not political statements, but sermons, casting all that was happening in an orthodox Catholic religious mould, thanking ' all our people through-out the world for the wonderful support they have given us, in our ordeal, by the innumerable Masses and prayers said on our behalf. The spiritual assistance afforded us has, I believe sustained us in a supernatural manner. . . .' He saw the protraction of his ordeal as God's mercy to the English, allowing them more time to repent to their intention to murder him and other hunger-strikers: ' I believe God has directly intervened to stay the tragedy for a while for a divine purpose of His own. . . . I believe He has, in His mercy, intervened for our enemy's sake. It is incredible that the people of England will allow this callous and cold-blooded murder to be pushed to the end. . . . If it is pushed through it will leave a stain on the name of England to which there is no parallel (even in her history) – that nothing will ever efface. . . .' Then, in the classic tradition of Christian martyrdom, MacSwiney accepted his fate and forgave his tormentors: ' We forgive all those who are compassing our death. . . . Between you and us it has been a veritable communion of prayer. I believe God is watching over our country and by his Divine decree her resurrection is at hand '.

This sense of Christian martydrom – and the old equation between England and Satan – are patent in the prayer MacSwiney issued from Brixton to his fellow hunger-strikers in Cork jail:

O my God, I offer my pain for Ireland. She is on the rack. My God, Thou knowest how many times our enemies have put her there to break her spirit, but, by Thy mercy, they have always failed. I offer my sufferings here for our martyred people, beseeching Thee, O God, to grant them nerve and strength and grace to withstand the present terror in Ireland. . . . The spirit of prayer will defeat the cunning of Satan. Thy power, O God, is stronger than the malice of the devil. I offer everything Thou askest for Ireland's resurrection. It is Thy Will. . . . May we, in dying, bring glory to Thy Name, and honour to our country, that has always been faithful to Thee. . . . God save, bless and guard the Irish Republic, to live and flourish, and be a model government of truth and justice to all nations.

Ireland – religious Ireland, identified with this man intensely, a man who claimed, without challenge, the clerical prerogative of composing prayers, whose body lay in state in Southwark Cathedral while thousands filed past, whose photograph appeared on little cards, ornamented and garlanded with flowers in the manner of a saint. Even in the sceptical Italian press, MacSwiney's fast was seen as the victory of the Soul over the Stomach, the triumph of Love over the World. There could be no question of the Church repudiating the cause consecrated by MacSwiney's death. Moreover, while MacSwiney starved, what Bishop

MacRory described as an anti-Catholic pogrom had begun in Belfast: 10,000 Catholics were expelled from their employment, Protestant mobs wrecked and looted the property of Catholics, 40 Catholics were killed between July and November 1920. Of the Partition Bill, MacRory said in August, ' I never took the Bill seriously; I don't take it seriously now; but I trust that the events of the past three weeks in Belfast and its neighbourhood will convince even the present Coalition Government of the intolerable conditions to which the Bill, if it ever become.an Act, would subject more than thirty-six per cent of the inhabitants of the " Six Counties ".' The Act, by which Northern Ireland is still governed, became law in December 1920: intolerable conditions there were to be.

The actuality was intolerable enough, but it was made much more hateful by its contrast with the dream. MacSwiney's hope that the new Irish Republic would be a model government was common at his time. Partition contradicted the secular version of this hope. In *The Path To Freedom*, Michael Collins held ' we can become a shining light in the world ' but he conceded that partition seriously impaired Ireland's freedom to achieve this. But it was the religious variety of Irish utopianism that partition aggrieved most: it cut across that hope for a holy nation that was the Church's greatest bond with Sinn Féin. How far this religious utopianism could go is illustrated by the proposal made in the *Catholic Bulletin* of February 1919, that the ancient Gaelic state be revived on the structural basis of Church areas, in an integral amalgam of Catholic Church and Gaelic Commonwealth:

> the statecraft of the Gaelic Commonwealth and of the Catholic Church by their strong points of resemblance mutually support each other in a most extraordinary manner. The sole difference between them is that in the Catholic Church all power comes from the Pope, as Vicar of Christ, whereas in the Gaelic State all power comes from the people. The religious power coming from above and the secular power from below dove-tail into each other, as it were, and together produce the nearest approach to Utopia ever likely to be realised on this earth.

Utopia was not to be realised, in this or any other form, but it was the dovetailing of religious and secular dispositions in Ireland after the 1916 rebellion which eventually forced England, in 1921, to renounce effective authority over all but six of Ireland's 32 counties. And in this, the religious disposition was the decisive one: if Ireland, in defiance of Froude's dictum, was to have a secular history, it was only by virtue of religious permission.

PART FOUR

The Question Answered?

I

The Question of the Twenty-Six Counties

The Anglo-Irish Treaty, which led to the establishment of the Irish Free State as a self-governing dominion within the British Empire, was signed on 6 December 1921 by representatives of the British government and of Dáil Éireann, the Irish republican Parliament which had been set up by the Sinn Féin candidates who had swept to popular victory in the elections of December 1918. In the mid-1960s, it was possible for British historians to regard the Treaty as ending the Irish question. According to A. J. P. Taylor 'Lloyd George conjured it out of existence', and to C. L. Mowat, 'It simply disappeared as a major factor in British politics'. The events of 1969-70 in Northern Ireland have seriously questioned the finality of such judgements, but they have always been misleading in their implicit assumption that once the Irish question had been removed from British politics it ceased to exist. The effect of the Anglo-Irish Treaty was not to dissolve the Irish question into virtual nothingness, but to transplant it to the soil of Ireland. In Northern Ireland it remained, until recently, largely buried under the oppressive weight of Unionist government: in the Free State it appeared immediately, to an exacerbated degree, in one of the forms it had always taken – that of the English question in Irish politics. Britain regarded the Treaty as a settlement of the Irish question, seen as the problem of the relationship between England and Ireland, but it thereby marked out the ground over which Irishmen fought a Civil War. The Treaty was Britain's answer to the Irish question: the Irish had yet to answer it for themselves.

The Irish delegates signed the Treaty under conditions of duress. To the extent that Sinn Féin and the Irish Republican Army had forced Britain to make a treaty, the Irish had won the Anglo-Irish war: they can hardly be said to have won the peace. In that, the victory went to Britain and Lloyd George. Not only was Britain adamant that any

settlement with nationalist Ireland must be on the basis of the exclusion
of Northern Ireland, and that Ireland must remain within and profess
loyalty to the Empire, but Lloyd George resorted to trickery, threats and
eventually an ultimatum of renewed and annihilating war in order to
extort the Irish signatures. It was this threat of reconquest which decided
the issue. This was, it seems, no bluff, though given the climate of English
opinion it seems highly likely, had it been put to the test, to have precipitated a major political crisis in Britain: but perhaps not, for if the Irish
had rejected the Treaty, the situation would have fulfilled the conditions
urged by General Macready from Ireland in August: 'if hostilities do
recommence we must be in a position in which the onus must be entirely on Sinn Féin'. And in that most of Ireland yearned for peace, and
thought the Treaty's terms acceptable, rejection of the Treaty would have
had serious repercussions within Ireland itself.

However, as it was, the circumstances of virtual coercion deprived
the settlement if not of all its moral authority, certainly of sufficient for
Irish zealots to have emotion as well as argument on their side in rejecting it. Far from being a great act of international reconciliation, as Asquith
chose to describe it, the Treaty was rather a coercive British political
device to put an end to a gravely embarrassing and highly discreditable
war, and to remove the baffling and ruinous Irish question from British
political life. Lloyd George told his Cabinet that the Treaty 'would
enormously increase Great Britain's prestige in the world and would
show that she was still capable of overcoming almost insuperable difficulties': rather was it a shrewd, ungenerous and hard-headed means of
avoiding further odium in Britain's dealings with Ireland. Its terms
were dictated not by beneficence, but by the realities of what were still,
essentially, anti-Irish politics. It was not, as Lloyd George called it 'A
just and righteous settlement of the Irish question', but what could be
piloted successfully through a Parliament specially summoned for the
occasion amidst all the panoply of Empire, massed bands, and companies
from all the Regiments of Guards – for it represented in the British
view, to sum it up in Lord Curzon's words 'an astonishing victory for the
Empire'. The Treaty was, in fact, all things to all men. Those who
supported it in the Dáil debates did so because they contended that it
recognised the substance of Ireland's national independence: those who
opposed it in the House of Commons did so for the same reason. Those
who supported the Treaty in the Commons contended that its qualifica-
tions, the inclusion of Ireland in the Empire and the oath of allegiance
were quite sufficient to keep Ireland subject to all necessary British control – which were precisely the grounds on which its Dáil opponents

rejected it. Or to put it with blunt simplicity: the anti-Treaty republicans fought the Irish Civil War because they held the same interpretation of the Treaty as did the British government.

So, even in ending the Union, Britain created a new source of hatred and dissension in Ireland. Of this Lloyd George and his Cabinet, caught up in a mood of self-congratulation, were blissfully unaware. Lloyd George believed, so it seems, that the Irish had abandoned the idea of a republic, had accepted a separate Ulster, and had agreed to an oath of allegiance better in many respects than that required in Great Britain. He saw the whole settlement as a tribute to the success of his government's policies, and congratulated the Black and Tans. Nor, when Ireland lapsed into Civil War did the Cabinet show any signs of understanding their own responsibility for bringing that situation about: for them, the Treaty seemed an end to the matter, and it was up to Ireland's Provisional Government to see that it was enforced, or Britain would have to intervene. Churchill observed to the Cabinet in May 1922, ' If Ireland fell into a state of anarchy, we should have to re-establish a pale again around Dublin prior to reconquest '.

Strange as it may seem, despite the nature of the Treaty negotiations, even the British Cabinet failed to appreciate that very few in Ireland regarded the Treaty as final. The Irish question which arose out of the Treaty was the simple question of what lengths its opponents, those who regarded it as unjust and insufficient – which included its Irish signatories – were prepared to go. It was a question of whether or not, in the circumstances of Anglo-Irish war, its terms were tolerable as a first step, as much as then could be gained, towards the objective of independence on which all were agreed. Popular feeling in Ireland held that it was tolerable, a view held by Arthur Griffith, Michael Collins and the others who made up the 64 Dáil votes which ratified the Treaty. But there were 57, most prominent among them de Valera, who rejected it as intolerable. From this point, the Irish situation degenerated into bitter and barbarous Civil War, with the Treaty as the central issue, from about mid-1922 to mid-1923.

It was the conflict between the British and the Irish solutions to the Irish question that was fought out in the Civil War. The Civil War was no simple internal struggle: it was the frontal collision between those Irishmen who – caught in the final prison of British politics – saw the imperative necessity of accepting a British settlement as the only chance of peace and eventual progress, and those Irishmen, still living under the spell of 1916, who clung to the grandiose dreams of Irish revolutionary principle and idealism. This opposition went deep into the past of Anglo-

Irish relations. When, at last, the future seemed to be opening up for Irish freedom, it was natural – given that Britain presided so decisively over the process – that this opposition should emerge as a focus of tension: that it produced Civil War reflected the fact that the 1921 definition of Irish freedom was not a viable compromise – it was too British. There was just too much inescapable evidence to support such definitions of the new Irish government as that promoted by Count Plunkett – ' an English agency set up in Ireland by Acts of the English Parliament, and based on the Partition Act '. If such definitions falsified the spirit of the new government, they had some formal truth. To the republican die-hards, the contest seemed one between Irish revolution and a variety of Home Rule dispensed by the English: the Free State was seen, as to some extent it was, as merely an extension of Home Rule. As the Free State used borrowed British weapons to fight the republicans, republican propaganda hit back: ' The enemy is the old enemy, England, using new weapons lent her, to their shame, by traitors to the Republic '. In the House of Commons, Winston Churchill declared that what was going on in Ireland was ' not our business at all '. It was very much Britain's business. The 1921 settlement was Britain's settlement. Had the Civil War overthrown it, Britain was prepared to settle the matter – her way – again.

This time, Britain's settlement had the support, or rather, exhausted acceptance, not only of Irish common sense and realism, but of Irish conservatism. This time, in contrast to 1916, the forces of Irish conservatism were not caught unawares. The majority of Irishmen stood by the Free State. So did the Church. The Church not only supported the Treaty but in October 1922 unequivocally condemned the republicans as conducting not war but ' a system of murder and assassination '. The Irish bishops, speaking as a body, went further still, denying to republicans the sacramental consolations of religion, absolution in Confession and admission to Holy Communion. Condemnation was bad enough, but excommunication was much more serious: political fortunes were one thing, the fate of one's soul another. The actual effect of the October 1922 Pastoral in weakening the republican cause was probably considerable, but difficult to determine: its immediate effect was to occasion the republicans to appeal to Rome against the bishops' decision to withhold the sacraments from them, an appeal sufficiently urgent and vigorous to bring a papal representative to Ireland to investigate the situation; but he achieved nothing.

The Church's attitude certainly damaged its relationship with those of strong republican viewpoint. Many active republicans felt betrayed:

having sided with the republican nationalism of 1916-21 – or so it seemed – the Church now seemed to have deserted its former position. But aggrieved republicans had their vengeance: there was much truth in Dan Breen's pungent summary, ' The Civil War was bad, but it saved us this much – it saved us from the government of Maynooth. The people were split on the issue of the Treaty but the Hierarchy went out and attacked the Republic, threw bell, book and candle at it in nearly every pulpit in the country. And they drove one half of the people against them with the result that they never regained the power they once had '.

This was so. The Church's stand in the Civil War disillusioned if it did not alienate many Irishmen. But there was more to the death of aspiring theocracy than that: it suffered multiple injuries. Many of these, perhaps those most fatal, were inflicted by the Civil War. Ireland, in the years immediately following the Anglo-Irish Treaty, was no environment for religious idealism. In that decisive period politics and violence dominated Irish life, pushing out everything else. Until late in 1923, the question was not one of building some new Ireland, but of whether the new government could survive as a government. After 1923 Ireland remained bitterly divided, political contention blotting out almost all other questions and issues, dividing everything and everybody, the Church included. And anyhow, by 1923, the atmosphere that might have produced theocracy was quite dispelled. The Civil War had engaged the Irish upon the slaughtering of their own dreams and ideals. The myth of the holy Irish was one of the major casualties of the Civil War. Not quite killed perhaps, but gravely wounded, as the world's most Catholic people set about destroying and maiming each other, one side in flagrant disregard of religious authority, all caught in the demoralising morass of fratricidal violence. Religion, nationalism, authority, all were challenged and trampled by that galloping anarchy; nothing of renascent Ireland emerged quite unscathed, and the things most fragile – dreams, hopes, utopian ideals of saints and scholars – were shattered.

There were other factors militating against a Church dominance of the new Irish state. One was partition. This cut across the diocesan structure of the Church, and by 1922, the religious situation in Northern Ireland had lapsed into a condition of intermittent and often murderous sectarian war: the attention of Catholics and their Church in the South was naturally focused on the fate of their brethren separated politically in the North. Moreover the Free State government, though in no way hostile to the Church, was anxious that its dominant Catholicism be not reflected formally: it sought to win the allegiance of Unionists, and, of course, wished to place no religious obstacles in the way of a prompt ending of partition. In consequence, the first constitution of the Irish Free State in 1922 was carefully secular in its whole approach to religion, and made no provision for episcopal representation: separation of church and state was complete. Partition, and the hope that it would be soon ended, made religious neutrality in politics essential.

As the Free State gradually settled down, this formal religious neutrality began to irk or scandalise some of the aggressively devout. In 1930, Rev. E. Cahill, s.j., began his *Ireland's Peril*, published by *An Rioghacht* (The League of the Kingship of Christ) with the observation, ' In Ireland we are confronted with the strange anomaly of a profoundly Catholic nation, devoid of many of the external features of a Catholic civilisation, and suffering from all the material, and very many of the mental defects which usually result from an un-Christian social *régime* '. There was a great deal of this kind of criticism, but it too was politically split. Father Cahill's comments implied censure of the Cosgrave government, which was also the *bête noir* of that paragon of Irish republican piety, the *Catholic Bulletin*. Against this, many Catholics, amongst them a substantial body of clergy, were distrustful – in a legacy of the Civil War condemnation – of de Valera and his Fianna Fáil party: in 1937 Leo McCabe published a book substantially devoted to the frenzied allegation that de Valera was still unrepentant of his disobedience to the teaching of the Church. In that same year, de Valera's government introduced a new constitution which had a distinctly Catholic flavour. In relation to religion it announced ' The State recognises the special position of the Holy Catholic Apostolic and Roman Church as the guardian of the faith professed by the great majority of the citizens '. Other clauses prohibited divorce legislation and were generally of such a kind as to attract the praise of Pope Pius XII for manifesting Catholic and Christian principles. But further than this – and it was not very far – into the realm of a confessional state Irish politicians would not go. As has been said, extremist religious pressure in that direction was divided in its political allegiance – or anathemas – between the two major parties that had emerged from the civil war. Besides, the traditional tendency in Irish religion to avoid social issues tended to make its proposals, so far as practical legislation went, confused, unreal, peripheral, naïve – and dominantly negative: prohibitions, restrictions and limitations had little appeal as a legislative programme, and the initiative remained with the politicians. It remained with them also because, on the whole they shared the Church's values and views. What champion of Irish religion could seriously criticise a politician who could say, and passionately mean, as de Valera did, ' The Ireland we dreamed of would be the home of a people who valued material wealth only as the basis of a right living, of a people who were satisfied with a frugal comfort and devoted their leisure to the things of the spirit. It would, in a word, be the home of a people living the life that God desires men to live '.

So, in the years that followed the Treaty it was not religion that dominated Irish politics, but the English question, the matter of the connection with England. Until 1927 the consequence was one party government in Ireland, because de Valera's party would have nothing to do with an English manufactured political system which incorporated an oath of allegiance and partition. After 1927 when Fianna Fáil entered the Dáil – with revolvers hidden in their pockets – the Civil War was fought again in fierce debate. In power from 1932 to 1948, de Valera launched a campaign to cut the ties with England. In 1933 he secured the removal of the oath of allegiance, in 1936 the abolition of the office of Governor-General. Meanwhile, from 1932 to 1938 he conducted economic war with Britain, a refusal on his part to pay annuities, mainly arising out of earlier land purchases, leading to six years of mutually injurious tariff war. This was ended by the London agreements of 1938 which settled the annuity dispute and also restored to Ireland the ports held by Britain since the Treaty. The natural culmination of this line of policy was Irish neutrality in the 1939-45 war, prompting Churchill, late in 1939, to urge the British Cabinet to repossess the Irish ports by force, but in fact not leading to any major crisis in the relationship between Ireland and Britain. In this, partition was a vital factor, for military access to Northern Ireland made it possible for Britain to be relatively indifferent to the existence of a neutral Éire. The 1949 declaration of an Irish Republic made formal a situation which had existed in fact since 1937.

But on one major aspect of the English question, no Irish government made any impression whatever. That was the situation created by the Government of Ireland Act of 1920 – partition. The only occasion on which Britain opened that matter was in the crisis of 1940 when the War Cabinet offered (apparently without the knowledge of the Northern Ireland Government) to approve the principle of a united Ireland, in return for the Free State's abandoning its neutrality – which de Valera refused.

2
The Continuing Question: Northern Ireland

Partition petrified Northern Ireland as a historical fossil. In the decade between 1911 and 1921 Anglo-Irish relations reached the point of decisive crisis, but all was not changed utterly. Britain answered the Irish question only in part: its answer to the Ulster question gravely qualified its answer to the Irish question *in toto,* and it was an answer which allowed Ulster to continue to opt out of history. In 26 counties, Counter Reformation Ireland, that historical and religious relic of the sixteenth and seventeenth centuries, went its way to face, within itself, the manifold problems of independent identity and adjustment in the twentieth century world. In six counties of the North, Reformation plantation Ireland, a determined vestige of the age of the battle of the Boyne, achieved for itself in 1920 – to be reinforced by the Ireland Act of 1949 – a charter of perpetuity from the British government. Northern Ireland received entitlement to preserve its own antiquity as a society based on Protestant Unionist ascendancy and anti-Catholic discrimination: as its first Prime Minister Sir James Craig put it, Northern Ireland had ' a Protestant Parliament for a Protestant people ', and the subsidiary political, social and economic structures followed suit. The outcome of partition was to reduce the traditional Irish question as it had formerly pertained to 32 counties, to the dimensions of six. The shrinkage converted a Protestant Unionist minority in Ireland as a whole to a majority in the Northern Ireland context, but it did not change the essential question, which remained, as it had always been, what was to be the status of Irish Catholics in the island of Ireland?

The partition question remained very much alive in Southern Ireland and among the Catholics of Northern Ireland, but the major effect of pressure towards all-Ireland unity, reaching occasional violent extremes in I.R.A. raids, was to tighten the hold of Protestant Ulster on its own anachronistic existence. And stagnant anachronism it was. Where other colonies of settlement – for such it was – diminished or severed their links with the mother country, Northern Ireland's whole rationale was based on being part of the United Kingdom. The creation of a subordinate legislature by the 1920 Act was something thrust on reluctant Ulster Unionists who did not want even that degree of weakening of the connection with Britain: in January 1969, Captain O'Neill, then Prime Minister, called on the Unionist party to make a right and generous response to times of stress and turmoil so that 'In what it says and what it does it can make the Union secure for all time'. In O'Neill's Ulster, attachment to Britain was preached as economic doctrine: 'It guarantees our standard of living; it makes it possible for us to develop here all the services of a modern industrial state.' O'Neill's 1969 Election manifesto was based on the premise that the economic benefits of the British connection should bridge the religious chasm – a premise which the totality of Irish history disproved. It was a premise based on invalid assumptions – 'let us assume that our [Catholic] fellow citizens have, for the most part, the same concerns as we do ourselves. They want a steady job. They want a decent home. They want the best for their children. They want, above all, to be allowed to live in peace.' To assume that economic interests and peace rated higher priorities with the Ulster minority than principles and emotion, than Catholicism, and nationalism and history and justice and hatred, was fatuity rather than creative hope. But the real and ultimate role of the British connection was demonstrated in August 1969 when Major Chichester-Clark made it clear that those who opposed or sought to overthrow the Unionist government were also facing the might of Britian, and when, in that month, the British army took over complete responsibility for law and order in Northern Ireland.

Ultimate reliance on British military force, demonstrated again in 1969-70, was, historically, the salient feature of Protestant ascendancy Ireland, and the broad similarities between the contemporary situation and that of the Protestant Irish Parliament of 1782-1800 are sufficient to be not lightly dismissed. The fact that, from 1920, Northern Ireland insisted on unchanging subordinate relationship with Britain, meant a good deal more than that Ulster was never forced (as the South was) to confront and deal with its own problems as an autonomous self-assessing unit. The North's refusal to stand on its own feet meant that it remained a gross and grotesque dependency, refusing to take ultimate responsibility for its own actions and policies – a disposition evident in the anger and concern shown by the government of Northern Ireland in April 1970 when General Freeland's comments were interpreted as warning that British troops would be withdrawn, and Ulster left to her fate. Seen thus, Britain's passive role in the half century following 1920 had been to provide the ultimate guarantee for the continued existence of an area of grave political irresponsibility within Britain's own realm. True, the irresponsibility was not evident, or at least not politically accountable, until it was seriously challenged, but it nonetheless damaged, diminished and warped all those involved in it. Although the causes of the situation lay within Northern Ireland, Britain was ultimately responsible, a fact which sustained and fed the odium and hatred in which Britain had been held by the Catholic Irish. That this could be overlaid by the recognition that Britain might be protection against the Ulster government and militant Protestantism, and the only power that could effect, by its pressure, reform in the North, did not alter the basic emotion: the I.R.A. stands in virtual declaration of war against the British army; and militant Catholics accept that army only in its anti-Protestant policing activities.

The British connection was not the only area of stagnant anachronism, though it sustained all the others. Northern Ireland's internal politics were dominated and dictated by the British connection. The political issue which dwarfed all others was the maintenance of the Union: politics consisted in being for or against that, which meant that the greatest internal, domestic question was always one essentially of external relations. The consequences have been pernicious – one party government since 1920, opposition identified with disloyalty, and destruction of the state, the vitiation of socio-economic forces – such as the labour movement – which had creative potential, the continuance of a conservative regime initially established on the basis of bigotry and sectarian discrimination, generally, the isolation of the North from the major forces of twentieth century change, other than the narrowly economic.

And at the core of everything lay religion, Reformation and Counter-Reformation confronting each other in intolerance as they had done for centuries. Just how stagnant was that situation can be illustrated only too readily: compare, for example, the Ulster situation of 1969-70 with a comment made by Sir Horace Plunkett in 1904 – ' I happened to remark to a friend that it was a disgrace to Christianity that Mussilman soldiery were employed at the Holy Sepulchre to keep the peace between the Latin and Greek Christians. He reminded me that the prosperous and progressive municipality of Belfast, with a population eminently industrious and predominantly Protestant, has to be policed by an Imperial force in order to restrain two sections of Irish Christians from assaulting each other in the name of religion.' The fact that, save for the 1935 riots, the situation between 1922 and 1964 was relatively quiet, evidenced the suppression of the religious question, not any temporary solution to it. Suppression drove the old hates and fears deeper, entrenched the old loyalties and prejudices, stored up more fuel for eventual fires. That Ulster was divided into two hostile religious camps seemed, into the 1960s, largely a mere fact of life, the necessary social essence of North-

ern Ireland as a state, at least in the view of the Unionist establishment –
which, in any case, strongly tended to regard Ulster as its preserve, to
which the question of Catholic access was hardly relevant. When this
situation came under liberal criticism as discreditable and wrong – a
relatively recent development – Unionists placed the entire blame for
Ulster's divisions on the Catholic Church. Captain O'Neill declared in
February 1964, 'Where there is "apartheid" in our society it comes
almost entirely from a voluntary separation from the mainstream of
our public and social life. This starts at an early age with the insistence
that certain children cannot attend State schools. . . . But it is not the
State which bars anyone from any of its institutions; the act of isolationism comes from another quarter'. Rendered down to its essentials, the
Prime Minister's analysis was not very different from that of extremist
Ulster Protestantism – that the Catholic Church and its policies were the
cause of all Ulster's discontents. All would be well if all the inhabitants
of Ulster accepted the the self-evident truths of Unionism: that a
minority did not was traceable to their perverse religious beliefs. Holding such views, it was hardly consistent or profound of the Prime
Minister to attempt to purchase peace with prosperity, as did his British
Unionist forebears in the 1890s but he did at least endeavour to build
necessary bridges between Catholics and Protestants on grounds of
equal civil rights: the Unionist foundation for these bridges collapsed
under him in April 1969 and he resigned.

Miss Devlin is right to say that the Northern Ireland situation should
be a question of economic and civil rights, a rectifying of injustice, the
abolition of discrimination – but this is the twentieth century reprimand-
ing the seventeenth. What should be and what is, can be readily distin-
guished. The economic interpretation of Irish history, whether pro-
pounded by conservative Unionists, or radicals, or Christian socialists,
has always been superficial, and misleading in its advocated solutions.
There can be no doubt that Unionists have traditionally encouraged religious bigotry to maintain their own privileged ascendancy. They have
also exploited the socialist aspects of minority agitation – dubbing Miss
Devlin 'Fidel Castro in a mini-skirt' – in attempts to divide Catholic
opposition. Nor can it be said that poverty, jobs and housing are not
vital, urgent and bitter grievances. Yet to diagnose the current Ulster
question as merely or mainly economic is shallow and unreal. The deepest
and most real division is religious. To argue that this cannot be so
because Christianity teaches fraternal love, or that the evident bigotry,
hatred and violence demonstrates that what purports to be religion is
not religion at all, but an outworn label for something else quite unholy,

misses the key point: in the stagnant anachronism that is Northern Ireland, popular religion – particularly that form of it held, or residually held, by the socially ascendant group – has not evolved past the age of the wars of religion, the seventeenth century. The fossil has lived so long that its living complexion seems but a mask.

Who can doubt the sincerity and power of the person and message of the Rev. Ian Paisley? Paisley's passionate crusade – for that is what it is – consists of a heady mixture of crude religious principles, traditional Ulster politics and fear. This brew does not accord with the modern recipe for religion, but its alchemy is very familiar to any student of the religion of the Reformation. The religious core of primitive Protestantism is clear in Paisleyism. All men are not children of God: some few are elected to be saved. Roman Catholicism is the Anti-Christ, Greatest of All Heresies, Mother of Harlots, Whore of Babylon, Enemy of Godliness and Freedom – the ancient clichés roll sonorously out. The tongue is, as with the first Protestors, lurid, unrestrained, violently abusive: ' Cardinal Conway cants with the hypocrisy dripping from his polluted lips . . . the scum of his distorted thinking . . . his corpulate belly, his extravagant (albeit effeminate) dress and luxurious surroundings . . . Rome's hatred of Protestantism seeps through almost every word and sentence . . . deep hatred and dark bigotry . . . blasphemy . . .' The religious oratory is seemingly innocent of charity, moderation, ideas: it is a fierce blast of righteousness and emotion. Added to this is a dash of traditional historical bitters. Mr Paisley's election posters in April 1970 carried the slogan ' Remember 1690 ', the date of William of Orange's victory over the Catholic Irish at the battle of the Boyne: a ludicrous absurdity in other political traditions, the backward look goes to the heart of the convictions and emotions on which modern Ulster was built. Then there is the linkage between religion and politics. Paisleyism's political message is that its religious truths must be enshrined for ever in Ulster's political structures. Reforms which would end discrimination against Catholics would be a betrayal: ' We call upon thee, O Lord, to rid us of the arch-traitor, the Prime Minister, Captain Terence O'Neill ', ' The Unionist Party cannot barter our heritage '. Then there is the appeal to fears which have ancient roots – the claim that the Unionist party has failed to stop the hideous growth of Catholicism and Irish nationalism, that there are two states and two governments in operation in Northern Ireland, that there is ' a monster in our midst ', that ' a rebellion will break out '. To top all this off is the burning sense of divine mission, the confidence that God is on Paisley's side. ' Tonight's victory ', said Mr Paisley at his election to the Northern Ireland Parliament in April 1970, 'belongs only to almighty God, whose intervention insured it'.

Paisley is no spectacular and isolated throw-back from by-gone ages. His evident grass-roots support, capped by his election, make it clear that he is seen by a very substantial portion of Ulster opinion as, to use the words of a supporter, 'the Man of God for our time'. Looking in on Ireland from the secular world of the 1970s, Paisley may seem on the eccentric fringe. In fact he is squarely in the continuing tradition of Protestant Ulster. As Captain O'Neill told the Ulster Unionist Council in 1965, 'Let no one in Ireland, North or South, no one in Great Britain, no one anywhere make the mistake of thinking that, because there is talk of a new Ulster, the Ulster of Carson and Craig is dead'. His emphasis in that context was on the indissolubility of the Union, but the proposition applied to old Ulster generally. That it was far from dead O'Neill acknowledged in his resignation in April 1969 where he testified to his failure to break the chains of ancient hatreds, that Ulster had not taken the chance he had tried to give it to cast off old loyalties, old prejudices, old fears.

Nor should it be supposed that the North's fossilisation applied to Protestant Unionists alone: it affected all involved. In order to survive, in order to retain its vitality under discrimination, Catholicism tended to retreat into its ghetto and to maintain rigidly its side of the apartheid mentality. Protestant ascendancy bred an assumption of moral superiority, a righteous anger and resentment against those whose very presence in the community seemed a threat to its existence. The usual Catholic reaction to this was passive withdrawal, but under provocation, when majority prejudice and contempt was blatantly asserted in triumphal public processions, or unleashed in passionate or scurrilous abuse or actual violence, the Catholic response was of the same kind. Side by side with the urge to withdraw from a hostile society, the Catholicism of Northern Ireland retained a residuum of that aggressive Catholic utopian-ism that had marked all Ireland from the late 1880s to the Civil War. The triumphalist impetus and aspirations remained: as Miss Devlin has pointed out, the Civil Rights Association 'moved from demanding something for the minority (that is, the Catholics), to demanding Catholic equality; to demanding Catholic power.' A religious cause awaited – in vain – a religious leader: despite her refusal to accept the holy mantle of popular Catholic leadership, Miss Devlin was showered with pious titles – 'St Bernadette', 'St Joan of Arc', 'The Maid of Bogside', 'The Saint of Tyrone'.

In contrast with the bigoted realism of Mr Paisley's crusade, Miss

Devlin's hopes – for an all-Ireland working class revolution – seem utopian. On her own admission she is making little headway with the Protestant working class, too many of whom believe with Mr Paisley that ' The veins of Miss Devlin are polluted with the venom of Popish tuition.' Her socialism has come under Catholic episcopal criticism. Above all, an agitation for civil and economic rights for the deprived minority in Northern Ireland must amount in fact to a crusade for the rights of those who are Catholic in religion. The Northern Ireland situation is not conducive to any effective distinguishing in the movement towards change between citizenship or economic status, and religious affiliation – particularly when the Paisleyite movement is utterly determined to maintain the religious division and the discriminatory apparatus which supports it.

The internal dynamics of the situation remain religious ones. This is not easily discerned by secularists and liberals who tend to believe that what they see as out-moded and absurd can have no real strength. The religious factor also tends to be undervalued by Irish Catholic intellectuals whose own religion is that of the twentieth century not the seventeenth, and who have long been obsessed, blinded even, by the social conservatism of their own Church at episcopal and clerical levels. Their own vigorous criticism of this alleged conservatism is itself part of the evidence which suggests that they misconstrue, if not the social role of their Church, certainly the social role of their religion. There is much more to Irish Catholicism than the official pronouncements of the hierarchy: it is a set of values, a culture, a historical tradition, a view on the world, a disposition of mind and heart, a loyalty, an emotion, a psychology – and a nationalism. These popular aspects of Irish Catholicism have moulded Irish history, and Anglo-Irish relations, no less than the deliberate interventions of the hierarchy, and it is these aspects which are engaged in the North. Given that the Paisleyite forces of counter-revolution are already in the field in Ulster, the possibility of the eruption of some violent irrevocable act of revolt is perhaps something more than remote contingency. If 1911-14 or 1916-21 are periods of Irish history which might still offer relevant lessons, the apparent prior outrageousness, irrationality, or hopelessness of an appeal to violence are no true guides to measuring the possibility or potential of such acts.

Nor can the situation be considered in isolation from the Irish Republic. Partition was a major political obsession in Southern Ireland until the late 1950s. All kinds of arguments and principles were mustered against it, but the really enduring question was that of the position of the Catholic minority in the Six Counties. Deep concern and anger on this score was the stimulus for the republic's call in August 1969 for a

United Nations peace keeping force for Northern Ireland, and for its positioning of Irish army refugee camps near the border. It was this also which lay behind that serious political crisis in the Republic in May 1970 when two cabinet ministers were dismissed and a third resigned in connection with the matter of an alleged plot to smuggle arms to Catholic extremists in Northern Ireland. That some responsible politicians should entertain the possibility of military intervention by the Republic if there was another outbreak of violence in Ulster on the scale of August 1969 points to the depth and intensity of a feeling which is not so much the nationalist one against partition, but rather a general one of religious solidarity, seeking to defend the lives and rights of co-religionists under a system seen as violent persecution.

One way or another it seems that Britain will have to answer this last Irish question, will have to face what was avoided half a century ago, will have to impose the twentieth century on the seventeenth. Left to itself, the Unionist party under Paisleyite pressure seems unlikely to move far and fast enough along the path of reform. Left to itself, Northern Ireland invites the polarising violence of religious extremists, perhaps descent into greater bloodshed under the living dead weight of its own history.

Bibliography

The purpose of this selected bibliography is two-fold, to specify the major sources used, and to provide a general guide for further reading: books so suggested are marked with an asterisk. For definitive bibliographies of work in Irish history, the reader is referred to Helen F. Mulvey 'Modern Irish History Since 1940: A bibliographical Survey (1600-1922)' *The Historian* XXVII August 1965, the annual 'Writings on Irish history' published in *Irish Historical Studies*, 'Thirty years' work in Irish history (I)' *Irish Historical* Studies, Vol. XV, No. 60, September 1967 and 'Thirty years' work in Irish history (II)' *ibid*, Vol. XVI, No. 61, March 1968. For older works on the period 1870-1921, an exhaustive bibliography is given by James Carty *Bibliography of Irish History 1870-1911* (1940) and *Bibliography of Irish History 1912-1921* (1936). A useful recent bibliography is appended to J. C. Beckett *The Making of Modern Ireland 1603-1923* (1966). A major and definitive bibliographical compilation is proceeding with work on the projected *A New History of Ireland* to be completed in 1974.

The relative paucity of analytic writing on the precise question of Anglo-Irish relations, and the particular thematic organisation used in this book, make for a good deal of overlap from section to section in the relevance of many of the sources cited. To avoid repetition, such publications are arranged under the heading of ' General ', or in relation to that part or subdivision of the book to which they principally but not exclusively refer.

Unpublished material, most notably ecclesiastical correspondence, has been extensively consulted, particularly in relation to the period 1870-1921. Reference to these sources has been made in the Preface, and a further note appears under Part Three of this bibliography. The extent and variety of this material, the absence of organisation and cataloguing in some of the archives consulted, the conditions and limits of access laid down by ecclesiastical authorities, the demands of space and the general nature of this present book, are factors which combine to make it impossible to do more than to indicate to scholars in the most general terms the source locations of these collections.

General Histories

*Beckett, J. C. *A Short History of Ireland*, London, 3rd ed. 1966

*Beckett, J. C. *The Making of Modern Ireland 1603-1923*, London, 1966

Cullen, L. M. *Life in Ireland*, London and New York, 1968

Cullen, L. M. *The Formation of the Irish Economy*, Cork 1969

Curtis, Edmund *A History of Ireland*, London and New York, 6th ed. 1950, 1961 reprint

Curtis, E. and McDowell, R. B. *Irish Historical Documents 1172-1922*, London, 1943

Edwards, O. D. 'Ireland' in Edwards, O. D., Rhys, I., and Evans, G., MacDiarmid, H., *Celtic Nationalism*, London, 1968

Gwynn, Denis 'England and Wales' in *A History of Irish Catholicism*. General Editor, Patrick J. Corish, Vol. VI. Dublin and Sydney, 1968

Hayes-McCoy, G. A. *The Irish at War*, Cork, 1964

Jackson, J. A. *The Irish in Britain*, London and Cleveland, 1963

*MacDonagh, Oliver *Ireland*, New Jersey, Spectrum Book, 1968

*Mansergh, Nicholas *The Irish Question 1840-1921*, New and Rev. Ed., London, 1965

Maxwell, Constantia *The Stranger in Ireland*, London, 1954

McCaffrey, Lawrence J. *The Irish Question 1800-1922*, Lexington, 1968

*Moody, T. W. and Martin, F. X. *The Course of Irish History*, Cork 1967

O'Connor, Sir J. *History of Ireland 1798-1924*, 2 Vols., London, 1925

*O'Faolain, Sean *The Irish*, Middlesex, Penguin Books, 1947, New ed., 1970

O'Hegarty, P. S. *A History of Ireland under the Union*, London, 1952

*Strauss, E. *Irish Nationalism and British Democracy*, London, 1951

PART ONE: *The Range of Answers 1534-1800*

General

Cullen, L. M. *Anglo-Irish Trade 1660-1800*, Manchester, 1968

*Froude, J. A. *The English in Ireland in the Eighteenth Century*, 3 Vols., London, 1887

*Lecky, W. E. H. *A History of Ireland in the Eighteenth Century*, 5 Vols., London, 1892-96

Moran, Right Rev. Patrick Francis, D.D. *Spicilegium Ossoriense: Being a Collection of Original Letters and Papers illustrative of the History of the Irish Church from the Reformation to the Year 1800*, First Series, Dublin 1874, Second Series, Dublin 1878

O'Brien, George *The Economic History of Ireland in the Eighteenth Century*, Dublin and London, 1918

O'Brien, George *The Economic History of Ireland in the Seventeenth Century*, Dublin and London, 1919

1 Conquest

Abbot, W. C. *The Writings and Speeches of Oliver Cromwell*, 2 Vols. Cambridge, 1939

Black, J. B. *The Reign of Elizabeth 1558-1603*, 2nd ed., Oxford, 1963

*Bagwell, R. *Ireland Under the Stuarts and During the Interregnum*, 3 Vols., London, 1909-16

*Bagwell, R. *Ireland Under the Tudors*, 3 Vols., London, 1885, 1890

*Coonan, T. L. *The Irish Catholic Confederacy and the Puritan Revolution*, Dublin, London, New York, 1954

*Corish, Patrick J. 'The Origins of Catholic Nationalism' in *A History of Irish Catholicism*, Vol. III, Dublin and Sydney, 1968

Clarke, Aidan *The Old English in Ireland 1625-42*, London, 1966

Conway, Agnes *Henry VIII's Relations with Scotland and Ireland 1485-1498*, Cambridge, 1932

Dunlop, Robert *Ireland under the Commonwealth. Being a selection of Documents relating to the government of Ireland from 1651 to 1659*, 2 Vols., Manchester, 1913

*Edwards, R. D. 'Ireland, Elizabeth I and the Counter Reformation' in Bindoff, S. T., et al, *Elizabethan Government and Society*, London, 1961

Elton, G. R. *England under the Tudors*, London, 1955

Hodgen, Margaret T. *Early Anthropology in the Sixteenth and Seventeenth Centuries*, Philadelphia, 1964

*Jones, Frederick M. (C.S.S.R.) 'The Counter Reformation' in *A History of Irish Catholicism*, Vol. III, Dublin and Melbourne, 1967

Kearney, H. F. *Strafford in Ireland 1633-41*, Manchester, 1959

Mackie, J. D. *The Earlier Tudors 1485-1558*, Oxford, 1952

*Millet, Benignus (O.F.M.) 'Survival and Reorganisation 1650-95' in *A History of Irish Catholicism*, Vol. III, Dublin and Sydney, 1968

Mooney, Canice (O.F.M.) ' The First Impact of the Reformation ' in *A History of Irish Catholicism*, Vol. III, Dublin and Melbourne, 1967

Moran, Cardinal P. F. *Historical Sketch of the Persecutions Suffered by the Catholics of Ireland under the rule of Cromwell and the Puritans*, Dublin, 1907

Murphy, Rev. Denis S.J. *Cromwell in Ireland*, Dublin, 1883

*Quinn, D. B. *The Elizabethans and the Irish*, Ithaca, New York, 1966

Rothe, David *Analecta*, Edited with an introduction by Patrick F. Moran, Dublin, 1884

Simms, J. G. *Jacobite Ireland 1685-91*, London and Toronto, 1969

Simms, J. G. *The Treaty of Limerick*, Irish History Series No. 2, Dublin Historical Association, Dundalk, 1961

Wedgwood, C. V. *The King's Peace 1637-1641*, London, 1955

Wedgwood, C. V. *The King's War 1641-1647*, London, 1958

2 Colonisation

As for 1 above. See also:

Bowen, Elizabeth *Bowen's Court*, 2nd ed., London, 1964

Prendergast, J. P. *The Cromwellian Settlement of Ireland*, 2nd ed., London, 1870

3 Legal Discrimination

Dowling, P. J. *The Hedge Schools of Ireland*, Cork, 1968

Edwards, R. D. *Church and State in Tudor Ireland. A History of Penal Laws Against Irish Catholics 1534-1603*, Dublin, n.d.

Moran, Cardinal P. F. *The Catholics of Ireland Under the Penal Laws in the Eighteenth Century*, London, 1899

*Wall, Maureen *The Penal Laws, 1691-1760*, Dublin Historical Association History Series No. 1, 2nd ed., Dundalk, 1967

Williams, Basil *The Whig Supremacy 1714-1760*, Oxford, 1962

4 Self Government

Gwynn, Stephen *Henry Grattan and His Times*, London, 1939

*Harlow, Vincent T. *The Founding of the Second British Empire 1763-1793*, Vol. 1, London, 1952

*Johnston, Edith M. *Great Britain and Ireland 1760-1800. A Study in Political Administration*, London 1963

Koebner, Richard *Empire*, Cambridge, 1961

Marshall, D. *Eighteenth Century England*, London, 1962

312 BIBLIOGRAPHY

*O'Connell, M. R. *Irish Politics and Social Conflict in the Age of the American Revolution*, London and Philadelphia, 1966

Staples, Hugh B. (editor) *The Ireland of Sir Jonah Barrington*, London, 1968

Palmer, R. R. *The Age of the Democratic Revolution*, 2 Vols, Princeton, 1964

Schuyler, R. L. *Parliament and the British Empire. Some Constitutional Controversies Concerning Imperial Legislative Jurisdiction*, London, 1963, reprint of 1929 edition

Watson, J. Steven *The Reign of George III 1760-1815*, Oxford, 1960

PART TWO: *The Elements of the Question 1800-1870*

General

*Black, R. D. C. *Economic Thought and the Irish Question 1817-70*, Cambridge 1960

Eversley, Lord *Gladstone and Ireland. The Irish Policy of Parliament from 1850-1894*, London, 1912

*Hammond, J. L. *Gladstone and the Irish Nation*, London, 1938

Leslie, Shane *Henry Edward Manning. His Life and Labours*, London, 1921

Magnus, P. *Gladstone*, London, 1954

McDowell, R. B. *Public Opinion and Government Policy in Ireland 1801-1846*, London, 1952

McDowell, R. B. *The Irish Administration 1801-1914*, London, 1964

Morley, John *The Life of William Ewart Gladstone*, 2 Vols., London, 1905

*Norman, E. R. *Anti-Catholicism in Victorian England*, London, 1968

Woodward, Sir Llewellyn *The Age of Reform 1815-1870*, Oxford, 1962

1 The Nature of the Union

Barnes, D. G. *George III and William Pitt 1783-1806*, New York, 1965

*Bolton, G. C. *The Passing of the Irish Act of Union. A Study in Parliamentary Politics*, London, 1966

2 The Question of Religion

A Catholic Layman. *The Catholic Case Stated. National Education 1859*

*Akenson, D. H. *The Irish Education Experiment. The National System of Education in the Nineteenth Century*, London and Toronto, 1970

*Bell, P. M. H. *Disestablishment in Ireland and Wales*, London, 1969
*Broderick, John F. (S.J.) *The Holy See and the Irish Movement for the Repeal of the Union with England 1829-1847*, Rome, 1951
Burke, Very Rev. T. N. (O.P.) *Lectures and Sermons to which is added Ireland's Case Stated in Reply to Mr Froude*, New York, 1872
*Corish, P. J. 'Political Problems 1860-1878' in *A History of Irish Catholicism*, (General Editor Patrick J. Corish) Vol. v, Dublin and Melbourne, 1967
Curry, Rev. John *Daniel O'Connell*, Catholic Truth Society of Ireland, Dublin, n.d.
Cusack, M. F. *The Speeches and Public Letters of the Liberator*, 2 Vols., Dublin, 1875
Gash, N. *Mr Secretary Peel*, London, 1960
Gwynn, D. *The Struggle for Catholic Emancipation*, London, 1928
*Hughes, P. *The Catholic Question 1688-1829*, London, 1929
Jupp, P. J. 'II. Irish Parliamentary Elections and the Influence of the Catholic Vote, 1801-20.' *The Historical Journal*, X, 2 (1967), pp. 183-196
Keane, Most Rev. J. J. *O'Connell: Panegyric. In the Church of the Irish College, Rome Saturday, 15th May 1897*, Dublin, 1897
Larkin, Emmet 'Economic Growth, Capital Investment, and the Roman Catholic Church in Nineteenth Century Ireland.' *American Historical Review*, April 1967
Larkin, Emmet 'Church and State in Ireland in the Nineteenth Century.' *Church History*, XXI, September 1962
Lecky, W. E. H. *Leaders of Public Opinion in Ireland*. Vol. 2, Daniel O'Connell. London, 1912
M'Gee, Thomas Darcy *A History of the Attempts to Establish the Protestant Reformation in Ireland and the Successful Resistance of that People (Time:1540-1830)*, Boston, 1853
*Machin, G. I. T. *The Catholic Question in English Politics 1820 to 1830*, Oxford, 1964
MacSuibhne, P. *Paul Cullen and his Contemporaries*, 3 Vols., Naas, 1961, 1962, 1965
Moran, P. F. (edit.) *The Letters of Rev. James Maher D. D.*, Dublin, 1877
*Norman. E. R. *The Catholic Church and Irish Politics in the Eighteen Sixties*, Irish History Series No. 5. Dublin Historical Association, Dundalk, 1965
*Norman, E. R. *The Catholic Church and Ireland in the Age of Rebellion 1859-1873*, London, 1965

*O'Faoláin, S. *King of the Beggars. A Life of Daniel O'Connell; the Irish Liberator, in a Study of the Rise of the Modern Irish Democracy 1775-1847*, London, 1938

O'Reilly, Bernard *John MacHale. Archbishop of Tuam. His Life, Times and Correspondence*, 2 Vols., New York and Cincinnati, 1890

*Reynolds, J. A. *The Catholic Emancipation Crisis in Ireland, 1823-1829*, New Haven, 1954

Tierney, M. (ed.) *Daniel O'Connell*, Dublin, 1948

Whately, E. Jane *Life and Correspondence of Richard Whately D.D.* London, 1868

*Whyte, John H. ' Political Problems 1850-1860.' in *A History of Irish Catholicism* (General Editor Patrick J. Corish) Vol. v, Dublin and Melbourne, 1967

Whyte, J. H. ' The Influence of the Catholic Clergy on Elections in Nineteenth-century Ireland.' *English Historical Review*, LXXV, 259, 1960

3 The Repeal Question

Fitzpatrick, W. J. *The Life, Times, and Correspondence of the Right Rev. Dr. Doyle*, 2 Vols., Dublin, 1880

J. K. L. (Bishop Doyle) *Letters on the State of Ireland*, Dublin, 1825

MacDonagh, M. *Bishop Doyle*, London and Dublin, 1896

MacIntyre, Angus *The Liberator. Daniel O'Connell and the Irish Party 1830-1847*, London, 1965

Maguire, J. F. *Father Mathew: A Biography*, London, 1863

McCaffrey, L. J. *Daniel O'Connell and the Repeal Year*, Kentucky, 1966

Murphy, J. A. ' The support of the Catholic Clergy in Ireland, 1750-1850.' in *Historical Studies V*, Papers read before the Sixth Conference of Irish Historians, London, 1965

Nowlan, Kevin B. ' The Meaning of Repeal in Irish History.' in *Historical Studies IV*, Papers read before the Fifth Irish Conference of Historians, London, 1963

*Nowlan, K. B. *The Politics of Repeal 1841-50*, London, 1965

O'Connell, D. *A Memoir on Ireland, Native and Saxon*, Dublin, 1854

4 The Question of Survival

Carleton, William *The Black Prophet. A Tale of Irish Famine*, With an introduction by D. J. O'Donoghue, London, 1899, First published 1847

*Edwards, R. D. and Williams, T. D. (editors) *The Great Famine. Studies in Irish History 1845-52*, Dublin, 1956

Freeman, T. W. *Pre-Famine Ireland. A Study in Historical Geography*, Manchester, 1957

Mitchel, J. *Jail Journal* with a preface by Arthur Griffith, Dublin, 1921

Mitchel, J. *The History of Ireland from the Treaty of Limerick to the Present Time*, Glasgow, 1869

Mitchel, J. *The Last Conquest of Ireland. (Perhaps)*, London, n.d.

*Woodham-Smith, Cecil *The Great Hunger. Ireland 1845-9*, London, 1962

5 The Land Question

Carleton, William *Traits and Stories of the Irish Peasantry*, 4 Vols., Boston 1911, first published 1830-33

*Connell, K. H. *Irish Peasant Society. Four Historical Essays*, Oxford, 1968

Danaher, Kevin *Irish Country People*, Cork, 1966

McDowell, R. B., (edit.) *Social Life in Ireland 1800-45*, Dublin, 1957

Richey, A. G. *The Irish Land Laws*, London, 1880

Steele, E. D. 'Ireland and the Empire in the 1860s. Imperial Precedents for Gladstone's First Irish Land Act.' *The Historical Journal*, XI, I, 1968, pp. 64-83

*Trench, W. Steuart *Realities of Irish Life*, with a Preface by Patrick Kavanagh, London, 1966, first published 1868

*Whyte, J. H. *The Independent Irish Party 1850-9*, Oxford, 1958

*Whyte, J. H. *The Tenant League and Irish Politics in the eighteen-fifties*, Irish History Series, No. 4, Dublin Historical Association, Dundalk, 1963

6 The Question of a Revolutionary Tradition

Ayres, Christopher V. H. 'A Comparative Survey of Major Irish Writings on Rebellion *c.* 1798 to 1922.' B.A. Honours Thesis, University of New South Wales, 1969

Boyle, J. W. (edit.) *Leaders and Workers*. Cork, n.d.

Cerowski, H. J. 'Poland in 1846-48 seen through Irish eyes.' M.A. Thesis, University College, Dublin, n.d.

Davis, Thomas *The Patriot Parliament of 1689*, edited with an Introduction by The Hon. Sir Charles Gavan Duffy, London, Dublin, New York, 1893

Dillon, William *Life of John Mitchel*, 2 Vols., London, 1888

Duffy, Sir C. G. *My Life in Two Hemispheres*, 2 Vols., London, 1898

Duffy, Sir C. G. *Young Ireland. A Fragment of Irish History 1840-45*, final revision, 2 Vols., London, 1896

Duffy's Irish Catholic Magazine, 1847

Edwards, R. D. 'The contribution of Young Ireland to the development of the Irish national idea' *Feilscribhinn Torna*, Cork, 1944

Fitzsimon, R. D. 'The Irish Government and the Phoenix Society' M.A. Thesis, University College Dublin, 1965

Fogarty, L. *James Fintan Lalor. Patriot and Political Essayist (1807-1849)* Dublin, 1918

*Harmon, Maurice (editor) *Fenians and Fenianism*, Dublin, 1968

MacDermot, Frank *Theobald Wolfe Tone*, Tralee, 1968

Madden, R. R. *The United Irishmen, their lives and Times*, First Series, 2nd ed. Dublin, 1858

*Moody, T. W. (ed.) *The Fenian Movement*, Cork, 1968

O'Hegarty, P. S. *John Mitchel*, Dublin and London, 1917

O'Leary, John *Recollections of Fenians and Fenianism*, 2 Vols., London, 1896

*Pakenham, Thomas *The Year of Liberty. The Great Irish Rebellion of 1798*, London, 1969

Penny Readings for The Irish People, (Compiled by the Editor of the 'Nation') Vol. 1, Dublin, 1879

Ryan, Desmond *The Fenian Chief. A biography of James Stephens*, Dublin and Sydney, 1967

Ryan, Desmond *The Phoenix Flame. A study of Fenianism and John Devoy*, London, 1937

Senior, H. *Orangeism in Ireland and Britain 1795-1836*, London 1966

Sullivan, A. M., *New Ireland: Political Sketches and Personal Reminiscences of Thirty Years of Irish Public Life*, Glasgow, 8th ed., 1882

Talmon, J. R. *Political Messianism. The Romantic Phase*, London, 1960

Tone, William Theobald Wolfe (ed.) *Life of Theobald Wolfe Tone*, 2 Vols., Washington, 1826

Wall, Maureen ' The United Irish Movement ' in *Historical Studies V.*, Papers read before the Sixth Conference of Irish Historians, London, 1965

7 *Some Questions of British Opinion*

*Curtis, L. P. *Anglo-Saxons and Celts. A Study in Anti-Irish Prejudice in Victorian England*, Connecticut, 1968

Neville, Henry Canon *A Few Comments on Mr Gladstone's Expostulation*, London, 1875

Fox, J. A. *A Key to The Irish Question. Mainly compiled from the Speeches and Writings of Eminent British Statesmen and Publicists, Past and Present*, London, 1890

PART THREE: *The Question Posed 1870-1921*

In this part, particular use has been made of unpublished materials, notably those drawn from the following ecclesiastical archives, within the various limits of access laid down by the appropriate authorities: All Hallows College, Dublin; the Archdiocese of Sydney; the Archives of the Primate of Ireland at Armagh; the Diocese of Limerick; the Irish College, Rome; the Irish College, Salamanca. Other unpublished materials used were: 'Denis McCullough' and 'P. McCarten Memo' (Typescripts lent by Fr F. X. Martin); Rev. Bernard Smith 'Maynooth Mission Booklet' (Typescript lent by Fr C. Hally).

Extensive use has been made of the collections of pamphlets and clippings from Irish newspapers 1873-1940 held in the archives of the Archdiocese of Sydney, and of the files of the following newspapers and periodicals: *Catholic Bulletin; Irish Catholic; Irish Messenger of the Sacred Heart; Irish Review, Irish Rosary; Little Flower Monthly; Lyceum; New Ireland Review.*

General

Ensor, Sir Robert *England 1870-1914*, Oxford, 1936

Hay, Ian *The Oppressed English*, Sydney, 1918

*Lyons, F. S. L. *John Dillon. A Biography*, London, 1968

*Lyons, F. S. L. *The Irish Parliamentary Party 1890-1910*, London, 1951

MacVeagh, J. *Home Rule in a Nutshell*, Dublin and London, 1911

*Mansergh, Nicholas *The Commonwealth Experience*, London, 1969

MacDonald, W. *Reminiscences of a Maynooth Professor*, edited with a memoir by Denis Gwynn. Cork, 1967

Miller, D. W. 'The Roman Catholic Church in Ireland: 1898-1918', *Eire-Ireland*, Vol. III, No. 3, Autumn 1968

O'Casey, Sean *Autobiographies*, 2 Vols., London, 1963

O'Donnell, F. H. *A History of the Irish Parliamentary Party*, 2 Vols., London, 1910

Walsh, P. J. *William J. Walsh. Archbishop of Dublin*, London and New York, 1928

1 The Home Rule Question

Koebner, R. & Schmidt, H. D. *Imperialism. The Story and Significance of a Political Word, 1840-1960*, Cambridge, 1965

MacDonagh, M. *The Home Rule Movement*, Dublin and London, 1920

MacNeill, J. G. Swift *The Constitutional and Parliamentary History of Ireland Till the Union*, Dublin and London, 1917

'*One of Them*' *Ireland and the English Catholics With Some Account of Events Leading up to the Appointment of Monsignor Persico as Papal Commissioner*, London, 1887

Thornley, D. *Isaac Butt* London, 1964

2 The Question of Land War

Cashman. D. B. *The Life of Michael Davitt, Founder of the National Land League to which is added, the Secret History of the Land League by Michael Davitt*, Glasgow, n.d.

Clancy, John J. *The Position of the Irish Tenant: A Reply*, London, 1888

Davitt, Michael *The Fall of Feudalism in Ireland or The Story of the Land League Revolution*, London and New York, 1904

Mahon, Hugh *The Land League: A Narrative of Four Years of Irish Agitation*, Sydney, 1883

Moody, T. W. 'The New Departure in Irish Politics 1878-9', In Cronne, H. A. *et al* (ed.) *Essays in British and Irish History in Honour of James Eadie Todd*, London, 1949

*O'Brien, C. C. *Parnell and His Party 1880-90*, Oxford, 1964

Pomfret, J. E. *The Struggle for Land in Ireland*, Princeton, 1930

McCarthy, Michael J. F. *The Irish Revolution*. Vol. 1. The Murdering Time, from the Land League to the First Home Rule Bill. Edinburgh and London, 1912

Savage, D. C. 'The Irish Unionists: 1867-1886', *Eire-Ireland*, Vol. 2, No. 3, Autumn 1967

3 The Question of Parnell's Ascendancy

Cooke, A. B. & Vincent, J. R. 'Select documents: XXVII Ireland and Party Politics, 1885-7: An Unpublished Conservative Memoir', *Irish Historical Studies*, Part I in Vol. XVI, No. 62, Sept., 1968, Part II in No. 63, March 1969, Part III in No. 64, Sept., 1969

*Lyons, F. S. L. *Parnell*, Irish History Series No. 3, Dublin Historical Association, Dundalk, 1963

4 Religious and Moral Questions

Historicus Dr. O'Dwyer, *The Pope, and the Irish Party*, 1890

Larkin, E. ' Mounting the Counter-Attack: The Roman Catholic Hierarchy and the Destruction of Parnellism ', *Review of Politics*, xxv, April 1963

Larkin, E. ' Launching the Counter-attack: Part II of The Roman Catholic Hierarchy and the Destruction of Parnellism ', *Review of Politics*, xxviii, July 1966

Larkin, E. ' The Roman Catholic Hierarchy and the Fall of Parnell ', *Victorian Studies*, IV, June 1961

*Lyons, F. S. L. *The Fall of Parnell 1890-91*, London, 1964

Stead, William T. *The Discrowned King of Ireland*, London, 1891

5 The Question Avoided

Colins, Mary E. ' Irish Public Opinion and the Boer War ', M.A. Thesis, University College Dublin, n.d.

*Curtis, L. P. Jr. *Coercion and Conciliation in Ireland 1880-1892. A Study in Conservative Unionism*, New Jersey, 1963

Dicey, A. V. *England's Case Against Home Rule*, London, 1887

Dunraven, The Earl of, *The Outlook in Ireland: The Case for Devolution and Conciliation*, Dublin and London, 1907

Good, J. W. *Irish Unionism*, Dublin, 1920

National League *Mr. Balfour's Coercion Record in Ireland, From August 18th, 1887 to February 6th 1888*, Dublin, 1888

Rosenbaum, S., (ed.) *Against Home Rule. The Case for Union*, London and New York, 1912

6 The Education Question

An Irish Priest *Wanted – An Irish University*, Dublin, 1909

Archbishop of Dublin (W. J. Walsh) *Statement of the Chief Grievances of Irish Catholics in the matter of Education, Primary, Intermediate, and University*, Dublin, 1890

Auchmuty, J. J. *Irish Education. A Historical Survey*, Dublin and London, 1937

Curry, Rev. John *Dr Starkie and the Catholic Clerical National School Managers of Ireland*, Dublin, 1903

Delany, W. (s.j.) *Irish University Education. A Plea for Fair Play,* Dublin, Belfast, Cork, 1904

Halinan, Right Rev. Monsignor *The Management of Primary Schools in Ireland,* Dublin, 1911

Nulty, Most Rev. T. *Supplemental Appendix to the Essay entitled The Relations existing between Convent Schools, and the Systems of Intermediate and Primary National Education,* Dublin, 1884

O'Dwyer, Bishop Edward Thomas *A University for Catholics in relation to the material interests of Ireland,* Catholic Truth Society of Ireland, Dublin, n.d.

O'Hickey, Rev. M. P. *An Irish University, or else* – Dublin and Waterford, 1909

O'Riordan, Rev. M. *A Reply to Dr. Starkie's Attack on the Managers of National Schools,* Dublin, 1903

Sacerdos (D.D.) *Primary Schools and their Management,* Privately Printed, 1907

Walsh, William J. *The Convent National Schools of Ireland,* reprinted from the *Contemporary Review,* March, 1892, for private circulation

7 The Question of Irish Nationalism

Arnold, Matthew *Irish Essays,* London, 1891

Boyle, J. W. 'The Rise of the Irish Labour Movement 1888-1907' Ph.D. Thesis, University of Dublin. Trinity College, 1961

Brown, Stephen J. (s.j.) *A Readers' Guide to Irish Fiction,* London 1910

Corkery, Daniel *The Fortunes of the Irish Language,* Cork, 1954

Coxhead, Elizabeth *Daughters of Erin,* London, 1965

Cullen, Rev. J. A. (s.j.) *Temperance Catechism and Total Abstinence Manual,* Dublin, 1891

Cullen, Rev. J. A. (s.j.) *The Pioneer Movement. Its Story and Origin,* Dublin, n.d.

Davis, R. P. 'The Rise of Sinn Féin 1891-1910', M.Litt. Thesis, University of Dublin, Trinity College, 1958

Davitt, Michael *The Rise of the Irish Movement,* Dublin and Waterford, 1910

Denson, A. (ed.) *Letters from AE,* London, New York, 1961

Dineen, Rev. P. S. *Lectures on the Irish Language Movement,* Dublin, 1904

Father Mathew Record, April 1911

Hallinan, Right Rev. Monsgr. *The Drink Question. Its relation to Church and State. Duties of both in regard to it,* Dublin, 1902

Healy, Most Rev. John *Papers and Addresses,* Dublin, 1909

Horgan, John J. *Parnell to Pearse. Some Recollections and Reflections,* Dublin, 1948

Hurley, James 'The Nationalism of Canon Sheehan' M.A. Thesis, University College, Cork, 1955

Hyde, Douglas *A Literary History of Ireland,* London, and Leipsic, 1910

Irish Association for the Prevention of Intemperance *Opinions of Irish Bishops and Other Divines, in favor of Sunday Closing and Saturday Early Closing of Public Houses in Ireland,* Dublin, 1888

Kingston, William 'The Genesis of Sinn Féin' M.A. Thesis, University College, Dublin, 1949

Lynd, Robert *Ireland a Nation,* London, 1919

Maher, L. *Temperance in Ireland,* Catholic Truth Society of Ireland, Dublin, 1959

McCarthy, Michael J. F. *Priests and People in Ireland,* Dublin and London, 1903

McKenna, Rev. J. *Life and Work of Rev. James Aloysius Cullen S. J.,* London, 1924

Moran, Cardinal P. F. *The Priests and People of Ireland in The Nineteenth Century,* Dublin, n.d. [1905]

Murphy, Rev. Thomas A. *The Literature Crusade in Ireland,* Limerick, 1912

*O'Brien, C. C. (ed.) *The Shaping of Modern Ireland,* London, 1960

O'Connor, U. *Oliver St. John Gogarty,* London, 1964

Official Record of the National Catholic Total Abstinence Congress and All-Ireland Demonstration, Dublin June 24th-28th 1914, Dublin, 1914

O'Hegarty, P. S. *Sinn Féin. An Illumination,* Dublin and London, 1919

O'Riain, W. P. *Lessons from Modern Language Movements. What Native Speech has achieved for Nationality,* Gaelic League, Dublin, n.d.

O'Riordan, Rev. M. *Catholicity and Progress in Ireland,* London and St Louis, 1906

O'Rourke, Canon *The Battle of The Faith in Ireland,* Dublin, 1887

Plunkett, Sir Horace *Ireland in the New Century,* London, 1904

Sheehan, Canon P. A. *Luke Delmege,* London and New York, 1932, first published, 1901

Sheehan, Canon P. A. *Geoffrey Austin: Student,* Dublin, n.d.

Sheehan, Canon P. A. *The Graves at Kilmorna,* London, 1926, first published, 1914

Sheehy, Michael *Is Ireland Dying? Culture and the Church in Modern Ireland,* London, 1968

Summary Statement of Reasons for The Establishment of a Catholic Association for Ireland, n.d. [1902]

*Thompson, William Irwin The Imagination of an Insurrection Dublin, Easter 1916, New York, 1967

Yeats, W. B. Autobiographies, London, 1955

Yeats, W. B. Collected Poems, London, 1952

8 The Ulster Question

Blake, R. The Unknown Prime Minister. The Life and Times of Andrew Bonar Law 1858-1923, London, 1955

Boyd, Andrew Holy War in Belfast, Tralee, 1969

Boylan, Rev. Patrick Catholicism and Citizenship in Self-Governed Ireland, Dublin, 1914

Buckland, P. J. 'The southern Irish unionists, the Irish question, and British politics, 1906-14', Irish Historical Studies, Vol. xv, No. 59, March 1967

Bulfin, William Rambles in Eirinn, Dublin, 1920, first ed. 1907

Churchill, W. S. The World Crisis 1911-18, London, rev. ed., 1951

Cross, C. The Liberals in Power 1905-14, London, 1963

*Dangerfield, G. The Strange Death of Liberal England, London, 1966, first published, 1935

Fanning, Ronan 'The unionist party and Ireland, 1906-10', Irish Historical Studies, Vol. xv, No. 58, September, 1966

Flynn, William J. How Irish County Councils Work, Dublin, 1907

Gill, Rev. Henry V. (s.j.) Catholic Ireland and its Future. No. 4. Irishmen As We Need Them, Dublin, 3rd ed., 1921

Handbook of the Ulster Question, Issued by the North Eastern Boundary Bureau. Dublin, 1923

Jenkins, R. Asquith, London, 1965

MacNeill, Eoin Shall Ireland be Divided, Dublin 1915

MacVeagh, Jeremiah 'Home Rule or Rome Rule.' The Truth about Religious Intolerance in Ireland, Sheffield, 1912

Marjoribanks, E. and Colvin, I. D. Life of Lord Carson, 3 Vols., London, 1932-6

Moody, T. W. & Beckett, J. C. Ulster Since 1800, London, rev. ed., 1957

*O'Broin, Leon The Chief Secretary. Augustine Birrell in Ireland, London, 1969

*Paor, Liam de Divided Ulster, Penguin Special, Middlesex, 1970

Ryan, A. P. *Mutiny at the Curragh*, London, 1956

Sibbitt, R. M. (A Member of the Order) *Orangeism in Ireland and Throughout the Empire*, 2 Vols, London, 1939

*Stewart, A. T. Q. *The Ulster Crisis*, London, 1967

9 The Question of the Irish Party

Gwynn, D. *John Redmond*, London, 1932

O'Brien, W. ' *The Party* ' *Who They Are and What They Have Done*, Dublin and London, 1917

O'Connor, James *A Plea For Home Rule*, Dublin, 1909

Pope Pius X *Some Errors respecting the Rights of Democracy*, foreword by His Eminence Cardinal Logue, Dublin, 1911

Redmond-Howard, J. *John Redmond. The Man and the Demand*, London, 1910

Spain, S. L. ' William O'Brien, the Reunion of the Irish Parliamentary Party in 1900, and the Land Act of 1903 ', M.A. Thesis, University College, Dublin, 1962

Stansky, P. *Ambitions and Strategies. The Struggle for Leadership in the Liberal Party in the 1890s*, Oxford, 1964

10 The Question of Rebellion

Barrett, Rev. E. Boyd *Effects of Strikes*, Dublin, 1914

Brinton, Crane *An Anatomy of Revolution*, Vintage Books, 1957

Caulfield, Max *The Easter Rebellion*, London, 1964

Choille, Breandon MacGiolla (ed.) *Intelligence Notes 1913-16, Preserved in the State Paper Office*, Dublin, 1966

' Coilin ' *Patrick H. Pearse. A Sketch of his Life*, Dublin, 1917

Colum, Pádraic *et al. The Irish Rebellion of 1916 and its Martyrs: Erin's Tragic Easter*, New York, 1916

Connolly, James *Labor, Nationality and Religion. Being a Discussion of the Lenten Discourses against Socialism delivered by Father Kane, S.J., in Gardiner Street Church, Dublin 1910*, Wellington, 1921

Connolly, J. *Labour in Ireland*, Dublin, 1948

Edwards, O. D. & Pyle, F. (eds.) *1916. The Easter Rising*, London, 1968

Greaves, C. D. *The Life and Times of James Connolly*, London, 1961

*Holt, E. *Protest in Arms*, London, 1960

Hurley, M. F. ' The tone of popular nationalist sentiment in Ireland as the setting for the policy of armed insurrection in 1916, M.A. Thesis, University College, Dublin, 1954

Jones, Francis P. *History of the Sinn Féin Movement and the Irish Rebellion of 1916*, New York, 1920

Larkin, Emmet *James Larkin. Irish Labor Leader 1876-1947*, London, 1965

Le Roux, L. N. *Patrick H. Pearse*, trans. D. Ryan, Dublin, Cork, Belfast, n.d. [1932]

Lynch, Diarmuid *The I.R.B. and The 1916 Rising*, (edited by Florence O'Donoghue), Cork, 1957

*Martin, F. X. (O.S.A.) (ed.) *Leaders and Men of the Easter Rising: Dublin 1916*, London, 1967

Martin, F. X. (O.S.A.) (ed.) *The Irish Volunteers 1913-1915*, Dublin, 1963

Martin, F. X. (O.S.A.) (ed.) 'The McCarten Documents, 1916', in *Glogher Record*, 1966

Martin, F. X. (O.S.A.) '*1916* – Myth, Fact and Mystery', *Studia Hibernia*, No. 7, 1967

McCay, Hedley *Padraic Pearse*, Cork, 1966

McDonnell, Rev. J. (S.J.) *Socialism and the Working Man*, Dublin, 1914

Newman, Jeremiah *Studies in Political Morality*, Dublin and London, 1962

*O'Broin, L. *Dublin Castle and the 1916 Rising*, Dublin, 1966

O Cathasaigh, P. *The Story of the Irish Citizen Army*, Dublin and London, 1919

Pearse, Padraic *Plays Stories Poems*, Dublin, 1966 reprint

Pearse, Padraic H. *Political Writings and Speeches*, Dublin, 1962 printing

Plunkett, Geraldine 'Joseph Plunkett's Diary of his Journey to Germany in 1915', *University Review*, Vol. 1, No. 11, 1958; 'The Insurrection of 1916' *ibid*. Vol. 2, Nos. 1-9, 1959

Snoddy, Patrick, O. P. 'Irish Revolutionary Movements 1913-1916', M.A. Thesis, University College, Dublin, 1963

11 The Question Changes

Beaslai, Piaras *Michael Collins and the Making of a New Ireland*, Dublin, 1926

Bennett, Richard *The Black and Tans*, London, 1959

Blácam, A. de *Towards the Republic. A Study of New Ireland's Social and Political Aims*, Dublin, 1919

Blácam, A. de *What Sinn Féin Stands For*, Dublin, 1921

Búrca, P. de, and Boyle, J. F. *Free State or Republic*, Dublin and London, 1922

Childers, Erskine *Military Rule in Ireland*, Dublin, 1920

Collins, Michael *The Path to Freedom*, Dublin and London, 1922

De Valera, Eamon *Ireland's Case Against Conscription*, Dublin and London, 1918

Ferris, William *The Gaelic Commonwealth*, Dublin, 1923

Figgis, Darrell *A Chronicle of Jails*, Dublin, 1918

Figgis, Darrell *A Second Chronicle of Jails*, Dublin, 1919

Figgis, Darrell *The Economic Case for Irish Independence*, Dublin and London, 1920

Figgis, Darrell *The Gaelic State in the Past and Future or ' The Crown of a Nation'*, Dublin and London, 1917

Gleeson, James *Bloody Sunday*, London, 1962

Gnáthai Gan Iarraidh *The Sacred Egoism of Sinn Féin*, Dublin and London, 1918

*Hancock, W. K. ' Saorstat Eireann ' in *Survey of British Commonwealth Affairs*, Vol. 1, London, 1937

Hughes, Katherine *English Atrocities in Ireland*, New York, 1920

Letter of His Lordship the Bishop of Down and Connor to the Committee of the Belfast Expelled Workers Fund November 20 1920

Macardle, Dorothy *The Irish Republic*, Dublin, 4th ed., 1951

McDonald, Rev. Walter *Some Ethical Questions of Peace and War with Special Reference to Ireland*, London, 1919

McDowell, R. B. *The Irish Convention 1917-18*, London and Toronto, 1970

MacSwiney, Terence *Principles of Freedom*, Dublin, 4th ed., 1964

O'Braonain, Cathaoir and others *Poets of the Insurrection. Padraic H. Pearse, Thomas MacDonagh, Joseph M. Plunkett, John F. MacEntee*, Dublin and London, 1918

O'Brien, William *The Downfall of Parliamentarianism*, Dublin and London, 1918

O'Duffy, Eimar *The Wasted Island*, London, 1919

O'Hegarty, P. S. *Ulster. A Brief Statement of Fact*, Dublin and London, 1919

O'Riordan, Right Rev. Monsignor *The Mission of St Patrick. A Witness to the Supernatural*, Rome, 1918

Taylor, A. J. P. *English History 1914-1945*, Oxford, 1965

*Williams, Desmond (ed.) *The Irish Struggle 1916-1926*, London 1966

PART FOUR: *The Question Answered?*

General

Breen, Dan *My Fight for Irish Freedom*, Dublin, 1924
*Coogan, T. P. *Ireland Since the Rising*, London, 1966
Donaldson, A. G. *Some Comparative Aspects of Irish Law*, Durham and London, 1957
Edwards, O. D. *Conor Cruise O'Brien introduces Ireland*, London, 1969
Gray, Tony *The Irish Answer*, London, 1966
*MacManus, Francis (ed.) *The Years of the Great Test 1926-39*, Cork, 1967
Medlicott, W. N. *Contemporary England 1914-1964*, London, 1967
*Nowlan, K. B. & Williams, T. D. *Ireland in the war years and after 1939-51*, Dublin, 1969
Report of the Irish Boundary Commmission 1925, introduction by Geoffrey J. Hand, Shannon, 1969

1 The Question of the Twenty-Six Counties

Cahill, Rev. E., (S.J.) *Ireland's Peril*, Dublin, 1930
Gallagher, F. *The Anglo-Irish Treaty*, London, 1965
*Harkness, D. W. *The Restless Dominion. The Irish Free State and the British Commonwealth of Nations 1921-31*, London and Dublin, 1969
McCabe, L. *Wolfe Tone and the United Irishmen. For or Against Christ?*, Vol. 1, London, 1937
McCracken, J. L. *Representative Government in Ireland. A Study of Dail Eireann 1919-48*, London, 1958
Neeson, Eoin *The Civil War in Ireland 1921-23*, Cork, 1966
*Pakenham, Frank *Peace by Ordeal*, London, 1935
Squires, J. H. ' A Comparison of the Attitudes of Dáil Eireann and the House of Commons to the " Articles of Agreement for a Treaty between Great Britain and Ireland December 6, 1921 " '. B.A. Honours Thesis, University of New South Wales, 1969
Stephan, E. *Spies in Ireland*, London, 1963
Taylor, Rex *Assassination. The death of Sir Henry Wilson and the tragedy of Ireland*, London, 1961
Taylor, Rex *Michael Collins*, London, 1958
White, Terence de Vere *Kevin O'Higgins*, Tralee 1966, first published, 1948
*Younger, Carlton *Ireland's Civil War*, London, 1968

2 The Continuing Question: Northern Ireland

Devlin, Bernadette *The Price of My Soul*, London, 1969
Edwards, O. D. *The Sins of Our Fathers*, Dublin, 1970
Hastings, Max *Ulster 1969*, London, 1970
Mansergh, N. *The Government of Northern Ireland*, London, 1936
O'Neill, Terence *Ulster at the Crossroads*, London, 1969
Riddell, Patrick *Fire Over Ulster*, London, 1970
Target, G. W. *Unholy Smoke*, London, 1969

Index